1001 Oriental RECIPES

BEEKMAN HOUSE
New York

Contents

Introduction

This treasury of over 1,000 recipes includes dishes from countries throughout the Orient—including Burma, China, India, Indochina, Indonesia, Korea, Japan, Malaysia, the Philippines, and Thailand. You'll learn how to prepare a full-course Oriental meal, from appetizers through dessert.

Many of the recipes included here use ingredients that can be readily found in any supermarket. Others use foods and spices that can only be purchased in Oriental grocery stores. The Glossary on page 356 will give you a definition or explanation of the unfamiliar terms and ingredients that appear in this book.

The key to successful Oriental cooking is the advance preparation. Generally, the cooking time itself is very brief, so that the ingredients remain crisp. The time-consuming part of the recipes is the cutting, chopping, and slicing—preparing and organizing all the ingredients before you begin cooking.

Although there are certain utensils—such as a wok—commonly used to prepare Oriental dishes, ordinary Western cooking utensils can be used just as successfully. A heavy skillet, a good chopping surface, some sharp knives, and a mallet are invaluable tools.

Oriental cooking is not a difficult art. This comprehensive collection of recipes will help you master that art by making you familiar with the techniques of Oriental cooking.

Appetizers

Fried Bread with Pork, Beef, or Shrimp

THAILAND   Yield: 28 pieces

> 1 cup raw pork, beef, or shrimp,
>   coarsely ground
> 2 tablespoons onions, finely chopped
> 1 teaspoon salt
> ½ teaspoon pepper
> 2 eggs
> 7 slices bread, crusts removed and
>   quartered
> Vegetable shortening or oil

Season your choice of pork, beef, or shrimp with onions, salt, pepper, and eggs. Be sure the meat is blended well with the rest of the ingredients. Spread this mixture on each quarter piece of bread.

Melt 2 or 3 tablespoons of shortening in a skillet. Allow the fat to get very hot; then lower the flame. Place each piece of meat-covered bread into the fat, meat side down. When the meat side is nicely browned, turn to brown the other side. Remove and drain on paper towels. Keep warm until all of the pieces are fried. Serve at once.

Imitation Chinese Egg Rolls

CHINA   Yield: 12 egg rolls

> 1 cup cooked pork, chopped
> 1 16-ounce can Chinese vegetables,
>   drained
> ¼ cup green onions, minced
> ½ teaspoon ground ginger
> 2 teaspoons soy sauce
> 1 teaspoon sugar
> 12 warm cooked crepes
> Hot oil for deep-fat frying

Mix pork with Chinese vegetables, onions, ginger, soy sauce, and sugar. Place about 2 tablespoons mixture on each crepe, fold over sides, and roll up. Seal edges with leftover crepe batter or a little flour-water mixture. Cook in hot oil at 375°F until golden brown. Drain. Serve hot.

Appetizers

Egg Rolls I

CHINA   Yield: 8 egg rolls

Dough

  ½ pound flour
  1½ cups water
  Salt
  1½ teaspoons peanut oil

Filling

  ½ pound green cabbage
  1 leek
  1 medium onion
  1 8-ounce can bamboo shoots
  1 4-ounce can mushrooms
  4 tablespoons oil
  4 ounces ground beef
  4 ounces ground pork
  2 cups fresh bean sprouts
  4 tablespoons soy sauce
  2 tablespoons sherry
  Salt
  Cayenne pepper

  Peanut oil
  Beaten egg yolks
  6 cups oil for deep frying

Place flour in a bowl. Slowly stir in water, making sure that you always stir in the same direction. Add salt and 1½ teaspoons peanut oil and cover bowl. Let rest for 30 minutes.

Meanwhile, prepare filling. Wash and drain cabbage and leek and cut into thin slices. Chop onion. Drain bamboo shoots and cut into fine strips. Drain and coarsely chop mushrooms. In skillet, heat 4 tablespoons oil and add ground meats; cook until lightly browned. Stir in cabbage, leek, onion, and bamboo shoots. Cook for 5 minutes. Add mushrooms and bean sprouts

and cook for an additional 2 minutes. Season to taste with soy sauce, sherry, salt, and cayenne pepper. Remove from heat and set aside.

Brush an 8-inch skillet with peanut oil. Pour in ⅛ of the egg-roll dough; tilt skillet to spread batter evenly. Over low heat, cook until set. Turn out onto moistened paper toweling. Cover with another moistened paper towel. Continue until all dough is used up.

Cut egg-roll rounds into 6-inch squares. Divide filling among the 8 egg rolls. Fold two opposite corners of egg rolls toward the middle. Starting with corner closest to you, roll up egg roll. Brush inside of opposite corner with small amount of beaten egg yolk; seal egg roll. Heat oil in deep frypan. Add rolls and fry until done. Put paper toweling on cake rack; place egg rolls on rack and drain. Keep them warm and serve on preheated platter.

Egg Rolls II

CHINA   Yield: About 24 egg rolls

You can purchase ready-made egg-roll skins in supermarkets or Oriental specialty stores.

Dipping batter

  1 egg
  1 tablespoon cornstarch
  1½ teaspoons baking powder
  1 cup flour
  1 tablespoon sugar
  2 teaspoons salt
  1¼ cups milk
  1¾ cups water

Filling

1 cup bamboo shoots, shredded
½ pound bean sprouts, rinsed and well
  drained
1½ cups water chestnuts, shredded
3½ cups cooked chicken, slivered
¾ cup barbecued pork, slivered
¾ cup fresh parsley, finely chopped
1 cup fresh mushrooms, chopped
½ cup scallion, finely chopped
Salt and freshly ground black pepper to
  taste
Oil

Beat egg slightly. Sift together dry in-gredients. Mix with egg. Slowly stir in milk and water and stir until smooth.

All filling ingredients should be cut finely. Mix filling ingredients (except oil) together and sauté in a little oil for about 10 minutes, stirring occasionally. Let mixture cool. Spoon about ½ cup onto egg-roll skin. Fold like an envelope. Dip in batter and fry in hot oil for about 5 minutes, turning carefully to brown both sides. Serve with Chinese mustard and/or duck sauce.

Egg Rolls III

CHINA   Yield: 45 to 50 egg rolls

2 eggs
2¾ cups water
2 cups all-purpose flour
4 tablespoons peanut oil
2 cups bamboo shoots, chopped
3 cups fresh bean sprouts or 1 1-pound
  can bean sprouts
3 tablespoons soy sauce
2 tablespoons green onion or scallions,
  minced
½ cup dried mushrooms, slivered
1 tablespoon sherry
2 tablespoons cornstarch
1 teaspoon salt
1 pound ground pork
1 tablespoon fresh gingerroot, minced

Beat the eggs and water together with a whisk until blended; then add the flour, mixing until smooth. With a pastry brush, brush a thin layer of the batter into a 5-inch square in a hot, lightly greased 7-inch skillet. Brush in a small amount of batter crosswise if holes appear in the batter. Cook for about 1 minute or until just set. Repeat until all batter is used, stacking the pancake squares on a platter.

Heat 2 tablespoons of the oil in a large skillet. Add the bamboo shoots and bean sprouts (canned bean sprouts must be drained) and sauté, stirring constantly, until heated through. Add 2 tablespoons of the soy sauce and sauté for about 30 seconds longer. Remove the bean sprout mixture from the skillet and set aside.

Add 1 tablespoon of the oil to the same skillet and sauté the onion and mushrooms for about 5 minutes or until onion is just tender. Remove the onion mixture from the skillet and set aside. Combine remaining soy sauce, sherry, 1 tablespoon of the cornstarch, and salt in a bowl. Add the pork and mix well. Add the remaining oil to the skillet and sauté the pork mixture for about 15 minutes or until the pork is cooked, stirring frequently.

Add the bean sprout mixture, the onion mixture, and gingerroot and cool. Combine remaining cornstarch and ½ cup of cold water. Place 1½ teaspoons of the filling across the bottom end of each pancake square about 1 inch from the edge. Moisten the side edges of the squares with the cornstarch mixture, then fold the bottom edge over the filling. Fold in the right and left sides about 1 inch, then moisten the top edge with the cornstarch mixture. Roll up the squares, sealing well.

Fry in 390°F oil in a deep-fat fryer until golden brown, then drain well on paper toweling. You may serve these with Duck Sauce (see Index). The egg rolls may be frozen before frying. One pound of cooked, cleaned, minced shrimp may be used instead of the pork.

Vegetarian Egg Rolls

CHINA

Experiment with this recipe. These are very good.

Vegetables such as:
 cabbage
 bok choy
 celery
 carrots
 fresh mushrooms
 onions
 scallions
 green pepper
 bean sprouts

The sauce

Apricot preserves
Plum preserves
Soy sauce
Dijon mustard
Peanut butter

Use as many of the above vegetables as you wish, in whatever amounts you desire. Shred or finely chop all the vegetables. Stir-fry quickly in small amount of oil. Add soy sauce to taste, garlic powder, and some peanut butter. Fill egg-roll skins, or wonton skins (for cocktail size), and fry in oil in wok or deep frying pan. Serve immediately or freeze and warm in oven before serving.

Make sauce by combining amounts of above ingredients to taste. Some prefer the sauce somewhat sweet, while others like it sharp.

Ground-Beef Filling for Egg Rolls

CHINA   Yield: About 24 egg rolls

1 pound ground beef
¼ cup margarine
4 cups cabbage, very finely shredded
½ cup scallion, finely chopped
1 cup celery, finely chopped
2 cups fresh bean sprouts
¼ cup soy sauce
1 tablespoon sugar (or to taste)
Salt to taste
Freshly ground black pepper to taste

Brown beef in margarine until just browned. Add rest of ingredients; cook 5 minutes, stirring frequently. Adjust seasonings if necessary. Drain; cool. Use purchased egg-roll skins as a shortcut.

Pork Egg-Roll Filling

CHINA   Yield: 6 or 8 egg rolls

2 tablespoons vegetable oil
¼ pound pork, finely shredded
1 teaspoon gingerroot, grated
4 to 5 mushrooms, shredded
2 scallions, cut into ¼-inch slices
¼ cup bamboo shoots, shredded
1 stalk celery, minced
2 cups bean sprouts
1 tablespoon soy sauce
1 teaspoon vinegar
1 teaspoon sugar
½ teaspoon salt
2 teaspoons cornstarch in ¼ cup cold water
6 to 8 egg-roll wrappers (6 × 6 inches each)
1 egg, beaten (for sealing)
2 cups oil for deep-frying

Heat 2 tablespoons oil in wok and stir-fry pork and ginger until pork is done. Push aside. Stir-fry mushrooms, scallions, bamboo shoots, and celery for 2 to 3 minutes. Add the bean sprouts. Return the pork. Stir together the soy sauce, vinegar, sugar, salt, and cornstarch mixture. Add to the wok and heat and stir until the sauce is thickened. Place in egg-roll wrappers and seal with beaten egg. Deep-fry a few at a time in oil at 375°F until brown and crisp.

Shrimp Egg-Roll Filling

CHINA   Yield: 6 or 8 egg rolls

    2 tablespoons vegetable oil
    12-ounces cooked shrimp, minced
    2 cups Chinese celery cabbage, sliced
        across the head into very fine shreds
    8 to 10 water chestnuts, shredded
    2 stalks celery, minced
    1 cup bean sprouts
    1 teaspoon salt
    1 tablespoon soy sauce
    1 teaspoon sugar
    6 to 8 egg-roll wrappers (6 × 6 inches
        each)
    1 egg, beaten (for sealing)
    2 cups oil for deep-frying

Heat 2 tablespoons oil in the wok and stir-fry shrimp, cabbage, water chestnuts, and celery for 2 to 3 minutes, until the green vegetables become brighter. Add the bean sprouts. Stir in the salt, soy sauce, and sugar. Place mixture in egg-roll wrappers and seal with beaten egg. Deep-fry a few at a time in oil at 375°F, until brown and crisp. Serve at once.

Egg-Roll Wrappers

CHINA   Yield: 16 squares

    2 cups sifted all-purpose flour
    ¾ cup cold water
    1 egg
    ½ teaspoon salt

Combine all the ingredients with a fork and stir until the flour is moistened. Knead the dough until smooth (about 5 minutes). Cover and set aside for 30 minutes. Roll out on a well-floured board into 1/16-inch-thick 6- or 7-inch squares.

Skillet Egg-Roll Wrappers

CHINA   Yield: About 20 wrappers

    2 cups sifted all-purpose flour
    2 tablespoons cornstarch
    1 teaspoon salt
    1 teaspoon sugar
    1 egg, beaten
    2 cups water

Combine the dry ingredients. Add the egg and gradually stir in the water until the batter is smooth. Oil a 6-inch skillet. Pour ¼ cup batter into the center of the pan and tilt it to spread the batter evenly over the bottom. Cook over low heat until the edges pull away from the sides. Turn over and cook the other side. Remove and cool before using.

5

Egg-Roll Skins

CHINA   Yield: About 24 skins

18 eggs
3 tablespoons cornstarch
3 teaspoons salt
2¼ cups water
Oil

Beat eggs. Add cornstarch and salt. Beat in water. Heat oil in bottom of 8-inch frying pan or wok and pour about ¼ cup of batter into pan. Fry lightly, turn, and fry on other side.

How to Fold Egg Rolls

1. Fold one corner in beyond the center:

2. Fold both side-corners in:

3. Roll down the top corner and seal:

Cocktail Meatballs

CHINA   Yield: 4 servings

1 20-ounce can pineapple chunks
1 jar red cherry jelly or preserves
¼ cup catsup
3 whole cloves
1 stick cinnamon
1 teaspoon salt
1 teaspoon cornstarch
1 tablespoon soy sauce
1 pound ground chuck, made into cooked meatballs

Drain pineapple and reserve juice. Combine juice with jelly or preserves, catsup, cloves, cinnamon, and salt. Heat to boiling. Dissolve cornstarch in enough liquid (either water or a small amount of the pineapple juice mixture) to make a smooth paste and stir into the boiling mixture. Cook until cornstarch thickens and clears.

Add the pineapple chunks and soy sauce. Pour over the cooked meatballs in a chafing dish and serve warm.

Kabobs with Raisin Stuffing

INDIA   Yield: 20 or more

The kabob

1 pound lean ground beef
2 teaspoons garlic, finely chopped
1½ teaspoons fresh gingerroot, finely chopped
1 teaspoon ground cumin
1 teaspoon ground coriander
1 teaspoon paprika
1 teaspoon garam masala
½ teaspoon black pepper

¼ cup bread crumbs
1 tablespoon sweet butter
1 large egg, lightly beaten
1¼ teaspoons Kosher salt

Stuffing

2 tablespoons blanched almonds,
   chopped
2 tablespoons seedless raisins
2 tablespoons light vegetable oil for
   frying

In a large bowl, mix all of the ingredients for the kabobs. When thoroughly mixed, cover and set aside for at least ½ hour. This may be made and refrigerated up to two days in advance.

Put the well-chopped almonds and raisins together. Divide the prepared kabob mixture into equal portions. Shape into cocktail-size sausages, about 1½ inches long and ½ inch thick. Make a lengthwise slit in each sausage and fill this with stuffing. Pinch the meat together to seal the stuffing inside. (This too can be done ahead and refrigerated until ready to fry the kabobs.)

Heat the oil in a large frying pan; add the kabobs. Cook them for about 8 to 10 minutes, until they are browned all over. Serve piping hot.

Meat and Potato Croquettes

INDONESIA   Yield: About 30-36 balls

When formed into 1-inch-size balls, these are ideal as an appetizer. When made into egg-shaped balls, these croquettes can be a main dish.

3 pounds potatoes, cooked, drained,
   and mashed
1 tablespoon butter
1 small onion, finely chopped
2 to 3 cloves garlic, finely chopped
1 pound ground beef
Salt and pepper to taste
¼ teaspoon nutmeg
4 shallots, finely sliced, including
   green tops
2 or 3 eggs, separated
Oil for deep frying
Parsley for garnish

Prepare mashed potatoes and set aside. Stir-fry onion and garlic in butter until onion is lightly browned. Add meat, salt, pepper, and nutmeg, stirring constantly until meat browns evenly. Add shallots and cook 2 minutes more.

In a large bowl, combine mashed potatoes, meat mixture, and egg yolks. When all is well blended, form into 1-inch balls and refrigerate for at least 1 hour.

In a small bowl, use a whisk or a fork to beat the egg whites until light and frothy. Dip each meatball into the egg white to coat it thoroughly. This will prevent the meatball from breaking up when fried.

Heat oil in deep-fat fryer and fry the meatballs until golden brown. Transfer to a platter, which can be kept warm in the oven until all are fried. Serve hot.

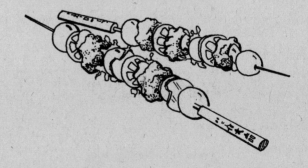

Pineapple Cocktail Barbecue

CHINA   Yield: 6 to 8 servings

1 can pineapple chunks (approximately
    16 ounces), drained; reserve syrup
1 jar red-cherry preserves or jelly
    (approximately 10 ounces)
¼ cup catsup
3 whole cloves
1 stick cinnamon
1 teaspoon salt
1 teaspoon cornstarch
2 teaspoons water
1 tablespoon soy sauce
Meatballs, cooked, made from 1 pound
    ground chuck

Combine pineapple syrup with cherry preserves, catsup, cloves, cinnamon, and salt. Heat to boiling. Dissolve cornstarch in water until it makes smooth paste. Stir into boiling sauce. Cook until cornstarch thickens and turns clear.

Add pineapple chunks and soy sauce. Pour over meatballs. Keep warm in chafing dish. Serve with toothpicks.

Savory Pastries

INDIA   Yield: 32 to 36 pastries

Pastry

1½ cups flour
¾ teaspoon salt
1 tablespoon ghee or oil
½ cup warm water

Filling

1 tablespoon ghee or oil
1 clove garlic, finely chopped
1 teaspoon fresh ginger, finely chopped
2 medium onions, finely chopped
2 teaspoons curry powder
½ teaspoon salt
1 tablespoon vinegar or lemon juice
½ pound ground beef or lamb
1 teaspoon garam masala
2 tablespoons fresh mint or coriander
    leaves, chopped
Oil for frying

In a large bowl, sift together the flour and salt. Combine the ghee and water with the dry ingredients, mixing thoroughly. If needed to form a workable dough, add a little extra water. Knead the dough until it is elastic to the touch, about 10 minutes. Cover and set aside while preparing the filling.

To make the filling, fry garlic in hot ghee with half the onion until onion is transparent. Mix in the curry powder, salt, and vinegar. Next, add ground beef and stir constantly until meat changes color. Reduce the heat, add hot water, and cover. Cook until all liquid has been absorbed and meat is tender. Stir frequently to prevent sticking to the pan. Then add the garam masala and fresh mint. Allow mixture to cool and then mix in the remaining onion.

Shape the dough into 1-inch pieces. On a lightly floured board, roll one piece into a 6-inch circle. Cut the circle in half. Working with one half at a time, fold the dough around your dampened hand to a cone shape. Brush the edges with water to seal. Fill the cone with some of the meat mixture and close the opening by pinching together.

Heat oil for deep frying. Put a few pastries at a time into the fat. When golden brown on all sides, remove from the fat; drain on paper towels. Transfer finished pastries to an oven dish to stay hot until all are cooked and ready to eat.

Galloping Horses

THAILAND　　　　　Yield: 4 to 6 servings

　　5 cloves garlic
　　2 or 3 tablespoons oil
　　2½ pounds mixed lean and fat pork
　　3 tablespoons roasted peanuts, coarsely
　　　　ground
　　2 tablespoons sugar
　　1½ tablespoons fish sauce
　　2 small fresh pineapples
　　Coriander leaves
　　1 fresh chili, cut in slivers

Place garlic cloves in a press until well crushed. Then, fry garlic in oil until light brown. Add the pork, peanuts, sugar, and fish sauce. Stir this mixture until the pork is well cooked, dry and dark brown in color.

Peel and core the pineapples and cut them into mouth-size pieces, about 1-inch square. Spoon the pork mixture on top of each piece of fruit. Arrange on a platter and decorate with coriander leaves and chili slivers.

Pork and Crab Balls

THAILAND　　　　　Yield: 12 servings

　　8 ounces pork, ground
　　2 ounces pork fat, ground
　　6 ounces crab meat, flaked and picked
　　　　over for bones
　　2 tablespoons coriander leaves, finely
　　　　chopped
　　1 teaspoon salt
　　¼ teaspoon ground black pepper
　　2 tablespoons beaten egg
　　1 tablespoon cornstarch
　　6 sheets dried bean curd skin or
　　　　wonton pastry
　　Oil for deep frying

Mix the ground pork, pork fat, and crab meat together until well blended. Add the coriander leaves, salt, pepper, and beaten egg. Put in the cornstarch and blend well.

Use slightly warm water to soften the bean curd skin. When it is easy to handle, cut it into 4-inch squares. Place 1 scant tablespoon of the meat filling in the center of each square. Gather up the edges and tie with a plastic-covered wire twist. Steam the balls for 10 to 12 minutes over boiling water. Remove wire twist.

Deep-fry the balls in hot oil until golden brown all over. Drain on paper towels and keep warm until ready to serve. These may be served with a spicy dip.

Stuffed Soybean Cake

THAILAND　　　　　Yield: 12 servings

　　Oil for frying
　　4 ounces pork, finely minced
　　3 cloves garlic, crushed
　　¼ teaspoon salt
　　⅛ teaspoon pepper
　　1 tablespoon fresh coriander, chopped
　　2 teaspoons fish sauce
　　12 cubes bean curd

In a medium-size skillet, heat enough oil to cover the pan. Add pork, garlic, salt, and pepper and cook until pork is well done, stirring frequently. Add coriander and fish sauce; then remove from heat.

Cut dried bean curd into 12 cubes. Make a hole in the center of each square big enough to hold some of the pork stuffing. When the bean curd is stuffed, deep-fry in heated oil. Drain on paper towels. Just before serving, refry the bean curds and serve hot. Garlic and vinegar sauce may be served with these.

Sweet-and-Sour Spareribs

CHINA   Yield: 24 to 28 pieces

    5 tablespoons soy sauce
    2 tablespoons sherry
    2 cloves garlic, minced
    1 teaspoon sugar
    1½ pounds spareribs
    1 tablespoon cornstarch
    2 tablespoons sugar
    1 tablespoon vinegar
    1 teaspoon cornstarch
    Oil for cooking

Combine 3 tablespoons soy sauce, 1 tablespoon sherry, garlic, and 1 teaspoon sugar; blend well.

Have butcher cut crosswise through bones of spareribs at about 1- to 1½-inch intervals. Cut bones apart. Pour soy-sauce mixture over spareribs. Let stand at room temperature 1 hour; stir occasionally. Blend in 1 tablespoon cornstarch.

Blend 2 tablespoons sugar, 2 tablespoons soy sauce, 1 tablespoon sherry, vinegar, and 1 teaspoon cornstarch together in saucepan. Cook over medium heat, stirring constantly, until thickened. Set aside.

Heat approximately 3 inches oil in deep pot.

Drain marinade from spareribs. Add one portion of meat at a time to hot oil; cook until well browned. Drain on paper toweling. Place cooked spareribs into cooked sauce; coat well. Cover; chill. Serve spareribs at room temperature.

Wonton

CHINA   Yield: About 120 wonton

    ½ pound pork, minced
    ¼ cup fresh mushrooms, minced
    1 tablespoon scallion, minced
    ¼ teaspoon salt
    ⅛ teaspoon freshly ground black
        pepper
    1 egg yolk
    Wonton squares
    Peanut oil

Mix minced pork, mushrooms, and scallion with salt, pepper, and egg yolk. Place ½ teaspoonful of the mixture in center of wonton square. Fold one corner up over the filling at an angle to make two askew triangles. Pull the bottom corners of the triangles gently down below their base. Overlap the tips of the two corners slightly and pinch them together. Fry in hot peanut oil and drain. Serve with Chinese mustard or catsup mixed with a little horseradish.

Cocktail Kabobs

CHINA   Yield: 40 to 50 kabobs

    1 15¼-ounce can pineapple chunks,
        drained
    1-pound package brown-and-serve
        sausages, cooked according to pack-
        age directions, cut into thirds
    1 8-ounce can water chestnuts, halved
    2 green peppers, cut into ¾-inch
        squares
    ¼ pound small mushrooms, stemmed
    Reserved syrup from drained pineapple

4 tablespoons soy sauce
3 slices fresh gingerroot
3 tablespoons brown sugar
2 tablespoons dry sherry

Alternate pieces of pineapple, sausage, water chestnuts, green pepper, and mushrooms on toothpicks.

Combine remaining ingredients; heat in skillet. Add kabobs. Cover; simmer 10 minutes. Remove from skillet and serve warm.

Curried Nuts

INDIA   Yield: 2 cups

¼ cup olive oil
1 tablespoon curry powder
1 tablespoon Worcestershire sauce
⅛ teaspoon cayenne pepper
2 cups nuts (assorted are best)

Combine oil and seasonings in medium-size skillet. When mixture is hot, add nuts; stir constantly until nuts are completely coated.

Line baking pan with brown paper. Spread out nuts. Bake at 200°F for 10 minutes. Nuts should be crisp.

Peanut Wafers

INDONESIA   Yield: About 1 dozen

These crunchy snacks can be served as hors d'oeuvres or with dinner.

½ cup rice flour
2 tablespoons ground rice
½ teaspoon ground cumin
¼ teaspoon ground turmeric
¾ teaspoon salt
1 cup coconut milk
1 clove garlic, peeled and very finely crushed

1 small onion, peeled and finely chopped
¼ pound roasted, unsalted peanuts
Oil for frying

Combine flour, ground rice, and seasonings in a small bowl. Stir in the coconut milk and beat until the batter is very smooth. Stir in garlic, onion, and peanuts and continue to stir until all spices are evenly spread throughout the batter.

Heat about ½ inch of oil in a skillet. Drop the batter by tablespoons into the oil. Each spoonful should spread into a lacy wafer as it cooks. If it is too thick, add an extra spoonful of coconut milk and stir well. Fry the wafers until golden brown on both sides, turning once. Cool wafers on paper towels over a wire rack to allow air to come through them. Store in an airtight container.

Chicken Wings in Oyster Sauce

CHINA   Yield: 4 servings

3 tablespoons oil
2 cloves garlic, crushed
8 chicken wings, each divided into 3 parts
2 tablespoons soy sauce
3 tablespoons oyster sauce
1 tablespoon sugar
½ cup water

Preheat wok. Coat bottom and sides with oil. Rub bottom and sides with garlic; discard garlic. Add middles and tips of wings; brown on both sides. Add rest of wing pieces; brown.

Mix together soy sauce and oyster sauce; stir into chicken. Stir in sugar and water. Cover wok; cook over medium-low heat for 15 minutes.

Chicken Wings

CHINA   Yield: 8 to 12 servings

1 10-ounce bottle soy sauce
2 teaspoons freshly grated ginger or 1
    teaspoon powdered ginger
2 cloves garlic, minced
⅓ cup brown sugar
1 teaspoon dark mustard
24 chicken wings
Garlic powder

Mix together soy sauce, ginger, garlic, brown sugar, and mustard. Blend well. Marinate chicken wings in mixture for two hours or longer. Drain wings, reserving marinade. Bake 1½ hours at 350°F, turning and basting with marinade frequently. Sprinkle with garlic powder and place under broiler for a minute or two just before serving to get crispy.

This may also be served as a main dish (makes 4-5 servings).

Fried Chicken Balls

JAPAN   Yield: 4 servings

½ large onion, chopped
1 pound chicken, finely chopped
1 tablespoon sugar
1½ tablespoons mirin (sweet rice
    wine)
2 tablespoons soy sauce
1 egg
2 tablespoons oil
3½ tablespoons water
1½ tablespoons sherry

Soak chopped onion in water; squeeze out moisture. Combine chicken and onion with sugar, mirin (or sherry mixed with sugar: 1 part sugar to 2 parts sherry), 1 tablespoon soy sauce, and egg. Stir until thoroughly mixed. Roll into bite-size balls.

Heat oil in pan; brown meatballs on all sides. Combine water, sherry, and remaining 1 tablespoon soy sauce. Add to meat in pan; cook until liquid is almost evaporated.

Salted Chicken

CHINA   Yield: 12 servings

1½ tablespoons salt
1 tablespoon rice wine
2 small slices gingerroot
2 scallions, cut into 1-inch pieces
1 whole chicken, 2½ to 3 pounds
Cold water
1 cup chicken stock
¼ teaspoon salt
1 tablespoon sesame oil

Mix together salt, wine, gingerroot, and scallions. Rub chicken with mixture; let stand 30 minutes. Place chicken in pot; cover with cold water. Bring to boil; simmer 40 minutes over medium heat. Remove from pot; chill. Remove skin; cut into pieces approximately 2 inches long and 1 inch wide.

Mix together stock, ¼ teaspoon salt, and sesame oil. Pour over chicken. Garnish with additional scallions if desired.

Appetizers Wrapped in Bacon

CHINA   Yield: 4 servings

    8 slices bacon, cut in half
    1 pound chicken livers, cut in half
    1 6-ounce can whole water chestnuts,
        drained and sliced

Lay bacon slices flat; place chicken livers and water chestnuts on top and roll up. Secure with toothpicks. Place appetizers in small amount of hot oil in frying pan or wok and cook until bacon is browned.

Chicken Liver Teriyaki

JAPAN

    Chicken livers, as many as are needed
    Equal amounts of soy sauce, sugar, and
        water
    Soy sauce or mustard for dipping

Marinate livers in mixture of soy sauce, sugar, and water. Skewer the livers; place on hibachi or grill, turning while cooking. When done, dip livers into soy sauce or mustard. Use approximately 4 livers per person.

Oriental Chicken Livers

CHINA   Yield: 4 servings

    8 ounces chicken livers, cut in half
    ⅓ cup soy sauce
    ½ cup flour
    1 small onion, sliced, or onion flakes

Marinate chicken livers overnight in soy sauce. Remove livers from marinade and dredge in flour. Heat small amount of oil in frying pan and fry livers and onion until browned.
    This may also be served as a main dish (serves 2).

Abalone Appetizer

CHINA   Yield: 5 to 6 servings

    1 teaspoon fresh gingerroot, grated
    1 tablespoon soy sauce
    1 tablespoon sherry
    1 can abalone, drained, cut into bite-
        size pieces

Mix together ginger, soy sauce, and sherry. Pour over abalone. Refrigerate several hours.

Hot Fish Balls

THAILAND   Yield: 20 to 25 balls

    4 cloves garlic, peeled and chopped
    20 peppercorns
    4 coriander roots, finely chopped
    Pinch of sugar
    3 dried chilies
    1½ pounds cod fillets, skinned
    1 tablespoon all-purpose flour
    1 tablespoon soy sauce
    ⅓ cup vegetable oil

Using a mortar, pound the garlic, peppercorns, coriander roots, and chilies to a paste. Gradually add the fish, continuing to pound the mixture to a paste. Lastly, put in flour and soy sauce and pound the mixture for another minute. Shape into 1-inch balls.
    Use either a wok or a deep-fat fryer and heat the oil. Drop a few of the fish balls into the fat. When golden brown all over, remove them from the fat with a slotted spoon. Drain on paper towels and put on a platter to keep warm. When all of the fish balls are fried, serve at once.

Fried Prawns

BURMA   Yield: 4 servings

  16 large prawns, peeled
  1 teaspoon salt
  1 teaspoon ground turmeric
  1 teaspoon chili powder
  2 tablespoons sesame oil
  2 tablespoons peanut oil
  Thin bamboo skewers

Mix salt, turmeric, and chili powder together and thoroughly coat prawns with the mixture. Bend prawns into a semicircle and put on skewer through top and tail. Thread 4 prawns to a skewer. Heat both kinds of oil in a shallow pan. Fry prawns until golden on both sides. Serve at once.

Scallops

CHINA   Yield: About 25 appetizers

  1 cup soy sauce
  1 tablespoon lemon juice
  2 teaspoons fresh gingerroot, finely
    chopped, or substitute powdered
    ginger
  2 tablespoons sugar
  1 pound scallops, cut into bite-size
    pieces

In large saucepan combine soy sauce, lemon juice, ginger, and sugar. Bring to a boil. Add scallops and cook over medium-high heat until all the liquid has evaporated.

Shrimp Crisps

INDONESIA

Uncooked shrimp crisps, sometimes called prawn crisps, are sold in most Oriental food stores. When used as an appetizer, smaller-size wafers are preferred.

  Shrimp crisps
  Oil for deep frying

Pour enough oil into wok or frying pan for deep frying. Allow the oil to get hot. Test it with a small piece of the shrimp crisp. Temperature is right if the crisp swells up within 3 seconds of being in the fat.

When the crisps are golden and puffy, remove from the fat to drain on paper towels. If you plan to store these in an airtight container, be sure they are thoroughly cool before sealing.

Shrimp Hors d'Oeuvres

CHINA   Yield: 6 servings

  6 tablespoons oil
  1 pound small cleaned shrimp
  Salt to taste
  1 tablespoon sherry, or to taste

Heat oil; stir-fry shrimp just until color changes. Drain; sprinkle with salt and sherry.

Shrimp Toast I

CHINA   Yield: 16 shrimp toasts

  ¼ teaspoon sesame-seed oil
  ¼ teaspoon soy sauce
  Pinch of white pepper
  Pinch of salt
  ½ pound uncooked shrimp, cleaned,
    deveined
  8 slices 2-day-old white bread, sliced
    thin
  1 quart vegetable oil

Add sesame-seed oil, soy sauce, pepper, and salt to shrimp; mix thoroughly. Cut 32 rounds from bread slices. Spread shrimp mixture evenly on 16 rounds. Top each circle with another round; press edges together.

Heat oil in deep pot until very hot. Drop each round into oil; turn to brown evenly. Takes approximately 2 minutes. Drain on paper toweling.

Shrimp Toast II

CHINA   Yield: 16 shrimp toasts

½ pound shrimp, shelled and deveined
4 water chestnuts, finely chopped
1 egg, beaten
1 teaspoon salt
1 teaspoon dry sherry
1 teaspoon cornstarch
Oil for frying
4 slices bread (older bread is better)

Mince shrimp. Mix thoroughly with water chestnuts, egg, salt, sherry, and cornstarch. Let this stand for 30 minutes. Trim crusts from bread. Spread 1½ tablespoons shrimp mixture evenly over bread. Cut each slice into four squares.

Heat oil in skillet. Deep-fry bread, shrimp-side-down first, then turn and fry until golden brown. Drain on paper towels and serve hot.

Shrimp Toast III

CHINA   Yield: 24 shrimp toasts

½ pound shrimp
2 green onions, cut into ½-inch
   lengths
2 eggs
2 tablespoons cornstarch

2 teaspoons salt
½ teaspoon pepper
1 teaspoon sugar
4 water chestnuts
8 slices day-old white bread
Oil for frying (about 3 cups)

Place first 7 ingredients into blender. Cover and blend until well mixed and paste is formed. Remove to a bowl and stir in the water chestnuts.

Trim the crusts from the bread. Spread shrimp mixture generously on the bread. Cut each slice diagonally in quarters forming 4 triangles.

In Dutch oven or medium skillet, heat oil; cook 4 to 6 pieces of breaded shrimp in hot oil until golden brown. Turn and fry until the other side is brown. Remove with slotted spoon.

Shrimp Wrapped in Bacon

JAPAN   Yield: 4 servings

8 cleaned shrimp with tails intact
8 slices bacon

Wrap shrimp with bacon; fasten with toothpicks. Bake in 350°F oven for 15 to 20 minutes.

Simple Fish Appetizer

JAPAN   Yield: 5 to 6 servings

1 6-ounce can tuna
1 teaspoon soy sauce (more, if desired)
2 tablespoons chopped onion

Drain tuna. Mix with soy sauce and chopped onion; spread on rice crackers (or another cracker of your choice).

Skewered Fish Meat

JAPAN   Yield: 3 servings

    6 pieces white fish meat, each about 2
      ounces
    Salt
    7 ounces white miso (soybean paste)
    ½ cup rice wine or sherry
    2 tablespoons sugar

Sprinkle fish meat lightly with salt; re-frigerate for 12 hours.

Mix soybean paste, rice wine or sherry, and sugar together until well blended. Drain fish, place in mixture, and refrigerate for 24 hours.

Thread fish on skewers; broil in oven, on grill, or on a hibachi.

Cucumber Hors d'Oeuvres

CHINA   Yield: 6 servings

    2 tablespoons oil
    3 small red chili peppers, seeded, cut
      into very thin slices
    4 medium to large cucumbers, cut into
      2-inch lengths, quartered, seeded
    1 teaspoon soy sauce
    2 tablespoons sugar
    ¼ teaspoon salt
    1 tablespoon vinegar

Heat oil in skillet. Add chili peppers; stir-fry 4 seconds. Add cucumbers; stir-fry 30 seconds. Add soy sauce, sugar, and salt; stir until well blended. Refrigerate at least 24 hours; remove cucumbers from liquid. Sprinkle with vinegar.

Onion Fritters

INDIA   Yield: 6 to 8 servings

This filling and delicious first course may be made ahead, several hours before being served. If this is done, refry fritters about 1 minute in hot oil just before serving to have them piping hot.

Batter

    1 cup unsifted chick-pea flour
    2 teaspoons peanut or corn oil or
      melted vegetable shortening
    1 teaspoon ground cumin
    1½ teaspoons Kosher salt
    1-2 green chilies, seeded and minced
    ½ cup warm water

Onions

    2 medium-size onions, peeled and
      thinly sliced
    Peanut or corn oil, enough to fill a
      fryer 2 inches

Use a large bowl to sift the flour. Using your fingers, rub the 2 teaspoons oil into the flour, until no more lumps of fat can be seen. Add cumin, salt, and chilies. Grad-ually, add the water while constantly beating the mixture. Use electric beater or wire whisk. Beat the batter vigorously for 10 minutes; cover and let rest in a warm place for at least ½ hour.

After the batter has rested, add the onions and coat thoroughly. This will make the mixture coarse and lumpy. Heat oil in frying pan until very hot but do not allow to smoke. Drop the onion batter mixture from a large spoon (about 2 tablespoons at a time). Fry about 6 at a time, keeping the heat medium-low for slower cooking. Each batch will take about 10 minutes until they are golden brown and crisp. Remove the finished fritters with a slotted spoon and drain on paper towels. Keep warm until ready to serve.

Stuffed Mushrooms

CHINA   Yield: 24 mushrooms

    24 large mushrooms, stems removed
    1 pound ground meat
    4 tablespoons scallions, chopped
    3½ tablespoons soy sauce, divided
    ⅛ teaspoon salt
    Freshly ground black pepper to taste
    1½ tablespoons flour
    1¼ cups beef broth

Wash mushrooms, remove stems, and put mushrooms aside. Chop the meat and scallions together, until fine. Add 1 tablespoon soy sauce, salt, pepper, and flour. Shape mixture into small balls and stuff mushrooms.

Heat large skillet to medium heat. Add remaining soy sauce and beef broth. Place mushrooms in skillet stuffed-side-up; cover and let cook for about 20 minutes, or until meat is done.

Water Chestnuts with Bacon

CHINA   Yield: About 20 appetizers

    ⅓ to ½ pound bacon
    1 6-ounce can water chestnuts
    1 tablespoon soy sauce
    1 tablespoon dry sherry
    Toothpicks

Wrap ½ slice bacon around each water chestnut; fasten with toothpick. Place water chestnuts in ovenproof dish; brush with mixture of soy sauce and sherry. Bake at 350°F 15 to 20 minutes.

Soups

Egg Drop Soup

CHINA   Yield: 4 servings

4 cups chicken broth, homemade or
    canned
1 tablespoon cornstarch
¼ cup cold water
1 tablespoon soy sauce
Pinch of grated fresh gingerroot, or a
    sprinkle of powdered ginger
Few sprinkles freshly ground pepper
2 eggs, slightly beaten
1 tablespoon fresh parsley, coarsely
    chopped

Garnish

A few chopped pea pods, or a small
    amount chopped scallions

Bring chicken broth to a boil. Dissolve cornstarch in water, stir into broth, and bring to a boil again. Add soy sauce, ginger, and pepper. Holding eggs above soup, slowly pour them into soup in a slow steady stream while whisking eggs into soup to form long threads. Turn off heat, add parsley, and garnish soup with pea pods or chopped scallions. If desired, warm chow mein noodles can be served with this soup.

Chicken Egg Drop Soup

CHINA   Yield: 4 servings

6 cups chicken broth
2 tablespoons cornstarch in 2
    tablespoons water
1 tablespoon soy sauce

½ teaspoon sugar
2 eggs, lightly beaten
Salt and pepper
2 scallions, sliced (green tops
    included)

Bring the chicken broth to a boil. Combine the cornstarch mixture with the soy sauce and sugar. Slowly stir into the broth. Heat and continue stirring until the soup is thickened and clear. Remove from the heat. Gradually add eggs, stirring with a fork until eggs separate into shreds. Season to taste with salt and pepper. Serve immediately garnished with sliced scallions.

Peking Egg Drop Soup

CHINA   Yield: 4 to 6 servings

¼ pound lean pork shoulder, cut
    into fine strips
2 ounces bamboo shoots, finely sliced
4 or 5 dried black Chinese mush-
    rooms, soaked 30 minutes in warm
    water and cut into small pieces
2 tablespoons vinegar
2 teaspoons soy sauce
¼ teaspoon (or less) ground pepper
1 quart chicken broth
½ teaspoon salt (or salt to taste)
1½ tablespoons cornstarch in 2
    tablespoons water
1 egg, beaten

Brown the strips of pork well in the wok or in a large saucepan. Add bamboo shoots, mushrooms, vinegar, soy sauce, pepper, chicken broth, salt, and cornstarch mixture. Bring mixture to a full boil, stirring constantly. Reduce heat. Add egg, a small amount at a time, stirring with a fork to separate it into shreds as it coagulates. Remove from heat and serve at once.

Egg-Flower Soup

CHINA: Yield: 4 servings

    4 cups chicken broth
    ½ medium onion, chopped
    ½ cup celery, sliced
    Pinch of salt
    1 egg, beaten
    ½ cup spinach, chopped

    Place chicken broth in pot and bring to boil. Add onion, celery, and salt. Bring to boil again. Stir in beaten egg. Add spinach and let simmer for 1 minute.

Egg-Flower Soup with Water Chestnuts

JAPAN   Yield: 6 servings

    1 quart chicken broth
    ½ cup finely chopped water
        chestnuts
    2 eggs, beaten
    ¼ teaspoon pepper

    Bring chicken broth to a boil. Add water chestnuts, cover, and simmer for 4 minutes. Add beaten eggs slowly while stirring soup. Add pepper; stir through once.

Egg Soup

CHINA   Yield: 5 servings

    2 cups Basic Beef Stock
    2 tablespoons cornstarch
    3 cups clam juice
    2 tablespoons soy sauce
    2 eggs, beaten
    ½ cup chopped green onions

    Combine ¼ cup of the stock with the cornstarch and blend until smooth. Pour the remaining stock and the clam juice into a large saucepan and place over medium high heat. Stir in the cornstarch mixture and soy sauce and bring to a boil, stirring constantly. Pour the eggs carefully onto the surface of the boiling soup and cook until the eggs are set. Ladle into soup bowls and sprinkle with the green onions.

Miso Soup with Egg

JAPAN   Yield: 4 servings

    4 cups chicken broth
    ¼ cup white miso (soybean paste)
    ¼ teaspoon salt
    1 egg, beaten
    2 teaspoons sherry or sweet rice wine
        (sweet sake)
    Lemon-peel twists

    Bring broth, miso, and salt to a boil. While slowly mixing the soup, gradually pour in the egg. Remove from heat, stir in the sherry or sake. Place a twist of lemon peel in each bowl before adding soup.

Beef and Chinese Cabbage Soup

CHINA   Yield: 4 servings

    ¼ pound rump steak, thinly sliced
    1 teaspoon cornflour
    ½ teaspoon soy sauce
    ½ teaspoon dry sherry
    2 teaspoons oil
    3 cups water
    2 cups Chinese cabbage, shredded
    1 teaspoon salt
    ¼ teaspoon monosodium glutamate

    Marinate steak in cornflour, soy sauce, dry sherry and oil. Bring water to boil and add Chinese cabbage. Return to boil and add salt and MSG. Cover and simmer for 10 minutes and serve immediately.

Beef Balls with Noodles

INDONESIA   Yield: 4 to 6 servings

12 ounces egg noodles, parboiled and
  set aside to drain

Beef balls

2 onions, grated
2 cloves garlic, crushed
1 tablespoon oil or margarine
1½ pounds ground beef
4 slices slightly stale bread, diced
1 egg, beaten lightly
½ teaspoon nutmeg
1 teaspoon salt
¼ teaspoon freshly ground pepper

Broth

1 onion, peeled and thinly sliced
2 cloves garlic, crushed
1 tablespoon oil
4 cups chicken stock (canned will do)
1-inch piece green ginger, scraped and
  bruised
4 shallots or spring onions, sliced
4 stalks celery, sliced
4 cabbage leaves, finely shredded
Celery leaves or parsley for garnish

In a small skillet, lightly brown onions
and garlic in the oil. Combine them in a
large bowl with the rest of the beef balls ingredients in the order given. When completely blended, form into balls, making between 12 and 18, depending on the size. Set
aside.

To make the broth, stir-fry onion and
garlic in bottom of large saucepan. Add soup
stock and ginger and bring to a boil. With a
slotted spoon, lower meatballs into stock and
allow to return to a boil. Reduce heat to
medium and cook for 15 minutes or until
meat is cooked through. Add the vegetables
and cook 5 minutes more or just until they
are slightly crunchy in texture.

Divide noodles into individual soup
bowls. Put 2 or 3 meatballs on top, along
with some of the vegetables. Fill to the top
of the bowl with the broth. Garnish with
celery leaves or parsley.

Indian Beef Soup

INDIA   Yield: 6 servings

Butter or oil
1 pound beef, cut into large chunks
1 cup onions or scallions, chopped
1 cup green pepper, chopped
1 clove garlic, minced
1 16-ounce can tomatoes
1 16-ounce can creamed corn
1 16-ounce can mixed vegetables
1 to 2 teaspoons mustard
Catsup to taste
Salt and pepper to taste

In Dutch oven, brown the beef in small
amount of butter or oil. Add the onions,
green pepper, and garlic. Cover, let steam
until lightly browned. Add tomatoes, corn,
mixed vegetables, mustard, catsup, and salt
and pepper. Simmer gently about one hour.

Refrigerate overnight and simply reheat
for next day's dinner.

Indian Stew

INDIA   Yield: 4 servings

1 tablespoon margarine or cooking oil
1 large onion, chopped
½ pound ground beef
1 tablespoon Worcestershire sauce

1 tablespoon sugar
2 cups corn
1 can tomato soup
2 or 3 drops Tabasco

Brown onion and ground beef in margarine. Add other ingredients and simmer 15 minutes. Serve in soup bowls with saltines.

Sour Soup of Beef

PHILIPPINES   Yield: 6 to 8 servings .

1 pound shank beef
1 pound soup bones
8 ounces pork chop with fat removed
Water to cover the meat and bones
1 medium onion, peeled and sliced
2 underripe tomatoes, sliced
2 teaspoons salt
1 tablespoon dried tamarind pulp
1 cup boiling water
1 large sweet potato, peeled and diced
1 giant white radish, sliced
2 cups shredded greens (such as
    spinach)
Fish sauce to taste
Lime or lemon wedges

Cover the beef, bones, and pork with water in a large soup pot. Add onions, tomatoes, and salt. After this has come to a boil, cover and reduce heat to a simmer. Cook until the meat is tender. Lift out the meat and set aside to cool.

While it is cooking, pour boiling water over tamarind pulp. When cool, squeeze to dissolve the pulp and strain into the simmering soup. Discard the seeds and fiber of tamarind.

Thinly slice the pork and dice the beef. Remove and discard the bones from the broth. Return the meat to the soup, adding the sweet potatoes and radish. When the sweet potato is almost soft, put in the greens and season the soup to taste with fish sauce. Simmer for 5 minutes more or until the leaves are soft. Garnish each soup bowl with a wedge of lemon or lime.

Meatball Soup

JAPAN   Yield: 4 servings

½ pound ground beef or pork
2 eggs
1 tablespoon flour
2 teaspoons freshly grated ginger or 1
    teaspoon ground ginger
5 cups beef or chicken stock
1 teaspoon soy sauce
Pinch of salt
3 carrots, parboiled and sliced ¼ inch
    thick
Very thin spaghetti, enough for 4 small
    servings, cooked and drained
4 sprigs of parsley

Mix together beef or pork, eggs, flour, and ginger. Set aside. Mix the stock with the soy sauce and salt. Bring to a boil. Add the carrots. Make very small meatballs from the meat mixture; drop them gently into the boiling soup, and boil gently for about 15 minutes.

Divide the spaghetti into 4 individual bowls; add the soup and meatballs. Garnish with parsley.

Pork and Chicken Soup

THAILAND   Yield: 6 servings

    1 pound sweet pork (see Index),
       divided in 2 parts
    6 cups water
    2 chicken legs
    1 teaspoon peppercorns
    1 whole coriander plant, including root
    ½ teaspoon salt
    5 dried Chinese mushrooms
    3 ounces cellophane noodles
    3 tablespoons spring onions, including
       leaves, chopped
    3 tablespoons fresh coriander leaves,
       chopped
    1 red chili, seeded and sliced, optional

Prepare pork; divide in half and set aside.

In a large saucepan, place water, chicken legs, peppercorns, well-washed coriander, and salt. After the water has come to a boil, reduce heat and simmer for 20 minutes until chicken is tender.

Cover the mushrooms in hot water while the chicken is cooking. Cut off stems and add them to the broth. Slice the caps thinly and set aside. Soak noodles in hot water for 15 minutes. Drain well and slice into 2-inch lengths.

Remove cooked chicken legs from the broth. Cut the meat into small pieces and discard the skin and bones. Cook the soup down to about 4 cups; strain.

Dice half the pork and set aside. (Use the other half as a side dish of sweet pork.) Add 2 cups of the pork stock to the chicken stock. Allow to come to a boil; then add noodles and mushrooms and simmer for about 10 minutes. Add the chicken, pork, spring onion, and coriander. Serve at once, garnished with chili slices.

Pork and Lotus Root Soup

INDOCHINA   Yield: 4 servings

    1 pound lean pork ribs, cut into short
       lengths
    1 pound fresh lotus root or 8 slices
       canned lotus root
    3 spring onions, sliced, including
       greens
    ½ teaspoon salt
    6 cups water
    1 to 2 tablespoons fish sauce

Peel fresh lotus root and cut into slices. Along with prepared spring onions, place lotus root in saucepan with salt, water, and pork ribs. Bring to a boil. Then cover the pan, reduce heat, and simmer for at least 1½ hours. Just before serving, add fish sauce to taste. Serve with hot white rice as an accompaniment.

Pork and Watercress Soup

CHINA   Yield: 4 to 6 servings

    ½ pound lean pork, shredded
    6 cups chicken broth
    1 small onion, thinly sliced
    1 celery stalk, thinly sliced
    1 teaspoon salt
    ¼ teaspoon pepper
    1 cup firmly packed, washed watercress,
       cut into 1-inch pieces

Simmer the pork in the chicken broth for 10 minutes. Add the onion, celery, salt, and pepper and simmer for 10 minutes longer. Add the watercress and heat briefly.

Pork with Bamboo Shoots Soup

THAILAND   Yield: 4 to 6 servings

2½ pounds bamboo shoots, finely sliced
Saltwater
2½ pounds pork, cut into 1½-inch squares
10 cloves garlic
Pepper
Coriander seeds
Enough chicken stock to cover meat and vegetables, about 4 to 5 cups
Nam pla
Palm sugar or light brown sugar to taste

Place bamboo shoots in salted water and boil until the shoots become light yellow. Drain and set aside. Prepare the pork in squares.

Pound the spices together with a mortar and pestle. Then mix thoroughly with the meat in a large saucepan. Add the soup stock, bamboo shoots, nam pla, and sugar. Cover the saucepan and cook the soup until the pork is quite tender; at least 1 hour. Serve piping hot.

Chicken Soup I

INDONESIA   Yield: 6 to 8 servings

3- to 4-pound chicken
2 quarts water
2 teaspoons salt
1 small onion, peeled and quartered
2 cloves garlic, peeled and finely sliced
1 tablespoon ginger powder
Dash of white pepper

7 ounces soybean paste
4 sticks celery, cut into ½-inch pieces
1 cup sherry
4 hard-boiled eggs, shelled and cut in half
Chopped chives for garnish

Wash chicken inside and out and dry with paper towels. In a soup pot, bring the water to a boil. Add salt. Add the chicken and simmer for an hour or until chicken is tender. Remove chicken from broth. Discard skin and bones of the chicken and cut meat into bite-size pieces. Set aside and keep warm.

Add onion, ginger, and pepper to broth. Cook over low heat for 15 minutes. In a small bowl, mix soybean paste, celery, and sherry.

Place chicken in preheated, individual soup dishes. Add some broth to each dish. Add a portion of the soybean-paste mixture to each dish. Top with half a hard-cooked egg. Garnish with chives and serve at once.

Chicken Soup II

JAPAN   Yield: 4 servings

5 cups chicken broth
1 4-ounce can mushroom stems and pieces, or slices (drain and reserve liquid)
2 teaspoons soy sauce
1 cup cooked fine noodles
1 chicken breast, cooked, boned, and thinly sliced
4 thin slices lemon with rind

Bring chicken broth to a boil. If there is not 5 cups of broth, add mushroom liquid to make 5 cups. Simmer, covered, for 5 minutes. Add mushrooms; heat through. Add soy sauce and noodles. Stir well; heat for 3 minutes.

Divide sliced chicken equally into 4 bowls. Pour soup into bowls. Garnish each with a lemon slice.

Chicken Sub Gum Soup

CHINA   Yield: 8 servings

1 can mixed Chinese vegetables
6 cups canned chicken broth
Soy sauce
Pepper
3 eggs, beaten

Drain vegetables and chop. Add to boiling broth and cook 5 minutes. Pour eggs slowly into soup, stirring slowly until eggs form small "flowers." Season to taste with soy sauce and pepper.

Chinese Chicken Soup I

CHINA   Yield: 4 to 6 servings

4-5 spring onions
5 cups of strongly flavored, clear
   chicken stock
6 small mushrooms, finely sliced
2 cups shredded white chicken meat
2 beaten eggs
2-3 teaspoons soy sauce

Finely slice the white part of the spring onions and reserve the green part for garnish. Heat the chicken stock until boiling. Add the mushrooms and onions, and cook for 2-3 minutes. Add the shredded white chicken meat.

Beat the eggs until frothy with a little salt and pepper. Stir the soup well. Then pour the beaten egg steadily into the soup, stirring constantly, so that it remains in shreds. Allow to cook for a minute or two to set egg.

Add soy sauce to taste and serve in soup bowls, sprinkled with the finely chopped green parts of the spring onions.

Chinese Chicken Soup II

CHINA   Yield: 4 to 6 servings

1 3-4 pound boiling fowl
1½ quarts water
1 small onion
Pinch of salt
2 slices of ginger

Pour water (cold) into a heavy pot and put in fowl. Bring to boiling point. Add chopped onion, salt, and ginger. Reduce heat and simmer for about 3 hours.

Cream Chicken Soup

INDIA   Yield: 4 to 6 servings

3 to 4 pounds whole soup chicken
6 cups water
1 leek, cut into coarse pieces
2 dried pepper pods
10 peppercorns
Salt to taste
3 egg yolks
1 cup cream
1 tablespoon curry powder
Pinch of sugar
Chopped parsley for garnish

Wash chicken inside and out and drain. Place in a pot with cold water. Bring to a boil. Add pepper pods, peppercorns, and salt. After mixture comes to a boil, skim off the top. Boil until the chicken is tender, 30 minutes or more. Remove chicken from the pot and allow to cool. Strain the broth.

Remove the skin and loosen the meat from the bones. Cut white meat only into small pieces. (Reserve dark meat for another meal.) Keep white meat warm.

In a pot, stir egg yolks, cream, curry, and sugar. Place in a double boiler. Add 3 cups lukewarm chicken broth. Beat this mixture as it heats into a creamy mass. Pour into preheated soup dishes. Divide chicken into bowls and garnish with parsley.

Spiced Chicken Soup

MALAYSIA   Yield: 4 to 6 servings

    6¼ cups water
1 small chicken, quartered
4 jumbo shrimp, cleaned, deveined,
    and cut in half
Salt and pepper to taste
2 kemiri nuts, chopped
4 shallots, peeled and chopped
2 cloves garlic, peeled and chopped
1 teaspoon ginger powder
Pinch of turmeric powder
Pinch of chili powder
Vegetable oil for frying
1 tablespoon light soy sauce
1¼ cups bean sprouts, cleaned
1 potato, peeled and sliced into very
    thin rounds
Lemon slices
Coriander leaves

Use a large saucepan and bring water to a boil. Put in chicken, shrimp, and salt and pepper to taste. When water has again come to a boil, reduce heat and simmer for 40 minutes. Remove chicken and shrimp from broth. Take meat from chicken bones and discard bones. Peel shrimp, discard heads, and cut shrimp into 4 or 5 pieces. Set aside.

Pound the kemiri, shallots, and garlic to a smooth paste. Mix in ginger, turmeric, and chili powder.

In a wok or deep frying pan, heat about 2 tablespoons oil. Stir-fry the spice paste for a few seconds. Add 1 cup reserved liquid, soy sauce, chicken, and shrimp and allow to simmer for 10 minutes. Put in remaining broth and simmer for another 10 minutes. Add the bean sprouts and adjust seasoning to taste. Continue to simmer for 3 minutes.

Fry potato slices in a skillet until crisp on both sides. Divide potatoes equally into soup bowls. Spoon soup over the potatoes. Garnish with lemon slices and coriander if desired.

Chicken Rice Soup

THAILAND   Yield: 4 to 6 servings

    5 cups chicken stock
2 large boneless chicken breasts,
    skinned and cut into ½-inch cubes
¼ pound boneless pork loin, cut into
    ½-inch cubes
1½ cups rice, cooked
2 celery stalks, with leaves, cut into
    ½-inch lengths
2 scallions, chopped
Nam pla (fish sauce) to taste
Freshly ground black pepper
1 tablespoon vegetable oil
4 cloves garlic, peeled and finely
    chopped
¼ pound bacon, cut into ½-inch
    squares

Add the chicken and pork to boiling stock; cook until meat turns white, at least 10 minutes. Add the rice and simmer for 5 minutes. Remove from heat. Add celery, scallions, nam pla, and pepper. Check the seasonings and add more if needed.

In a small skillet, fry garlic in oil until golden brown. Drain and set aside the garlic. Then fry the bacon until crisp.

Ladle the soup into individual bowls and garnish with garlic and bacon.

Chicken Vegetable Soup

CHINA   Yield: 4 to 6 servings

    6 cups chicken broth
    ½ cup bean sprouts
    ¼ cup water chestnuts, thinly sliced
    1 scallion, minced
    ½ cup bok choy, sliced (use leafy part
        also)
    3 Chinese mushrooms, soaked and
        drained and sliced
    ½ cup snow pea pods
    ½ cup cooked chicken, diced
    2 teaspoons soy sauce
    1 tablespoon sherry
    Pepper to taste

Bring chicken broth to boil in soup pot. Add vegetables and chicken and simmer about 1 minute. Add soy sauce and sherry. Add pepper to taste. If desired, cellophane noodles or very fine egg noodles may be added.

Fondue-Pot Japanese-Style Chicken Soup

JAPAN   Yield: 4 servings

    ½ uncooked boned chicken breast
    8 fresh mushrooms
    4 cups hot chicken broth
    1 cup cooked rice
    4 strips lemon peel

Cut chicken meat into thin slices. Wash and cut mushrooms into thin slices. Put chicken broth in fondue pot over medium-high heat, add chicken and mushrooms, and cook for 4 minutes.

Place ¼ cup of rice in each of 4 bowls; put 1 lemon-peel strip in each bowl. Spoon in the chicken-broth mixture.

Duck Soup

INDOCHINA   Yield: 8 servings

    1 3- to 5-pound duck
    1 tablespoon salt
    ¼ teaspoon freshly ground black
        pepper
    5 shallots, peeled and crushed
    5 cups water
    1 cup dried bamboo shoot, soaked in
        hot water for 2 hours
    1 lump rock sugar
    ¼ cup fish sauce
    ½ pound medium rice vermicelli
    1 tablespoon scallion, green parts only,
        chopped
    1 tablespoon coriander leaves, chopped
    Nuoc Cham (see Index)

Rub the duck with salt, pepper, and crushed shallots. Set aside for at least 1 hour.

Bring water to a boil in a large saucepan. Add the duck and prepared bamboo shoot. Return to boil and then simmer for 15 minutes. Skim off any scum that may form. Then, add the rock sugar; cover and simmer for 1 hour.

Next, add the fish sauce and simmer covered for another 30 minutes or until bamboo shoot is tender.

Cook the rice vermicelli in another pan according to package directions for just 5 minutes. Drain and rinse. Remove the duck from the soup and cut into 8 pieces. Divide the vermicelli into 8 soup bowls and put a piece of duck on top. Cover with the hot soup. Garnish with scallion and coriander leaves and serve with Nuoc Cham.

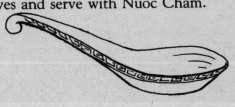

Clam Soup I

CHINA   Yield: 5 to 6 servings

    2 cups chicken broth
    2 cups clam juice
    2 cups minced clams
    1 small onion, minced
    2 tablespoons fresh parsley, minced
    2 tablespoons soy sauce
    1 tablespoon sherry

In large saucepan, combine chicken broth and clam juice. Add clams and onion and bring to a boil. Simmer for 10 minutes. Add parsley, soy sauce, and sherry and heat through.

Clam Soup II

JAPAN   Yield: 4 servings

    16 small clams
    4 cups boiling water
    ½ teaspoon salt
    ¾ teaspoon rice wine or sherry
    1 tablespoon soy sauce
    Lemon slices for garnish

Thoroughly wash the clams. Put them into boiling water; boil them until the shells crack. Put in the salt, rice wine or sherry, and soy sauce. Serve the clam soup with a garnish of lemon slices.

Spiced Fish Soup

KOREA   Yield: 4 servings

If you don't like food spicy and hot, skip this one.

    1½ pound cod fillets, skinned and cut
        into large chunks

    3 cups water
    2 tablespoons vegetable oil
    1 medium onion, peeled and finely
        chopped
    2 tablespoons scallions, chopped
    2 teaspoons garlic, crushed
    1 teaspoon fresh gingerroot, crushed
    2 to 6 teaspoons chili powder,
        according to taste
    2 to 3 teaspoons salt
    1 cup zucchini, thinly sliced
    1 medium green pepper, cored, seeded,
        and finely sliced

Cover cod chunks with water and bring to a boil. Lower the heat and simmer for 5 minutes. Set aside.

In a medium-size skillet, heat the oil. Put in all ingredients except the zucchini and green pepper. Stir-fry for 1 minute. Add the zucchini and pepper and continue to stir-fry for 1 minute more. Place this mixture in the saucepan with the fish and simmer gently until well heated. Serve at once.

Oyster Soup

JAPAN   Yield: 4 servings

    8 ounces shucked oysters
    4 cups dashi
    ¾ teaspoon cornstarch
    Small amount of cold water
    ½ teaspoon Tabasco

Wash the oysters. Add them to the boiling dashi; cook until the oysters are done. Mix the cornstarch with enough cold water to make a smooth paste; add to soup. Flavor with the Tabasco.

Soups

Oyster Soup with Miso

JAPAN   Yield: 4 servings

    8 ounces shucked oysters
    3½ ounces miso (soybean paste)
    4 cups dashi
    ¾ teaspoon cornstarch
    Cold water
    ½ teaspoon red pepper

Wash oysters; set aside. Blend the miso and dashi; bring to a boil. Gradually add oysters to the boiling mixture.

Mix the cornstarch with enough cold water to make a smooth paste; add this to the oyster mixture, stirring constantly. Simmer until done. Flavor with red pepper.

Hot-and-Sour Cuttlefish Soup

CHINA   Yield: 5 to 6 servings

    2 cups carp, cut in irregular pieces
    5 cups abalone stock
    ½ cup dried shrimp, well soaked
    2 dried cuttlefish, about 10 × 6 inches
      cut into 1 × 1½-inch cubes properly
      soaked and cleaned
    ½ cup bamboo shoots cut in small
      strips
    ½ cup celery, cut in 1-inch sections
    4 tablespoons light soy sauce
    2 tablespoons vinegar
    Salt and pepper to taste

Bring abalone stock and carp to a boil uncovered over high heat. Add shrimp and cook for 3 minutes. Add cuttlefish, bamboo shoots, and celery and cook uncovered for another 3 minutes. Add salt, vinegar, and pepper. Serve hot.

Crab Soup

CHINA   Yield: 4 to 6 servings

    2 tablespoons oil
    ½ pound crab meat
    ¼ teaspoon salt
    2 medium tomatoes, chopped coarsely
    1½ teaspoons fresh gingerroot,
      chopped
    5 cups chicken broth
    2 eggs, beaten
    1½ tablespoons vinegar
    1½ tablespoons sherry
    1½ tablespoons soy sauce
    3 scallions, sliced

In large pot, heat oil. Sauté crab meat, salt, tomatoes, and ginger for 5 minutes. Add chicken broth and cook over low heat 10 minutes. Beat eggs, and add vinegar, sherry, and soy sauce. Pour into the soup slowly. Stir in the scallions and let soup simmer for about 3 minutes.

Lobster Soup

JAPAN   Yield: 4 servings

    6 ounces lobster meat
    2 teaspoons salt
    1½ teaspoons soy sauce
    4½ cups dashi
    2 medium cucumbers, thinly sliced
    8 dried mushrooms
    4 pieces lemon rind

Mince the lobster meat, pour ½ teaspoon of the salt over it, and boil. Gradually add ¾ teaspoon of soy sauce and ¼ cup of dashi to the lobster.

Peel and slice the cucumbers. Boil the mushrooms in ¼ cup of dashi and ¾ teaspoon of salt. Into each of 4 bowls place pieces of boiled lobster, cucumbers, and mushrooms.

Heat together 4 cups of dashi, ¾ teaspoon of salt, and ¾ teaspoon of soy sauce; pour some into each bowl. Garnish lobster soup with floating lemon rind.

Prawn and Eggplant Soup

INDONESIA   Yield: 4 servings

4 ounces fresh prawns, shelled, deveined, and chopped into small pieces
2 tablespoons peanut oil
1 medium onion, finely chopped
2 cloves garlic, finely chopped
2 fresh red chilies, seeded and chopped
1 ripe tomato, peeled and chopped
2 daun salam or curry leaves
2 cups chicken stock
1 medium eggplant
1 cup coconut milk
½ teaspoon brown sugar
1 teaspoon salt

In a large saucepan, fry onion, garlic, and chilies until onions are golden. Add tomato and daun salam leaves and sauté for 5 minutes. Mash the tomato to a pulp while frying. Add soup stock, bring to a boil, and then allow to simmer.

Peel and dice the eggplant and add to the simmering stock. Cook for 10 minutes or until eggplant is tender. Add the coconut milk, sugar, and salt. Stir continuously while all the ingredients heat through. Pour into bowls and serve with rice and curries.

Prawn Soup with Lily Buds

THAILAND   Yield: 6 to 8 servings

3 ounces cellophane noodles

30 dried lily buds
8 dried Chinese mushrooms
4 or 5 cloves garlic, peeled
3 whole fresh coriander plants, including roots
1 pound small raw prawns, well washed and drained
3 tablespoons peanut oil
1 medium onion, peeled and sliced
8 cups water
6 spring onions, sliced diagonally
4 tablespoons fish sauce
1 tablespoon light soy sauce
1 teaspoon sugar
2 eggs

Soak noodles in a bowl with warm water. Soak the lily buds and dried mushrooms in a bowl of hot water for 30 minutes. After they have soaked, pinch off the ends of the lily buds. The Thais and Chinese tie a knot in each lily bud. You may prefer to cut them in two. Discard the stems of the mushrooms and thinly slice the caps. Cut noodles to about 2 inches long.

Place garlic and washed coriander in electric blender, reserving some coriander leaves for garnish. Add 2 tablespoons water and purée.

Shell and devein the prawns, saving the shells and heads. Heat 1 tablespoon oil in a large saucepan. Fry the shells and heads until the shells turn bright pink. Add water; cover and simmer for 20 minutes. Strain the stock into a large bowl and discard shells.

Heat remaining 2 tablespoons oil in clean saucepan. Fry onions until transparent; add garlic and coriander paste, stirring until oil separates from the mixture. Put in prawns and stir-fry for 3 minutes. Add the hot stock, lily buds, mushrooms, and noodles. Bring all to a boil and then lower heat; simmer for 5 minutes. Add spring onions, fish sauce, soy sauce, and sugar. Gradually pour beaten eggs into the boiling soup. Serve at once, garnished with coriander leaves.

Black-Mushroom Soup

CHINA   Yield: 8 servings

¼ cup dried black mushrooms
1 clove garlic, crushed
1 tablespoon sesame oil
8 cups rich chicken broth
1 piece of gingerroot, size of hazelnut
2½ tablespoons soy sauce
½ cup cooked chicken, finely diced
½ cup cooked ham, finely diced
½ cup bamboo shoots, diced
½ cup scallions, finely chopped

Soak mushrooms in warm water until soft and spongy, about 10 minutes. Squeeze out liquid and chop very fine. Crush garlic and sauté in oil for 2 or 3 seconds; remove from oil and set aside. Sauté the mushrooms in the same pan for about 5 minutes.

In soup kettle, bring chicken broth to boil. Add mushrooms, garlic, ginger, and soy sauce. Simmer about 4 hours. Strain the broth and add chicken, ham, bamboo shoots, and scallions. Simmer until heated through.

Celery Cabbage and Pork Soup

CHINA   Yield: 6 servings

1 small head celery cabbage
5 water chestnuts
4 green onions (with tops), very finely
    chopped
½ cup ground pork
1 egg yolk
¾ teaspoon salt
4 cups boiling water

Wash and cut the cabbage crosswise into 1½-inch strips. Wash, peel, and cut the water chestnuts in cross sections ¼ inch

thick. Chop the onions very fine and mix with the pork. Add the egg yolk.

Combine the salt, boiling water, and water chestnuts; cook for 15 minutes. Add the cabbage and cook until it is nearly tender. Drop the pork mixture, a teaspoonful at a time, into the soup. Boil for 5 minutes and serve hot.

Celery Cabbage and Shrimp Soup

CHINA   Yield: 6 servings

1 small head celery cabbage
5 water chestnuts
½ cup large dried or 1 cup canned
    shrimp
1 cup water
1 tablespoon vegetable oil
3½ cups boiling water
1 teaspoon salt
4 green onions (with tops), finely
    chopped

Wash and cut the cabbage crosswise into 1-inch strips. Wash, peel, and cut the water chestnuts crosswise into ¼-inch slices. Soak the dried shrimp in 1 cup water for ½ hour. Drain the shrimp, but save the liquid. Heat the oil until it is very hot, add the shrimp, and fry for 2 to 3 minutes. Add the shrimp liquid, water chestnuts, 3½ cups boiling water, and salt. Bring the liquid to the boiling point and simmer for ½ hour. Add the cabbage and boil for 5 to 10 minutes, until the cabbage is tender but has not lost all its crispness. Add the finely chopped green onions and serve hot.

If wet-packed shrimp are used, substitute ⅔ cup liquid from the canned shrimp for ⅔ cup water. Clean the shrimp by removing the black vein along the back.

Celery Soup

CHINA   Yield: 4 servings

1 heaping tablespoon dried Chinese
   mushrooms
2 small celeriac roots, with green tops
   (celery stalks may be substituted)
4 tablespoons oil
½ pound pork shoulder, cut into
   1½-inch-long, ½-inch-thick strips
2 small onions, minced
1 clove garlic, minced
3 cups hot chicken broth, from cubes
   or homemade
2 quarts salted water
1 ounce Chinese transparent noodles
2 tablespoons soy sauce
⅛ teaspoon ground ginger

Soak mushrooms in cold water 30
minutes.

Cut off celeriac tops; set aside. Brush celeriac roots under running cold water. Peel;
cut into ½-inch cubes. Heat oil in saucepan.
Add pork, brown on all sides, stirring constantly, about 3 minutes. Add onions, garlic,
and celeriac root; cook 5 minutes. Drain
mushrooms; cut in halves, or quarters if very
large. Add to saucepan. Pour in broth.
Cover; simmer over low heat 25 minutes.

Meanwhile, bring salted water to boil in
another saucepan. Add noodles. Remove
from heat immediately; let stand 5 minutes.
Drain noodles. Five minutes before end of
cooking time of soup, add coarsely chopped
celeriac tops. Season to taste with soy sauce
and ground ginger. Place noodles in soup
tureen or 4 individual Chinese soup bowls.
Pour soup over noodles. Serve immediately.

Cucumber and Mung Bean Soup

INDIA   Yield: 6 to 8 servings

¾ cup yellow split mung beans,
   cleaned and washed
⅛ teaspoon turmeric
3 cups water
¾ cup potatoes, grated
2 cups cucumbers (about 2 large
   cucumbers), grated
1½ teaspoons Kosher salt
4 tablespoons ghee or light oil
¾ teaspoon cumin seeds
¼ teaspoon black pepper
Juice of ½ lemon
2 tablespoons fresh coriander leaves,
   minced

In a large saucepan, place beans, turmeric, and water. Bring to a boil; reduce
heat and simmer for 30 minutes. Stir the
soup from time to time. When cooking time
is finished, transfer soup to a bowl and puree
with electric beater or wire whisk. Add
enough hot water to make 5 cups in all. Return to saucepan.

Bring the puree to a boil along with the
potatoes, onions, cucumbers, and salt. Simmer about 5 minutes. In a small frying pan,
heat the ghee. Put in the cumin and black
pepper just until coated with ghee. Remove
from heat. Pour this mixture on top of the
soup. Add lemon juice and coriander leaves
and serve at once.

Corn and Chicken Soup

CHINA   Yield: 4 to 6 servings

6 ounces raw chicken meat, minced
1 tablespoon dry sherry
1 teaspoon salt
2 egg whites
1 quart chicken broth
1 10-ounce can cream-style corn
2 tablespoons cornstarch in ¼ cup
    cold water
Thin strips of ham

Combine the chicken with the sherry, salt, and egg whites. Bring the chicken broth to a full, rolling boil. Add minced-chicken mixture and corn. Simmer 2 minutes. Add cornstarch mixture and simmer an additional 2 minutes, stirring continuously. Add more salt, if needed. Pour into serving bowls and garnish with thin strips of ham.

Cucumber Soup

CHINA   Yield: 6 servings

¾ tablespoon salt
¼ teaspoon cornstarch
1 teaspoon soy sauce
½ cup pork, sliced in pieces ½ × ¼
    × ¾ inch
1 tablespoon vegetable oil
4 cups water
10 medium-size mushrooms, cut into
    ½-inch strips
5 red dates, if desired
¾ cup bamboo shoots, sliced in pieces
    ½ × ¼ × ¾ inch
3 cucumbers
Fish balls, optional

Add ¼ teaspoon salt, cornstarch, and soy sauce to the pork and allow them to

stand for 5 minutes. Heat the oil and brown the pork for 3 minutes. Add the water, mushrooms, red dates, bamboo shoots, and remaining salt, and simmer for 30 to 45 minutes. Discard the red dates. Peel the cucumbers and cut them into cross sections. Add the cucumber pieces to the soup and boil it for 3 minutes. Serve immediately.

Fish balls may be added. Drop them into the boiling soup and boil for 3 minutes after they come to the surface. Then add the cucumber pieces and boil the soup for 3 minutes.

Fig and Pork Soup

CHINA   Yield: 8 servings

1 pound partially ripe figs
4 dried red dates, if desired
¼ roll salted mustard cabbage root, if
    desired
¼ pound pork liver
1 pound pork soup bone (with very
    little meat)
½ pound lean pork
5 cups boiling water
1½ teaspoons salt

Remove stem ends, wash, and cut the figs into quarters. Wash red dates and cabbage root. Remove white tissue from the liver. Combine all the ingredients and boil slowly for 1½ hours.

Remove the liver and pork and slice them into strips. Discard red dates, cabbage root, and the soup bone. Serve the figs and soup in a bowl garnished with slices of pork and liver.

Green Mustard Cabbage and Dried Shrimp Soup

CHINA   Yield: 6 servings

1 bunch green mustard cabbage
    (¾ pound), cut crosswise into
    1½-inch pieces
½ cup large dried shrimp
4½ cups water
1 tablespoon vegetable oil
1 teaspoon salt

Keep the cabbage leaf and stalk pieces separate. Wash and soak the dried shrimp in 1 cup water for ½ hour. Drain the shrimp but save the liquid. Add the shrimp to very hot oil and fry them for 2 or 3 minutes. Add the remaining water and the shrimp liquid and simmer for ½ hour. Add the cabbage stalks and boil them for 1 minute; add the leaves, and boil for 2 minutes. Serve the soup immediately.

Finely sliced lean pork or beef may be substituted for the shrimp. Combine ½ cup meat with water or soup, add salt, and simmer for ½ hour. Add the cabbage with stalks and leaves separated. Watercress, celery cabbage, or spinach may be substituted for mustard cabbage.

Soup with Fresh Greens

BURMA   Yield: 4 servings

This soup can be as varied as the greens you use in it. Any fresh green vegetable will do, from watercress to spinach to mustard leaves. It's quick and easy too.

5 cups water
1 medium onion, peeled and sliced
3 cloves garlic, peeled and sliced

3 tablespoons pounded dried shrimp
½ teaspoon shrimp paste, optional
2 teaspoons soy sauce
1 teaspoon salt
½ pound green leaves, washed and
    drained

Bring the water, onion, and garlic to a boil. Reduce the heat and add shrimp, shrimp paste, soy sauce, and salt. Stir well to blend all the flavors. Then, put in the green leaves. Boil all together for just 5 minutes. Add extra seasonings if desired. Serve at once.

Melon and Dried Shrimp Soup

INDOCHINA   Yield: 4 to 6 servings

½ cup dried shrimp
6 dried Chinese mushrooms
1 pound melon (any variety) or
    cucumbers
8 cups chicken stock
1 to 2 tablespoons fish sauce
6 thin slices fresh ginger
2 tablespoons Chinese wine or dry
    sherry

Soak dried shrimp in water overnight. Drain.

Soak mushrooms in hot water for 30 minutes. Discard the stems and slice the caps finely.

Peel the melon and scrape out the center portion with seeds. Cut into bite-size pieces.

In a saucepan, place stock, fish sauce, ginger, mushrooms, and dried shrimp. Bring all to a boil and then reduce heat. Simmer for 30 minutes. Remove and discard ginger slices. Add the melon and simmer for 5 minutes more. Then, add the wine and stir once. Dish into individual serving bowls.

Soups

Lentil and Vegetable Soup

INDIA   Yield: 4 to 6 servings

1 cup yellow split peas or red lentils,
    soaked overnight and drained
6 cups water
1 tablespoon tamarind pulp
1 cup hot water
1 pound mixed vegetables such as
    eggplant, carrots, and beans
2 tablespoons ghee or oil
1 tablespoon ground coriander
2 teaspoons ground cumin
½ teaspoon ground black pepper
½ teaspoon ground turmeric
1 peppercorn-size grain of asafetida
2 green chilies, seeded and sliced
2½ teaspoons salt
½ teaspoon black mustard seeds
1 small onion, finely sliced

Place lentils in 6 cups water and cook
until soft. At the same time, soak tamarind
pulp in hot water. When the water cools,
squeeze the tamarind pulp and strain, keeping only the seasoned liquid. Add this to
lentils. Prepare vegetables by cutting into
small bite-size pieces.

In a small skillet, heat 1 tablespoon ghee.
Stirring constantly, fry the ground spices and
asafetida for 2 minutes. Put them in with the
lentils, along with the chilies, salt, and vegetables. This will cook for about 30 minutes
or until vegetables are soft.

In the remaining tablespoon of ghee, fry
the mustard seeds and onion slices until
onion is brown. Add this to the soup mixture and simmer for 2 minutes more. Serve
at once.

Indian Pea Soup

INDIA   Yield: About 5 cups

1 1-pound can peas, drained, liquid
    reserved
3 cups chicken broth or bouillon
2 teaspoons curry powder
1 teaspoon sugar
¼ cup all-purpose flour, shaken in a
    jar with ⅓ cup cold water until
    lump-free
¼ cup slivered almonds
¼ cup raisins
½ cup light cream
Salt and pepper to taste

Place drained peas in food processor bowl
and process with metal blade until smooth.
Place in saucepan with reserved liquid,
broth, curry, sugar, and flour mixture. Bring
to a boil, stirring constantly. Add almonds
and raisins. Simmer 5 minutes. Remove from
heat and add cream. Season to taste with salt
and pepper. Serve at once.

Pumpkin or Squash Soup

BURMA   Yield: 4 to 6 servings

1 cup uncooked shrimp, shelled and
    deveined
6 cups beef broth
1 large onion, finely chopped
2 teaspoons anchovy paste
2 cloves garlic, minced
4 cups pumpkin or winter squash, cut
    into small squares
¼ teaspoon ground dried chili peppers
Salt to taste

Dice the raw shrimp very finely. Put into
saucepan with the beef broth, onion, anchovy paste, and garlic. Bring this mixture to
a boil. Add the remaining ingredients. When
mixture has again come to a boil, reduce
heat and simmer for 15 minutes. Serve at
once.

34

Radish and Fish Soup

BURMA   Yield: 4 servings

A substitute for the long white radishes can be white turnips. Other substitutes can be spinach, eggplant, or okra.

½ pound white fish fillets, cut into
  chunks
1 teaspoon salt
½ teaspoon turmeric powder
2 tablespoons vegetable oil
1 medium onion, peeled and pounded
  or finely grated
3 cloves garlic, peeled and crushed
½-inch piece of fresh gingerroot,
  peeled and pounded
½ teaspoon chili powder
4 tomatoes, chopped
½ teaspoon shrimp paste, optional
1 tablespoon shrimp-flavored soy sauce
5 cups cold water
5 sprigs coriander leaves
3 tablespoons dried tamarind pulp
6 tablespoons hot water
¾ pound long white radishes including
  green tops, peeled and thinly sliced

Rub the fish with salt and turmeric and set aside.

Heat the vegetable oil and lightly brown onion, garlic, ginger, and chili powder, stirring well to mix the flavors. Add the fish and stir-fry until the pieces are well coated. Next add tomatoes, shrimp paste, and soy sauce. Add water and coriander and bring to a boil. Reduce heat to a simmer for 15 minutes.

In a bowl, pour the hot water over the tamarind pulp and knead to get the flavor. Strain off the liquid and discard the pulp. Add the tamarind liquid and radishes to the soup pot and simmer for 15 minutes more. Check the seasoning and add any if needed. Allow the soup to stand for at least 30 minutes.

When ready to serve, reheat just to the boiling point and serve at once.

Spinach Soup with Pork

CHINA   Yield: 6 servings

1½ bunches spinach (1½ pounds)
1 tablespoon soy sauce
2¼ teaspoons salt
½ cup sliced lean pork, sliced 1½ ×
  ½ × ¼ inches
1 tablespoon vegetable oil
1 clove garlic, mashed
6 cups boiling water

Remove the tough stems from the spinach and wash the leafy portions thoroughly. Add the soy sauce and ¼ teaspoon salt to the pork. Heat the oil in a wok, add the mashed garlic and pork, and fry them for 3 minutes. Remove the garlic if desired. Add the boiling water, 2 teaspoons salt, and simmer for 10 minutes. Add the spinach and simmer for 5 minutes. Serve hot.

One-fourth cup dried shrimp may be substituted for the pork and the salt reduced to 1½ teaspoons. Wash and soak the shrimp for 15 minutes. Drain, but keep the liquid. Fry the shrimp, add the liquid, and simmer for 10 minutes; then add the spinach.

Rice Chowder

JAPAN   Yield: 4 servings

2 cups leftover cooked chicken, diced
5 cups chicken stock
2 tablespoons soy sauce
2 tablespoons sherry
Pinch of salt
½ teaspoon ground ginger
4 cups leftover rice
4 scallions, chopped

Add diced chicken to the boiling stock that has been mixed with the soy sauce, sherry, salt, and ginger. Simmer slowly for about 10 minutes. Add the leftover rice; heat through.

Put ¼ of the chopped scallions into each of 4 individual bowls. Pour in the soup; serve.

Soup of Soybean Sprouts

KOREA   Yield: 4 to 6 servings

1 pound soybean sprouts, washed,
   drained, and tails pinched off
1 pound lean steak, cut into thin strips
1 tablespoon soy sauce
1 tablespoon sesame oil
¼ teaspoon ground black pepper
2 cloves garlic, peeled and crushed
8 cups water
Finely chopped green leaves of 2 spring
   onions

Prepare bean sprouts, chopping them if they are too long. Marinate the meat in soy sauce, sesame-seed oil, pepper, and garlic for 30 minutes.

Heat wok or large saucepan and stir-fry beef until it browns nicely. Add water and bean sprouts and bring to a boil. Cover and simmer for 30 minutes. Remove from heat and add onion leaves. Let stand covered for 5 minutes. Adjust seasoning with soy sauce and salt if desired and serve at once.

Chinese Tomato Soup

CHINA   Yield: 4 to 6 servings

1 pound tomatoes
1 tablespoon peanut oil
1 scallion, chopped
5 cups chicken or beef broth
1 egg, slightly beaten
1¼ teaspoon salt
Dash of pepper

Peel tomatoes, cut into wedges, and remove seeds. Heat oil in saucepan over high heat. Add tomato wedges and chopped scallion; stir-fry 2 minutes. Add broth; bring to boil and slowly stir in egg, salt, and pepper. Cook until egg is lightly set (about ½ minute).

Watercress Soup

CHINA   Yield: 5 servings

4 cups watercress, cut in 2-inch pieces
4½ cups water
1 teaspoon salt
¼ cup fresh lean pork, sliced 1½ ×
   ½ × ¼ inches

Wash the watercress thoroughly and discard the tough stems. Cut the watercress and keep the tougher portions separate. Combine the water, salt, and pork and simmer for 30 minutes. Add the tough watercress and boil for 1 minute. Add the watercress tips, boil for 1 minute, and serve immediately.

Japanese Vegetable Soup I

JAPAN   Yield: 1½ quarts

    1 pound lean pork
    1 carrot
    12 dried mushrooms
    4 cups chicken stock
    1 4-ounce can bamboo shoots, drained
    1 tablespoon soy sauce
    ½ cup fresh spinach leaves, chopped
    1 teaspoon powdered ginger

Cut the pork and carrot into julienne strips. Place the dried mushrooms in a small bowl. Add enough of the chicken stock to cover and let stand for 1 hour. Remove the mushrooms from the stock and slice, then place in a large saucepan. Add the stock from the bowl, the remaining stock, and the pork and bring to a boil. Reduce the heat to low and simmer for 10 minutes.

Add the carrot, bamboo shoots, and soy sauce and cook for 5 minutes longer. Stir in the spinach and ginger and boil rapidly for 2 minutes.

Japanese Vegetable Soup II

JAPAN   Yield: 4 servings

    2 ounces dried mushrooms
    Cold water
    ½ pound lean pork
    1 carrot
    4 ounces canned bamboo shoots
    2 celery stalks
    4 cups hot beef broth
    4 ounces fresh spinach
    3 tablespoons rice wine or sherry
    1 tablespoon soy sauce
    ⅛ teaspoon ground ginger
    3 drops Tabasco sauce

Soak mushrooms in a generous amount of cold water for 30 minutes, covering the bowl. Cut pork into very thin strips. Cut the carrot and bamboo shoots into matchstick-size pieces. Cut the celery into thin slices. Drain the mushrooms; cut them into halves or quarters, depending on size. Bring beef broth to a boil. Add pork, mushrooms, and other vegetables. Cook over low heat for 10 minutes.

Meanwhile, thoroughly wash the spinach; chop it coarsely. Remove soup from heat, add spinach, and let stand for 3 minutes. Season soup with rice wine (or sherry), soy sauce, ginger, and Tabasco sauce. Return it to heat; heat through, but do not boil again.

Serve soup in preheated soup bowls or cups.

Vegetable Soup

INDONESIA   Yield: 2 to 3 servings

    2 ears corn, husked and sliced from the
        cob
    2 tablespoons onions, chopped
    1 teaspoon chopped garlic, optional
    2 tablespoons sugar
    1 teaspoon salt
    3 cups water
    2 bouillon cubes, optional
    4 ounces spinach

Put all ingredients except the spinach into a saucepan. Bring to a boil; reduce heat and simmer for 2 minutes. Add spinach and cook for 2 more minutes. Spoon into soup bowls.

Chinese Soup

CHINA   Yield: 4 to 6 servings

1 quart chicken broth
½ teaspoon salt (or salt to taste)
¼ teaspoon pepper (or less)
2 teaspoons soy sauce
2 ounces whole, cooked shrimp
2 ounces cooked ham, cut into thin
strips
2 ounces cooked chicken, cut into thin
strips

Bring the chicken broth to a boil and add all the remaining ingredients. Simmer 3 to 4 minutes and serve immediately.

Clear Soup I

JAPAN   Yield: 4 servings

This is a nice soup to start off with before enjoying a dinner of Sukiyaki or Tempura.

4 cups chicken broth
1 teaspoon soy sauce
1 teaspoon sugar
Pinch of salt
1 cup chicken, cubed
1 scallion, finely chopped
Few sprigs of parsley

Combine chicken broth, soy sauce, sugar, and salt; bring to a boil.

In each of 4 bowls, put a few cubes of chicken, a few pieces of scallion, and parsley for garnish. Pour soup into bowls; serve without spoons.

Clear Soup II

BURMA   Yield: 4 servings

Add cabbage, cauliflower, bean sprouts, or noodles to this if you choose. It is tasty clear or with vegetables.

6 cups water
¾ pound pork bones
5 peppercorns, crushed
3 cloves garlic, peeled and crushed
2 teaspoons soy sauce
Salt and pepper to taste
Finely chopped celery and/or
Finely chopped scallions plus tops for
garnish

Measure the water into a large saucepan. Add pork bones, peppercorns, garlic, and soy sauce and bring to a boil. Then reduce the heat and simmer for about 30 minutes. Remove the bones from the soup. Season to taste. Serve in warmed soup bowls and garnish with celery and/or scallions.

Soup with Dumplings

PHILIPPINES   Yield: 6 to 8 servings

Dough

3 cups flour
¼ teaspoon salt
3 egg yolks, beaten lightly
¼ cup water

Filling

1 cup ground pork (½ pound)
1 egg yolk
½ teaspoon salt
Dash of pepper

Broth

2 cloves garlic, peeled and crushed
½ medium onion, chopped
1½ cups shrimp, shelled and deveined
About 3 tablespoons lard or oil
Salt to taste
3 cups shrimp juice (pound heads of shrimp, squeezing out juice, adding enough water to make 3 cups)
1 chicken, cooked and cut into small pieces
3 quarts chicken broth
Salt and pepper to taste
2 tablespoons parsley, chopped

To make the dough, combine the flour and salt; make a well in center of mixture and add the egg yolks. When well mixed, gradually add water. Knead until dough is elastic. Pat down very thin on a floured board. Cut into 3-inch triangles.

Mix all of the filling ingredients in a bowl in the order given. Spoon 1 teaspoon into the center of each triangle, folding the dough over the filling. Seal the edges of the dough and set aside.

To make the broth, melt lard and sauté garlic, onion, and shrimp until brown. Add salt and shrimp juice; bring to a boil for 1 minute. Add chicken and broth. When all has come to a boil again, drop in the prepared dumplings. Check seasonings, adding salt and pepper if needed. Lower heat and allow to simmer for 20 minutes. Add more pepper if desired. Dish into soup bowls and garnish with chopped parsley.

Soup with Vegetables and Meat Dumplings

CHINA   Yield: 4 to 6 servings

Meat dumplings

2 slices bread
½ pound lean ground beef
Salt
White pepper
5 cups beef bouillon

Soup

¾ head savoy cabbage (green cabbage can be substituted), sliced
1 leek, sliced
2 ounces fresh mushrooms, sliced
1 celery stalk, sliced
1 tablespoon oil
1 small onion, chopped
2 ounces frozen peas
4 ounces egg noodles
Salt
White pepper
1 tablespoon soy sauce
3 tablespoons sherry

Soak bread in small amount of cold water. Squeeze as dry as possible and mix with ground beef and salt and pepper to taste. Bring bouillon to a boil. Using 1 teaspoon of meat mixture, form little dumplings and drop into boiling broth. Reduce heat and simmer for 10 minutes.

For soup, slice cabbage, leek, mushrooms, and celery. Heat oil in a large saucepan. Add onion and cook until golden. Add sliced vegetables and cook for 5 minutes. Remove dumplings from beef broth with a slotted spoon, drain on paper toweling, and keep warm. Strain broth and add to vegetables. Add peas and noodles and simmer for 15 minutes. Return dumplings to soup. Season with salt, pepper, soy sauce, and sherry. Serve immediately.

Cold Noodle Soup

KOREA   Yield: 4 to 6 servings

1 pound fresh wheat noodles
Boiling water
½ pound cooked beef brisket or top
    round
4 cups chicken stock
8 whole black peppercorns
2-inch piece of fresh gingerroot, peeled
1 to 2 teaspoons salt
1 teaspoon soy sauce
4 dried chilies
24 cucumber slices
1 large, hard pear, peeled, cored, and
    thinly sliced
3 hard-cooked eggs, shelled and cut in
    half lengthwise
Prepared mustard and vinegar to taste

Cook noodles in boiling water for 5
minutes. Drain and set aside to cool.

Slice the meat into strips about 2 inches
long by ½ inch wide.

Place all ingredients in a saucepan except
the noodles. Reduce heat after mixture has
come to a boil and simmer for 5 minutes. Allow to get cold; remove peppercorns, ginger,
and chilies.

Divide noodles into individual serving
bowls. Divide cucumber and pear slices as
well, alternating the slices in layers on top of
the noodles. Place a half egg on top of each
bowl. Spoon the cold soup over all that is in
the bowl. Top with mustard and vinegar.
This soup is served cold.

Noodles in Broth

INDONESIA   Yield: 4 to 6 servings

6 ounces egg noodles, parboiled and set
    aside to drain

2 cloves garlic, thinly sliced
1 onion, peeled and thinly sliced
1 tablespoon oil or margarine
7 cups water
2 slices fresh ginger
1 pound chicken breasts
Salt and freshly ground pepper to taste
4 cabbage leaves, shredded
1 cup bean sprouts, cleaned
2 shallots or spring onions including
    green tops, cut in ½-inch pieces
¼ cup snipped celery tops
¼ cup fried onion flakes

Stir-fry garlic and onion slices in oil in
the bottom of a deep saucepan. Add water,
chicken breasts, and salt and pepper to taste.
When this comes to a boil, reduce the heat
and cook for 20 minutes or until the chicken
is tender. Remove the chicken and allow to
cool. When you can handle the chicken,
remove bones and cut breast meat into strips.
Set aside.

Add cabbage, bean sprouts, and shallots
to the stock and simmer for 2 minutes. Put
cut-up chicken strips in and continue to
simmer until chicken is hot. Adjust salt and
pepper to taste.

Divide the noodles into individual soup
bowls. Fill each bowl with piping hot soup
stock and garnish with celery tops and onion
flakes. Serve at once.

Transparent Vermicelli Soup

THAILAND   Yield: 4 to 6 servings

¼ pound wun sen, soaked in water for
    10 minutes
2 coriander roots, finely chopped
2 cloves garlic, peeled and chopped
1 teaspoon freshly ground black pepper

½ cup ground pork, firmly packed
5 cups water
3 large shrimp, shelled and deveined
⅓ cup dried shrimp, optional
1 ounce dried squid, sliced, optional
½ onion, peeled and sliced
2 tablespoons tree ears, soaked in warm
  water for 20 minutes
1 egg
Few scallions, finely chopped to
  garnish

Separate the wun sen and drain; then cut it into 2-inch lengths. Grind the coriander roots, garlic, and pepper to a fine paste. Continue pounding the mixture as you add the pork. When the paste is smooth, shape into small balls about ½ inch in diameter.

In a large saucepan, bring water to a boil; add pork balls and cook for 5 minutes. Add the shrimp. If any scum rises to the surface, spoon it off. Allow to simmer for 5 minutes, stirring constantly.

Add remaining ingredients, except for egg and scallions, and continue to simmer for 5 more minutes. Gradually stir in the egg, and then remove the soup from the heat. Garnish with scallions and serve at once.

Wonton Soup

CHINA   Yield: 6 servings

Dough for dumplings

4 ounces flour
Salt
1 tablespoon milk
2 tablespoons oil
1 small egg

Filling

4 ounces fresh spinach, chopped
4 ounces ground pork
½ tablespoon soy sauce
⅛ teaspoon powdered ginger

Soup

5 cups chicken broth
2 tablespoons chives, chopped

In bowl, stir together flour and salt. Add milk, oil, and egg. Knead dough until it is smooth. On a floured board, roll out dough until it is paper thin. Cut into 3-inch squares. Cover with a kitchen towel while you prepare the filling.

Thoroughly wash spinach; remove coarse stems. Place in bowl and barely cover with boiling water; let stand for 3 minutes. Drain well and coarsely chop. Add ground pork, soy sauce, and ginger. Blend thoroughly. Place 1 teaspoon of filling on each dough square, giving filling a lengthy shape. Fold over dough from one side and roll up jelly-roll fashion. Press ends of roll together to seal.

Bring chicken broth to a boil. Add wontons and simmer over low heat for 20 minutes. Spoon soup into bowls. Garnish with chopped chives.

Coconut Milk Soup

MALAYSIA   Yield: 4 to 6 servings

2 cups thin coconut milk
2 medium onions, peeled and sliced
6 curry leaves
2 fresh red or green chilies, seeded
½ teaspoon ground turmeric
1½ teaspoons salt
2 tablespoons prawn powder
1½ cups thick coconut milk
2 tablespoons lemon juice

Place coconut milk, onions, curry leaves, chilies, and seasonings in a large saucepan. Bring to a boil and then simmer for 15 minutes. Add thick coconut milk, stirring constantly with a wooden spoon. When all is heated, remove from burner. Add lemon juice and stir to blend. Spoon over boiled rice and serve with a dry curry.

Bird's Nest Soup

CHINA   Yield: 8 servings

1½ cups bird's nest soaked overnight in 1 quart of water, feathers and debris removed
1½ pounds chicken (including bones)
6 cups cold water
4 teaspoons salt
5 dried red dates, if desired
½ cup cooked ham, finely chopped

Cook the bird's nest and water slowly for 1 hour in a wok and drain off the water. Cold water may be added to cool the bird's nest. Take a small portion of the bird's nest in the hand and squeeze out the excess water; remove and discard the black and brown particles. Look over the entire quantity in this manner.

Place the chicken in 6 cups cold water, add the salt, and skim off the substance that rises to the top as the liquid comes to the boiling point. Cook slowly for 1½ hours. Add the dates and cleaned bird's nest and continue simmering for 3 to 4 hours. Remove the chicken, separate the meat from the bones, and finely chop the meat. Add 1 cup chopped chicken and ½ cup chopped ham to the soup.

Mix slightly and serve hot. This soup is usually served as the first course of a banquet or elaborate dinner.

Long-Rice Soup

CHINA   Yield: 6 to 8 servings

This is also known as Imitation Bird's Nest Soup.

1 cup soaked long rice (½ bunch—available in Oriental food stores)
¾ teaspoon salt
5 cups boiling water or chicken broth
⅜ cup fresh lean pork, finely minced
⅓ cup smoked ham, finely minced
1 tablespoon water chestnuts, finely chopped
½ tablespoon soy sauce
1 teaspoon (or ½ cup, optional) green onions with tops, finely chopped
½ cup mushrooms, finely chopped, optional
½ cup bamboo shoots, finely chopped, optional
¼ teaspoon cornstarch, optional

Soak the long rice in cold water for ½ hour. Drain, and cut in 6-inch lengths. Add long rice and salt to the boiling water and boil for 20 minutes. Combine the pork, ham, water chestnuts, and soy sauce. Shape into balls ¾ inch in diameter. Drop into the soup mixture and boil 10 minutes. Do not stir. Add the green onions and serve immediately. To improve the flavor, ½ cup finely chopped mushrooms and ½ cup finely chopped bamboo shoots may be added to the soup and the green onions increased to ½ cup.

One-fourth teaspoon cornstarch may be mixed with the soy sauce and meat mixture so that the balls will retain their shape during cooking.

Chrysanthemum Soup

INDOCHINA   Yield: 4 servings

Use chrysanthemum choy, a cultivated, edible form of the flower, available in Oriental groceries.

½ cup ground pork
Freshly ground black pepper to taste
2 tablespoons plus 1 teaspoon fish sauce

1 shallot, peeled and finely chopped
6 cups chicken stock
1 pound chrysanthemum choy
2 scallions, cut into 2-inch lengths

In a bowl, mix the pork, pepper, 1 teaspoon fish sauce, and shallot. Allow to stand for about 15 minutes. Take 1 teaspoon of meat mixture and shape into a small ball. Continue until all of meat is used and rolled.

Bring the soup stock to a boil and add the pork balls. Cook for 12 minutes. Put in remaining fish sauce and black pepper to taste.

Line a warmed soup tureen with chrysanthemum choy and scallions. Over this, pour the hot stock and the meatballs. Rice and fish sauce make a nice accompaniment for this soup.

Curry Soup

INDONESIA   Yield: 2 to 3 servings

1 teaspoon ground chestnuts or
    cashews
½ cup meat or chicken, cubed
2 tablespoons butter or margarine
¼ teaspoon curry powder
1 cup beef broth
½ cup potatoes, peeled and diced
½ cup green beans, sliced
½ cup carrots, diced
1 bay leaf
1 cup coconut milk
Salt to taste
1 tablespoon dried onion flakes,
    sautéed in 2 teaspoons oil

Stir nuts and meat in the melted butter along with the curry powder. Slowly pour in the beef broth and bring to a boil. Put in the vegetables and the bay leaf and cover. Re-

duce heat to medium and cook about 10 minutes or until the vegetables are tender.

Add the milk and extra salt if desired. Once again, bring the soup to a boil. Garnish with onion flakes and serve at once.

Hot-and-Sour Soup

CHINA   Yield: 5 to 6 servings

¼ cup cloud ears
¼ cup golden needles
¼ pound pork, shredded into
    1½-inch-long strips
3 tablespoons cornstarch
2 teaspoons sherry
½ cup water
3 tablespoons white-wine vinegar (or
    to taste)
White pepper to taste
½ teaspoon hot oil
2 teaspoons sesame-seed oil
4 cups chicken stock
Salt to taste
1 tablespoon soy sauce
2 bean curds, each cut into 8 pieces
1 egg, beaten
2 scallions, chopped

Soak cloud ears and golden needles in hot water about 15 minutes or until noticeably increased in size; drain. Shred cloud ears. Cut golden needles in half. Combine pork with 1 tablespoon cornstarch and sherry.

Mix 2 tablespoons cornstarch with water; set aside.

Combine vinegar, pepper, hot oil, and sesame oil in bowl; set aside.

Bring chicken stock, salt, and soy sauce to boil in large soup pot. Add pork; boil 1 minute. Add cloud ears, golden needles, and bean curds; boil 1 minute. Add cornstarch mixture; stir until thickened. Lower heat. Add vinegar mixture. Taste; adjust seasoning if necessary. Slowly stir in egg. Garnish with scallions.

Lime Soup

INDIA   Yield: 6 to 8 servings

1 cinnamon stick, 3 inches long,
  broken into 3 pieces
6 whole cloves
3 green cardamom pods
1 teaspoon black peppercorns
4 tablespoons ghee or oil
2 medium-size onions, peeled and
  chopped
5 medium-size potatoes, peeled and
  cubed
¼ teaspoon turmeric
6 cups homemade beef, vegetable, or
  chicken broth
¼ cup firmly packed fresh coriander
  leaves or 2 tablespoons dried
  coriander leaves
Kosher salt to taste
⅔ cup coconut milk
⅓ cup heavy cream
Juice of 1 small lime or lemon

Tie cinnamon, cloves, cardamom, and
peppercorns in a piece of cheesecloth and
crush spices together with a wooden mallet.
  Heat the ghee in a large saucepan; add
onions and potatoes. Stir often and cook for
10 minutes. Add the turmeric, broth, and
spice bag. When soup has come to a boil,
reduce heat and simmer for about 30
minutes. Turn off heat and add coriander
leaves and salt. Allow to cool. When broth
is cool, remove spice bag and purée in a
blender, food processor, or food mill.
  Reheat the soup and add coconut milk
and heavy cream. Simmer until all liquid is
heated. When serving, garnish each individual soup bowl with a little lime juice on
top.

Lotus Root and Pork Soup

CHINA   Yield: 6 servings

1 pound lotus root (4 sections)
5 cups cold water
1 pound soup bone (with very little
  meat)
⅓ pound lean pork
1½ teaspoons salt

Place the scraped lotus root in cold
water. Bring the water to a boil, add the
soup bone and piece of pork, and simmer for
3 to 4 hours. Add the salt near the end of
the cooking period. Remove the lotus root
and pork. Cut them into thin slices, place in
a serving dish, and pour in the soup stock.
  The lotus root and pork may also be
served separately and the soup served clear.

Milk Soup

INDONESIA   Yield: 2 to 3 servings

2 tablespoons butter or margarine
2 tablespoons onions, chopped
1 teaspoon garlic, chopped
1 bay leaf
Dash of ground coriander
1 teaspoon salt
2 cups chicken broth
1 small stalk Chinese cabbage,
  chopped
1 cup coconut milk

Melt butter in a saucepan; gently sauté
the onions and garlic. Put in spices and
chicken broth and bring to a boil. Add cabbage and reduce heat to medium. Cook a few
minutes, until the cabbage is just tender.
Then, put in the milk and stir constantly until soup comes to a boil once more. Serve at
once.

Mulligatawny Soup

INDIA   Yield: 4 to 6 servings

Mullaga means pepper and tanni means water and broth. The combination of flavors used here was first created about two centuries ago in India for the British.

3 to 4 tablespoons butter or oil
1 large onion, chopped
1 carrot, chopped
1 or 2 stalks celery, chopped
1 medium sour cooking apple
1 tablespoon curry powder or paste
1½ tablespoons flour
1 tablespoon tomato purée
4 to 5 cups stock
1 bay leaf
3 or 4 sprigs parsley
Pinch of thyme
Salt and pepper
2 tablespoons shredded coconut
1 teaspoon sugar
4 to 6 tablespoons cooked rice
2 teaspoons lemon juice
4 to 6 slices lemon
Paprika

Melt butter. Add onion, carrot, celery, and apple; stir well. Cook gently 5 to 6 minutes. Add curry; cook a few minutes. Add flour; mix well. Cook a few minutes to brown slightly. Add tomato purée and stock; blend well. Bring slowly to boil; reduce heat. Add herbs, seasoning, coconut, and sugar; simmer 30 to 45 minutes with lid on pan.

Remove bay leaf. Blend soup in electric blender or put through fine food mill; return to pan. Add rice; adjust seasoning. Reheat; add lemon juice just before serving. (If preferred, rice can be served separately.) Serve hot with slice of lemon; sprinkle with paprika.

Pepper Water

INDIA   Yield: 4 to 6 servings

Rasam, or pepper water, is frequently served in southern India. It can be a course by itself or an accompaniment to the meal.

1 tablespoon dried tamarind pulp
1 cup hot water
2 cloves garlic, peeled and sliced
1 peppercorn-size grain of asafetida
1 teaspoon ground black pepper
1 teaspoon ground cumin
4 cups cold water
2 teaspoons salt
2 tablespoons fresh coriander leaves, chopped
2 teaspoons oil
1 teaspoon black mustard seeds
8 curry leaves

Allow tamarind pulp to soak in hot water for 10 minutes. Squeeze and strain, keeping only the seasoned liquid. Bring the tamarind liquid, garlic, asafetida, pepper, cumin, water, salt, and coriander leaves to a boil in a saucepan. Reduce heat and simmer for 10 minutes.

Heat the oil in a small frying pan; sauté mustard seeds and curry leaves until leaves are brown. Add this to the simmering soup. Serve at once.

Oxtail Soup

KOREA   Yield: 6 to 8 servings

  1 oxtail, cut into 8 pieces
  8 cups water
  2 slices fresh ginger
  1 teaspoon salt

Dipping Sauce

  3 tablespoons light soy sauce
  1 tablespoon sesame oil
  1 tablespoon toasted crushed sesame
    seeds
  ¼ teaspoon ground black pepper
  3 tablespoons spring onions, finely
    chopped
  3 teaspoons garlic, finely chopped
  1 teaspoon ginger, finely chopped

Put oxtail, water, 2 slices ginger, and 1 teaspoon salt into a saucepan and bring to a boil. Reduce heat and simmer for about 2 hours or until the meat is tender to the fork. Lift off any froth or scum that forms during the cooking. Remove oxtail and cut meat from the bones and into bite-size pieces; return meat to broth.

Combine the sauce ingredients in a bowl; mix well until all flavors blend. Serve dipping sauce with the soup.

Cold Senegalese Soup

SENEGAL   Yield: About 8 servings

  2 medium onions, chopped
  2 stalks celery, chopped
  4 tablespoons margarine or butter
  2 tablespoons flour
  1 tablespoon curry powder
  2 quarts chicken broth
  1 bay leaf
  2 apples, peeled and chopped

  1 cup light cream
  1 cup cooked chicken, diced
  1 tablespoon dill weed

Sauté onion and celery in butter until limp. Add flour and curry powder; cook slowly, stirring, for 5 minutes. Add broth, bay leaf, and apples. Cook 30 minutes; strain and chill. Before serving, add cream and sprinkle with chicken. Garnish with dill. If this soup is not served very cold, it will lose all its zest.

Sharks'-Fin Soup

CHINA   Yield: About 8 servings

  ¾ pound dried sharks' fins
  1 tablespoon oil
  2 tablespoons fresh gingerroot, sliced
  ¼ cup scallions, sliced
  1 tablespoon sherry
  3 quarts chicken broth, divided
  2 tablespoons cornstarch
  1 teaspoon soy sauce
  ¼ cup water
  ½ pound crab meat

Wash sharks' fins and cover with cold water. Drain, cover with fresh water, and boil 3 hours. Drain, add fresh water, and boil again for 3 hours. Drain and let dry.

Heat oil in large saucepan. Sauté the ginger and scallions for 3 minutes. Add the sherry, 1 quart of the chicken broth, and the sharks' fins. Cook over medium-high heat for 15 minutes. Drain off any remaining liquid. Add the remaining broth; bring to a boil. Mix together the cornstarch, soy sauce, and water. Slowly stir into the soup. Stir in the crab meat. Heat through.

Fish and Seafood

Fish with Sweet-and-Sour Sauce

MALAYSIA   Yield: 4 to 6 servings

1 teaspoon gingerroot, finely chopped
Salt and pepper to taste
1½ pounds bass, cleaned and wiped
   dry with paper towels
2 teaspoons cornstarch
Fat for deep frying
2 tablespoons catsup
1 cup water
1 teaspoon sugar
Salt and pepper
1 small cucumber, finely minced
Parsley greens for garnish

Add salt and pepper to gingerroot. Marinate the fish in this mixture for 15 minutes. Sprinkle 1 teaspoon cornstarch over fish and let stand for 15 to 20 minutes more. Heat fat in a deep frying pan and fry the fish until it is golden brown. Remove from fat and drain on paper towels. Put on a heated serving plate.

Put remaining cornstarch together with rest of ingredients in a saucepan. Allow the sauce to thicken over medium heat, stirring occasionally. Pour over the prepared fish and garnish with parsley greens.

Cod Fillets in Shrimp Sauce

JAPAN   Yield: 4 servings

4 cod fillets, about 6 ounces each
Juice of 1 lemon
Salt
White pepper
2 tablespoons butter

1 medium onion, sliced
2 tablespoons parsley, chopped
½ cup dry white wine

Shrimp sauce

2 tablespoons butter
1½ tablespoons flour
1 cup hot beef broth
½ cup dry white wine
6 ounces fresh mushrooms
4 ounces fresh shrimp
2 teaspoons lemon juice
Salt
2 egg yolks

Garnish

Lemon slices
Parsley

Sprinkle cod fillets with lemon juice. Let stand for 10 minutes. Season to taste with salt and pepper. Heat butter in large skillet. Add fish; brown well for about 10 minutes on each side. Add sliced onion; cook until golden. Stir in chopped parsley. Pour in white wine; simmer for another 5 minutes. Remove cod fillets to preheated platter; keep them warm. Reserve pan drippings.

To prepare sauce, melt butter in a saucepan. Stir in flour; pour in hot beef broth, as well as reserved pan drippings. Add white wine. Let simmer over low heat. Cut mushrooms into thin slices and add, together with shrimp, to sauce; simmer for 15 minutes. Season to taste with lemon juice and salt. Remove small amount of sauce; blend with egg yolks. Return to sauce; stir thoroughly. Heat through, but do not boil, since yolks will curdle.

Pour sauce over cod fillets. Garnish with lemon slices and parsley.

Steamed Sea Bass

Yield: 4 servings

2 sea bass, about 1½ pounds each,
  cleaned but with heads and tails left on
1 teaspoon salt
4 mushrooms, chopped
1 tablespoon soy sauce
1 tablespoon dry sherry
1 tablespoon fresh gingerroot, peeled
  and finely shredded
1 scallion, including the green top, cut
  into 2-inch lengths
1 tablespoon vegetable oil
½ teaspoon sugar
2 whole shrimp

Wash the bass with cold water and dry with paper towels. With a sharp knife make diagonal cuts ¼ inch deep at ½-inch intervals on both sides of each fish. Sprinkle the fish, inside and out, with the salt.

Lay the fish on a heat-proof platter ½ inch smaller in diameter than the bamboo steamer. Pour the chopped mushrooms and seasonings over the fish, and arrange the pieces of ginger and scallion on top.

Pour enough boiling water into the lower part of the wok so that it comes within an inch of the bamboo steamer. Bring the water to a rolling boil and place the platter of fish into the steamer with the shrimp arranged around it. Steam the fish for about 15 minutes, or until they are firm to the touch. Serve at once in their own steaming platter.

Crab-Meat Dumplings

CHINA   Yield: 2 to 3 servings

12 ounces fresh crab meat, or frozen, if
  fresh is unavailable

3 tablespoons bread or cracker crumbs
1 egg, beaten
Flour for hands

Batter

1 cup flour
1 egg
1 cup water

Oil for frying

Mix together thoroughly the crab meat, bread or cracker crumbs, and egg. Make small balls with floured hands; refrigerate for about 30 minutes.

Meanwhile, make batter of flour, egg, and water; blend until well mixed. If it remains lumpy, it's all right. Heat oil; dip balls into batter, then fry in hot oil. Drain on paper toweling. Serve with soy sauce, if desired.

Crab Rangoon

CHINA   Yield: About 95 filled squares

¼ pound crab meat, chopped
¼ pound cream cheese
¼ teaspoon A-1 sauce
⅛ teaspoon garlic powder
Wonton squares
1 egg yolk, beaten
Oil for deep frying

Blend chopped crab meat with cream cheese, A-1 sauce, and garlic powder. Put ½ teaspoon of mixture in center of each wonton square. Fold corners of the square over, moisten edges with beaten egg yolk, and twist together. Fry in oil until lightly browned. Drain and serve hot.

Japanese Crab Cakes

JAPAN   Yield: 3 servings

12 ounces fresh crab meat, or canned,
    if fresh is unavailable
1 cup frozen peas
3 eggs
1 cup fresh mushrooms, chopped
1 teaspoon freshly grated ginger or ½
    teaspoon ground ginger
Oil
Soy sauce for dipping

Combine crab meat, peas, eggs, mushrooms, and ginger. Mix well. Heat oil in large frying pan; fry all the batter at once, like a pancake. Fry well on one side, then turn carefully and fry well on the other side. Cut into slices and dip into soy sauce.

Qari Vakasoso

INDONESIA   Yield: 4 servings

1 large crab (about 2 cups meat)
1 bunch Chinese cabbage
1 medium-size onion
1 tomato
1 coconut
¼ cup very thick coconut cream

Boil and remove the meat from 1 large crab. Shred the Chinese cabbage finely and boil in salted water. Strain and put aside. Finely chop the onion. Peel and chop the tomato; grate the coconut, leaving a good coating of coconut in the shell. Put the shell aside.

Mix crab, tomato, onion, cabbage and 2 tablespoons grated coconut together. Place in coconut shell and squeeze the very thick coconut cream over the top. Place the lid on the coconut and put in a saucepan with water to steam for 10 minutes. Serve in shell.

This may be prepared with crab as given, or with any available combination of seafood or fish. Excellent for a buffet dinner.

Note: Care must be taken to cut the coconut shell neatly in half.

Eel Kabobs I

JAPAN   Yield: 6 servings

2 pounds eel (2 to 3 eels)
1½ cups dry sherry
2 tablespoons honey
¼ cup teriyaki sauce

Skin eels; cut off heads. Remove eel fillets from bone; cut into 1½-inch pieces. Combine sherry, honey, and teriyaki sauce. Heat to simmer. Pour marinade over eels; let stand 2 hours.

Thread eel on skewers. Place over hot coals; grill 15 to 20 minutes or until fish flakes easily with fork. Baste and turn frequently during cooking period.

Eel Kabobs II

JAPAN   Yield: 2 to 3 servings

2 eels, about 1 pound each

Marinade

¾ cup rice wine or sherry
3 teaspoons honey
5 tablespoons soy sauce

Skin eels, cut off heads, and, with a very sharp knife, remove eel fillets from bone. Cut into 1½-inch pieces; place in deep bowl. Combine rice wine (or sherry), honey, and soy sauce. Heat. Pour marinade over eel pieces. Let marinate for 30 minutes.

Light coals in your barbecue grill; wait until white hot. Thread eel pieces on metal skewers; place on grill. Turn skewers occasionally; baste with marinade. Grill for 15 minutes. This can also be done under the oven broiler or on a hibachi.

Baked Spiced Fish

INDIA   Yield: 4 servings

1¼ cups unflavored yogurt
1 medium onion, peeled and chopped
1 clove garlic, peeled and chopped
1 tablespoon vinegar
1½ teaspoons cumin powder
Pinch of chili powder
1½ pounds fish fillets (sole or
    haddock, preferably)
Juice of 1 lemon
1 teaspoon salt
1 lemon slice
Coriander leaves

Mix yogurt, garlic clove, vinegar, cumin, and chili powder together. An electric blender or food processor is good for this. Work the ingredients into a well-blended sauce.

Score the fish and place in an ovenproof dish. Dot with lemon juice and sprinkle with salt. Pour the prepared marinade over the fish, cover, and refrigerate overnight.

When ready to cook, cover fish with foil. Bake at 350°F for 30 minutes. Garnish with lemon slice and coriander.

Deep-Fried Fish with Sweet-and-Sour Sauce

CHINA   Yield: 4 to 6 servings

1½ to 2 pounds fish fillets
Salt

Batter for frying

1½ cups biscuit mix
1 cup water
2 eggs
¾ teaspoon salt
2 cups oil for frying

Sauce

1 cup water
½ cup cider vinegar
6 tablespoons catsup
2 cups brown sugar
2 teaspoons soy sauce
2 tablespoons cornstarch
1 tablespoon sesame seeds, toasted in
    the oven on a baking sheet until
    light brown

Cut the fish into 1-inch cubes or ½-inch strips. Salt lightly. Combine the ingredients for the batter and stir until smooth and free of lumps. Dip fish pieces into batter and deep-fry at 375°F until golden brown, turning once. Drain on paper towels and keep warm, uncovered.

Combine the ingredients for the sauce in a small saucepan. Stir constantly over moderate heat until mixture thickens. Pour over fish. Sprinkle with sesame seeds. Serve at once while the batter coating is still crisp.

Deep-fried Fish with Vegetables

INDOCHINA   Yield: 4 to 6 servings

> 1½ pounds white fish fillets, cut into finger pieces
> 1 tablespoon egg white
> 1 teaspoon salt
> 1 tablespoon cornstarch
> 6 tablespoons oil
> 1 clove garlic, peeled and crushed
> ½ teaspoon fresh ginger, finely grated
> 2 cups white Chinese cabbage, sliced
> 6 spring onions, cut in 2-inch lengths
> 2 tablespoons fish sauce
> ½ cup water
> 1 teaspoon extra cornstarch

Dip fish in egg white, then in a mixture of salt and cornstarch. Heat oil and fry fish on high heat. Do not crowd the pan. Each batch should cook 2 minutes. Drain on paper towels and keep warm.

Leaving just 1 tablespoon oil in frying pan or wok, stir-fry garlic, ginger, and cabbage for 1 minute. Stir-fry spring onions with the other vegetables for 1 minute more. Add fish sauce and water and bring to a boil. Mix cornstarch with cold water and pour in. Continue stirring until sauce thickens. Arrange a platter with a bed of rice, the thickened sauce, and fish pieces on top; serve piping hot.

Fried Fish I

CHINA   Yield: 4 servings

> 2 eggs, beaten
> 2 tablespoons water
> 4 fish fillets

> Bread or cracker crumbs
> Oil for frying
> Soy sauce

Beat eggs, add water, and mix together. Dip fish in egg mixture, then into bread or cracker crumbs. Fry fish in heated oil until done. Sprinkle with soy sauce to taste, and serve with rice, if desired.

Fried Fish II

KOREA   Yield: 4 to 6 servings

> 6 small fillets of fish, washed and dried
> 2 tablespoons light soy sauce
> 2 tablespoons toasted, crushed sesame seeds
> Pinch of ground black pepper
> 2 tablespoons spring onions, finely chopped
> 2 teaspoons sesame oil
> 2 tablespoons vegetable oil

In a bowl, combine soy sauce, sesame seeds, pepper, spring onions, and sesame oil. Dip each fillet in the mixture, coating both sides. Heat vegetable oil in frying pan and fry for a few minutes on each side until fish is golden brown. Serve at once.

Spiced Fried Fish with Onions

BURMA   Yield: 4 servings

1½ pounds white fish fillets, cut into
    4-inch squares
½ teaspoon turmeric powder
1 tablespoon shrimp-flavored soy sauce
2 tablespoons dried tamarind pulp
6 tablespoons hot water
7 tablespoons vegetable oil
2 medium onions, peeled and sliced
1½ teaspoons chili powder

Rub the fish lightly with turmeric and soy sauce. Set aside.

Prepare tamarind by covering pulp with hot water. Soak 10 minutes. Knead to extract flavor (squeeze until tamarind mixes with the water) and strain, discarding pulp.

Heat oil in large skillet. Fry onions over brisk heat until crisp and light brown. Remove onions from oil and drain on paper towels.

Pour off half the oil. Add chili powder, then fish, and fry quickly for 1 minute over high heat. Add tamarind liquid, cover, and simmer for 20 minutes. Check liquid as fish cooks and add more oil if needed to prevent sticking.

Transfer to a warm serving platter. Garnish with reserved onions and serve hot.

Fish Curry I

INDONESIA   Yield: 4 to 6 servings

2 pounds fish fillets
Juice of half a lemon
Sprinkle of salt
Flour for dredging
3 tablespoons oil

1 large onion, peeled and chopped
1 large apple, peeled, cored, and diced
4 tablespoons butter or margarine
1½ tablespoons curry powder
1 cup clear fish broth
2 tablespoons raisins

Wash the fillets, wipe dry, and put on a platter. Sprinkle with lemon juice and salt and dredge in flour. When fish is floured on both sides, heat oil and cook fillets in a skillet until they are golden brown on both sides. Set aside and keep warm.

Melt the butter in a small saucepan and cook onions and apples until onions are transparent. Add curry powder and fish broth and simmer until apples are soft. Return fish to skillet, add the broth, and simmer 10 minutes or until the fish is tender. Place in a serving dish and sprinkle with raisins. Serve hot.

Fish Curry II

MALAYSIA   Yield: 4 to 6 servings

2 pounds fish fillets, cod or red perch
    preferred
2 tablespoons lemon juice
2 teaspoons salt
2 tablespoons curry
3 tablespoons flour
4 tablespoons peanut oil
1 tablespoon butter or margarine
3 onions, peeled and thinly sliced in
    rings
4 tablespoons milk
1 tablespoon flour
¼ cup peanuts
½ teaspoon ground ginger
½ cup cream

Cut fish into 2-inch cubes and put on a platter. Sprinkle with lemon juice. Cover and allow to soak for 10 minutes. Then, sprinkle on both sides with salt and 1 tablespoon curry. Coat with flour. Fry in hot peanut oil for 3 minutes, until light brown. Remove, place in a heated dish, and keep warm.

Heat butter in a second skillet. Place onion rings in milk, then in 1 tablespoon of flour. Fry in the hot fat for 5 minutes, until golden brown. Keep warm.

Break peanuts in half. Add them to the fish skillet along with ginger, cream, and the remaining curry. Simmer for 2 minutes. Pour over fish. Garnish with onion rings and serve.

Fish Curry with Tomato

INDIA   Yield: 4 servings

1 pound fish fillets or fish steak
2 tablespoons ghee or oil
1 medium onion, peeled and finely chopped
2 cloves garlic, peeled and finely chopped
2 tablespoons fresh coriander leaves or mint, chopped
1 teaspoon ground cumin
1 teaspoon ground turmeric
½ to 1 teaspoon chili powder to taste
1 large, ripe tomato, chopped
1 teaspoon salt
1½ teaspoons garam masala

Wash fish in cold water and cut into serving pieces. Heat ghee in a saucepan. Fry

onion, garlic, and coriander on a low setting until onion is soft and golden in color. Add cumin, turmeric, and chili powder and stir for 1 minute. Add tomato, salt, and garam masala. Continue stirring until tomato has cooked down to a pulp. Add lemon juice and more salt if needed. Place fish in frying pan, spooning sauce over it. Cover and simmer for 10 minutes. Especially good over cooked white rice.

Fish Fillets

INDIA   Yield: 4 servings

1 pound fresh or frozen fish fillets
½ cup flour
2 teaspoons curry powder
¼ teaspoon salt
½ cup butter or margarine
½ cup blanched almonds, chopped
Chives, chopped
Chutney

Thaw fish if frozen; pat dry with toweling.

Mix flour, curry powder, and salt well. Thoroughly coat each piece of fish with mixture.

Heat butter in large skillet. Brown fish over moderate heat about 4 minutes per side. When fish flakes easily, it is done through. Remove fillets; put them onto a heated serving dish.

Add almonds to butter left in skillet; stir until browned. Pour over fish. Garnish with chopped chives; serve chutney as a relish.

Fish Fillets India

INDIA   Yield: 4 servings

½ cup flour
2 teaspoons curry powder
¼ teaspoon salt
1 pound fresh or frozen fillets (your choice of favorite fish)
½ cup margarine
½ cup blanched almonds, chopped
Chutney

Mix flour, curry powder, and salt well. Thoroughly coat each piece of fish with this mixture. Heat margarine in a large skillet. Brown the fish over moderate heat, about 4 minutes per side. When fish flakes easily, it is done through. Remove fillets; put them on a heated serving dish.

Add almonds to shortening left in skillet; stir until nuts are browned. Pour over fish.

Serve the chutney as a relish.

Fish and Vegetables in Foil

JAPAN   Yield: 4 servings

4 fillets of white fish meat, about 4 ounces each
1 teaspoon salt
1 tablespoon rice wine or sherry
12 shrimp, with shells
Pepper to taste
4 fresh mushrooms
Aluminum foil, heavy duty
Salad oil
20 gingko nuts, canned, optional

Wash fish, pat dry, and sprinkle with ½ teaspoon of the salt and the rice wine or sherry. Set aside while preparing shrimp.

Keeping the shrimp in their shells, slit the shells in the backs and remove veins.

Sprinkle with ½ teaspoon salt and pepper. Wash mushrooms; set aside. Brush a piece of foil (large enough to wrap the fish, shrimp, mushrooms, and gingko nuts in) with oil. Lay the fish, shrimp, mushrooms, and nuts on foil; pinch ends together to seal it.

Heat frying pan over medium heat; place foil package in pan. Cover; bake for approximately 15 minutes.

Fish in Brown Bean Sauce with Vegetables

INDONESIA   Yield: 4 to 6 servings

1½ pound fish steaks (any firm fish such as mackerel)
Salt
2 small onions
6 sweet chili peppers, seeded and cut in strips
½ cup fresh green beans, sliced diagonally
1 cup sliced, canned bamboo shoots
2 cloves garlic, peeled and finely chopped
1½ teaspoons fresh ginger, finely grated
2 tablespoons bean sauce (tauco)
4 tablespoons peanut oil
1 teaspoon dried shrimp paste, optional
1 tablespoon light soy sauce
⅔ cup water

Cut fish into serving pieces. Salt on both sides and set aside.

Peel onions. Cut one onion in 8 long sections. Then slice each section in half. Separate the layers. Set aside. Prepare peppers, beans, and bamboo shoots; set each aside separately. Chop remaining onion very fine and mix with garlic, ginger, and bean sauce; set this aside also.

Remove excess moisture from fish with paper towels. Brown both sides of each piece of fish in peanut oil on high heat. Set aside. To remaining fat, add onion, ginger, garlic, and bean sauce mixture. Stir constantly until onions are soft. Add shrimp paste and green beans and stir for 2 minutes. Add peppers and remaining onion and stir-fry for 1 minute more. Put in bamboo shoots, soy sauce, and water and stir well. Cover and reduce heat to simmer for 3 minutes. Then add the fish. When fish is heated through, serve at once. Delicious over white rice.

Fish in Coconut Milk and Spices

INDONESIA   Yield: 6 servings

1½ pound fish steaks, 6 portions (tuna or mackerel)
Salt to taste
Juice of ½ lemon
2 onions, finely chopped
3 cloves garlic, peeled and crushed
2 teaspoons fresh ginger, finely grated
1 teaspoon ground turmeric
½ teaspoon dried shrimp paste
1 teaspoon sambal ulek or chili powder
1 stalk lemon grass or 2 strips lemon rind
1 teaspoon salt
1½ cups thin coconut milk
2 tablespoons fresh basil, chopped
¼ cup tamarind liquid
1 cup thick coconut milk

After washing, rub fish with salt and lemon juice and set aside.

In a saucepan, combine onions, garlic, ginger, turmeric, shrimp paste, chili, lemon rind, and 1 teaspoon salt with the thin coconut milk. Simmer uncovered until onions are quite soft and coconut milk has thickened. Next, add fish, basil, and tamarind liquid. Allow to simmer until fish is tender, 10 to 15 minutes. Stir in thick coconut milk, continuing to stir until all is hot through. Serve at once.

Fish in Coconut Cream

BURMA   Yield: 4 to 6 servings

1 teaspoon dried chili peppers
2 pounds fish fillets, cut into 1-inch squares
1 medium onion, peeled and chopped
1 heaping teaspoon powdered ginger
3 cloves garlic, peeled and minced
2 tablespoons lemon juice
1½ teaspoons salt
1 tablespoon cornstarch
½ teaspoon turmeric
1 medium onion, peeled and sliced
¾ cup oil
1 cup coconut cream

Pound the first five ingredients until very fine. You may use an electric blender or food processor. To this pounded mixture, add lemon juice, salt, cornstarch, and turmeric. When well mixed, shape into small balls and set aside.

Use a large skillet to brown onion slices in oil. Remove onions and set aside to drain on paper towels. Add fish balls to oil and cook until brown. Remove. Drain all but 1 tablespoon of oil from the skillet. Add coconut cream and bring to boiling point. Add the fish and reduce heat to simmer for 15 minutes. Place on warmed platter and garnish with browned onions.

Fish in Red Sauce

THAILAND   Yield: 4 to 6 servings

- 1½ pounds fish fillets
- 4 tablespoons oil
- 2 onions, peeled and finely chopped
- 4 ripe tomatoes, chopped
- 2 tablespoons vinegar
- Salt and pepper to taste
- 2 or 3 fresh chilies, seeded and chopped
- 3 to 4 tablespoons fresh coriander leaves, chopped

Fry onions in oil until they are golden. Add tomatoes, vinegar, salt, pepper, and chilies. Cover and simmer the sauce for 20 minutes until it is thick. Add fish and cover again. Cook for 10 to 15 minutes or until fish is fork tender. Garnish with coriander leaves and serve hot.

Fish in Sweet-and-Sour Sauce

CHINA   Yield: 3 to 4 servings

- 1 to 1½ pounds fish fillet (cod, haddock, or turbot)
- Juice of half a lemon
- 2 tablespoons soy sauce
- Salt
- 3 tablespoons cornstarch

Sweet-and-sour sauce

- 5 tablespoons vinegar
- ½ cup water
- 6 teaspoons sugar
- 3 tablespoons soy sauce
- 3 slices lemon
- 3 tablespoons cornstarch
- Cold water

- 4 cups oil for frying

Wash fish thoroughly; pat dry. Sprinkle with lemon juice and soy sauce. Cut into 1½-inch-wide strips. Set aside for 15 minutes and let marinate. Season to taste with salt and roll in cornstarch.

To prepare sauce, bring vinegar, water, sugar, soy sauce, and lemon slices to a boil over high heat. Reduce heat to lowest point; simmer sauce for 20 minutes. Blend cornstarch with small amount of cold water; add to sauce. Stir until smooth and bubbly.

About 5 minutes before sauce is done, place fish in hot oil, and fry for about 8 minutes. Fish is done when it floats to the surface. Remove fish pieces with slotted spoon; drain on paper towels.

Arrange on serving platter and spoon sauce over fish. Serve immediately. Sauce can also be served separately.

Fish Portions Oriental

CHINA   Yield: 4 servings

- 1 12-ounce package frozen breaded fish portions
- 1 13¼-ounce can pineapple chunks
- 2 tablespoons sugar
- 2 tablespoons vinegar
- 1 tablespoon soy sauce
- 1 tablespoon cornstarch
- ½ teaspoon garlic salt
- ½ medium green pepper, cut in strips
- 4 servings hot cooked seasoned rice

Heat fish portions as directed on package label. Drain pineapple chunks; save syrup. Add water as needed to pineapple syrup to make ¾ cup liquid. Combine liquid, sugar, vinegar, soy sauce, cornstarch, and garlic salt in saucepan; mix well. Cook stirring constantly until sauce is thickened and clear. Add pineapple chunks and green pepper strips; heat. Serve fish portions on rice and spoon sauce over fish.

Fish with Coconut Cream

INDOCHINA   Yield: 4 servings

1 pound fish fillets
2 large, dried chilies
15 cloves garlic, peeled
3 tender lemon leaves
1 teaspoon laos powder, optional
2 stalks lemon grass, finely sliced, or 2
  strips lemon rind
1 cup thick coconut milk
3 cups thin coconut milk
1 tablespoon fish sauce
2 tablespoons roasted peanuts, finely
  chopped
Fresh basil leaves for garnish
5 or 6 small dried chilies
Oil for frying

Cut fillets into serving pieces. Remove stalks and seeds from large, dried chilies; soak in hot water for 10 minutes. With mortar and pestle, pound chilies, garlic, lemon leaves, laos powder, and lemon grass to a fine paste.

Place thick coconut milk in saucepan and cook about 10 minutes until oil floats on top. Add pounded mixture and stir constantly until well blended. Add fillets to mixture, coating well. Then add thin coconut milk and fish sauce and simmer for 10 minutes. Last, add the peanuts and stir for 1 minute more. Garnish with basil and small chilies that have been fried for 15 seconds in hot oil.

Fish with Ginger

PHILIPPINES   Yield: 4 servings

1½ to 2 pounds flathead or other delicate white fish
3 tablespoons oil

3 tablespoons fresh ginger, finely
  chopped
1 teaspoon ground black pepper
Rice washings (the water in which rice
  has been washed prior to cooking the
  rice)
Salt to taste
4 spring onions
1 sprig coriander leaves for garnish

Tomato sauce

2 tablespoons pork fat, chopped
2 cloves garlic, peeled and crushed
1 medium onion, peeled and chopped
2 tomatoes, chopped
2 tablespoons red misu (salted bean
  curd paste)
1 tablespoon vinegar
¼ teaspoon ground black pepper

Have fish cleaned and scaled. Rub cavity with salt and then rinse lightly.

In a large skillet, heat oil; fry ginger until soft and golden. Add pepper and stir. Place fish in pan with enough rice water to almost cover. Season with at least ½ teaspoon salt and place a spring onion on top. Cover the skillet and simmer for about 15 minutes, or until fish is tender. Transfer to a serving dish. Garnish with uncooked onions and coriander leaves. Pour liquid around the fish. Serve with white rice and tomato sauce.

To make tomato sauce, heat pork fat, garlic, and onions in a medium skillet. Stir until the onions are soft. Add tomatoes and continue stirring until the tomatoes cook down. Add remaining ingredients and stir well. Simmer for several minutes and serve.

Fish with Peanut Sauce

INDONESIA   Yield: 4 to 6 servings

2 large fish steaks
Lemon juice
Salt
Black pepper
Oil for frying
2 tablespoons light soy sauce
2 tablespoons Peanut Sauce (see Index)
½ cup thick coconut milk
1 tablespoon tamarind liquid or vinegar
1 tablespoon fresh coriander leaves, chopped

Wash and dry fish steaks; cut into serving pieces. Rub each piece on both sides with lemon juice, salt, and pepper. Let sit for at least 15 minutes. Before frying fish, dry again with paper towels.

Heat oil and brown fish on both sides. Remove all but 1 tablespoon of oil. Mix the remaining liquid ingredients together and put into a pan. Place the fish over the sauce. Sprinkle coriander on top and cover. Simmer for 5 minutes more and serve at once.

Simmered Pineapple with Fish

INDOCHINA   Yield: 4 servings

2 tablespoons vegetable oil
1 pound fish steaks
1 shallot, peeled and sliced
1 cup fresh pineapple, cut into 1-inch squares
6 tablespoons fish sauce
¼ cup sugar
Freshly ground black pepper

Heat 1 tablespoon oil in skillet; fry fish until lightly browned on both sides. In a separate skillet, heat remaining oil. Add shallot slices and fry until lightly browned. Add pineapple squares and cook for 3 minutes. Lift out shallots and pineapple and discard juice.

In medium-size saucepan or flameproof casserole, place half of the pineapple mixture. Add fish steaks and cover with remaining pineapple, fish sauce, sugar, and pepper. Cover and simmer for 25 to 30 minutes. Serve at once.

Indian Fish

INDIA   Yield: 4 servings

Potatoes and spinach go well with this recipe.

4 white-flesh fish steaks, each ¾ to 1-inch thick (about 1½ pounds)
½ teaspoon salt
⅛ teaspoon cayenne pepper
½ teaspoon ground turmeric
3 or 4 tablespoons vegetable oil

Wipe the fish with damp paper towel; dry with more toweling. Stir together the salt, cayenne, and turmeric; rub over both sides of the fish. In a large heavy skillet—one with a non-stick lining produces the best results—heat the oil; add the fish and cook over moderate heat until browned on both sides and fish has lost its opaque color when flaked in the center—about 10 minutes.

Japanese Fish Kabobs

JAPAN   Yield: 6 servings

1½ to 2 pounds white fish, cut into
    2-ounce pieces
Salt
14 ounces white miso (soybean paste)
1 cup rice wine or sherry
¼ cup sugar

Sprinkle fish with salt. Cover; leave in refrigerator 12 hours.

Mix remaining ingredients. Place fish in mixture; cover. Marinate in refrigerator overnight.

Thread fish on skewers; grill over hot coals about 5 minutes or until fish flakes easily with fork.

Oriental Fish Kabobs

JAPAN   Yield: 4 servings

2 pounds fish fillet (cod, haddock,
    turbot, etc.)
Juice of 2 lemons
1 clove garlic, minced
Salt to taste
8 small tomatoes
4 small onions

Basting sauce

4 tablespoons olive oil
2 tablespoons sherry
1 teaspoon sugar
Salt to taste
Pepper to taste

Sauce (served separately)

½ cup sour cream
1 cup yogurt
2 tablespoons parsley, chopped
2 tablespoons chives, chopped

Wash fish under cold running water. Cut into 2-inch-wide strips. In bowl blend lemon juice, garlic, and salt to taste. Add fish strips; marinate for 15 minutes, turning often.

Meanwhile, quarter tomatoes. Peel and quarter onions; drop into boiling water for a few minutes. Drain fish strips; roll up jelly-roll fashion. Thread fish rolls, tomatoes, and onions on skewers.

Prepare sauce for basting by combining and blending thoroughly oil, sherry, sugar, salt, and plenty of freshly ground pepper. Place skewers in broiler pan and broil. Baste generously with sauce. Broil for about 8 minutes, turning and basting often.

To prepare sauce, beat yogurt and sour cream together until smooth. Stir in parsley and chives; add salt to taste. Serve separately.

Raw Fish

JAPAN   Yield: About 4 servings

1 pound fresh salmon, tuna, or other
    fish of your choice
Handful of fresh dill, parsley, water-
    cress, or other type of greens
2 teaspoons horseradish
4 tablespoons soy sauce

Slice fish; arrange on platter along with greens.

Mix horseradish and soy sauce; dip the fish into sauce before eating. If desired, freshly grated ginger may be substituted for the horseradish.

Capers may be used for garnish.

Hot Pickled Fish

PHILIPPINES   Yield: 4 to 6 servings

2¼ pounds cleaned white fish (red
  snapper, sea bass, etc.)
Salt
Flour for coating
3 tablespoons oil
3 cloves garlic, peeled and ground
1 teaspoon grated fresh gingerroot
1 large onion, peeled and thinly sliced
  into rings
1 large green pepper, cored, seeded,
  and sliced into thin strips
1 tablespoon cornstarch
1¼ cups water
3 tablespoons cider vinegar
1½ tablespoons brown sugar

Slice the fish into steaks; pat dry and
sprinkle lightly with salt and flour. Heat 2
tablespoons oil in skillet. Fry fish until it is
crisp and brown. Set aside.

Add remaining oil to pan with garlic and
ginger. Fry until brown. Then add onion and
green pepper. Stir-fry for one minute, remove from pan, and set aside.

Make paste of the cornstarch with ¼ cup
of water. Add to pan with remaining water,
vinegar, and sugar. Stir constantly over a low
heat until thickened. Add the fish and bring
to a boil. Cover and simmer for 5 minutes
more. Return onions and green pepper and
stir until heated through. Lift fish to a warm
serving dish. Arrange vegetables around it.
Check remaining sauce, adding seasoning if
required. Pour over the fish and serve.

Salted Fish

KOREA   Yield: 4 servings

1 pound perch or mackerel, skinned
  and boned

¼ cup water
1 tablespoon sugar
4 tablespoons soy sauce
Dash of pepper to taste
1 scallion, chopped with greens
1 clove garlic, peeled and minced
½ teaspoon candied ginger

Prepare the fish by cutting it into small
squares. In a saucepan, place the fish with
remaining ingredients and stir gently until all
flavors blend. Cook over medium heat for 5
to 10 minutes or until fish is tender. Serve
hot with white rice.

Smoked Fish Oriental

KOREA   Yield: 6 servings

1 pound smoked white fish or other
  smoked fish
1 can (1 pound) bean sprouts, drained
6 eggs, beaten
½ cup green onion, finely chopped
Dash pepper
1 tablespoon toasted sesame seeds

Foo yung sauce

2 chicken bouillon cubes
½ teaspoon sugar
2 cups boiling water
2 tablespoons cornstarch
2 tablespoons soy sauce

Remove skin and bones from the fish.
Flake the fish. Combine all ingredients except sauce and sesame seeds. Pour ⅓ cup
fish mixture onto a hot greased griddle or frying pan. Fry at moderate heat for 2 to 3
minutes or until brown. Turn carefully and
fry 2 to 3 minutes longer or until brown.
Drain on absorbent paper. Pour Foo Yung
Sauce over patties and sprinkle with sesame
seeds.

To make the sauce, dissolve bouillon cubes and sugar in boiling water. Combine cornstarch and soy sauce. Add cornstarch mixture to bouillon mixture and cook until thick and clear, stirring constantly. Makes approximately 1⅔ cups sauce.

Spiced Coconut Fish

MALAYSIA   Yield: 4 servings

1 pound fish fillets, washed, cleaned,
    and scaled
½ cup desiccated (dehydrated)
    coconut
¾ cup hot water
1 clove garlic, peeled
½ inch fresh ginger
1 teaspoon ground cumin
1 teaspoon ground coriander
1 teaspoon garam masala
1 teaspoon salt
1½ tablespoons lemon juice
1 tablespoon fresh coriander leaves,
    chopped
Banana leaves or foil

Cut fish into 4-inch lengths. In a blender or food processor, or with mortar and pestle, combine coconut, hot water, garlic, ginger, cumin, coriander, garam masala, and salt until all is very finely ground. Add lemon juice and coriander leaves.

On a square of foil or banana leaves, place 1 fillet. Spoon 2 to 3 teaspoons of coconut mixture on top. Wrap to make a sealed parcel. Continue in this way until all the fish is used. Steam the parcels over boiling water for 15 minutes. Serve at once, piping hot, with white rice.

Steamed Fish Parcels

BURMA   Yield: 10 servings

The native way to prepare the parcels is in banana leaves. If you can't obtain banana leaves, use aluminum foil as a substitute.

1¼ pounds thick white fish fillets
    (cod, haddock, etc.) cut into
    3 × 1½-inch pieces
2 teaspoons salt
½ teaspoon turmeric powder
3 small onions, peeled
2 cloves garlic, peeled and crushed
1-inch piece of fresh gingerroot, peeled
    and pounded
½ teaspoon chili powder
1 tablespoon rice flour
⅔ cup coconut milk
2 teaspoons vegetable oil
½ teaspoon powdered lemon grass
Banana leaves or foil for wrapping
10 bok choy leaves, washed and cut in
    half

Rub the fish all over with 1 teaspoon salt and turmeric. Set aside.

Thinly slice 1 onion and pound or chop the remaining onions. Make a paste of the onions, remaining salt, garlic, ginger, chili powder, and rice flour. Add coconut milk to onion paste; add oil, lemon grass, and sliced onions. Mix well.

Cut foil or banana leaves, if available, into ten 7-inch squares. Place a piece of bok choy on each piece of foil. Top with some of the paste mixture and 1 piece of fish. Add more paste to this and cover with another piece of bok choy. Fold foil over the filling to form a sealed parcel. Steam these parcels over boiling water for 20 minutes.

Steamed Fish with Black Bean Sauce

CHINA   Yield: 4 servings

2 tablespoons black bean sauce
1 clove garlic, grated
1 teaspoon fresh gingerroot, grated
½ teaspoon sugar
1 teaspoon vegetable oil (for non-oily fish)
2 cups water
1 to 1½ pounds fish fillets (flounder, trout, etc.)
1 scallion, sliced

Combine the bean sauce, garlic, ginger, sugar, and oil. Place 2 cups water in the wok and arrange fish on a rack 1 to 2 inches above the water so the water will not boil up onto the fish but the steam can circulate freely around it. Spread the bean sauce mixture evenly over the surface of the fillets. Sprinkle with scallion slices.

Cover wok and steam until fish separates into flakes with a fork. Serve immediately. (Rack may be covered with one layer of cheesecloth before fish are placed on it. This will prevent fish from adhering to the rack.)

Steamed Fish with Scallions and Ginger

CHINA   Yield: 4 servings

2 tablespoons vinegar
2 cups water
2 teaspoons whole pickling spices
1 to 1½ pounds fish fillets (flounder, perch, etc.)
1 teaspoon salt
1 teaspoon fresh gingerroot, grated
3 tablespoons scallions, minced

Combine vinegar, water, and pickling spices in the wok. Place fish on a metal rack 1 to 2 inches above the vinegar and water so the water will not boil up onto the fish but steam can circulate freely around it. Combine the salt, ginger, and scallions and spread evenly over the surface of the fillets. Place the lid on the wok and steam for 10 to 20 minutes or just until the fish will separate into flakes with a fork. Serve immediately. (The vinegar and spices in the cooking water eliminate the characteristic odor in the kitchen of cooked fish.)

Steamed Fish

CHINA   Yield: 4 to 6 servings

3 pounds dressed sea bass, rockfish, bluefish or other fish
3 cloves garlic, crushed
1 tablespoon soy sauce
2 teaspoons shredded fresh ginger or ginger powder
½ teaspoon sugar
Water for steaming
3 tablespoons vegetable oil
2 spring onions, finely cut
2 to 3 cups hot cooked rice

Wash and dry fish. Place fish in shallow pan.

Mix garlic, soy sauce, ginger, and sugar together in a bowl. Spread mixture over fish.

Put a rack in large pan (such as turkey roaster). Add water to just under rack. Place pan of fish on rack and cover tightly. Bring water to a boil, lower heat, and simmer until fish flakes easily when tested with a fork, about 30 minutes. Remove fish to a warmed serving platter.

Heat oil in small pan. Pour hot oil over fish and sprinkle with onion. Serve with rice.

Sweet-and-Sour Fish

CHINA   Yield: 4 servings

3 to 3½ pounds fish fillets (carp, bass, or fish of your choice)
4 tablespoons onions, finely chopped
2 teaspoons fresh gingerroot, chopped
Pinch of salt
¼ teaspoon freshly ground black pepper
1 teaspoon soy sauce
1 teaspoon sherry
½ cup cornstarch (more if needed)
Fat for deep frying

Sweet-and-sour sauce

¾ cup cider vinegar
1 tablespoon cornstarch
1 green pepper, cut into julienne strips
1 carrot, peeled, cut into julienne strips
2 teaspoons fresh gingerroot, chopped
4 scallions, sliced into ½-inch pieces
2 tablespoons sweet pickle relish
Salt to taste
¼ cup sugar

Sprinkle fish with onions, gingerroot, salt, pepper, soy sauce, and sherry. Let stand 30 minutes. Roll in cornstarch; let stand 10 minutes.

Heat fat in deep-fryer or deep skillet over medium-high heat. Fry the fish 10 to 15 minutes or until done. Drain. Serve with sweet-and-sour sauce.

To make the sauce, mix all ingredients together. Cook over low heat, stirring constantly, until thickened.

Easy Fish Teriyaki

JAPAN   Yield: 4 servings

4 fish fillets
Soy sauce
Oil

Place fish on broiler; brush with soy sauce and oil. Broil fish, turning frequently and basting with soy sauce, until fish flakes.

Fish Teriyaki

JAPAN   Yield: 4 to 6 servings

2 pounds fish fillets, cut into 2-inch pieces
Teriyaki sauce to cover the fish
1 cup rice
2 cups canned tomatoes with juice
½ cup water

Marinate the fish in enough teriyaki sauce to cover for at least 1 hour.

Place both fish and marinade in pressure cooker. Add rice, tomatoes, and water. Close cover and put pressure control in place. When pressure is reached, cook for 5 minutes. Cool cooker normally for 5 minutes, then reduce pressure under running water.

Use bamboo shoots and water chestnuts in your salad to complete the dinner.

Fish Tempura

JAPAN   Yield: 4 to 6 servings

2 pounds fresh fish fillets
Salt to taste
Lemon juice
½ recipe Basic Tempura Batter
Oil
Chili-horseradish sauce
Soy sauce

Basic tempura batter

2 cups all-purpose flour, sifted
3 egg yolks
2 cups ice water

Chili-horseradish sauce

1 cup mayonnaise
⅓ cup chili sauce
3 tablespoons horseradish

Cut the fish fillets into bite-size pieces and drain well on paper toweling. Prepare other ingredients. Season the fish with salt and squeeze desired amount of lemon juice over fish. Make up the batter.

Sift flour 3 times. Combine the yolks and water in a large bowl over ice and beat with a whisk until well blended. Gradually add the flour, stirring and turning the mixture with a spoon. Don't overmix. Keep the batter over ice while frying. Makes approximately 4½ cups.

Place all the fish in the batter. When ready to fry, remove the fish from the batter with a fork and drain slightly. Heat the oil in a wok, an electric skillet, or deep-fat fryer to between 350° and 375°F. Fry the fish, a few pieces at a time, for about 5 minutes, turning to brown evenly. Remove the fish from the oil with a slotted spoon and drain well on paper toweling. Keep fish warm until all is cooked. Serve with chili-horseradish

sauce or just dipped into soy sauce. Use this batter for vegetables also, or meat, or seafood. Skim off loose particles of food as they appear, to keep the oil clean. Keep the batter cold.

To make chili-horseradish sauce, combine all ingredients in small bowl and mix thoroughly. Chill well before serving.

Chinese Fish

CHINA   Yield: About 4 servings

1 whole trout, about 1 pound
1 whole carp, about 3 pounds
Juice of 1 lemon
Salt
White pepper
2 slices lean bacon
Margarine to grease pan
4 large leaves savoy cabbage (if unavailable, use regular cabbage)
1 pound fresh mushrooms
2 pieces sugared ginger
3 tablespoons soy sauce
Pinch of ground anise
1 cup hot water
2 teaspoons cornstarch
2 tablespoons bacon drippings
Juice of half a lemon

Garnish

2 tablespoons parsley, chopped
Lemon slices

Have fishmonger scale and clean out the insides of the fish, but leave whole. At home, wash fish thoroughly under running water, pat dry, and rub with lemon juice. With sharp knife, make shallow incisions in backs of both fish and rub with salt and pepper. Cut bacon into small strips and insert one strip in each incision. Grease ovenproof baking dish with margarine and line with cabbage leaves. Place fish on top. Slice mushrooms and sugared ginger. Mix together and spoon over fish.

Sprinkle with soy sauce and ground anise. Pour in small amount of hot water. Cover with lid or aluminum foil and place in preheated oven at 350°F. Bake for 30 minutes. While baking, gradually add rest of hot water and baste fish with pan drippings.

Remove fish and cabbage leaves from pan. Arrange on a preheated platter. Bring pan drippings to a boil, scraping all brown particles from bottom of pan and adding some more water, if necessary. Blend cornstarch with small amount of cold water, add to pan drippings, and stir until sauce is smooth and bubbly. Correct seasonings if necessary, and serve separately. Melt and heat bacon drippings. Pour over fish and sprinkle with lemon juice. Garnish fish with chopped parsley and lemon slices.

Whole Fried Fish with Ginger Sauce

THAILAND   Yield: 2 to 3 servings

Ginger sauce
8 dried Chinese mushrooms
Hot water
6 tablespoons vinegar
6 tablespoons sugar
¾ cup water
2 tablespoons soy sauce
2 tablespoons spring onion, finely chopped
1 tablespoon cornstarch
1 tablespoon cold water
4 tablespoons red ginger, chopped

The fish
1 whole fish, about 2 pounds
Flour seasoned with salt
Oil for frying

Prepare the sauce first. Soak the mushrooms in hot water for 30 minutes. Trim off and discard tough stems. Finely slice mushroom caps. Boil the mushrooms, vinegar, sugar, water, and soy sauce together for 5 minutes. Add the spring onion. Blend cornstarch with cold water and gradually stir it into the sauce. When the sauce is clear and thick, remove it from the heat and add the red ginger. Simmer until fish is ready.

Keeping the head on the fish, trim fins and tail. Dry the cavity with paper towels. Slash the fish diagonally on both sides to form diamond shapes in the meat. Dip it in seasoned flour. Deep-fry in hot oil until fish is fork tender. Remove to a serving dish. Spoon ginger sauce over the fish.

If other dishes are served as a main course along with the fish, this will serve more than the 2 or 3 people listed above.

Chinese Egg-Lobster

CHINA   Yield: 6 servings
1 cup canned bean sprouts
½ cup canned bamboo shoots
½ cup canned water chestnuts, thinly sliced
2 cups boiled lobster, cubed
4 tablespoons vegetable oil
6 eggs
1 teaspoon salt

Sauté bean sprouts, bamboo shoots, water chestnuts, and lobster in hot oil 3 minutes. Remove mixture from frying pan and drain water off top of oil. Reheat fat and drop eggs whole into it. Immediately spread first mixture over the top of eggs and stir constantly, but gently until the eggs are cooked.

Fried Fish with Tamarind

THAILAND   Yield: 4 to 6 servings

1 whole fish, about 2 pounds
Salt
Lard or oil for frying
3 cloves garlic, peeled and crushed
3 tablespoons soy sauce
1 tablespoon palm sugar
2 tablespoons fish sauce
4 tablespoons tamarind liquid
1 tablespoon fresh ginger, finely shredded
3 spring onions, cut into 1-inch pieces
3 tablespoons fresh coriander leaves, chopped
3 fresh red chilies, sliced

Have fish cleaned and scaled but keep the head on. Trim off fins and tail. Salt the cavity of the fish and then wipe it dry with paper towels. Heat lard and fry fish on both sides until brown and tender, 5 to 10 minutes. Drain on paper towels. Put on a warmed platter and cover with foil to keep warm.

Pour off excess fat, leaving about 1 tablespoon in pan. Lightly brown garlic. Add soy sauce, sugar, fish sauce, and tamarind liquid and bring to a boil. Now add ginger and spring onions. Cook for 1 minute, stirring. Spoon mixture over the fish. Garnish with coriander leaves and chilies and serve at once.

Steamed Whole Fish

JAPAN   Yield: 3 servings

1½ pounds whole fish (flounder, pike, trout, or sea bass)
1 teaspoon salt
½ teaspoon freshly ground pepper
¼ teaspoon powdered ginger
3 cups water
2 teaspoons mixed pickling spices (more, if you prefer it spicier)
2 bay leaves
2 cloves garlic, cut in half
2 tablespoons scallion, chopped

Garnish

Lemon slices
Tomato
Parsley

Have fish scaled and cleaned and head removed, if you prefer. Lightly score the skin so seasonings will flavor the fish. Combine salt, pepper, and ginger; rub on fish thoroughly.

Pour water into large frying pan or wok; add pickling spices, bay leaves, garlic, and scallion. Place rack in pan so that the fish will sit above the liquid, in order to allow the steam to circulate. Place the fish on the rack, cover, and let simmer for approximately 30 minutes, or until fish is tender.

Garnish fish with lemon slices, tomato, and parsley.

Fish Roll

JAPAN   Yield: 5 to 6 servings

3 eggs, beaten
1 tablespoon water
2 tablespoons oil
¾ cup flounder, chopped
2 tablespoons water chestnuts, chopped
2 tablespoons scallions, chopped
Salt to taste
1 tablespoon soy sauce
Flour

Sauce

1½ tablespoons soy sauce
1 tablespoon cornstarch
¾ cup water
½ teaspoon sugar

Beat the eggs with the water. Heat a little of the oil in a large skillet and fry half of the egg mixture until it's set. Turn it over and cook the other side. Repeat this with the rest of the egg mixture.

Mix together the fish, water chestnuts, scallions, salt, and soy sauce. Put half of it on one of the egg pieces, covering the whole thing. Roll it up jelly-roll style, put some flour on the edges and press together. Repeat with the other piece of egg. With a sharp knife, cut the rolls into ¼-inch slices. Heat oil in skillet and fry the slices until golden brown.

To make the sauce, mix together the soy sauce and cornstarch until smooth. Blend in water and sugar and place in small saucepan. Boil slowly for about 3 minutes. Serve the sauce separately.

Halibut Cantonese

CHINA   Yield: 2 servings

1½ pounds halibut, cut into small chunks
1 tablespoon oil
1 medium onion, chopped

Sauce

1½ cups water
1 tablespoon oil
Pinch salt
3 teaspoons soy sauce
1 teaspoon MSG, optional
Pinch of freshly ground pepper
2 tablespoons cornstarch dissolved in 3 tablespoons water

2 cloves garlic, minced
1 scallion, sliced
1 tablespoon celery, chopped
1 egg, beaten

Boil the halibut in a pot of water for 2 minutes. Heat the oil in a skillet and brown the onion. Transfer the fish to the skillet. Mix together the sauce ingredients, except for the cornstarch and water. Pour the sauce on the fish, and add the garlic, scallion and celery.

Cover the skillet and simmer for 2 minutes. Pour the beaten egg slowly into the sauce, mixing constantly. Mix cornstarch with water and stir into sauce. Cook until thickened.

Hong Kong Lobster

CHINA   Yield: 2 servings

2 large lobster tails
2 tablespoons oil
½ teaspoon salt
1 small can button mushrooms, drained
½ cup bamboo shoots, thinly sliced
½ cup celery, thinly sliced
⅓ teaspoon sugar
1 teaspoon soy sauce
½ teaspoon MSG, optional
1 cup chicken stock
1 tablespoon cornstarch
1 tablespoon water

Remove lobster meat from shells and slice into half-inch pieces. In a preheated skillet, place oil and salt. Turn heat high. Bring oil to sizzling point. Add lobster and toss rapidly for 2 minutes. Add remaining ingredients. Turn lightly until thoroughly mixed. Cover and cook at high heat for 7 minutes.

Uncover. Add gradually 1 tablespoon cornstarch, which has been smoothed into a paste with 1 tablespoon water. Toss and cook over high heat until sauce is thickened.

Lobster Cantonese

CHINA   Yield: 4 servings

2 tablespoons vegetable oil
2 tablespoons black beans, rinsed and
    mashed
2 cloves garlic, grated
1 teaspoon grated gingerroot
2 to 3 ounces minced or ground pork
1½ to 2 pounds live lobster, cleaned
    and chopped into 1-inch pieces or
    1 pound lobster tails, split
    lengthwise
1 cup chicken broth or water
1 teaspoon soy sauce
½ teaspoon sugar
1 tablespoon cornstarch in 2 table-
    spoons cold water
Salt and pepper
1 egg, beaten
1 scallion, sliced

Heat the oil in the wok and brown the
black beans, garlic, and ginger briefly. Add
pork and stir-fry for 1 minute. Add lobster
and stir-fry for 1 minute. Add the broth, soy
sauce, sugar, and cornstarch mixture. Cover
and heat for 5 minutes.

Remove from heat, season with salt and
pepper, and slowly pour in the egg while stirring with a fork. This sauce should not be so
hot as to completely coagulate the egg and
turn it white. The egg should give the sauce
a yellowish color. Serve at once with rice.
Garnish with scallion slices.

Lobster Indian Style

INDIA   Yield: 4 to 6 servings

1 carrot, scraped and cut in 4 pieces
1 leek, coarsely cut
4 to 5 quarts water

1 tablespoon salt
1 live 3-pound lobster
4 tablespoons butter
1 onion, peeled and finely chopped
1 piece of celery root, diced
½ bunch each parsley, dill, and
    chervil
2 cups white wine
2 teaspoons flour
½ cup cream
1 teaspoon curry
Pinch sugar

In a large pot, bring water with salt, carrot, and leek to a boil. Boil for 10 minutes.
Place lobster, head first, into the boiling
water. Boil for 15 minutes. Remove lobster.
Cut in half lengthwise, and take meat carefully out of the shell. Remove the innards.
Cut legs open and remove meat. Rinse lobster meat under cold water and pat dry. Discard water.

Heat butter in a pot. Steam lobster meat
with onion, celery, and herbs for 5 minutes.
Add white wine. Bring to a boil and then
simmer for 20 minutes. Remove lobster and
place in a preheated serving dish. Keep
warm.

Strain the liquid into a different pot to
make the sauce. Mix flour with a little cold
water and stir into the sauce. Boil for 5
minutes. Mix cream with curry and add.
Season to taste with sugar, adding salt if
needed. Pour sauce over the lobster and
serve at once.

Steamed Rock Lobster

JAPAN   Yield: 6 servings

3 (8-ounce) packages frozen South
    African rock lobster tails
6 large mushrooms, cut into slices

6 scallions, cut into long, thin strips
1 cup celery, thinly sliced
1 bunch broccoli, trimmed and cut
   into florets
1 tablespoon soy sauce
1 envelope dehydrated chicken broth
¼ cup water

Remove thin underside membrane from lobster tails with scissors. Push bamboo skewer lengthwise through tail to prevent curling.

Place colander over boiling water in large pot, or use steamer. Place lobster tails in colander; place vegetables on top and around tails.

Combine soy sauce, broth, and water; brush over tails and vegetables. Cover pot; steam 20 minutes or until vegetables are crisp-tender and lobster meat loses translucency and is opaque.

Fried Oysters

KOREA   Yield: 4 servings

   1 pound oysters, washed and shelled
   ½ cup flour
   2 eggs, beaten
   ¼ cup oil
   1 teaspoon salt

Vinegar soy sauce

   ½ cup soy sauce
   1 tablespoon sugar
   3 tablespoons vinegar
   Pine nuts, finely chopped, for garnish

Dredge each oyster in flour. Just before frying, dip oysters in the egg and place gently in heated fat. When nicely browned all over, remove to drain on paper towels. Salt lightly. Keep cooked oysters warm until all are ready. Serve with vinegar-soy sauce.

To make the sauce, mix soy sauce, sugar, and vinegar in a small bowl until sugar is completely dissolved. Sprinkle with chopped pine nuts and serve.

Fried Salmon Steaks Japanese Style

JAPAN   Yield: 4 servings

   1 pound skinless, boneless salmon
      fillets
   1 large egg
   3 tablespoons water
   Salt and freshly ground pepper to taste
   ⅓ cup flour
   2 cups fresh bread crumbs
   Fat for deep frying
   Lemon slices for garnish
   Pickled ginger sprouts (hajikami),
      available in Japanese groceries,
      optional

Cut the salmon into four pieces approximately the same size and weight. Beat the egg with water, salt and pepper. Dip the salmon pieces in flour to coat well. Shake off excess. Dip the flour-coated pieces in egg to coat well.

Dip the pieces in bread crumbs until coated all over. Place the pieces on a flat surface and tap with the flat side of a knife to help the crumbs adhere. Set aside.

Heat the oil and when it is quite hot, add the salmon pieces. Cook two to three minutes. Do not overcook or the fish will dry out. Drain on absorbent toweling. Serve garnished with lemon slices and pickled ginger sprouts.

Broiled Scallops

JAPAN   Yield: 2 to 3 servings

1 pound fresh scallops
Melted butter
Lemon juice
Freshly ground pepper, optional
Soy sauce
Rice

Place scallops on broiler; brush with melted butter mixed with lemon juice. Sprinkle with pepper; broil just until done. Sprinkle with soy sauce and serve with rice.

Deep-fried Scallops with Sweet-and-Sour Sauce

CHINA   Yield: 4 servings

1 pound scallops (cubed fish fillets may be substituted)

batter

1 cup all-purpose flour, sifted
¾ cup water
1 large egg
½ teaspoon salt
2 cups oil for frying

Sweet-and-sour sauce

4 pineapple rings, cut into small pieces
Reserved pineapple syrup and water to make 1 cup
1 tablespoon cornstarch in 2 tablespoons cold water
2 tablespoons vinegar
¼ cup brown sugar
1 teaspoon soy sauce
1 small onion, sliced
Few strips each of carrots and green pepper
2 cups hot boiled rice

Combine the batter ingredients and beat just until smooth. Allow to stand for 1 hour. Dip scallops a few at a time into the batter and deep-fry in oil at 375°F just until golden brown and done, about 3 to 4 minutes. Drain on paper towels.

Combine the sauce ingredients in a saucepan. Stir constantly while bringing to a boil. Heat until thickened and the carrot and pepper strips are heated through.

Place scallops on a bed of boiled rice and cover with the sauce. Serve at once while the scallop batter coating is still crisp.

Scallops Chinese Style

CHINA   Yield: About 25 appetizers

1 cup soy sauce
1 tablespoon lemon juice
2 teaspoons fresh gingerroot, finely chopped, or substitute powdered ginger
2 tablespoons sugar
¼ teaspoon MSG, optional
1 pound scallops, cut into bite-size pieces

In large saucepan combine soy sauce, lemon juice, ginger, sugar, and MSG. Bring to a boil. Add scallops and cook over medium-high heat until all the liquid has evaporated.

Boiled Shrimp

JAPAN   Yield: 2 servings

2 ounces cabbage, thinly sliced
8 ounces cucumbers, peeled and cut
   into ¼-inch cubes
8 ounces shrimp

Sauce

2 teaspoons horseradish
¼ cup soy sauce

Dip cabbage quickly into boiling water; let dry. Peel and slice cucumbers. Boil the shrimp in salted water for about 5 minutes.

Serve the cabbage, cucumber, and shrimp in small bowls. The shrimp is dipped into a sauce made from the horseradish and soy sauce.

Boiled Shrimp with Bamboo Shoots

JAPAN   Yield: 3 to 4 servings

2 cups boiling water
2 tablespoons mirin (sweet rice wine)
3 tablespoons soy sauce
12 shrimp, shelled and cleaned
1 pound bamboo shoots

Bring water to a boil; add mirin and soy sauce to it. If substituting sherry for the mirin, add 1 tablespoon sugar. Cook the shrimp in the mixture until done.

Cut the bamboo shoots into small pieces; cook them in the same liquid used for the shrimp. Serve shrimp and bamboo shoots with rice.

Butterfly Shrimp Cantonese Style

CHINA   Yield: 2 servings

1 pound shrimp
½ pound bacon
Shredded lettuce
Green onions, chopped

Sauce

1 large can tomato sauce
½ lemon, juice
⅓ cup brown sugar
⅓ cup vinegar
1 tablespoon Worcestershire sauce
3 pieces sour salt

Split shrimp, remove shell, devein, and open butterfly-style. Flatten. Meanwhile, cut bacon strips in half and fry on low heat, light to light brown, not crisp. Drain. Wrap each shrimp in bacon, roll and secure with toothpick. Bake in a 350°F oven for 10 to 15 minutes.

Combine all sauce ingredients and cook 10 minutes. After baking shrimp, add to sauce and cook 5 minutes. Put lettuce in bottom of serving bowl. Pour shrimp and sauce over it. Top with green onions. Serve with cooked rice. This may also be used as an hors d'oeuvre.

Butterfly Shrimp with Flower Drum Sauce

CHINA   Yield: 4 to 6 servings

2 pounds large raw shrimp, peeled and deveined
2 eggs
3 tablespoons water
Bacon
Oil for frying
1-2 tablespoons sherry or brandy

Sauce

2 cups water
1 cup catsup
2 tablespoons plus 2 teaspoons sugar
3 tablespoons vinegar
2 teaspoons cooking oil
1 slice lemon
1 tablespoon ground almonds
1½ teaspoons cornstarch
Spring onions and part of green stems, thinly sliced

Butterfly the shrimp by slitting down the back without actually cutting all the way through, and flatten. Beat eggs with water. Place a piece of bacon cut in pieces the length of the shrimp (each strip yields about 4 to 5 pieces) on the cut side of the shrimp. Hold in place and dip them together in egg mixture.

Fry bacon-side-down in a little oil about 3 to 4 minutes or until bacon starts to crisp. Sprinkle sherry or brandy on top of each shrimp. Cover and cook a few more minutes until shrimp turns pink. Drain on paper towels. Serve on fried rice and pour sauce on top or pass separately.

To make sauce, simmer all sauce ingredients except cornstarch for 15 minutes. Dissolve cornstarch in a little cold water, add it to the sauce, and cook until slightly thickened, about 10 minutes. Garnish with thin onion slices.

Shrimp Cantonese

CHINA   Yield: 6 servings

3 tablespoons vegetable oil
1 pound shrimp
1 clove garlic, mashed
¼ cup green onions (scallions)
½ teaspoon ginger
1 teaspoon salt
Dash of pepper
1 cup chicken stock (1 bouillon cube in 1 cup water)
1 package Italian green beans
1 tablespoon cornstarch
1 tablespoon cold water

Heat oil in skillet; sauté shrimp, garlic, onion for 5 minutes. Stir in ginger, salt, pepper, stock, and beans. Cover and simmer for 6 minutes. Combine cornstarch and cold water. Stir into shrimp mixture. Simmer 1 minute longer. Serve with rice.

Cantonese Shrimp and Beans

CHINA   Yield: 6 servings

1½ pounds frozen raw, peeled, deveined shrimp
1½ teaspoons chicken-stock base
1 cup boiling water
¼ cup green onion, thinly sliced
1 clove garlic, crushed
1 tablespoon salad oil
1 teaspoon salt
½ teaspoon ginger

Dash of pepper
1 9-ounce package frozen cut green
  beans, thawed
1 tablespoon cornstarch
1 tablespoon cold water

Dissolve chicken-stock base in boiling water.

Cook onion, garlic, and shrimp in oil 3 minutes; stir frequently. If necessary, add a little broth to prevent sticking. Stir in salt, ginger, pepper, beans, and broth; cover. Simmer 5 to 7 minutes, until beans are cooked but still slightly crisp.

Combine cornstarch and water. Add to shrimp; cook until thick and clear, stirring constantly.

Chinese Shrimp Casserole

CHINA   Yield: 8 servings

3 cups celery
1 cup onion, chopped
½ cup water
1 5-ounce box mushrooms
2 tablespoons butter
1 5-ounce can water chestnuts, sliced
  or diced
¾ cup green pepper, chopped
1 6-ounce package cashew nuts,
  chopped
1 small can (4½ ounces) pimientos,
  sliced
2 pounds fresh shrimp in shells or ¾
  pound cooked shrimp
2½ cups medium white sauce
2 cans (3 ounces each) crisp Chinese
  noodles

Cook celery, cut diagonally in ½-inch pieces, and onion until onion is tender. Wash and slice mushrooms and sauté in but-

ter. Combine celery, onion, mushrooms, water chestnuts, green pepper, cashew nuts, pimientos, shrimp, and cream sauce.

On the bottom of a buttered 3½-quart casserole, place can of the crisp noodles. Cover with the shrimp mixture; top with the other can of noodles. Bake at 350°F for 30 minutes.

Shrimp Curry

PHILIPPINES   Yield: 4 to 6 servings

4 tablespoons butter
2 onions, peeled and finely chopped
1 tablespoon curry powder
1 ounce candied ginger, finely cut
½ cup beef broth
½ cup coconut milk
½ cucumber, diced, unpeeled
1 pound shrimp, cooked, shelled, and
  deveined
Juice of ½ lemon
1 tablespoon soy sauce
1 teaspoon cornstarch
¼ cup water
Dash of cayenne pepper

Heat butter and cook onions until they are golden. Add curry and ginger. Pour in beef broth and coconut milk. When hot, add cucumber and shrimp. Season with lemon juice and soy sauce. Simmer.

Mix cornstarch in water and add to pan. Stir until the sauce thickens slightly. Season with cayenne pepper to taste and serve at once.

Fish and Seafood

Curried Shrimp I

CHINA   Yield: 4 servings

1 pound fresh shrimp, shelled, cleaned
Juice of 1 lemon
1 egg white
1 tablespoon cornstarch
2 cups sesame-seed or vegetable oil
1 tablespoon dried Chinese mushrooms
1 can (approximately 6 ounces)
   bamboo shoots
1 medium onion, chopped
½ teaspoon ground ginger
1 green pepper, thinly sliced
2 teaspoons curry powder
1 teaspoon sugar
2 tablespoons soy sauce
8-ounce can tiny peas, drained
2 tablespoons rice wine or sherry

Sprinkle shrimp with lemon juice. Blend egg white and cornstarch; coat shrimp with mixture. Heat oil in heavy, deep skillet or deep-fryer. Fry shrimp 2 or 3 minutes; remove with slotted spoon. Set aside; keep warm.

Break mushrooms into small pieces; cover with boiling water. Let soak 15 minutes.

Drain bamboo shoots; reserve liquid. Cut shoots into thin strips. Pour 2 tablespoons oil used for frying into skillet. Add bamboo shoots and onion; cook until transparent. Pour ½ cup reserved liquid from bamboo shoots. Season with ground ginger. Add green pepper; cook 5 minutes. Pepper should be crisp. Add curry powder, sugar, and soy sauce.

Drain soaked mushrooms. Add mushrooms, peas, and shrimp to skillet. Fold in carefully; heat through.

Heat wine in small saucepan; pour over dish just before serving.

Curried Shrimp II

INDIA   Yield: 4 servings

1½ teaspoons vinegar
1 clove garlic, minced
1½ teaspoons ground coriander
½ teaspoon salt
½ teaspoon turmeric
¼ teaspoon cumin
¼ teaspoon dry mustard
⅛ teaspoon freshly ground pepper
⅛ teaspoon ground ginger
1 small piece stick cinnamon
Dash of cayenne pepper
1 cardamom seed
1 bay leaf
1 pound fresh, large shrimp, peeled,
   deveined
1½ tablespoons butter
½ cup onions, chopped
½ sweet green pepper, chopped
½ cup coconut milk
1 tablespoon all-purpose flour
1½ teaspoons lemon juice

Combine vinegar, garlic, coriander, salt, turmeric, cumin, mustard, pepper, ginger, cinnamon, cayenne pepper, cardamom, and bay leaf in medium-size bowl. Add shrimp; mix well. Cover; refrigerate 2 hours.

Melt butter in chafing dish over direct flame. Add onions and green pepper; cook, stirring occasionally, until tender. Remove cinnamon stick, cardamom seed, and bay leaf; add shrimp mixture. Cook, stirring occasionally, 10 minutes or until shrimp are tender.

Combine coconut milk and flour; stir into shrimp mixture. Cook about 3 minutes, until sauce thickens and comes to a boil. Stir in lemon juice. Serve with rice, toasted coconut, plumped raisins, peanuts, and chutney.

Shrimp Curry with Tomatoes

BURMA   Yield: 4 servings

1¼ pounds shrimp, shelled and
    deveined
2 tablespoons shrimp-flavored soy sauce
½ teaspoon salt
½ teaspoon turmeric powder
¼ cup vegetable oil
1 large onion, peeled and pounded
4 cloves garlic, peeled and crushed
½-inch piece fresh gingerroot, peeled
    and pounded
½ teaspoon chili powder
3 tomatoes, chopped
2 tablespoons coriander leaves,
    chopped
¼ cup water
Coriander leaves for garnish

Marinate shrimp with soy sauce, salt, and turmeric. Marinate for at least 15 minutes.

Heat vegetable oil with onion, garlic, ginger, and chili powder until spices are fragrant but not dry. Add the shrimp, tomatoes, and coriander. Cover the pan and cook for 5 minutes. Gradually add the water, cover again, and simmer for 15 minutes. The shrimp should be nicely pink and the water absorbed. Place in a warm serving dish and garnish with coriander leaves.

Golden Shrimp

JAPAN   Yield: 2 servings

12 large fresh shrimp

Marinade
3 tablespoons soy sauce
1 tablespoon rice wine or sherry

Ginger to taste, either ground or grated
    gingerroot
Cornstarch

Oil for frying

Rinse shrimp. Mix together soy sauce, rice wine or sherry, and ginger. Marinate shrimp in the marinade for 30 minutes. Drain well. Sprinkle shrimp with cornstarch; set aside for 3 minutes. Heat oil in deep fryer or frying pan; fry shrimp.

The shrimp may be left whole for a main course or cut into approximately 3 pieces each for an appetizer. Makes 4 servings as an appetizer.

Grilled Oriental Shrimp

JAPAN   Yield: 2 to 3 servings

1 pound shrimp, cleaned
⅓ cup soy sauce
¼ cup sesame oil
1 tablespoon brown sugar
1 tablespoon fresh gingerroot, finely
    chopped, or ¾ teaspoon powdered
    ginger
3 scallions, finely chopped

Combine all ingredients and marinate in refrigerator 6 hours. Drain the shrimp, reserving the marinade. Skewer the shrimp and grill over a grill or hibachi approximately 5 minutes, turning frequently and basting with marinade.

Hot-Mustard Shrimp

CHINA   Yield: 2 to 3 servings

   3 tablespoons powdered mustard
   ¼ teaspoon salt
   1 teaspoon sugar
   1 teaspoon horseradish
   ¾ cup flat beer
   1 pound shrimp, cleaned
   4 tablespoons melted butter
   Duck sauce

   Mix mustard, salt, sugar, and horseradish together. Add enough beer to make a smooth paste. Gradually add rest of beer to make sauce thin. Let mixture stand for 1 hour. If it becomes too thick, add more beer or cold water.

   Dip shrimp in mustard sauce, skewer, and brush with melted butter. Grill on hibachi or grill for approximately 8 minutes. Turn frequently for even browning. Serve with duck sauce.

Oriental Shrimp

CHINA   Yield: Approximately 4 servings

   1 teaspoon curry and, perhaps, some
      paprika powder
   4 tablespoons margarine or butter
   2 red and 2 green paprikas
   2 yellow onions or 2 pieces of leek
   2 cloves garlic or garlic powder
   2 pounds shelled and deveined shrimp
   6 tablespoons tomato purée
   ½ cup water
   ½ cup dry white wine
   ½ cup heavy cream
   Salt
   2 cups fresh mushrooms

   In a wok, fry the curry and paprika powder in the margarine or butter; add paprika strips, onions, garlic, and shrimp to soften. Add the tomato purée, water, wine, and cream and let simmer for a few minutes. Heat the shrimp in the mixture, taste, and correct seasoning. Stir in the mushrooms and finish cooking.

   This mixture can be served hot in shells or eaten with white bread or rice. The mixture can also be used as filling in crepes.

Sesame Shrimp

KOREA   Yield: 2 to 3 servings

   ½ cup sesame seeds, toasted
   1 pound shrimp, cleaned
   Salt
   Freshly ground black pepper
   6 tablespoons melted butter

   Place sesame seeds in ungreased skillet over low heat and stir until browned. Set aside. Sprinkle shrimp lightly with salt and pepper. Dip in melted butter. Roll in toasted sesame seeds. Skewer shrimp and grill approximately 8 minutes over a grill or hibachi, turning frequently to brown evenly.

Shrimp and Asparagus

CHINA   Yield: 6 servings

   1 pound cooked shrimp, shelled and
      deveined
   1 can water chestnuts, drained and
      sliced
   1 medium onion, sliced
   1 cup fresh mushrooms, sliced
   1 cup celery, sliced diagonally
   1 small can mandarin oranges, drained

1½ pounds fresh asparagus, steamed
2 tablespoons oil
¼ teaspoon salt
½ teaspoon freshly ground black
  pepper
2 tablespoons sugar
2 tablespoons soy sauce
Cooked rice

Prepare the shrimp and set aside. Drain and slice the water chestnuts. On a large tray, arrange the shrimp, chestnuts, onion, mushrooms, celery, mandarin oranges, and asparagus. Heat the oil in a wok. Add onion, celery, salt, pepper, and sugar. Stir-fry until the vegetables are tender, but still on the crisp side.

Add asparagus and shrimp. Place the water chestnuts and mushrooms over the shrimp. Sprinkle with the soy sauce and place the orange sections on top. Cover and cook until mixture steams. Reduce heat and simmer about 10 minutes. Serve with rice.

Shrimp and Lobster Tempura with Sauce

JAPAN   Yield: 4 servings

4 frozen lobster tails
2 dozen fresh shrimp
1 recipe Basic Tempura Batter (see
  Index)

Sauce

¾ cup fish stock
⅓ cup soy sauce
1 tablespoon sugar
½ teaspoon MSG, optional
⅓ cup sake
1 teaspoon ginger
¼ cup white radish, grated

Thaw the lobster tails. Shell and devein the shrimp, leaving the tails intact. Slit the shrimp down the back without separating the halves and press flat. Remove the lobster meat from the lobster tails and cut into cubes. Drain the shrimp and lobster meat thoroughly. Dip into the batter, then drain slightly. Fry in oil, a few pieces at a time, for about 5 minutes, turning to brown evenly. Drain well on paper towels.

Combine the fish stock, soy sauce, sugar, MSG, and sake, stirring to mix well. Pour into individual serving bowls. Sprinkle each bowl with the ginger and radish just before serving. This makes about 1⅔ cups of sauce.

Foo Chow (Shrimp Balls)

CHINA   Yield: 12 to 15 portions

1 pound cooked shrimp in shell
10 water chestnuts
1 tablespoon cornstarch
1 teaspoon sherry
½ teaspoon salt
1 egg, beaten lightly
Enough oil for deep frying

Shell and devein shrimp and mince finely. Peel and mince water chestnuts, and add to the shrimp. Mix well. Add cornstarch, sherry, salt and egg. Mix well. Form into balls the size of a small walnut.

Heat 2 inches of oil in a pan and, when hot, lower the balls into it with a draining spoon. Fry about 5 minutes or until golden brown. Serve very hot on toothpicks as an appetizer.

Shrimp Balls

INDIA   Yield: 4 to 6 servings

1 pound canned shrimp
2 onions, peeled and finely chopped
½ bunch parsley, finely chopped
3 branches fresh mint or ½ tablespoon
  dried mint
1 slice fresh white bread, minus crusts
  and crumbed
1 teaspoon salt
Pepper to taste
½ teaspoon ground ginger
1 egg
4 tablespoons lemon juice
6 tablespoons flour
1 teaspoon ground coriander
Dash of tabasco sauce
2 tablespoons cold water
4 tablespoons oil
Lemon slices for garnish

Drain liquid off shrimp. In a bowl, mix shrimp, onions, parsley, mint, bread crumbs, salt, pepper, and ginger. Add egg and lemon juice. Mix ingredients well. With a spoon, beat them into a smooth mass. Let rest at room temperature for 30 minutes.

Stir flour, coriander, tabasco, and cold water to a thick, smooth dough. Form the shrimp mixture into round balls 1 inch thick. Heat oil in a skillet. Roll shrimp balls in the flour mixture and fry on each side for 5 minutes, until golden brown. Garnish with lemon and serve at once.

Shrimp Bombay

INDIA   Yield: 4 to 6 servings

1 pound fresh shrimp
1 cup water
1 teaspoon salt

Sauce

2 tablespoons butter or margarine
1 shallot, peeled and finely cut
1 green pepper, seeded and diced
2 teaspoons curry powder
2 tablespoons flour
1 cup shrimp broth
Scant 1 cup beef broth
2 tablespoons tomato paste
½ cup cream
Pinch sugar
Pinch salt
Parsley for garnish

Rinse shrimp in cold water and drain. Place in 1 cup boiling water with salt. Boil shrimp until pink and drain, reserving the broth. Shell and devein the shrimp.

Heat butter or margarine in a pot. Add shallot and green pepper and cook for 3 to 5 minutes. Sprinkle with curry and then stir in flour. Pour in reserved shrimp broth and beef broth. Stir constantly for about 5 minutes. Remove from the heat.

Mix the tomato paste and cream together. Add the mixture to the hot sauce. Season to taste with sugar and salt. Return sauce to stove at a simmer and add shrimp. Heat only until the shrimp is hot through. Place in a serving dish and garnish with parsley. Delicious with a side dish of rice.

Shrimp in Coconut Milk

PHILIPPINES   Yield: 6 servings

1½ pounds raw shrimp
2 cups thick coconut milk
1 tablespoon garlic, finely chopped
1 teaspoon ginger, finely chopped
1 teaspoon salt
¼ teaspoon black pepper

Do not shell shrimp, but wash well and drain. In a saucepan, place the shrimp and remaining ingredients listed. Bring this mixture to a boil, stirring constantly. Reduce heat and simmer for 15 minutes, continuing to stir. Serve at once over hot white rice.

Shrimp in Garlic Sauce

CHINA   Yield: 4 servings

2 tablespoons vegetable oil
1 small onion, chopped
1 teaspoon grated gingerroot
4 cloves garlic, sliced
5 or 6 Chinese dried black mushrooms, soaked 30 minutes in warm water and sliced
1 cup peas, fresh or frozen defrosted
1 pound cooked shrimp
½ cup chicken broth or water
2 teaspoons soy sauce
1 teaspoon salt
1 tablespoon cornstarch in 2 table- spoons water

Heat oil in wok and stir-fry onion, ginger, and garlic for 1 to 2 minutes. Add mushrooms and peas and stir-fry 1 to 3 minutes. Add shrimp and continue to stir-fry 1 to 2 minutes. Combine broth, soy sauce, salt, and the cornstarch mixture. Add to wok and heat until sauce boils and has thickened. Serve immediately with boiled rice.

Shrimp in Hot Sauce

CHINA   Yield: 4 servings

1 pound medium-sized fresh shrimp

Marinade

1 egg white (or 1 tablespoon corn- starch)
Few drops vegetable oil

2 cups vegetable oil
1 tablespoon fresh garlic, minced
½ tablespoon fresh ginger, minced
1 cup canned bamboo shoots, cut into ¾-inch squares (or same amount green or red bell pepper, or white or yellow onions, cut to same size)
1½ to 2 tablespoons chicken broth
1 tablespoon Szechuan hot bean sauce
1 tablespoon soy sauce
1 tablespoon minced scallions
½ tablespoon liquid cornstarch
1 teaspoon sesame oil, optional

Shell, devein, wash, and dry shrimp. Mix shrimp with marinade and let stand for 10 minutes.

Heat a wok over highest heat for 2 minutes; then add vegetable oil. As soon as the oil is smoking hot, stir-fry shrimp for about 10 seconds until they begin to change color. Remove shrimp quickly from wok and drain. Pour off all but 3 to 4 tablespoons oil from wok and reheat remaining oil until smoking hot.

Add garlic, ginger, bamboo shoots, and chicken broth; stir vigorously for 10 seconds. Return shrimp to wok and add hot bean sauce, soy sauce, scallions, and liquid cornstarch; stir until thoroughly hot (about 10 seconds). Serve at once, garnished with sesame oil if you wish.

Variations: For hot and sour shrimp, add 1½ tablespoons vinegar (with garlic, ginger, and bamboo shoots).

For fierce hot shrimp, just add 1 teaspoon hot red pepper powder at same point.

Shrimp or Chicken Chow Mein

CHINA   Yield: 4 servings

1 tablespoon oil
⅛ teaspoon garlic, minced
½ pound cut-up shrimp or ½ pound sliced chicken
1 onion, sliced
2 cups bok choy, diced
1 cup celery, sliced
½ cup bean sprouts
1½ cups meat stock
½ teaspoon salt
¼ teaspoon sugar
2 tablespoons cornstarch mixed with 2 tablespoons cold water

Place oil in frying pan with minced garlic. Add shrimp or chicken along with the vegetables. Stir-fry for 1 minute. Add meat stock. Simmer for 5 minutes. Add salt, sugar, and cornstarch mixture. Serve over crispy chow mein noodles.

Shrimp Puffs

JAPAN   Yield: About 16

1 pound shrimp, cleaned, deveined, chopped very fine
8 to 9 water chestnuts, minced
1 egg, beaten
1 teaspoon salt
½ teaspoon sugar
1 teaspoon cornstarch
2 teaspoons dry sherry
1 teaspoon soy sauce
2 cups oil for frying
Lemon wedges and soy sauce for dipping

Combine the shrimp, water chestnuts, egg, salt, sugar, cornstarch, sherry, and soy sauce. Heat oil in the wok to 375°F. Shape the shrimp mixture into balls the size of small walnuts and drop from a spoon into the hot oil. Fry until the balls float and turn pink and golden. Drain on paper towels. Serve hot with lemon wedges and a bowl of soy sauce for dipping.

Shrimp Rolls

THAILAND   Yield: 4 to 6 servings

2 bean-curd leaves
4 or 5 heaping tablespoons pork fat, finely diced
Boiling water
2 pounds whole raw shrimp, shelled, washed, and finely minced
3 cloves garlic, peeled and finely chopped
2 teaspoons salt
1 teaspoon ground pepper
4 tablespoons flour
2 eggs, beaten
Oil for deep frying

Pour water over bean-curd leaves and set aside to soften. Cover pork fat with boiling water; drain well and set aside.

Place prepared shrimp in a large bowl. Mix with garlic, adding salt, pepper, and flour. Add beaten eggs to this mixture. Add the prepared pork fat and mix again. Divide into 2 portions. Wrap each portion, like a sausage, in bean-curd leaves. Steam for 10 minutes and allow to cool.

When cool, cut into slices and fry in hot oil until brown and crisp on the outside. Although these shrimp rolls are good by themselves, they are even better when served with your favorite sweet-and-sour sauce.

Speedy Shrimp Stir-Fry

CHINA   Yield: 6 servings

½ cup creamy Italian salad dressing
3 tablespoons soy sauce
12 ounces peeled, deveined raw shrimp
1 large onion, sliced
1 large green pepper, cut in 1-inch
    pieces
¼ pound fresh mushrooms, sliced
1 tablespoon vegetable oil
13¼ ounce can pineapple tidbits,
    drain, reserve syrup
1 tablespoon cornstarch

Pour salad dressing mixed with soy sauce over shrimp and allow to marinate while preparing vegetables. Sauté onion, green pepper, and mushrooms in hot oil until tender crisp. Add pineapple, shrimp, and marinade.

Blend pineapple syrup into cornstarch. Stir into shrimp mixture. Cook and stir 2-3 minutes, or until thickened. Spoon over beds of fluffy rice.

Shrimp Tempura

JAPAN   Yield: 4 servings

1 pound fresh large shrimp
8 ounces bamboo shoots
4 peppers, green, red, and yellow
4 small onions
2 sugared or candied ginger

Tempura batter

2 ounces rice flour
6 ounces flour
1 cup water
4 jiggers rice wine or sherry
8 egg whites

4 cups oil for frying

Rinse shrimp. Drain bamboo shoots; cut into ½-inch pieces. Cut green peppers into ½-inch strips. Cut onions into thick slices; separate into rings. Slice sugared ginger. Arrange these ingredients in separate, small bowls.

To prepare the batter, place the flour in a bowl. In a separate bowl, combine water and rice wine or sherry and egg whites until well blended. Gradually stir into flour to form loose batter.

Heat the oil in a fondue pot or wok. Each person places a shrimp or piece of vegetable on a fondue fork, dips it in batter, and deep-fries it in hot oil.

Shrimp Teriyaki

JAPAN   Yield: 4 servings

1 pound shelled, deveined raw shrimp
½ pound Chinese pea pods
2 tablespoons soy sauce
3 tablespoons vinegar
¾ cup pineapple juice
3 tablespoons sugar
1 cup chicken broth

Put shrimp and pea pods in pressure cooker.

Combine the rest of the ingredients, mixing well so that sugar dissolves. Pour the liquid into the cooker and close cover. Set pressure control in place. When pressure is reached, cook for 2 minutes. Cool at once to lower pressure under running water. Serve.

Shrimp with Bean Sprouts

CHINA   Yield: 4 servings

1 green pepper (or a red, ripe one), cut
    into ¼-inch strips
1 cup bean sprouts
1 teaspoon ginger, grated
2 tablespoons vegetable oil
6 ounces cooked shrimp
1 tablespoon dry sherry
2 teaspoons soy sauce
Salt

Crispy fried noodles

12 ounces fine egg noodles
2 cups vegetable oil for frying

Combine green pepper, bean sprouts, and
ginger. Heat oil in a wok; stir-fry vegetables
about 2 minutes. Push aside. Add shrimp;
stir-fry until heated. Combine shrimp and
vegetables; add sherry and soy sauce. Salt to
taste. Serve hot with crispy fried noodles.

To make the fried noodles, cook noodles
in boiling, salted water according to package
directions. Drain; rinse thoroughly in cold
water. Dry on paper towels. Fry handfuls of
noodles in oil at 375°F, turning frequently,
about 5 minutes. Drain on paper towels.

Shrimp with Chicken and Cauliflower

CHINA   Yield: 4 servings

2 tablespoons vegetable oil
1 cup cauliflower, cut into bite-size
    florets and parboiled (cover with
    boiling water and let stand 5
    minutes)
1 cup fresh or frozen, defrosted peas

½ pound cooked chicken meat, cut
    into ½-inch cubes
¾ to 1 pound cooked whole shrimp
2 scallions, cut lengthwise into quarters

Sauce

½ cup chicken broth
1 tablespoon soy sauce
2 tablespoons tomato paste (or chili
    sauce)
1 tablespoon cornstarch in
    2 tablespoons cold water
¼ cup dry white wine

Heat oil in wok and stir-fry cauliflower
florets 1 to 2 minutes. Push aside. Stir-fry
peas 1 to 3 minutes. Push aside. Stir-fry
chicken, shrimp, and scallions 2 to 3
minutes, until heated. Combine sauce ingredients and add to the vegetables, chicken,
and shrimp. Heat until sauce boils and is
thickened. Serve at once with rice.

Shrimp with Cucumber

CHINA   Yield: 4 servings

1 pound shrimp, shelled and deveined
2 tablespoons white wine
2 teaspoons salt
1 teaspoon sugar
2 teaspoons cornstarch
2 tablespoons vegetable oil
2 cucumbers, quartered lengthwise,
    seeds removed, and cut into 1-inch
    pieces
1 scallion, sliced

Combine the shrimp, wine, salt, sugar,
and cornstarch. Let stand 30 minutes. Heat
vegetable oil in wok and stir-fry the cucumber 2 to 3 minutes. Push aside. Stir-fry
shrimp for 2 to 3 minutes or until they turn
pink. Return the cucumbers and heat briefly.
Serve at once garnished with scallion slices.

Shrimp with Lobster Sauce

CHINA   Yield: 4 servings

Lobster sauce is made with garlic, fermented black beans, and egg. The sauce does not contain lobster, but is used with lobster, shrimp, and other seafood. This is how the name was derived.

2 to 3 ounces pork, minced
2 tablespoons vegetable oil
1 pound cooked shrimp, cut into bite-size pieces
1 tablespoon gingerroot, grated
3 cloves garlic, grated
1 tablespoon black beans (dow sei), washed and mashed
1 cup chicken broth or water
1 teaspoon soy sauce
1 teaspoon salt
1 teaspoon sugar
2 tablespoons dry sherry
1 tablespoon cornstarch in 2 tablespoons cold water
1 egg, beaten
Scallion slices, leaves only

Stir-fry the pork in the vegetable oil until well done. Add shrimp, ginger, garlic, and beans. Stir-fry briefly. Combine broth, soy sauce, salt, sugar, sherry, and the cornstarch mixture. Stir and add to the wok. Heat until thickened.

Remove from heat and pour egg in slowly while stirring with a fork. Serve on rice and garnish with green scallion slices. The sauce must not be hot enough to coagulate the egg as it is stirred in with a fork. The purpose of the egg is to color the sauce and thicken it slightly.

Szechuan Shrimp

CHINA   Yield: 4 servings

½ cup scallions, minced
½ cup bamboo shoots, minced
¼ teaspoon fresh gingeroot, minced
3 large cloves garlic, minced
¼ teaspoon liquid hot pepper sauce
2 tablespoons sugar
½ cup catsup
3 tablespoons dry sherry
1 tablespoon soy sauce
1½ teaspoons sesame oil or 1 tablespoon toasted sesame seeds
1 tablespoon cornstarch
3 tablespoons water
1½ cups vegetable oil
1 pound shelled and deveined raw shrimp

Combine scallions, bamboo shoots, ginger, garlic, and pepper sauce in a small bowl. In second bowl, combine sugar, catsup, sherry, soy sauce, and sesame oil (or sesame seeds).

In third bowl, mix cornstarch and water. Heat vegetable oil in wok or large skillet to 400°F. Have ready a large strainer with a bowl underneath. Add shrimp to hot oil, stirring until done, about 2 minutes. Pour oil and shrimp into strainer to drain.

Heat 2 tablespoons of the strained oil in the same wok or skillet over high heat. Add scallion mixture and stir-fry 1 minute. Add drained shrimp and stir-fry 30 seconds. Add cornstarch mixture to wok. Cook and stir until slightly thickened.

Shrimp with Mandarin Oranges

CHINA   Yield: 2 servings

    2 teaspoons sherry
    1 teaspoon cornstarch
    ½ pound shrimp, cleaned
    Oil for cooking
    ½ cup drained canned mandarin
        orange segments
    ¼ teaspoon sugar
    ¼ teaspoon salt

Mix together sherry and cornstarch and marinate shrimp in mixture for 5 minutes. Heat oil in skillet or wok, enough to cover bottom of pan, and stir-fry shrimp just until color changes. Add mandarin orange segments, sugar, and salt and stir-fry just until heated through, no more than 1 minute.

Shrimp with Mushrooms and Celery

CHINA   Yield: 4 servings

    1 pound shrimp, cleaned and peeled
    1 teaspoon salt
    3 tablespoons white wine
    2 tablespoons vegetable oil
    1 slice fresh gingerroot
    ¼ pound mushrooms, sliced into "T"
        shapes
    2 cups celery, sliced diagonally into
        ½-inch slices
    1 scallion, sliced into ½-inch slices
    1 tablespoon cornstarch in ½ cup cold
        chicken broth

Combine shrimp, salt, and white wine. Marinate in the refrigerator for 30 minutes.

Heat oil in the wok and brown the slice of ginger to flavor the oil. Remove and discard the ginger. Stir-fry the mushrooms 1 to 2 minutes. Push aside. Stir-fry the celery and scallion 1 to 2 minutes, until the color brightens. Push aside. Stir-fry the shrimp and wine 2 minutes or until the shrimp turn pink. (Frozen, defrosted shrimp should only be heated through.) Return the vegetables to the shrimp in the wok. Add the cornstarch mixture and heat until the sauce boils. Serve at once with rice.

Skewered Shrimp

JAPAN   Yield: 2 servings

    4 large shelled shrimp

Sauce

    1 tablespoon (or less) salt
    4 tablespoons soy sauce
    ¾ tablespoon rice wine or sherry
    ¼ teaspoon ginger, freshly grated
    Asparagus tips

Cut shrimp into bite-size pieces. Make a sauce by blending together the salt, soy sauce, rice wine (sake) or sherry, and ginger. Dip shrimp into sauce; place on skewers.

Dip the asparagus tips into the sauce, then place on skewers. Broil in oven, basting with sauce, or use a grill or hibachi.

Sweet and Pungent Shrimp

CHINA   Yield: 4 servings

    1¼ pound shrimp, cleaned and pre-
        pared like butterfly shrimp
    1 egg
    4 tablespoons cornstarch
    1 cup vinegar

½ cup juice from sweet mixed pickles
2 tablespoons catsup
Dash of salt
2 teaspoons cornstarch
¼ cup cold water
1 green pepper, cut diagonally
1 large tomato, cut into 6 pieces
2 pineapple rings, cut into chunks
½ cup mixed pickles
1 cup sugar

Make batter with egg and 4 tablespoons cornstarch and add a little water. Dip shrimp in batter and fry. Set aside. In large skillet, put vinegar, pickle juice, catsup, and salt; bring to a boil. When mixture begins to boil, add cornstarch which has been in ¼ cup cold water. Add green pepper, tomato, pineapple, and mixed pickles. Cook for 2 minutes. Add shrimp and sugar; mix thoroughly, but do not cook any more.

Sweet-and-Sour Shrimp

CHINA   Yield: 4 servings

2 tablespoons honey
1 tablespoon vinegar
1 clove garlic, crushed
2 tablespoons soy sauce
1 tablespoon tomato paste
Pinch chili powder
12 large shrimp, peeled and deveined
2 tablespoons vegetable oil

Combine the honey, vinegar, crushed garlic, soy sauce, tomato paste, and chili powder in a small bowl. Add the shrimp and marinate in the refrigerator for 30 minutes.

Remove the shrimp from the marinade and stir-fry in the oil for 3 minutes (less if cooked shrimp are used). Add the marinade and heat for 2 minutes. Pour shrimp and sauce into a hot serving dish. Stir-fried vegetables may be added if you wish.

Pan Fried Fillet of Sole

INDIA   Yield: 6 servings

The hidden ingredient here is carom, which adds a special flavor. The fish should be marinated for at least 24 hours before cooking.

6 whole skinless, boned fillets, about ½ pound each

Marinade

1 teaspoon Kosher salt
2 tablespoons lemon juice
1 tablespoon garlic, finely minced
½ teaspoon carom seeds, crushed

Crumb coating

¼ cup flour
2 large eggs, beaten
2½ cups bread crumbs
½ teaspoon Kosher salt
½ teaspoon black pepper
Peanut or corn oil for frying

Dry each fillet with a paper towel and place in a bowl. Mix the marinade ingredients together and rub over each fillet. Cover and let stand in the refrigerator for 24 to 48 hours.

Just before frying, place 3 bowls on countertop. Put flour in one, beaten eggs in the second bowl, and bread crumbs and seasonings in the third. Dip each fillet in the flour, then the eggs, and finally the bread crumbs, making sure they are thoroughly breaded. Place on waxed paper until all fillets are covered.

Heat oil in a frying pan about ¾ inch deep. Gently add 2 or 3 fillets to oil. When brown on one side, about 3 minutes, turn with a large spatula until brown on the other side. Drain on paper towels. Then transfer finished fillets to warm serving dish and put in a low oven to keep warm until all fillets are cooked. Serve hot with your favorite relish.

Sole with Sweet-Sour Vegetables

CHINA   Yield: 4 servings

4 fillets of sole (about 1 pound)
1 tablespoon lemon juice
1 tablespoon oil
2 cups julienne-cut carrots (cut 2¼ ×
    ¼ inch)
½ cup onion, thinly sliced
2 tablespoons water
2 cups celery, sliced
½ cup water chestnuts, sliced
1 8¼-ounce can pineapple chunks
1½ tablespoons brown sugar
3 tablespoons cider vinegar
1½ tablespoons soy sauce
1½ teaspoons cornstarch

Prepare all ingredients before starting to cook. Roll sole fillets and place in skillet with enough boiling water to barely cover, and 1 tablespoon lemon juice. Simmer, covered, until fish flakes easily with a fork, about 8 to 10 minutes.

Meanwhile, heat oil in 10-inch skillet. Add carrots and onion, and stir-fry 5 minutes over moderately high heat. Reduce heat to moderate, add water, cover and steam 4 minutes. Uncover, add celery and water chestnuts, and stir-fry 2 minutes. Add un-drained pineapple.

Mix sugar, vinegar, soy sauce and corn-starch together. Stir slowly into skillet and cook, stirring, until sauce coats vegetables and pineapple. Remove fish rolls from liquid, drain well, and serve topped with sweet-sour vegetable mixture.

Note: Sweet-sour vegetables may be served with any poached, broiled or baked fish.

Baked Snapper

INDONESIA   Yield: 4 to 6 servings

1 3- to 4-pound snapper
1 medium onion, peeled and chopped
2 cloves garlic, peeled
1 teaspoon fresh ginger, finely chopped
2 tablespoons tamarind liquid
1 tablespoon dark soy sauce
1 tablespoon oil
1 teaspoon salt
1 teaspoon ground turmeric
3 tablespoons fresh coriander leaves,
    finely chopped
Banana leaves or foil for wrapping

Wash the fish and pat dry with paper towels. Score the flesh diagonally on each side. Use a blender or food processor to mix onion, garlic, ginger, tamarind liquid, soy sauce, oil, salt, and turmeric. When blended smooth, rub into body of fish on both sides. Rub remaining mixture into body cavity for extra flavor. Lay fish on banana leaves in a baking dish and sprinkle with coriander. Fold leaves to cover fish and secure with skewers. If banana leaves are unavailable, use foil.

Bake at 375°F for 35 to 40 minutes or until the fish flakes when tested with a fork. Reseal the fish after testing and serve closed. When opened, it will have a delightful fragrance.

Oriental Swordfish Steaks

CHINA   Yield: 6 servings

2 pounds swordfish steaks or other fish
    steaks, fresh or frozen
¼ cup orange juice
¼ cup soy sauce
2 tablespoons catsup
2 tablespoons melted fat or oil
2 tablespoons parsley, chopped

1 tablespoon lemon juice
1 clove garlic, finely chopped
½ teaspoon oregano
½ teaspoon pepper

Thaw frozen steaks. Cut into serving-size portions and place in a single layer in a shallow baking dish. Combine remaining ingredients. Pour sauce over fish and let stand for 30 minutes, turning once.

Remove fish, reserving sauce for basting. Place fish in well-greased, hinged wire grills. Cook about 4 inches from moderately hot coals for 8 minutes. Baste with sauce. Turn and cook for 7 to 10 minutes longer or until fish flakes easily when tested with a fork.

Chinese Tuna

CHINA   Yield: 2 to 3 servings

1 10¾-ounce can cream of mushroom
    soup
¼ cup water
2 cups chow mein noodles
1 6½- or 7-ounce can tuna, drained
    and flaked
1 cup celery, thinly sliced
½ cup salted, lightly toasted cashews
¼ cup onion, diced
Dash of freshly ground black pepper
1 small can mandarin oranges, drained

Combine soup and water. Add 1 cup noodles, tuna, celery, cashews, onion, and pepper. Toss lightly. Place in ungreased baking dish. Sprinkle with remaining noodles. Bake in 375°F toaster oven 10 minutes or until heated through. Garnish with mandarin oranges.

Tuna Stir-Fry

CHINA   Yield: 2 servings

1 6½- to 7-ounce can tuna
1 cup sliced mushrooms
1 cup diagonally sliced celery
½ cup chopped onion
1 clove garlic, minced
1 tablespoon chopped candied ginger
¼ cup water
1 10-ounce package frozen Chinese-
    style vegetables
2 tablespoons soy sauce
1 tablespoon sherry
¼ cup almonds or walnut halves
Cooked rice

Into large skillet or wok drain excess oil from tuna. If using water-pack tuna, add a tablespoon vegetable oil to the skillet. Add mushrooms, celery, onion, garlic and ginger; cook until tender. Add tuna and ingredients through nuts. Cook, stirring constantly, over moderately high heat until vegetables are crisp-tender. Serve over rice if desired.

Tuna Casserole

JAPAN   Yield: 2 to 3 servings

1 small can tuna
½ cup onion, diced
½ cup celery, diced
1 can bean sprouts, rinsed with cold
    water and drained
¼ cup green pepper, diced
Soy sauce to taste

Drain tuna; mix with onion, celery, bean sprouts, green pepper, and soy sauce to taste. Place in casserole; bake at 350°F for 30 minutes. Add additional soy sauce, if needed.

Mai Kai

CHINA   Yield: 4 servings

1 can tuna
1 can cream of chicken soup mixed
    with ¼ cup water
1½ cup celery, cut on the bias
1 green pepper, cut in strips
1 large onion, chopped
1 can mushrooms, drained
½ teaspoon salt
¼ cup slivered almonds
½ teaspoon MSG
1 can chow mein noodles

Mix all ingredients except tuna and noodles. Then gently add tuna and noodles. Place in a buttered baking dish (approximately 9 × 14″) and dot with butter and bake at 325°F for 1 hour.

Oriental Tuna

JAPAN   Yield: 5 to 6 servings

2 tablespoons cornstarch
¼ teaspoon ground ginger
1 13¾-ounce can chicken broth
3 tablespoons soy sauce
3 tablespoons cooking oil
1 cup bias-cut celery, ¼ inch thick
1 cup bias-cut carrots, 1 inch thick
1 clove garlic, minced
¼ cup green onions, sliced
2 7-ounce cans water-pack tuna,
    drained and broken in chunks
1 16-ounce can bean sprouts, drained
1 cup frozen peas, thawed
Hot cooked rice

Cut and assemble all ingredients before starting to cook. Blend together cornstarch, ginger, chicken broth, and soy sauce. Heat 12-inch skillet over high heat. Add cooking oil and heat. Stir in celery, carrots, and garlic. Cook and stir 3 minutes. Add onions; cook and stir 1 minute. Stir in cornstarch mixture. Cook and stir until mixture is thickened and bubbly, about 2 minutes. Stir in tuna, bean sprouts, and peas. Cover and reduce heat to low. Cook 3 minutes or until thoroughly heated. Serve over hot cooked rice.

Tuna Chop Suey

CHINA   Yield: 6 servings

¼ cup (½ stick) corn oil margarine
1 cup celery, sliced
1 medium onion, sliced
1 medium green pepper, cut in strips
1 clove garlic, minced
1 8-ounce can bamboo shoots, drained
1 8-ounce can water chestnuts, drained
    and sliced
1½ cups water
1 tablespoon soy sauce
½ teaspoon salt
2 tablespoons cornstarch
2 cans (7 ounces each) water-packed
    tuna, drained and flaked
Cooked rice

In a large skillet melt corn oil margarine over medium heat. Lightly sauté celery, onion, green pepper, garlic, bamboo shoots, and water chestnuts. Mix 1¼ cups water, soy sauce, and salt into skillet. Combine cornstarch with remaining water; slowly add to skillet, stirring constantly. Simmer until thickened. Fold in tuna and heat through. Serve over rice.

Tuna Chow Mein

CHINA   Yield: 6 servings

2 cans tuna
2 cans cream of mushroom soup
⅔ cup water
2 cups celery, cut on a slant
Few drops soy sauce
Dash of pepper
1 cup onion
1 can Chinese noodles

Mix together ingredients (only use ½ can noodles). Put in greased casserole. Sprinkle with remaining ½ can Chinese noodles. Bake at 375°F for 20 minutes or until bubbly. Serve on rice if desired. Do not mix more than 1 hour before baking or leave in oven too long.

Tuna Taipei

CHINA   Yield: 6 servings

2 6½- or 7-ounce cans tuna
½ cup green onion, chopped
¼ cup salad oil
4 cups cold unsalted cooked rice
3 tablespoons soy sauce
2 eggs, beaten
1 5-ounce can water chestnuts, drained and chopped

Drain and flake tuna. Cook onion in hot oil in a 10-inch frying pan until tender. Add rice and soy sauce. Stir over low heat until rice is hot. Push rice to one side. Pour in egg and cook, stirring frequently. Add water chestnuts and tuna. Mix well and heat.

Poultry

Baked Chicken Legs with Fruit

JAPAN   Yield: 6 servings

- 1 teaspoon paprika
- ½ teaspoon ground ginger
- 1 teaspoon seasoned salt
- ¼ cup flour
- 6 chicken legs, disjointed, using thigh and leg
- ¼ cup shortening
- 1 29-ounce can or jar fruits-for-salad
- 3 oranges, peeled and cut into bite-size pieces
- 1 tablespoon brown sugar
- 2 teaspoons soy sauce
- 1 tablespoon cornstarch

Mix together paprika, ginger, seasoned salt, and flour. Place in small paper or double-plastic bag. Drop chicken in bag, one piece at a time, until well coated. Set aside.

Heat shortening in skillet to low-medium heat. Brown chicken on all sides.

Tear 6 pieces of heavy-duty aluminum foil large enough to hold chicken and fruit. On each piece of foil, place 1 thigh and 1 leg. Drain fruits, reserving liquid. Mix the canned fruit with the orange pieces; place 1/6 of fruit on each piece of foil, along with chicken pieces.

Into small saucepan, place 1 cup of fruit syrup, brown sugar, soy sauce, and cornstarch. Mix well; bring to a boil. Simmer for 3 minutes. Spoon sauce over chicken and fruit. Fold foil; seal, by double-folding edges. Place packages in pan; bake at 425°F for 1½ hours or until chicken is tender.

Balinese-style Fried Chicken

INDONESIA   Yield: 4 servings

- 1 onion, peeled and roughly chopped
- 2 cloves garlic, peeled
- 1 teaspoon fresh ginger, chopped
- 3 fresh red chilies, seeded and chopped
- 4 kemiri nuts
- 1 tablespoon dark soy sauce
- 1 2½-pound frying chicken
- Peanut oil, at least ½ cup
- 2 teaspoons palm sugar
- 2 tablespoons lemon juice
- ½ teaspoon salt
- 1 cup coconut milk

Make a smooth paste, preferably in blender or food processor, of onion, garlic, ginger, chilies, kemiri nuts, and soy sauce.

Quarter the chicken and dry each piece with paper towels. Heat ½ cup peanut oil in wok or frying pan and brown chicken pieces quickly on both sides. Remove chicken and drain on paper towels.

Pour off excess oil, leaving 1 tablespoon in pan. Fry the prepared paste in this for a few minutes, stirring constantly. While stirring, add sugar, lemon juice, salt, and coconut milk, and allow to come to a boil. Put chicken into this sauce and simmer for 25 minutes, until chicken is tender and sauce has thickened. Serve with rice.

Braised Chicken with Mushrooms

KOREA   Yield: 4 to 6 servings

- 10 dried Chinese mushrooms
- 1 2-pound chicken, cut into small pieces
- 3 tablespoons light soy sauce

1 tablespoon sesame oil

2 cloves garlic, peeled and crushed

½ teaspoon cayenne powder or chili powder

½ teaspoon ground black pepper

2 tablespoons vegetable oil

1 large onion, cut into 8 wedges and then cut again

2 canned winter bamboo shoots

4 spring onions

2 tablespoons toasted sesame seeds, crushed

Soak mushrooms in boiling water for 20 to 30 minutes. Discard stems and then slice the mushroom caps into thin strips.

Marinate the chicken in a combination of soy sauce, sesame oil, garlic, cayenne pepper, and black pepper. Rub each piece of the chicken with this and allow them to marinate for at least 30 minutes.

Heat vegetable oil in skillet or wok. Over medium heat stir-fry the chicken until golden brown. Add mushroom strips and ½ cup of mushroom liquid. Add remaining marinade and cover. Simmer for 15 to 20 minutes.

Prepare the onion, separating the layers into pieces. Quarter the bamboo shoots and then slice. Cut spring onions into bite-size pieces. Add these to the already-simmering chicken and cook for 2 minutes more. Garnish with sesame seeds.

Chicken Cantonese

CHINA   Yield: 3 to 4 servings

½ pound white meat of chicken sliced in strips, about 1½ inches long and ½ inch wide

½ pound snow peas, strings removed

¼ cup peanut oil

¼ cup bamboo shoots

1 cup bok choy, sliced

1 cup fresh mushrooms, sliced

1 cup celery, sliced diagonally

¼ cup water chestnuts, sliced

1 teaspoon MSG, optional

4 cups chicken stock

2 tablespoons cornstarch mixed with ½ cup cold water

Slice chicken and set aside. Wash snow peas, remove strings, and set aside. Heat oil in skillet or wok and stir-fry chicken for about 10 seconds. Add bamboo shoots, bok choy, mushrooms, celery, water chestnuts, and MSG, and stir-fry for another 10 seconds.

Add chicken stock, bring to a boil, cover and simmer for about 1 minute. Stir in cornstarch mixture and mix thoroughly. Serve immediately.

Cantonese Chicken

CHINA   Yield: 4 servings

1 broiler or fryer, cut up

Salt

Pepper

Paprika

¼ pound butter

½ cup honey

½ cup prepared mustard

¼ teaspoon dry mustard

¼ teaspoon salt

Salt, pepper, and paprika chicken. Place skin-side-up in a roasting pan and add sauce of melted butter, honey, salt and mustards. Baste often. Cook without top at 375°F for 1½ hours or until tender. This is a crispy, barbecue-like chicken dish.

Cantonese Chicken Slices

CHINA Yield: 4 servings

2 whole chicken breasts
Celery
4 tablespoons soy sauce
4 tablespoons cornstarch
Twist of lemon
¼ cup peanut oil
1 cup chicken stock
2 cups Chinese vegetables (such as pea
  pods, bok toy, bean sprouts,
  celery, onion)
¼ cup water chestnuts, thinly sliced
1 teaspoon salt
Dash of pepper
¼ teaspoon garlic salt or chopped
  garlic
Green onions

With a sharp knife and fingers, bone chicken. Cook skin and bones for stock with celery. Cut chicken into strips ½ inch wide, 1½ inches long. Combine soy sauce and cornstarch and twist of lemon. Marinate chicken slices in this coating.

Fry chicken a little at a time in peanut oil, until golden brown. Remove to paper towel. Add ½ cup chicken stock and steam the vegetables for a few minutes. Add another ½ cup chicken stock with 2 tablespoons cornstarch. Cook until thick, add chicken and seasonings. Heat and serve. Garnish with chopped green onion. Serve on rice or Chinese fried noodles.

Chicken Adobo with Coconut Cream

PHILIPPINES Yield: 4 to 6 servings

1 3-pound chicken, skinned and cut
  into serving pieces

¼ cup vinegar
Ground black pepper to taste
2 tablespoons salt
3 cloves garlic, peeled
2 cups coconut cream

In a deep pot, boil the prepared chicken with vinegar, pepper, salt, and garlic until tender. Remove whatever liquid remains in the pot. Add coconut cream and reduce the heat to a low simmer. When the coconut cream thickens into sauce consistency, remove from heat and serve at once.

Chicken and Bamboo Shoot Curry

MALAYSIA Yield: 6 to 8 servings

1 3-pound roasting fowl, cut into
  serving pieces
1 can bamboo shoots, drained, quartered, and sliced
2 medium onions, finely chopped
4 tablespoons coconut or peanut oil
1½ tablespoons ground coriander
1 teaspoon dried shrimp paste
1 teaspoon laos powder
1 teaspoon chili powder
2 teaspoons salt
2 cups thin coconut milk
1 cup thick coconut milk

Having prepared chicken, bamboo shoots, and onions as directed, heat oil in a large frying pan. Stir onions over medium heat until soft and golden. Add coriander, shrimp paste, laos, chili, and salt, allowing spices to cook until lightly browned. Place chicken pieces in spices and mix well. Add thin coconut milk and allow to simmer for 20 to 25 minutes. Add bamboo shoots and stir thoroughly. Simmer for an additional 20 minutes.

When chicken is tender, add thick coconut milk and continue to simmer gently. Adjust salt if needed. Continue to simmer until oil rises to the top. Then serve at once.

Chicken and Noodles

INDONESIA   Yield: 4 to 6 servings

½ pound medium egg noodles
1 boned chicken breast
3 tablespoons peanut, vegetable, or corn oil
3 cloves garlic, finely minced
¼ teaspoon MSG, optional
1 tablespoon dark soy sauce, or preferably ketjap manis (sweet Indonesian soy sauce), available where fine Eastern imports are sold
3 Chinese cabbage leaves, shredded
Salt to taste
1 scallion, chopped
½ pound cooked, peeled shrimp, the smaller the better
Chicken broth, if needed

Cook the noodles according to package directions. Drain and run under cold water. Drain well. Set aside.

Cut the chicken meat into small cubes. Heat the oil and add the chicken, garlic, and MSG. Cook, stirring rapidly, just until chicken meat loses its raw look. Add the soy sauce and cook, stirring, about 30 seconds over high heat.

Add the shredded cabbage and cook, stirring, until cabbage is wilted. Add the noodles and salt and cook, stirring constantly, over low heat.

When the dish is piping hot, add the scallion and shrimp and cook, stirring often, about two minutes. If necessary, add a little broth to prevent sticking. Serve immediately.

Note: Shredded raw beef or pork can be substituted for the chicken in this recipe.

Chicken and Shrimp with Vegetables

CHINA   Yield: 4 servings

2 chicken-breast halves, skinned, boned, and cut into ¼-inch strips
1 tablespoon dry sherry
2 tablespoons soy sauce
2 tablespoons oil
2 cups mixed vegetables (green beans, sliced mushrooms, strips of green pepper, shredded carrots, etc.)
½ cup chicken broth
1 tablespoon cornstarch in 2 tablespoons cold water
½ pound cooked whole shrimp
8 ounces thin spaghetti noodles, cooked according to package directions and tossed with 1 tablespoon soy sauce
1 egg, beaten and cooked in a small skillet over moderate heat as an omelette

Marinate chicken in sherry and soy sauce for about 20 minutes. Heat oil in wok and stir-fry vegetables for 2 to 3 minutes. Push aside. Add chicken and stir-fry for 3 to 4 minutes, until done.

Return the vegetables to the chicken in the wok. Add the broth, cornstarch mixture, and the cooked shrimp. Heat until sauce boils and shrimp are heated through. Serve over spaghetti noodles and garnish with the 1-egg omelette cut into ¼-inch strips.

Chicken and Vegetable Balls

CHINA   Yield: 2 servings

  12 ounces leftover cooked chicken,
    chopped
  2 bamboo shoots, cut into very thin
    strips
  4 mushrooms, chopped
  2 small carrots, finely chopped
  1 egg, beaten
  5 teaspoons soy sauce
  2 teaspoons sugar
  3 cups chicken stock

Combine chicken, bamboo shoots, mushrooms, carrots, egg, 1 teaspoon of the soy sauce, and 1 teaspoon of the sugar. Form into balls after mixing very well.

Drop balls into the boiling chicken stock to which 4 tablespoons soy sauce and 1 tablespoon sugar have been added. Simmer about 8 minutes. Serve chicken balls hot or cold. The chicken-stock mixture is also served hot poured into individual bowls.

Chicken Balls in Oyster Sauce

CHINA   Yield: 4 servings

  2 raw chicken breasts, skin and bones
    discarded
  2 scallions
  1 teaspoon salt
  1 tablespoon cornstarch
  1 tablespoon sherry
  2 tablespoons water
  Oil for frying
  ½ cup onions, thinly sliced
  1 teaspoon sugar
  ½ teaspoon fresh gingerroot, chopped

  2 tablespoons oyster sauce
  ¼ cup chicken broth
  Freshly ground black pepper to taste

Chop the chicken and scallions together until very fine. Mix in the salt, cornstarch, sherry, and water. Shape into small balls. Heat oil in skillet, and fry the balls until browned on all sides. Pour off the oil. Add the onions, sugar, ginger, oyster sauce, and chicken broth. Cook and stir over low heat 5 minutes. Sprinkle with pepper.

Chicken Chop Suey

CHINA   Yield: 4 to 6 servings

  1 3-pound chicken
  4 onions
  2 carrots
  1 bunch herbs
  6 to 8 peppercorns
  1 chicken bouillon cube
  1 cup rice
  3 to 4 stalks celery
  6 to 8 mushrooms
  Squeeze of lemon juice
  1 can bean sprouts
  2 tablespoons soy sauce
  1½ tablespoons cornstarch

Boil chicken with 2 onions, carrots, herbs, and peppercorns until tender. Let cool in water. When cool, remove skin and bones, and boil up stock with these and a chicken bouillon cube to make a well-flavored stock.

Boil rice in usual way, drain well, and keep warm in oven.

Cut chicken into large chunks and reserve. Slice 2 onions and celery, and cook these in a little of the stock until just tender, 8 to 10 minutes. Cook sliced mushrooms in a little stock and lemon juice for 3 to 4 minutes; add to chicken. Mix chicken with drained vegetables, add drained bean sprouts, soy sauce, seasoning, and 1½ cups of chicken stock.

Heat gently. Meanwhile, mix cornstarch with cup of stock, add this to chicken mix ture. Heat until sauce thickens and serve with boiled rice.

Chicken Chow Mein I

CHINA   Yield: 4 servings

- ¼ cup cooking oil
- 1 teaspoon salt
- ¼ teaspoon pepper
- 2 cups Chinese cabbage (or Nappa), sliced
- 3 cups celery, thinly sliced
- 1-pound can bean sprouts, drained
- 4-ounce can water chestnuts, sliced and drained
- 2 teaspoons sugar
- 2 cups chicken broth
- 2½ tablespoons cornstarch
- ¼ cup water
- ¼ cup soy sauce
- 2 cups cooked chicken, chopped

Heat oil, salt, and pepper in deep skillet. Add cabbage, celery, bean sprouts, water chestnuts, and sugar. Stir in chicken broth; cook 10 minutes. Mix cornstarch and water and soy sauce until smooth. Add to vege-table mixture. Stir until mixture thickens. Add meat and heat through. Serve over hot chow mein noodles.

Chicken Chow Mein II

CHINA   Yield: 4 servings

- 2 whole chicken breasts, skinned, boned
- 3 tablespoons butter
- 1½ cups frozen loose-pack Oriental vegetables
- 4 tablespoons water
- 1 cup chicken broth
- 3 tablespoons soy sauce
- 3 tablespoons dry sherry
- 1 teaspoon fresh ginger, minced
- 2 tablespoons cornstarch

Cut chicken into 1-inch cubes; set aside. Put butter in 2-quart casserole. Cover and microcook on high 1 to 1½ minutes, or un-til butter is melted. Add chicken; cover and microcook 4 to 5 minutes, stirring three times, until chicken is cooked through. Let stand, covered.

Add vegetables and 2 tablespoons water to 3-quart casserole; cover and microcook on high 3 minutes, just until vegetables are completely thawed and hot through. Let stand, covered, while preparing sauce.

Measure chicken broth, soy sauce, sherry, and ginger into 2-cup measure. Microcook on high until boiling, 3½ to 4½ minutes. Blend cornstarch and 2 tablespoons water. Stir into sauce. Microcook ½ to 1 additional minute, until thickened and clear. Drain vegetables; stir sauce into vegetables.

Using slotted spoon, add chicken to sauce. Stir until mixed. Heat in microwave oven 1 to 2 minutes, until piping hot. Serve with chow mein noodles.

Chicken Chow Mein III

CHINA   Yield: 4 servings

1 green sweet pepper, cut into slices
1 red sweet pepper, cut into slices
1 cup boiling water
1½ tablespoons butter
1 small onion, chopped
2 stalks celery, sliced
1 tablespoon flour
1 cup chicken broth
2 tablespoons soy sauce
Freshly ground pepper to taste
1 4-ounce can sliced mushrooms, drained
8 ounces cooked chicken breast, cut into bite-size pieces
6 cups water
8 ounces egg noodles
Salt
1 tablespoon butter
Oil for frying
4 ounces sliced almonds, toasted and slightly salted

Cut green and red peppers into slices. Blanch in boiling water for 5 minutes. Remove and drain. Heat 1½ tablespoons butter in saucepan. Add onions and celery and sauté until onions are transparent. Sprinkle with flour, pour in chicken broth, and bring to a boil while stirring constantly. Simmer for 10 minutes. Season with soy sauce and pepper. Add pepper slices, drained mushrooms, and chicken pieces. Cover and simmer for 15 minutes.

Meanwhile, bring 6 cups of slightly salted water to a boil; add noodles and cook for 15 minutes. Drain and rinse with cold water. Set aside ⅓ of the noodles. Place rest of noodles in heated bowl, add 1 tablespoon butter, cover and keep warm.

Heat oil in skillet until very hot. Cut noodles that were set aside into approximately 2-inch-long pieces. Add to hot oil and fry until golden. Drain on paper towels. To serve, spoon chicken mixture over buttered noodles; top with fried noodles and toasted almonds.

Chicken Chow Mein IV

CHINA   Yield: 2 servings

2 tablespoons margarine
1½ cups celery, diced
1½ cups onion, diced
1 small can bean sprouts, drained
Mushrooms, optional
1 cup chicken stock
1 cup cooked chicken, diced
2 tablespoons cornstarch
2 tablespoons soy sauce
Salt and pepper
Chow mein noodles

Cook celery and onion in margarine until tender. Add sprouts, mushrooms, chicken, and chicken stock. Simmer slowly for 10 minutes. Add cornstarch to thicken. Season with salt, pepper, and soy sauce. Serve over rice with chow mein noodles.

Chow Mein I

CHINA   Yield: 6 to 8 servings

¾ cup Crisco oil
3 cups onions, sliced diagonally
3 cups celery, sliced diagonally
2 teaspoons salt
½ teaspoon pepper
1½ cups chicken broth
3 cups mixed Chinese vegetables

6 tablespoons cornstarch
3 tablespoons sugar
1 cup cold water
6 teaspoons soy sauce
4½ cups cut-up pieces of chicken
    or turkey

Melt oil in large pot; add onions, celery, salt, pepper, and broth. Cover and simmer until vegetables are soft.

In small bowl, stir together cornstarch, sugar, water, and soy sauce. Combine with Chinese vegetables in main pot. Add chicken, mix gently. Simmer 15 minutes.

You can add more soy sauce during the final simmer to get a richer color and more flavor. This freezes well.

Chow Mein II

CHINA   Yield: 4 servings

¼ cup shortening or oil
1 cup onions, finely cut
2 cups celery, finely cut
1 teaspoon salt
Dash pepper
1½ cups hot water or bouillon
1 can bean sprouts
1 can mixed Chinese vegetables or 1
    can water chestnuts and 1 can
    bamboo shoots
½ pound fresh mushrooms
2 cups cooked chicken or beef

2 tablespoons cold water
2 tablespoons cornstarch
1 tablespoon soy sauce
1 teaspoon sugar

Melt fat and add onions; fry for 3 minutes. Add celery, salt, pepper, and hot water or bouillon. Cover and cook 5 minutes. Add vegetables and meat; cook 5 more minutes. Add cornstarch mixed with cold water, soy sauce, and sugar. Cook 1 minute more, stirring gently. Serve hot over noodles or rice.

Chow Mein III

CHINA   Yield: 4 servings

3 cups celery
3 cups onions
3 tablespoons schmaltz
1½ cups chicken soup
1 can Chinese mixed vegetables
2 cups cooked chicken
1 tablespoon soy sauce
3 tablespoons cornstarch
2 tablespoons sugar
2 tablespoons soy sauce

Sauté celery and onions in schmaltz about 40 minutes until done. Add chicken soup, mixed vegetables, chicken, and 1 tablespoon soy sauce. Mix thoroughly and cook for 15 minutes. Add remaining ingredients; mix and serve.

Chow-Mein Chicken

CHINA   Yield: 4 to 6 servings

The fixings for this take time to do, but the cooking goes quickly. Rice and/or noodles make a fine complement for this dish.

2 cups raw chicken breasts, thinly sliced or julienne
2 tablespoons oil
1 small onion, thinly sliced
1 cup celery, finely diced
1 cup water chestnuts, sliced
1 5-ounce can bamboo shoots (1 cup)
1 10-ounce package snow pea pods
2 cups chicken broth
2 tablespoons soy sauce
1 teaspoon sugar
2 tablespoons cornstarch
¼ cup cold water
1 teaspoon salt
Slivered almonds for garnish

In a large skillet, sauté chicken in oil just 3 minutes, stirring. Add onion and celery; cook uncovered 5 minutes more. Add water chestnuts, bamboo shoots, pea pods, broth, and soy sauce. Cover; cook for 5 minutes.

Blend sugar, cornstarch, and cold water. Pour over chicken; stir until slightly thickened. Add salt. Serve, garnished with nuts if desired.

Chicken Curry I

BURMA   Yield: 4 to 6 servings

2 small frying chickens, cut into serving pieces
2 teaspoons curry powder
2 tablespoons soy sauce
Pinch of saffron

2 large onions, peeled and finely chopped
½ teaspoon ground dried chili peppers
3 cloves garlic, peeled
¼ cup oil
2½ cups water
1 teaspoon cinnamon
1 heaping teaspoon salt
3 bay leaves

Wipe chicken pieces dry with paper towels. Combine curry powder, soy sauce, and saffron; rub all pieces of the chicken with this mixture. Set aside.

Pound onions, chili peppers, and garlic very fine. Heat oil in large skillet and brown this onion mixture. Add the chicken, making sure each piece is seasoned with the onion mixture. Add remaining ingredients, cover, and simmer gently for at least 1 hour. When chicken is tender, remove from heat and serve.

Chicken Curry II

INDIA   Yield: 4 to 6 servings

1 frying chicken, cut into serving pieces
2 tablespoons vegetable oil
2 tablespoons butter or margarine
2 cups cooked barley
1 medium onion, minced
2 cups chicken broth
Salt and pepper to taste
2 teaspoons curry powder
1 teaspoon marjoram
1 cup plain yogurt
1 tomato, peeled, seeded, cut into bite-size pieces

Brown chicken in oil and butter in a large skillet. Remove chicken from pan; place on bed of barley in Dutch oven or flameproof casserole.

In the same skillet, cook onion in the remaining oil and butter until transparent. Remove; place on top of chicken. Pour 1½ cups broth over chicken and barley. Sprinkle with salt, pepper, curry powder, and marjoram. Cover; cook over low heat 30 minutes. Remove cover. Add yogurt, tomato, and ½ cup broth if needed. Cook uncovered, 20 to 30 minutes, until chicken is tender.

Chicken Curry III

INDIA   Yield: 4 to 6 servings

- 1 2½- to 3-pound frying chicken
- 4 tablespoons margarine
- 1 onion, peeled and finely chopped
- 2 cups beef broth
- 2 apples, peeled, cored, and diced
- 2 teaspoons curry
- 2½ tablespoons cornstarch
- 4 tablespoons powdered milk
- 1 teaspoon salt
- 1 teaspoon honey
- 1 teaspoon pepper
- 4 tablespoons cream
- 2 tablespoons raisins
- 1 banana, peeled and sliced

Wash the chicken and cut it into pieces. Dry thoroughly with paper towels. Heat margarine in a heavy skillet and brown chicken pieces on all sides. Place chopped onion on top of chicken. Cover and steam until onion is transparent. Pour broth over chicken and simmer for 30 minutes or until chicken is fork tender. Place apples with chicken. Add curry. When well mixed, remove chicken from pan and keep warm.

Remove 2 tablespoons of liquid and stir cornstarch into this to make a smooth paste.

Add to liquid in the skillet. Add remaining ingredients in order given, stirring constantly. When the sauce is thickened and hot, pour over the waiting chicken and serve at once.

Chicken Curry IV

INDIA   Yield: 4 to 6 servings

- 4 tablespoons oil
- 2 bay leaves
- 2 cardamoms
- 3 whole cloves
- 1 onion, chopped
- 2 cloves garlic, crushed
- ½ teaspoon ground ginger
- 1 teaspoon turmeric powder
- 2 tablespoons coriander leaves, chopped
- 1 teaspoon ground coriander
- ½ teaspoon ground cumin
- 1 teaspoon paprika
- 3 pounds chicken pieces, skinned
- 2 cups boiling water
- Salt to taste
- 2 tomatoes, quartered

Heat the oil; add bay leaves, cardamoms, and cloves and fry for 1 minute over medium heat. Add the chopped onion and fry until light brown. Mix garlic, ginger, turmeric, coriander, cumin, and paprika with 2 tablespoons water to make a paste. Add this spice paste to the pan with the fried onion mixture.

Fry for 5 minutes, sprinkling with water occasionally to prevent burning. Add chicken pieces to the pan; stir until all pieces are well coated. Cook chicken for 30 minutes, stirring occasionally to prevent burning.

Add boiling water, salt, and tomatoes to the pan and bring to a boil. Reduce heat to low, cover the pan, and cook for about 25 minutes until chicken is done. Sprinkle with fresh coriander leaves and serve with rice. Lamb can be cooked in a similar way.

Curried Chicken Cantonese

CHINA   Yield: 4 servings

1½ tablespoons vegetable oil
¼ teaspoon salt
1 2-pound frying chicken, cut in
  2-inch pieces
¼ cup dried onions, sliced
½ clove garlic, crushed
1 stalk celery, diced
½ teaspoon MSG, optional
¼ cup bell pepper, cut into 1-inch
  squares
1½ tablespoons curry powder
1 cup chicken stock
1 teaspoon soy sauce

In a preheated wok or skillet, put the oil and salt. Bring oil to sizzling point and add the chicken pieces. Brown chicken but do not overcook. Transfer to large pot. Add onions, garlic, celery, MSG, bell pepper, curry powder, chicken stock, and soy sauce.

Bring to high heat, stir and mix; then cover pot. Cook at medium-high heat for 30 minutes or until chicken is tender. If a thicker sauce is desired, add 1 tablespoon cornstarch mixed with 2 tablespoons water and add paste gradually. Stir and mix until gravy thickens.

Serve chicken with or over hot steamed rice.

Curried Chicken or Turkey

INDIA   Yield: 6 servings

1 chicken or 3 pounds turkey meat
4 tablespoons butter
1 onion, chopped
2 teaspoons flour

1 tablespoon curry powder
2 teaspoons curry paste
1 pint white stock
1 apple, chopped
2 teaspoons chutney
1 tablespoon lemon juice
Salt and pepper
3 tablespoons raisins
3 tablespoons blanched almonds
2 teaspoons coconut
2 teaspoons cream or milk, optional

Garnish

Fans of lemon
Gherkin fans
Red pepper

Divide the chicken into parts, remove skin; fry parts in hot butter, remove from saucepan, and drain. Fry the onion; add flour, curry powder and paste, and fry very well, stirring occasionally. Stir in the stock; bring to a boil. Put in all other ingredients except the cream. (Have the coconut tied in muslin and remove after 15 minutes.)

Put in chicken. Simmer gently about 1¼ hours, adding a little more stock if necessary. Dish the chicken, add the cream to the sauce, and pour the sauce over the chicken, after straining if liked.

Accompaniments: Dry boiled rice sprinkled with paprika and pepper, mango chutney, Bombay duck, fresh grated coconut, gherkins, pickled pimientos. These are served separately, not in the dish with the curry. Bombay duck is fried before serving.

Chicken Fritada

PHILIPPINES   Yield: 4 to 6 servings

1 3-pound chicken, cut into serving
  pieces
2 tablespoons lard

---

5 cloves garlic, peeled and crushed
1 large onion, finely sliced
2 ripe tomatoes, diced
1½ teaspoons salt
½ teaspoon black pepper
1½ cups hot chicken stock
1 pound new potatoes, scrubbed
1 red pepper, seeded and cut into strips
1 green pepper, seeded and cut into strips

Make chicken stock, using the neck, back, and wing tips of the chicken.

In a large skillet, heat lard and fry garlic and onion until soft. Gradually add chicken pieces, browning on both sides. Add tomatoes, salt, pepper, and 1½ cups of the stock. Cover and cook on medium heat until chicken is half done. Add potatoes and peppers and continue to cook until potatoes are tender. Serve at once, piping hot.

Chicken Ginger with Honey

THAILAND   Yield: 4 to 6 servings

Most of the work for this dish is done the day before.

5 scallions, cut into ½-inch pieces
1¼ cups fresh gingerroot, shredded
2 tablespoons vegetable oil
3 boneless chicken breasts, skinned and cut into bite-size pieces
3 chicken livers, chopped
1 onion, peeled and sliced
2 tablespoons tree ears, soaked in warm water for 20 minutes
2 tablespoons soy sauce
1 tablespoon honey

Cover the cut spring onions in a bowl with cold water. Allow to soak. Mix gingerroot with some cold water to reduce the hot taste. Squeeze and rinse under cold running water. Drain.

Fry the chicken and liver pieces in heated oil for 5 minutes. Remove from pan and drain on paper towels. Add onion to fat, followed by garlic and tree ears, and stir-fry for 1 minute. Return chicken to pan.

Mix the soy sauce and honey together well. Pour over the chicken. Add ginger and continue cooking for 2 to 3 minutes. Last, add the drained spring onions. Transfer all of this to a bowl, cover, and refrigerate overnight. When ready to serve, reheat until chicken pieces are hot through.

Chicken Go Wan

CHINA   Yield: 4 to 6 servings

2 whole chicken breasts, boned
¾ cup soy sauce
2 cups long grain rice
4½ cups chicken stock
1 teaspoon MSG
1 cup sliced fresh mushrooms

Cut chicken into ½-inch cubes. Combine chicken cubes and soy sauce in a mixing bowl and let stand for at least 1 hour to marinate. Combine rice, chicken stock, MSG, and mushrooms in a Dutch oven, mixing lightly. Spoon chicken and soy sauce over top.

Cover and cook over low heat for 30 minutes or until the chicken and rice are tender. Serve with cooked snow peas, if desired.

Chicken Grilled on Skewers

INDONESIA   Yield: 4 to 6 servings

    1½ pounds chicken breasts, boned and skinned
    2 red chilies
    2 medium onions, peeled and chopped
    3 teaspoons fresh ginger, finely chopped
    2 tablespoons lemon juice
    1½ teaspoons salt
    2 tablespoons light soy sauce
    2 tablespoons dark soy sauce
    2 tablespoons sesame oil
    2 tablespoons palm sugar
    ½ cup thick coconut milk

Cut chicken into small squares. Set aside.

Preferably in a blender or food processor, make a paste of the chilies, onions, ginger, lemon juice, salt, and soy sauce. When smooth, pour paste into a bowl and stir in oil and sugar. Add chicken, making sure that each piece is covered with the marinade. Cover and marinate for at least 1 hour. (If prepared the night before, it can be kept in the refrigerator overnight.)

Place pieces of chicken on skewers, leaving half the skewer free at the blunt end. Grill 2 inches from heat for 5 to 8 minutes, or until chicken is crisp and brown. Brush once with extra oil during the grilling period.

Place remaining marinade in saucepan with coconut milk. Simmer, stirring constantly, until smooth. Serve in a small bowl with the chicken.

Chicken Indonesian

INDONESIA   Yield: 4 to 5 servings

    1 package of 15-minute chicken marinade
    Orange juice

    1 tablespoon lemon juice
    ¼ cup peanut butter
    ½ small onion, grated or very finely chopped
    1 clove garlic, crushed
    2 tablespoons cooking oil
    ⅛ teaspoon cayenne
    2½- to 3-pound broiler-fryer, cut in quarters

In shallow 9 × 13-inch baking dish, thoroughly blend the 15-minute chicken marinade, 1 cup orange juice, lemon juice, peanut butter, onion, garlic, oil, and cayenne. Place rinsed and well-drained chicken in marinade; turn, pierce all surfaces of chicken deeply with fork. Marinate only 15 minutes, turning several times. Remove chicken from marinade.

Barbecue 6 inches from glowing coals a total of 35 to 40 minutes or until thoroughly cooked, turning frequently and basting occasionally with remaining marinade.

Combine remaining marinade with an equal amount of orange juice; heat to boiling; reduce heat and simmer 5 minutes. Serve sauce with chicken.

Chicken in Mild Sauce

INDONESIA   Yield: 4 to 6 servings

    1 2½- to 3-pound chicken, cut in serving pieces
    4 candlenuts or macadamia nuts
    3-inch piece green ginger, finely chopped
    2 onions, peeled and finely chopped
    3 cloves garlic, peeled and finely chopped
    2 tablespoons coriander
    ½ teaspoon cumin
    1 piece lemon grass
    2 salam leaves, optional

2 tablespoons oil
Salt and pepper to taste
4 cups coconut milk
2 tablespoons tamarind juice

Blend nuts, ginger, onions, and garlic into a fine paste. In a large saucepan, stir-fry the paste, coriander, cumin, lemon grass, and salam leaves in the oil long enough to bring out the aroma and flavor of the spices. Season the chicken with salt and pepper and add to saucepan. Allow to simmer for 10 minutes.

Slowly pour coconut milk over the chicken and stir as it comes to a boil. Reduce heat to medium and continue cooking until chicken is tender to the fork. Add additional salt and pepper if needed. Last, add tamarind juice and serve at once.

Chicken in Soy Sauce

KOREA   Yield: 4 servings

3¾ cups water
1 2½- to 3-pound chicken, cut into
    serving portions
1 medium green pepper, cored, seeded,
    and thinly sliced
2 carrots, peeled and thinly sliced
8 mushrooms, sliced

Sauce

1 cup soy sauce
2 cups water
4 scallions
2 teaspoons garlic, crushed
1 tablespoon sugar
2 teaspoons freshly ground black
    pepper
1 tablespoon fresh gingerroot, crushed

In a large saucepan, bring water and chicken to a boil. Allow to boil gently for 5 minutes. While this is being done, use another pan to make the sauce. Combine all sauce ingredients, stir well, and allow to come to a boil.

Drain the chicken and add to the sauce; add peppers, carrots, and mushrooms. Return to a boil, then lower heat and simmer for 20 minutes, or until the chicken is tender. Serve at once.

Chicken Kai Yang

THAILAND   Yield: 4 to 6 servings

1 3-pound roasting chicken, cut into
    serving pieces
6 cloves garlic, peeled
2 teaspoons salt
2 tablespoons black peppercorns
4 whole plants fresh coriander,
    including roots
2 tablespoons lemon juice

Crush garlic with salt. Coarsely crush peppercorns. (Use either mortar and pestle or blender.) Wash coriander carefully, drain, and finely chop entire plant. Mix all seasonings together and rub into the chicken pieces well. Allow to stand for at least 1 hour. Better still, cover and refrigerate overnight.

Grill the chicken pieces under a hot grill, turning every 5 minutes. When chicken is tender and skin crisp, the chicken is done.

Mandarin Chicken with Almonds

CHINA   Yield: 4 servings

1 teaspoon salt
2 teaspoons paprika
3-pound frying chicken, cut up
3 tablespoons vegetable oil
1 clove garlic
2 tablespoons raisins
½ cup dry red wine

Gravy

1 cup accumulated cooking liquid
2 tablespoons cornstarch in 2
  tablespoons cold water, mixed
  to a smooth paste
2 tablespoons soy sauce
½ teaspoon ground ginger
1 11-ounce can mandarin oranges,
  drained
½ cup heavy cream or sour cream
2 to 4 tablespoons sliced almonds

Combine salt and paprika and rub chicken pieces with the mixture. Brown chicken on all sides in hot oil in a heavy skillet, about 10 minutes. Place in the slow cooker with garlic and raisins.

Add the red wine to the skillet and stir to pick up the browned bits. Add to the chicken. Cover and cook on low about 8 hours.

Pour off accumulated cooking juices, reserving 1 cup. Place this in a saucepan with the cornstarch mixture, soy sauce, and ginger. Bring to a boil, stirring constantly until thickened. Add mandarin oranges. Blend in cream. Pour at once over chicken arranged on a hot platter. Garnish with almonds. Serve at once with rice.

Chicken Oriental I

CHINA   Yield: 4 servings

1 teaspoon MSG, optional
1 broiler, cut up
¼ cup margarine
1 can mushrooms; drain and reserve
  liquid
1 can pineapple chunks; drain and
  reserve juice
2 tablespoons vinegar
1 tablespoon soy sauce
2 tablespoons sugar
2 green peppers, cut up
2 onions, sliced
1½ tablespoons cornstarch
Water

Sprinkle MSG on chicken. Let stand 15 minutes. Brown in margarine. Drain and combine liquid (water from mushrooms, unless fresh cooked) and pineapple juice to make 2 cups. Add to chicken and bring to boil.

Cover and reduce heat. Simmer 1 hour. Stir in vinegar, soy sauce, and sugar. Add vegetables and pineapple chunks. Cook 15 minutes. Blend cornstarch with small amount of water. Stir into chicken. Heat.

Chicken Oriental II

CHINA   Yield: 4 to 6 servings

2 tablespoons shortening
3 chicken breasts, boned, halved, and
  skinned
Salt and pepper to taste
½ cup water chestnuts, sliced
1 green pepper, chopped
1 tablespoon ginger
¼ cup sugar
1 tablespoon soy sauce

½ cup pineapple juice
½ cup wine vinegar
1 cup drained, crushed pineapple
2 tablespoons cornstarch
¼ cup water

Heat shortening in pressure cooker. Season chicken breasts with salt and pepper. Brown them in the cooker. Add water chestnuts, green pepper, and ginger.

Dissolve the sugar in soy sauce, juice, and vinegar. (Add extra sugar if preferred.) Add to the chicken. Last, put pineapple over chicken and close cooker. Set pressure control in place. When pressure is reached, cook for 10 minutes. Cool at once under running water. Return open cooker to low flame.

Dissolve the cornstarch in water. Add to the chicken, stirring until liquid is slightly thickened. Serve chicken over rice or buttered noodles.

Chicken Oriental III

CHINA   Yield: 6 to 8 servings

1 cup onion, shredded
½ cup green pepper, slivered
3 tablespoons oil
2 cups cooked chicken
2 cups celery, sliced, including tops
2 cups canned bean sprouts
1½ cups chicken broth
1 tablespoon cornstarch
1 cup pineapple chunks
¼ cup soy sauce
1 cup toasted almonds

Sauté green pepper and onion in oil until tender, not brown. Add chicken, celery, bean sprouts, and broth. Cook gently 10 minutes. Stir in cornstarch made into a paste

by adding small amount of water. Add soy sauce and pineapple. Just before removing from heat, add almonds. Serve with hot rice.

Oriental Chicken I

CHINA   Yield: 2 servings

¾ cup chicken broth, canned or
   homemade, fat-skimmed
6-ounce can (¾ cup) pineapple juice,
   unsweetened
½ pound chicken fillets, (skinless,
   boneless breast of chicken)
2 bell peppers (1 green, 1 red)
1 large Spanish onion
2 tablespoons soy sauce
Pinch of anise seed or fennel seed,
   optional

Simmer broth and pineapple juice two minutes in a large nonstick skillet or electric frying pan, to reduce liquid. Cut chicken fillets into bite-size chunks. Cut peppers into 2-inch squares, discarding tops and seeds. Peel and halve onion, then slice thinly.

Simmer peppers two minutes in broth mixture. Stir in onion, soy sauce, and anise. Cook and stir one minute. Stir in chicken. Cook and stir until chicken is white and opaque, and nearly all the liquid has evaporated, forming a rich glaze.

Oriental Chicken II

CHINA   Yield: 4 servings

1 2- to 3-pound frying chicken, cut up
⅓ cup soy sauce
2 tablespoons dry sherry
2 tablespoons brown sugar
1 teaspoon ginger or 2 slices fresh
    gingerroot
1 clove garlic, minced
2 tablespoons cornstarch in 2 table-
    spoons cold water, stirred until
    smooth
¼ cup slivered almonds

Place chicken in a slow cooker. Combine soy sauce, sherry, brown sugar, ginger, and garlic. Pour over chicken. Cover and cook on low about 8 hours.

Pour cooking liquids into a measuring cup. Prepare gravy by combining 1 cup of the accumulated cooking liquid with the cornstarch mixture in a saucepan. Bring to a boil, stirring constantly until thickened. Serve over chicken. Garnish with slivered almonds.

Oriental Chicken III

CHINA   Yield: 4 servings

4 ounces almonds, whole, sliced, or
    slivered (blanched)
3 tablespoons oil, peanut or vegetable
¾ cup onion, chopped
4 chicken breasts, boned and thinly
    sliced
2 cans bamboo shoots, drained and
    sliced
1 can water chestnuts, drained and
    sliced
1 cucumber, unpeeled and thinly sliced
½ cup chicken stock

2 teaspoons sherry
¼ teaspoon ground ginger
1 teaspoon soy sauce
½ teaspoon cornstarch
1 tablespoon cold water
Salt to taste
Freshly ground pepper to taste

Brown almonds in 400°F oven for about 10 minutes. Watch closely. Pour oil into large frying pan or wok; heat to medium-high heat. Add onion; cook it until limp. Remove onion from pan (or push up the side, if using wok). Add chicken; toss gently for about 1 minute. Add bamboo shoots and water chestnuts; toss gently for 1 minute. Add cucumber; cook for 1 minute.

Combine chicken stock, sherry, ginger, and soy sauce. Add to pan; cook for 1 minute.

Combine cornstarch and water in a small dish. Stir slowly into hot mixture. Season with salt and pepper; cook until liquid is thickened. While it is cooking, return onions to mixture. Serve chicken with rice and the browned almonds.

Oriental Chicken IV

CHINA   Yield: About 6 servings

⅓ cup flour
¼ teaspoon nutmeg
¼ teaspoon grated gingerroot
2 chickens, cut up
Oil for cooking
1 can sliced pineapple, 20 ounces;
    drain and reserve juice
¼ cup soy sauce
2 tablespoons sugar
2 cloves garlic, crushed
Rice

Blend flour, nutmeg, and gingerroot. Coat chicken with this mixture and brown well in oil in skillet. Transfer chicken to casserole dish and cover with sauce made from pineapple juice, soy sauce, sugar, and garlic. Bake, lightly covered, at 350°F for 1 hour.

Brown pineapple slices in skillet and arrange on serving platter with chicken. Serve with rice.

Oriental Chicken V

CHINA   Yield: 3 to 4 servings

½ cup barbecue sauce
½ cup firmly packed brown sugar
¼ cup soy sauce
¼ cup vinegar
⅛ teaspoon pepper
3 pounds frying chicken pieces

Place all ingredients except chicken in saucepan. Heat and stir until sugar is dissolved. Bake chicken, skin-side-down, at 400°F for 15 minutes. Turn; bake 10 minutes more.

Pour sauce mixture over the chicken and bake, basting every 10 minutes until tender (about 30 minutes).

Oriental Chicken Casserole

CHINA   Yield: 2 servings

½ cup chicken broth
2 tablespoons soy sauce
3 teaspoons sugar
1 cup celery, thinly sliced
1 small onion, thinly sliced
2 tablespoons oil
1 cup cooked chicken, cut into bite-size pieces
¼ cup toasted almonds

Combine chicken broth, soy sauce, and sugar. Blend well; set aside. Sauté celery and onion in oil until lightly browned. Add chicken and sauce mixture to sautéed ingredients; mix thoroughly. Place in greased casserole; sprinkle with toasted almonds. Placed in 325°F oven 10 minutes or until heated thoroughly.

Oriental Chicken with Chinese Mushrooms

CHINA   Yield: 4 servings

2 tablespoons soy sauce
1 tablespoon cornstarch
1 small fryer chicken, boned, skinned, and cut into bite-size pieces
1 tablespoon vegetable oil
1 clove garlic, cut in half lengthwise
3 slices gingerroot, ⅛-inch thick
½ pound fresh mushrooms, quartered
4 dried black Chinese mushrooms (soaked in warm water for 30 minutes, drained, and diced)
2 tablespoons hoisin sauce

Combine soy sauce and cornstarch; pour over chicken and marinate ½ hour. In the hot oil, brown the garlic and ginger slices for 2 to 3 minutes. Remove and discard the garlic and ginger. Add the two types of mushrooms to the pan and stir-fry for 1 to 2 minutes. Remove mushrooms and reserve. Stir-fry the chicken 3 to 4 minutes or until done. Add the hoisin sauce and return mushrooms to pan. Heat through and serve over Oriental vegetables.

Secret Oriental Chicken

CHINA   Yield: 4 servings

¼ cup orange marmalade
1 package dry onion soup mix
1 frying chicken, quartered

Blend marmalade and soup mix together in a small bowl. Place chicken in baking dish and dab sauce evenly on each piece. Cook in slow (325°F) oven for one hour, or until chicken is tender.

Chicken Patties

JAPAN   Yield: 4 to 6 servings

¾ cup leftover cooked chicken, chopped
2 cups mashed potatoes
2 eggs
Bread or cracker crumbs
Oil for frying

Combine chicken, potatoes, and eggs. Mix well. Roll in bread or cracker crumbs; fry in hot oil. Dip patties in soy sauce, if desired, before enjoying.

Chicken-Peach Casserole

POLYNESIA   Yield: 6 servings

1 3½-pound frying chicken or 6-8 chicken joints
2 tablespoons butter or margarine
1 tablespoon oil
1 large onion, peeled and sliced
1 green pepper, seeded and cut into strips
1 large can (about 30 ounces) sliced peaches

1 tablespoon cornstarch
1 tablespoon soy sauce
3 tablespoons white wine vinegar
2 tomatoes, peeled and thickly sliced

Disjoint and skin the chicken. Heat the butter and oil in a skillet, brown the chicken pieces on all sides; then cover, reduce the heat, and cook for about 10 minutes. Remove the chicken and arrange in a large casserole.

Sauté the onion and pepper in the remaining fat until the onion is transparent.

Drain the peaches but reserve the syrup. Mix the cornstarch smoothly with the soy sauce and vinegar; add 1 cup peach syrup and pour into the skillet. Stir until boiling, and boil until clear. Add peaches and tomatoes. Then pour the contents of the skillet over the chicken.

Cover the casserole, and cook at 375°F for 30-40 minutes, removing the lid for the last 5 minutes.

Adjust the seasoning, and serve with wild rice to which some cooked green peas and a few strips of red pepper have been added.

Chicken Saté

MALAYSIA   Yield: 4 servings

Use bamboo skewers, if available, for this saté. The word saté, sometimes spelled satay, refers to the process of grilling or broiling the chicken.

2 pounds chicken, preferably breasts and thighs, boned and skinned
1 tablespoon dark soy sauce
2 shallots, peeled and finely sliced
1 clove garlic, peeled and crushed
Pinch of chili powder, optional
1 tablespoon lemon juice, optional

Cut the chicken meat into 1-inch cubes. In a large bowl, mix remaining ingredients together. Coat each piece of the chicken with this mixture. Marinate for at least 1 hour so flavors are absorbed.

Divide chicken pieces onto skewers. Grill for 5 to 8 minutes, being sure to turn the skewers so that all sides are cooked and crisp. Serve hot with your choice of sauces. Peanut sauce or chili sauce are recommended with this chicken.

Chicken Stew

KOREA   Yield: 4 to 6 servings

- 1 3-pound roasting chicken, cut into small serving pieces
- ¼ cup light soy sauce
- 2 tablespoons sesame oil
- 1 tablespoon garlic, finely chopped
- ½ teaspoon chili powder or cayenne pepper
- 3 spring onions, finely chopped
- ¼ teaspoon salt

Place chicken in a heavy pan with all other ingredients in order given. Mix well so that the chicken is covered with the seasonings. Let stand for 2 hours at room temperature. When ready to cook, place on a low heat, cover, and cook 30 minutes or until chicken is fork tender. Delicious with white rice.

Chicken Stir-Fry

CHINA   Yield: 6 to 8 servings

- 6-8 chicken breasts, skinned, boned, and cut into 1-inch pieces
- ¼ cup cornstarch
- ¼ cup peanut oil

- ⅛ teaspoon garlic powder
- 1 cup fresh bean sprouts
- ½ pound mushrooms, sliced
- 1 cup celery, sliced diagonally
- 1 cup scallions, sliced
- ¼ cup soy sauce
- 2 cups lettuce, shredded

Roll chicken in cornstarch. Heat oil in wok or frying pan over medium high heat. Add chicken and brown quickly. Sprinkle with garlic; add bean sprouts, mushrooms, celery, and scallions; stir. Blend in soy sauce. Cover and reduce heat; simmer 5 minutes. Remove from heat and toss in lettuce.

Monday Stir-Fry

CHINA   Yield: 2 servings

- 1 chicken breast, boned, and cut into ¾-inch pieces
- ¼ cup peanut oil
- 4 carrots, cut in diagonal pieces ¼ inch thick
- 1 small onion, coarsely chopped
- 2 cups broccoli, coarsely chopped
- 2 cloves garlic, minced
- ½-inch piece fresh ginger, slivered
- 2 to 3 cups green cabbage, coarsely chopped
- Soy sauce
- Salt

In a wok or large frying pan, heat one tablespoon of oil over a medium-high heat. Briefly fry chicken pieces until they turn white and salt them lightly. Remove chicken from pan, add a little more oil, and fry carrots 2 to 3 minutes. Add remaining oil and stir in onion, broccoli, garlic, and ginger. Continue to stir-fry for 3 to 4 minutes (depending on your taste for crispness in vegetables). Stir in cabbage last, salt all ingredients very lightly, and cook until cabbage softens slightly. Add soy sauce to taste and serve with brown rice and sliced tomatoes.

Stir-fried Chicken with Asparagus

CHINA   Yield: 4 servings

1 whole chicken breast (about 1 pound)
1 pound fresh asparagus
1 tablespoon cornstarch
1 teaspoon chicken bouillon granules
¾ cup water
3 tablespoons soy sauce
5 tablespoons cooking oil
¼ cup water
¼ pound fresh mushrooms, sliced
6 green onions, cut in 1-inch pieces
½ cup canned water chestnuts, sliced
1½ cups cherry tomatoes, halved
Hot cooked rice

Cut and measure all ingredients before starting to cook. Remove skin and bones from chicken breast. Cut chicken in 2 × 1-inch strips. Cut asparagus on the bias in 2 × ¼-inch slices. Blend cornstarch, chicken bouillon granules, ¾ cup water, and soy sauce; set aside. Heat 3 tablespoons of the oil in heavy 12-inch skillet over high heat.

Add chicken. Stir-fry until chicken is opaque, about two minutes. Remove chicken from skillet. Add one tablespoon of the oil to skillet. Add asparagus, stirring to coat with oil. Add ¼ cup water. Cover and cook three minutes.

Add remaining tablespoon oil. Add mushrooms, onions, and water chestnuts. Stir-fry until asparagus is tender-crisp, about four minutes. Add cherry tomatoes and chicken. Stir in cornstarch mixture. Cook and stir until mixture comes to a boil and tomatoes are heated, about 2 minutes. Serve over hot cooked rice.

Chicken Sub Gum

CHINA   Yield: 4 to 6 servings

2 cups chicken, cooked and cut into pieces
2 cups cabbage, shredded
1 cup green pepper, diced
1 cup celery, diced
1 cup chicken broth
1 tablespoon cornstarch
3 tablespoons soy sauce
2 tablespoons dark molasses
1 teaspoon salt
1 teaspoon vinegar
¼ cup water
2 tomatoes, cubed
½ cup blanched almonds

Combine chicken, cabbage, green pepper, celery, and chicken broth in pressure cooker. Close cover and set pressure control in place. When pressure is reached, cook for 2 minutes. Cool at once under running water.

Mix cornstarch, soy sauce, molasses, salt, and vinegar in water. Add to the chicken and vegetables, stirring gently. When mixture has thickened, add tomatoes and ¼ cup almonds. Cook for 1 minute more.

Sprinkle remaining almonds on top and serve with rice.

Chicken Sukiyaki

JAPAN   Yield: 2 to 3 servings

2 cups chicken stock
1 cup sugar
1 cup soy sauce
1 pound chicken meat, cut into bite-size pieces
8 large mushrooms, sliced

3 carrots, sliced diagonally and parboiled
6 scallions, cut into 2-inch lengths

Boil chicken stock that has been mixed with sugar and soy sauce. Add half of the chicken; simmer about 12 minutes. Add remaining ingredients; simmer another 3 minutes. Serve this with rice.

Chicken Tarts

MALAYSIA   Yield: 12 tarts

4 chicken breasts, skinned and boned

Sauce

3 tablespoons butter
1 medium onion, peeled and chopped
1 clove garlic, peeled and crushed
1 tart apple, peeled, cored, and diced
1 teaspoon tomato paste
1 heaping tablespoon flour
1 cup chicken broth
1 tablespoon grated coconut
1 teaspoon curry
Salt to taste

4 tablespoons oil
2 tablespoons mango chutney
12 small shortcake or puff pastry tarts
1 apple, peeled, cored, and cut in 8 slices
1 tablespoon butter
Ginger plums

Cut the chicken into bite-size pieces.
Heat the butter and fry the onion and garlic in it for 5 minutes, until onion is transparent. Add apple, then stir in tomato paste. Sprinkle with flour. Stir and cook for 3 minutes. Gradually stir broth into mixture and simmer gently for 20 minutes. Mix the sauce with coconut and curry and season with added salt if needed.

While the sauce is simmering, heat oil in a skillet and fry the chicken for about 6 minutes, until meat is golden brown. Dice mango chutney. Add this and the chicken to the finished sauce. Set aside and keep warm.
On a baking tin, bake pastry at 350°F for 5 minutes, until hot and crisp. While baking, fry apple slices in butter on each side for 2 minutes, until golden. Cut ginger plums into 8 slices.
Fill the baked tarts with the chicken mixture. Then cover with apple and ginger plum slices. Serve immediately.

Chicken Breasts Teriyaki

JAPAN   Yield: 2 to 3 servings

2 chicken breasts, halved, boned, and skin removed
4 tablespoons oil
4 tablespoons soy sauce
4 tablespoons sugar
½ teaspoon freshly grated ginger or ¼ teaspoon ground ginger

Parboil chicken breasts for only about 30 seconds. Drain. Heat oil medium high; brown the chicken. Pour off the oil. Add the soy sauce, sugar, and ginger to the pan; cover and simmer until sauce is like syrup. Serve chicken with rice, if desired.

Poultry

Chicken Teriyaki I

JAPAN   Yield: 4 servings

This is delicious served with rice that has pan drippings poured over it.

1 2½- to 3-pound broiler chicken, cut up

Marinade
¾ cup soy sauce
¼ cup sugar
¼ cup sherry or sake
2 teaspoons fresh gingerroot, grated
1 large clove garlic, crushed

Wash chicken; pat dry. Mix together marinade ingredients. Place chicken in marinade. Cover and refrigerate for several hours, turning occasionally.

Drain chicken, reserving marinade. Place skin-side-down in greased baking pan. Bake in 450°F oven for 15 minutes. Turn chicken; bake for another 15 minutes. Reduce oven temperature to 350°F. Pour off and reserve liquid in pan. Continue baking for approximately 30 minutes or until chicken is tender, brushing occasionally with reserved marinade. Broil (if desired) about 6 inches from heat until well browned.

Chicken Teriyaki III

JAPAN   Yield: 3 servings

2 tablespoons cooking oil
2 cloves garlic, finely chopped
2 pounds frying chicken, cut up
2 tablespoons water
1 teaspoon ginger
1 teaspoon MSG, optional
2 tablespoons sherry
½ cup soy sauce
¾ cup sugar

Brown chicken and garlic in skillet with oil. Add water; cover and steam 15 or 20 minutes. Mix together ginger, MSG, sherry, soy sauce, and sugar. Heat in separate pan. Pour over chicken and cook to glaze an additional 15 minutes, or until tender. Turn chicken several times during final cooking.

Chicken Teriyaki III

JAPAN   Yield: 4 to 6 servings

3 to 4 pounds chicken parts
Teriyaki sauce to cover the chicken
½ cup water

Marinate the chicken parts in the teriyaki sauce for at least 1 hour.

Place the chicken and marinade in a pressure cooker. Add the water. Close cover securely and put the pressure control in place. When pressure is reached, cook for 15 to 20 minutes, depending on age of the chicken. Allow to cool naturally. Serve.

Chicken Teriyaki for the Outdoor Grill

JAPAN   Yield: 5 servings

1 large can pineapple slices
1 cup teriyaki marinade
¼ cup Sauterne
5 chicken breasts, boned and skinned

Drain ¼ cup syrup from pineapple and combine with teriyaki sauce and wine. Pour over chicken breasts and pineapple slices. Cover and marinate in refrigerator several hours.

Grill drained chicken over hot coals, turning and basting frequently with the marinade until tender and browned. Grill pineapple quickly on both sides and serve 2 slices with each chicken breast.

Chicken Tinola

PHILIPPINES   Yield: 4 to 6 servings

1 3-pound chicken, cut into serving
  pieces
1 onion, peeled and sliced
2 cloves garlic, peeled and crushed
1 tablespoon fresh ginger, finely grated
1 tablespoon lard
2 cups water
1 green papaya, peeled and sliced
Fish sauce to taste
Pepper to taste

In a heavy saucepan, melt lard and fry onion, garlic, and ginger until tender. Add chicken pieces, stirring until browned on all sides. Put water in, cover pan, and simmer gently until chicken is tender. Add sliced papaya and continue to simmer until papaya is tender. Season with fish sauce and pepper to taste.

Chicken with Almonds

JAPAN   Yield: 4 servings

4 ounces almonds, whole, sliced, or
  slivered (blanched)
3 tablespoons oil, peanut or vegetable
¾ cup onion, chopped
4 chicken breasts, boned and thinly
  sliced
2 cans bamboo shoots, drained and
  sliced

1 can water chestnuts, drained and
  sliced
1 cucumber, unpeeled and thinly sliced
½ cup chicken stock
2 teaspoons sherry
¼ teaspoon ground ginger
1 teaspoon soy sauce
½ teaspoon cornstarch
1 tablespoon cold water
Salt to taste
Freshly ground pepper to taste

Brown almonds in 400°F oven for about 10 minutes. Watch closely.

Pour oil into large frying pan or wok; heat to medium-high heat. Add onion; cook it until limp. Remove onion from pan (or push up the side, if using wok). Add chicken; toss gently for about 1 minute. Add bamboo shoots and water chestnuts; toss gently for 1 minute. Add cucumber; cook for 1 minute.

Combine chicken stock, sherry, ginger, and soy sauce. Add to pan; cook for 1 minute.

Combine cornstarch and water in a small dish. Stir slowly into hot mixture. Season with salt and pepper; cook until liquid is thickened. While it is cooking, return onions to mixture.

Serve chicken with rice and the browned almonds.

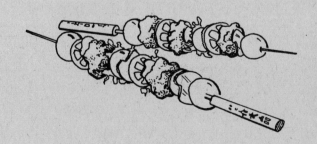

Chicken with Almonds and Mushrooms

CHINA   Yield: 4 servings

2 tablespoons vegetable oil
¼ cup whole blanched almonds
1 green pepper, cut into ½-inch cubes
1 medium onion, cut into ½-inch cubes
¼ pound mushrooms, sliced in "T" shapes
4 chicken-breast halves, skinned, boned, and cut into ½-inch cubes
4 to 5 water chestnuts, sliced
2 teaspoons soy sauce
2 teaspoons dry sherry (or white wine)
½ cup chicken broth or water
1 tablespoon cornstarch in 2 tablespoons cold water

Heat oil in wok and stir-fry almonds until lightly browned. Remove from pan. Stir-fry green pepper and onion 2 to 3 minutes. Push aside. Stir-fry mushrooms 1 to 2 minutes. Push aside. Stir-fry chicken 3 to 4 minutes, until done. Return the vegetables to the chicken. Add water chestnuts.

In a small bowl, combine soy sauce, sherry, chicken broth, and the cornstarch mixture. Stir and add to ingredients in the wok. Heat until sauce is thickened. Add almonds. Serve at once with noodles.

Chicken with Asparagus

CHINA   Yield: 4 servings

2 tablespoons vegetable oil
1 clove garlic
1 pound asparagus, cut diagonally into ½-inch slices (discard tough, white portions)

4 chicken breasts, boned, skinned, and cut into ¾-inch cubes
1 tablespoon dry sherry
2 tablespoons black bean sauce, optional
1 tablespoon cornstarch in ½ cup cold chicken broth
1 teaspoon salt

Heat oil in the wok and brown the garlic to flavor the oil. Remove and discard the garlic. Stir-fry asparagus 2 to 3 minutes. Push aside. Stir-fry chicken 3 to 4 minutes, until done. Return the asparagus.

Combine the sherry, bean sauce, cornstarch mixture, and salt. Add to the chicken and asparagus and heat until sauce thickens. Serve at once with rice or noodles.

Chicken with Bean Sprouts and Snow Pea Pods

CHINA   Yield: 4 servings

4 chicken-breast halves, skinned, boned, and cut into bite-size pieces
¼ cup white wine or dry sherry
1 teaspoon salt
2 tablespoons vegetable oil
2 cups fresh bean sprouts
1 cup snow pea pods, strings removed
½ cup chicken broth
1 tablespoon cornstarch in 2 tablespoons water
Sesame seeds, toasted, optional

Combine the chicken, wine, and ½ teaspoon salt. Let stand about 20 minutes. Heat oil in the wok and stir-fry bean sprouts 1 minute. Push aside. Stir-fry pea pods 1 to 2 minutes, until their green color intensifies.

Push aside. Add the chicken and wine mixture and stir-fry 3 to 4 minutes, until the chicken is done. Return the bean sprouts and pea pods to the chicken in the wok. Add the combined ½ teaspoon salt, chicken broth, and the cornstarch mixture. Heat and stir gently until mixture thickens. Serve at once garnished with sesame seeds.

Chicken with Celery and Mushrooms

CHINA   Yield: 4 servings

2 tablespoons vegetable oil
3 to 4 stalks celery, cut into ¼-inch slices
¼ pound whole small mushrooms
1 broiler-fryer chicken, skinned, boned, and cut into ½-inch strips
½ cup chicken broth or water
1 tablespoon soy sauce
1 tablespoon cornstarch in 2 tablespoons water
¼ cup dry sherry

Heat oil in wok and stir-fry celery and mushrooms 2 to 3 minutes. Push aside. Stir-fry chicken 3 to 4 minutes or until done. Combine chicken and vegetables. Add broth, soy sauce, cornstarch mixture, and sherry. Heat until sauce boils and is thickened, stirring constantly. Serve at once with rice.

Chicken with Chinese Mushrooms

CHINA   Yield: 4 servings

2 tablespoons soy sauce
1 tablespoon cornstarch
1 small fryer chicken, boned, skinned, and cut into bite-size pieces
1 clove garlic, cut in half lengthwise
3 slices gingerroot, ⅛ inch thick

1 tablespoon vegetable oil
½ pound fresh mushrooms, quartered
4 dried black Chinese mushrooms (soaked in warm water for 30 minutes, drained, and diced)
2 tablespoons hoisin sauce

Combine soy sauce and cornstarch. Pour over chicken; marinate ½ hour.

Brown the garlic and ginger slices in hot oil 2 to 3 minutes. Remove and discard garlic and ginger. Add both types of mushrooms to pan; stir-fry for 1 to 2 minutes. Remove mushrooms; reserve.

Stir-fry chicken 3 to 4 minutes or until done. Add hoisin sauce; return mushrooms to pan. Heat through. Serve over Oriental vegetables.

Chicken with Coconut Milk

INDOCHINA   Yield: 4 to 6 servings

1 medium onion, peeled and chopped
1 clove garlic, peeled and minced
½ pound ground pork
¼ package fried, cured pork rinds
Red or white pepper to taste
Salt or nam pla to taste
1 cup coconut milk
1 2-pound chicken

Make a stuffing of the onion, garlic, ground pork, pork rinds, pepper, salt, and ¼ cup coconut milk. When this is all mixed and blended, stuff the cavity of the chicken with the mixture.

Put the chicken in a deep pan, half filled with coconut milk. (If ¾ of a cup of coconut milk is not enough to half fill the pan, add more.) Cover the pan and cook on low heat until the chicken is fork tender and the coconut milk has thickened, about 30 minutes. Serve when chicken is tender, using the coconut milk as a gravy.

Chicken with Coconut Milk Gravy

MALAYSIA   Yield: 6 servings

1 3-pound roasting chicken, cut into
    serving pieces
2½ teaspoons fresh ginger, finely
    grated
2 medium onions, peeled and chopped
3 stalks lemon grass or rind of 1 lemon
6 fresh red chilies, seeded, or
    2 teaspoons sambal ulek
1 teaspoon ground turmeric
3 tablespoons oil
3 cups thick coconut milk
3 strips (2 inches) daun pandan or
    few fresh basil leaves
2 teaspoons salt

After the chicken is cut, set aside. Make
a paste of the ginger, onions, lemon grass,
and chilies, adding a little oil to make the
paste. Thoroughly coat the chicken with
turmeric.

Heat oil in a heavy saucepan and gently
fry the paste for about 15 minutes. Stir constantly. Add chicken and fry for another 10
minutes. Add coconut milk, pandan or basil,
and salt. Allow to simmer uncovered for at
least 20 minutes or until the chicken is tender. Serve at once.

This is a spicy dish.

Chicken with Fresh Coconut

INDIA   Yield: 4 servings

½ cup ghee
1 large onion, peeled and sliced
2 cloves garlic, peeled and sliced
4 whole cardamoms

4 whole cloves
1-inch piece of cinnamon stick
2 teaspoons garam masala
1 teaspoon turmeric powder
1 teaspoon chili powder
1 teaspoon salt
1 3-pound chicken, skinned, boned,
    and cut into 8 pieces
Flesh of ½ fresh coconut, thinly sliced
1 tablespoon tomato paste
1¼ cups water

In a large pan, melt ghee. Fry onions and
garlic until both are soft. Add spices and salt
and stir-fry for 3 minutes more. Add the
chicken pieces and brown on both sides,
about 10 minutes. Add coconut, tomato
paste, and water. Bring to a boil, stirring
constantly. Lower the heat, cover, and simmer for 45 minutes. When chicken is fork
tender, serve at once.

Chicken with Dates

CHINA   Yield: 4 to 5 servings

1 chicken, approximately 3 to 3½
    pounds
Salt
Pepper
Curry powder
2 tablespoons oil
1 medium onion, chopped
2 green peppers, cut into thin strips
1 cup beef bouillon
½ pound rice
1 teaspoon cornstarch
12 dates, pitted, cut into halves
1 cup yogurt
3 tablespoons sliced almonds, toasted

Divide chicken into 8 pieces. Remove all bones except wing and leg bones. Rub chicken with salt, pepper, and curry powder. Heat oil in heavy skillet. Add chicken; cook until golden on all sides. Add onion; cook until golden. Add green peppers. Pour in bouillon; simmer over low heat 30 minutes.

Meanwhile, cook rice according to package directions.

Remove chicken from sauce; keep warm. Strain sauce. Blend cornstarch with small amount cold water. Slowly stir into sauce; cook until thick and bubbly. Add dates.

Beat yogurt with fork; stir into sauce. If necessary, correct seasonings. Heat through, but do not boil. Spoon rice into bowl or platter; arrange chicken on top. Pour sauce over chicken; top with almonds.

Chicken with Ginger

INDOCHINA   Yield: 4 servings

1½-pound frying chicken, cut into
  serving pieces
Salt to taste
Oil
Water
1 piece of fresh ginger
1 clove garlic, peeled and minced
1 medium onion, peeled and sliced

Bone the chicken and cut meat into small pieces. Sprinkle liberally with salt. Fry the meat in a small amount of oil until yellow. At the same time, add small amounts of hot water and continue to simmer until meat is tender.

Wash and skin ginger; cut into long pieces. Fry ginger in a small amount of oil until it gives a pleasant aroma. Remove from pan and set aside. In the same pan, fry the garlic and onion until they also give out a pleasant aroma. Remove and add to the ginger.

Place ginger, garlic, and onion in pan with the chicken meat. Add a small amount of hot water and allow all to blend and heat for 10 minutes more. Serve hot.

Chicken with Green Peppers and Bamboo Shoots in Oyster Sauce

CHINA   Yield: 4 servings

2 tablespoons vegetable oil
1 large green pepper, cut into
  ¾-inch cubes
¼ cup bamboo shoots, sliced
¼ pound small whole mushrooms
  (or large ones, quartered)
4 chicken-breast halves, skinned,
  boned, and cut into bite-size pieces

Sauce

1 small onion, sliced, or 1 scallion,
  sliced
2 tablespoons soy sauce
2 tablespoons oyster sauce
½ cup chicken broth
1 tablespoon brown sugar
1 teaspoon gingerroot, grated
1 tablespoon cornstarch in
  2 tablespoons cold water

Heat oil in wok and stir-fry green pepper 2 to 3 minutes. Push aside. Add bamboo shoots and mushrooms. Stir-fry 2 to 3 minutes. Push aside. Add chicken and stir-fry 3 to 4 minutes, until done. Return vegetables to the chicken in the wok.

Immediately add a sauce made by simmering together the sliced onion, soy sauce, oyster sauce, broth, sugar, gingerroot, and cornstarch mixture for about 10 minutes. Heat this mixture with the chicken and vegetables for 2 to 3 minutes. Serve at once with rice.

Chicken with Green Pepper and Cashews

CHINA   Yield: 4 servings

    2 tablespoons vegetable oil
    1 large green pepper, cut into
        ¼-inch strips
    4 chicken-breast halves, skinned,
        boned, and cut into ½-inch strips
    2 tablespoons soy sauce
    1 tablespoon cornstarch
    ½ cup cold chicken broth
    2 tablespoons dry white wine
    ½ cup cashews

Heat oil in the wok. Add the green pepper and stir-fry for 2 minutes. Push aside. Stir-fry the chicken 3 to 4 minutes, until done. Return the green pepper to the chicken in the wok. Combine and stir in the soy sauce, cornstarch, chicken broth, and wine. Heat and stir gently until the sauce is thickened and clear. Add the cashews and serve at once with rice.

Chicken with Hoisin Sauce

CHINA   Yield: 4 servings

    4 chicken-breast halves, boned,
        skinned, and cut into ¾-inch cubes
    1 tablespoon cornstarch
    1 tablespoon dry sherry
    1 tablespoon soy sauce
    1 green pepper, cut into ½-inch
        squares
    1 tablespoon vegetable oil
    ½ pound mushrooms, cut into
        ½-inch cubes
    2½ tablespoons hoisin sauce
    ¼ cup cashews

Sprinkle the cubed chicken with cornstarch, dry sherry, and soy sauce. Toss to coat well and set aside. Stir-fry the green pepper in the oil for 1 minute. Push aside. Add mushrooms. Stir-fry for 1 to 2 minutes. Push aside. Stir-fry chicken 2 to 3 minutes, until done. Add hoisin sauce and cashews. Reheat and stir briefly. Serve at once.

Chicken with Lentils

INDIA   Yield: 4 servings

This recipe should be made from two types of dried beans. If you cannot find chenna dal or moong dal, substitute the more familiar lentil.

    ½ pound chenna dal
    ½ pound moong dal
    5 cups water
    ¾ cup ghee
    2 large onions, peeled and sliced
    4 cloves garlic, peeled and sliced
    6 whole cloves
    6 whole cardamoms
    2 teaspoons garam masala
    2½ teaspoons salt
    1 3-pound chicken, skinned, boned,
        and cut into 8 pieces
    1 pound frozen whole leaf spinach
    4 large tomatoes, chopped

After washing the dals, place them in a saucepan with water. Bring to a boil, then cover and simmer for 15 minutes. While the dals are cooking, melt ghee in a large skillet. Fry the onions and garlic until soft. Add the spices and salt and stir-fry for 3 minutes. Add the chicken pieces and brown on both sides. Drain cooked chicken on paper towels.

Add spinach and tomatoes to skillet and fry gently for 10 minutes. Mash the dals in cooking water and stir into spinach. Return chicken to the pan. Cover and simmer for 45 minutes or until chicken is tender. Serve at once.

Chicken with Mandarin Oranges and Almonds

CHINA   Yield: 6 servings

2 ounces seedless raisins
1 jigger Madeira
1 3½- to 4-pound chicken, cut into serving pieces
2 teaspoons paprika
1 teaspoon white pepper
5 tablespoons oil
1 11-ounce can mandarin oranges, drained
1 clove garlic, minced
½ cup hot beef bouillon
1 tablespoon cornstarch
1 tablespoon soy sauce
½ teaspoon powdered ginger
½ cup heavy cream, lightly beaten
1 tablespoon butter
2 tablespoons sliced almonds

Cover raisins with Madeira and soak. Cut chicken into serving pieces. Mix paprika and pepper together, and rub chicken with this mixture. Heat oil in skillet or Dutch oven. Add chicken and fry until golden on all sides, about 10 minutes. Drain mandarin oranges, reserving juice. Measure ½ cup of juice and pour over chicken. Add minced garlic. Pour in beef bouillon, cover, and simmer for 30 minutes. Drain raisins and add them to pot; cook for another 5 minutes.

Remove chicken with slotted spoon; arrange on preheated platter and keep warm. Blend cornstarch with small amount of cold water; add to sauce, stirring constantly until thickened and bubbly. Season with soy sauce and powdered ginger. Add mandarin oranges and lightly beaten heavy cream. Heat through, but do not boil. Heat butter in small skillet. Add sliced almonds and cook until golden. Pour sauce over chicken and top with almonds.

Chicken with Soy Sauce

INDONESIA   Yield: 4 servings

1 3-pound chicken
Salt
2 tablespoons dark soy sauce
2 shallots, peeled and finely sliced
2 cloves garlic, peeled and crushed
½ teaspoon chili powder
Juice of ½ lemon or lime
2 teaspoons sesame-seed oil
Oil for basting

Gently rub the outside of the chicken with salt. Roast at 375°F for 45 minutes or until chicken is golden brown all over. Allow to cool.

Divide the chicken into four pieces. Use a mallet to beat the chicken flesh and loosen the fibers. Mix together the remaining ingredients to form a marinade for the cooked chicken. Allow the chicken to marinate for 1 hour, turning the pieces from time to time.

When ready to serve, place the chicken under the broiler. Brush each piece with oil and broil just long enough to heat through.

Chicken with Mushrooms (Moo Goo Gai Pan)

CHINA   Yield: 4 servings

4 chicken-breast halves, boned,
    skinned, and cut into ½-inch cubes
¼ cup dry white wine
1 teaspoon salt
2 scallions, cut into ½-inch slices
½ cup celery, cut into ½-inch cubes
1 tablespoon vegetable oil
12 snow pea pods, strings removed
¼ pound mushrooms, sliced into
    "T" shapes
6 water chestnuts, sliced
½ cup chicken broth
1 tablespoon cornstarch in
    2 tablespoons cold water
Whole, blanched almonds, optional

Combine the chicken with the wine and
½ teaspoon salt. Set aside. Stir-fry the scallions and celery in oil for 1 minute. Push
aside. Stir-fry the snow pea pods 2 minutes.
Push aside. Stir-fry mushrooms and water
chestnuts 1 to 2 minutes. Push aside. Add
the chicken and wine and stir-fry 2 to 3
minutes, until chicken is done.

Combine the chicken and vegetables in
the wok. Stir together the broth, cornstarch
mixture, and another ½ teaspoon salt. Add
slowly to the chicken and vegetables in the
wok and heat until thickened and clear.
Serve over rice and sprinkle with almonds, if
desired.

Chicken with Noodles and Coconut

BURMA   Yield: 6 to 8 servings

This is typical of Burmese cooking because of the split-pea and lentil flours. You
may substitute chick-pea flour for the split-
pea flour. You can make the Burmese flours
easily with your blender, food processor, or
mortar and pestle.

1 3½-pound chicken, cut into large
    pieces
1 tablespoon salt
½ teaspoon turmeric powder
3 quarts water
7 tablespoons vegetable oil
4 medium onions, peeled and pounded
4 cloves garlic, peeled and crushed
1-inch piece of fresh gingerroot, peeled
    and pounded
2 teaspoons chili powder
5 tablespoons split-pea flour
5 tablespoons lentil flour
1⅔ cups thick coconut milk
2 pounds fresh or dried egg noodles

To serve

6 tablespoons oil
12 cloves garlic, peeled and sliced
    crossways
3 hard-cooked eggs, shelled and
    quartered
2 onions, peeled and sliced
5 scallions, including green tops, finely
    chopped
1 tablespoon chili powder, optional
2 lemons, quartered

Rub chicken with salt and turmeric. Place the chicken in a large can or kettle with water. Bring to a boil, then simmer for 25 minutes. The chicken will be cooked but still firm. Remove chicken but continue to simmer the liquid.

Remove skin and bones from chicken and add to liquid. Cut the chicken meat into chunks.

Using a large skillet, heat oil and add onions, garlic, ginger, and chili powder. Stir-fry for 5 minutes. Add chicken meat and continue stir-frying for 10 minutes. Turn off the heat.

Mix the flours to a paste with 1 cup of the cooking liquid. Strain remaining liquid into pan with chicken. Slowly stir in the flour paste and bring to a boil. Reduce heat and add coconut milk. Simmer for 20 minutes. Mixture should be consistency of thick pea soup. Adjust seasonings, cover pan, and set aside.

Cook noodles, drain, and keep hot. In a small frying pan, fry small quantities of noodles until crisp. When all are fried in this way and drained on paper towels, place in a serving bowl. Add garlic to pan and stir-fry until golden and crisp. Transfer to small bowl.

Reheat chicken mixture and place in serving bowl. Surround this with noodles and other accompaniments, such as oil, hard-cooked eggs, onions, and scallions.

Chicken with Peas and Mushrooms

CHINA   Yield: 4 servings

4 chicken-breast halves, skinned, boned, and cut into ¼-inch strips
2 tablespoons soy sauce
2 tablespoons dry sherry
½ teaspoon gingerroot, grated
1 tablespoon cornstarch
2 tablespoons vegetable oil
¼ pound mushrooms, sliced in "T" shapes
1 cup peas, fresh or defrosted frozen
¼ cup whole blanched almonds
½ cup chicken broth or water

Marinate the chicken strips in the combined soy sauce, dry sherry, grated ginger, and cornstarch for 20 to 30 minutes. Heat oil in the wok and stir-fry mushrooms for 1 to 2 minutes. Push aside and stir-fry peas 1 to 3 minutes, until they are heated through. Push aside. Stir-fry the chicken 3 to 4 minutes. Combine chicken, mushrooms, and peas. Stir in the almonds and chicken broth. Heat until sauce boils. Serve with rice.

Chicken with Sesame Seeds

JAPAN   Yield: 2 servings

This may also be made with pork or beef.

12 ounces boned chicken wings or breast meat
2 tablespoons rice wine or sherry
½ teaspoon (scant) salt
½ teaspoon oil
2 teaspoons sesame seeds

Sprinkle chicken with rice wine or sherry and salt. Set aside for 30 minutes. Heat oil in frying pan, brown meat on both sides, and remove to preheated platter. Heat sesame seeds in frying pan; sprinkle on the chicken.

Chicken with Pineapple

CHINA   Yield: 4 servings

1 chicken, approximately 2½ to
    3 pounds, boned

Marinade

2 tablespoons cornstarch
3 tablespoons oil
4 tablespoons soy sauce
1 tablespoon sherry
Salt
Pepper

2 tablespoons oil
1 cup pineapple chunks, drained,
    reserving pineapple juice

Gravy

1 tablespoon oil
1 clove garlic, minced
½ cup pineapple juice
2 tablespoons sherry

Bone chicken and cut meat into bite-size
pieces. Combine ingredients for marinade
and blend thoroughly. Pour over chicken
pieces, cover, and refrigerate for 30 minutes.
Heat 2 tablespoons oil in heavy skillet. Drain
chicken, reserving marinade. Add chicken to
skillet and brown for about 5 minutes, while
stirring constantly. Add drained pineapple
chunks. Cover skillet and simmer over low
heat for 12 minutes.

Remove chicken and pineapple chunks
with slotted spoon. Arrange on preheated
platter and keep warm. Add additional 1
tablespoon oil to pan drippings. Stir in
minced garlic and cook for 5 minutes.

Blend pineapple juice with reserved
marinade and sherry. Pour into skillet and
heat through. Strain sauce through sieve,
spoon over chicken and pineapple, and serve
immediately. Delicious over rice.

Chicken with Pork in Peanut Sauce

PHILIPPINES   Yield: 6 to 8 servings

1 3-pound chicken, skinned and boned
1 pound pork, with excess fat removed
4 ounces raw ham, diced
Salt and pepper
Water to cover

Sauce

½ cup uncooked rice
4 tablespoons lard
1 teaspoon annatto seeds
1 clove garlic, peeled and crushed
2 onions, peeled and finely chopped
2 tablespoons pork fat, diced
½ cup peanut butter
Salt to taste

Put chicken and prepared meats in a
large saucepan with salt and pepper and
water to cover. Bring to a boil; reduce heat
and simmer until meat is fork tender.

Use a dry pan to toast rice over low heat
until golden. Then grind to a powder with
mortar and pestle, electric blender, or food
processor. Heat lard in skillet and fry annatto
seeds for 1 minute. (Cover pan to prevent
seeds from spattering.) Lift out seeds and discard. The remaining oil will be colored. Fry
onions, garlic, and pork fat in this oil until
soft.

Use enough stock from the chicken and pork to combine with ground rice and make a smooth cream. Add this plus the peanut butter to the frying pan. Bring sauce to a boil. Add more liquid if necessary. Heat through the chicken and meat in the sauce so that all flavors blend. Serve hot.

Chicken with Rice

CHINA   Yield: 2 servings

This is a quick, tasty dish—excellent for using up leftover chicken.

    2 tablespoons oil
    2 medium onions, diced
    1 green pepper, diced
    2 cups cooked rice
    2 cups cooked chicken breast, diced
    Soy sauce to taste
    Dash of ginger

Heat oil in large skillet and brown onion. Add remaining ingredients and stir frequently while cooking over moderate heat 20 minutes.

Chicken with Sweet-and-Sour Tomato Sauce

CHINA   Yield: 4 servings

    2 tablespoons vinegar
    3 tablespoons orange marmalade
    1 8-ounce can tomato sauce
    2 tablespoons vegetable oil
    1 green pepper, cut into bite-size
      squares

    1 medium onion, cubed
    1 carrot, very thinly sliced
    4 chicken-breast halves, skinned,
      boned, and cut into bite-size pieces
    1 cup pineapple chunks

In a small saucepan, heat the combined vinegar, orange marmalade, and tomato sauce.

Heat oil in a wok and stir-fry the green pepper, onion, and carrot slices for about 2 minutes. Push aside. Stir-fry the chicken 3 to 4 minutes, until done. Return the vegetables to the chicken. Add the vinegar sauce and the pineapple and heat through. Serve with rice.

Chinese-style Barbecued Chicken

CHINA   Yield: 4 servings

    ¼ cup soy sauce
    1 tablespoon oil
    ¾ teaspoon dry mustard
    Pepper
    1 small clove garlic, minced
    1 frying chicken, cut up

Mix all ingredients except chicken. Put chicken in shallow baking pan and brush on all sides with mixture. Let stand 30 minutes. Then bake 50 minutes in a 350°F oven. Baste with sauce occasionally.

Poultry

Chicken with Vegetables

KOREA   Yield: 4 servings

    1 pound boneless chicken, cut into
      1-inch cubes
    Vegetable oil for deep frying
    2 medium carrots, peeled and sliced
    2 medium potatoes, peeled and cubed
    ½ small red pepper, cored, seeded,
      and thinly sliced
    ½ small green pepper, cored, seeded,
      and thinly sliced
    1 medium onion, peeled and chopped

Batter

    1 cup all-purpose flour
    2 eggs, well beaten
    Approximately 2 tablespoons water

Sauce

    2 tablespoons soy sauce
    2 tablespoons water
    1 tablespoon sugar
    2 teaspoons fresh gingerroot, crushed
    2 teaspoons garlic, peeled and crushed
    2 tablespoons sake
    1 tablespoon sesame oil
    2 scallions
    ½ teaspoon salt

After the chicken is cubed and set aside, make the batter. Combine flour and eggs in a bowl. Add the water, stirring constantly until batter is smooth. Coat each piece of the chicken in the batter. Heat the oil in a deep-fat fryer and fry chicken pieces until all are golden brown. Remove from the fat and set aside to drain on paper towels.

Gently blanch the carrots and potatoes in boiling water for 3 minutes. Drain and dry thoroughly. Then deep-fry these vegetables for 5 minutes. Drain on paper towels.

Place all sauce ingredients in a saucepan and bring to a boil. Remove from heat.

Place oil in the bottom of a large skillet. Add chicken, carrots, potatoes, peppers, and onions. Stir-fry for 1 minute very gently. Increase the heat a little and then add the hot sauce. Stir constantly; when sauce has covered all other ingredients, serve at once.

Chicken with Walnuts

CHINA   Yield: 4 servings

    4 chicken-breast halves, skinned,
      boned, and cut into ¾-inch cubes
    3 tablespoons soy sauce
    1 teaspoon sugar
    2 tablespoons vegetable oil
    1 cup English walnuts
    1 teaspoon gingerroot, grated
    1 clove garlic, grated
    ½ cup chicken broth or water
    1 tablespoon cornstarch in
      2 tablespoons cold water
    1 8-ounce can bamboo shoots, drained
      and sliced

Marinate chicken in soy sauce and sugar in a small bowl for 20 minutes. Heat oil in a wok and stir-fry walnuts 2 minutes. Remove from pan. Add chicken, ginger, garlic, and the marinade to the wok and stir-fry 3 to 4 minutes, until chicken is done. Combine the broth and cornstarch mixture. Add to the chicken along with the bamboo shoots. Heat and stir gently until sauce is thickened and bamboo shoots are hot. Add walnuts and serve at once with rice.

124

Chicken with Yellow Bean Sauce

THAILAND   Yield: 3 servings

1 large chicken breast
1 tablespoon egg white, slightly beaten
2 teaspoons water chestnut flour or
   cornstarch
Oil for deep frying
1 tablespoon lard
1 tablespoon yellow bean paste
1 teaspoon sugar
2 tablespoons Chinese wine or sherry
½ teaspoon sesame oil

After skinning and boning the chicken breast, dice the meat into small pieces. Pour egg white over the chicken meat and add flour or cornstarch. Mix to make a batter. Heat oil and deep-fry chicken just until the color changes. Since these are small pieces, they will cook fairly quickly. Remove from frying pan and drain on paper towels.

In the hot lard, fry the bean paste for a few seconds. Add remaining ingredients and mix well. Return the chicken to the frying pan and allow to heat through in the sauce. Serve with white rice.

Chinese Barbecued Chicken

CHINA   Yield: 6 servings

4 tablespoons peanut oil
2 tablespoons fresh gingerroot, chopped
¼ cup scallions, chopped
2 cloves garlic, chopped
⅓ cup soy sauce
1 tablespoon sugar
1 tablespoon sesame oil
17 chicken thighs, or 3 pounds
   chicken parts

In a small skillet or saucepan, heat peanut oil until hot. Add ginger, scallions, and garlic and stir-fry for 1 minute. Add soy sauce and sugar and bring to a boil. Turn off heat and add sesame oil.

Marinate the chicken in this mixture for 1 to 2 hours.

Remove chicken from marinade and barbecue or broil until golden brown. Baste with marinade, turn pieces over, and cook until done. Skin should be crispy.

Chinese Chicken I

CHINA   Yield: 4 servings

1 chicken, about 2½ pounds
1 can water chestnuts, sliced
3 tablespoons salad oil
1½ tablespoons soy sauce
2 tablespoons sherry
3 tablespoons water

Clean chicken and chop into 2-inch pieces. Drain chestnuts. Brown chicken in a mixture of oil and soy sauce. After chicken has fried for several minutes, add sherry.

Cook over brisk heat until sherry partly evaporates, then add water chestnuts and water. Cover and simmer about 45 minutes. Serve with hot rice.

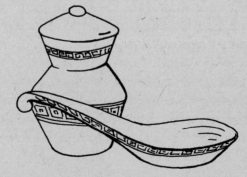

Chinese Chicken II

CHINA   Yield: 4 servings

    1 frying chicken, cut up
    4 tablespoons garlic powder
    1 cup pineapple juice
    ½ cup soy sauce
    ½ pound brown sugar

Blend ingredients, pour over chicken. Marinate 2 days. Bake in marinade in 370°F oven for 1 hour. Serve over rice. Great as party finger food if you use chicken wings.

Chinese Chicken with Sweet Peppers

CHINA   Yield: 4 servings

    2 whole chicken breasts, boned
    1 clove garlic, pressed
    4 tablespoons olive oil
    3 tablespoons soy sauce
    ½ teaspoon salt
    ½ teaspoon pepper
    2 tablespoons cornstarch
    2 green sweet peppers
    1 red sweet pepper
    8 green onions
    3 celery stalks
    ¼ teaspoon sugar
    ¼ cup cold water

Cut chicken into 1-inch pieces. Combine chicken, garlic, 1 tablespoon oil, 2 tablespoons soy sauce, salt, pepper, and 1 teaspoon cornstarch in a mixing bowl and let stand for at least 30 minutes to marinate.

Cut the peppers into 1-inch pieces, removing seeds and membrane. Cut onions and celery in ½-inch pieces. Heat the remaining 3 tablespoons of oil in a wok. Add the peppers and stir-fry for 3 minutes. Add the onions and celery and stir-fry for 2 minutes. Remove the peppers and onions, using a slotted spoon. Keep warm. Place the chicken in the hot oil in the wok and stir-fry for 5 minutes. Combine the remaining 1 tablespoon of soy sauce, remaining 1 teaspoon of cornstarch, sugar, and water and pour over the chicken. Add the vegetables and combine carefully, cooking over low heat for about 3 minutes.

Chinese Lemon Chicken

CHINA   Yield: 4 servings

    1 3-pound chicken
    1½ teaspoons salt
    2 tablespoons soy sauce
    2 tablespoons brandy
    5 tablespoons safflower oil
    ½ teaspoon powdered ginger
    1 cup chicken broth
    ¼ cup lemon juice
    ½ teaspoon sugar

Rub inside of chicken with 1 teaspoon of the salt. Rub the outside with the soy sauce. Place in a deep bowl and pour the brandy over the chicken. Marinate for 6 hours, turning the chicken frequently. Drain and reserve marinade.

In a wok over medium-high heat, combine the oil and ginger. Brown the chicken on all sides. Reduce the heat to low and add the marinade, chicken broth, lemon juice, sugar and remaining ½ teaspoon salt. Cover wok and simmer for about 25 minutes, or until the chicken is tender. Place on serving platter, cut into pieces and pour juices in wok over chicken.

Deep-fried Chicken with Lemon Sauce

CHINA   Yield: 4 servings

4 chicken-breast halves, skinned, boned, and cut into ½-inch strips

Frying batter
1 large egg
¾ cup water
1 cup sifted all-purpose flour
2 cups vegetable oil for deep frying

Lemon sauce
1 cup chicken broth
¼ cup dry white wine
1 tablespoon soy sauce
1 tablespoon honey
Grated rind of 1 lemon
3 tablespoons lemon juice
1 tablespoon cornstarch
Lemon slices for garnish

Combine the ingredients for the frying batter and allow to stand for 1 hour. Dip the chicken strips in the batter and deep-fry in oil at 400°F a few strips at a time until light golden in color and the chicken is done. Use a deep-fat thermometer and control the temperature of the oil carefully. Remove chicken from the oil with a slotted spoon and drain on paper towels.

Combine the ingredients for the lemon sauce in a small saucepan. Stir constantly and bring to a boil over moderate heat. Simmer 1 to 2 minutes. Arrange chicken in a serving bowl and cover with the sauce. Garnish with lemon slices. Serve at once while batter coating is still crisp.

Garlic Chicken

THAILAND   Yield: 4 servings

4 boneless chicken breasts, skinned
3 cloves garlic, peeled and crushed
1 tablespoon freshly ground black pepper
2 tablespoons soy sauce
1 teaspoon sugar
1 teaspoon salt
1 teaspoon sesame-seed oil
Vegetable oil for shallow frying

With a sharp knife, cut the surface of the chicken breasts on both sides. In a bowl, mix all of the remaining ingredients, except vegetable oil, well. Rub this mixture into the chicken breasts and allow to marinate for at least 2 hours.

Using your wok or skillet, heat about 5 tablespoons vegetable oil. When hot, add 2 pieces of chicken and cook for about 4 minutes per side until both sides are golden brown. Remove from the pan and drain on paper towels. Proceed in the same way with the remaining chicken. Add more oil when needed.

Cut each piece of cooked chicken in half with a sharp knife. Return to skillet and cook until edges are no longer pink. Serve at once.

Poultry

Deep-fried Sweet-and-Sour Chicken

CHINA — Yield: 4 to 6 servings

- 2 tablespoons cornstarch
- 2 tablespoons soy sauce
- 1 teaspoon salt
- 2 eggs
- Oil for cooking
- 1 4-pound cooked chicken, boned, skinned, meat cut into 1-inch cubes

Sweet-and-sour sauce

- ¾ cup sugar
- 2 tablespoons soy sauce
- 1 tablespoon dry white wine
- 3 tablespoons wine vinegar
- 3 tablespoons catsup
- 2 tablespoons cornstarch
- ½ cup water

Combine cornstarch and soy sauce; mix well. Combine salt and eggs in mixing bowl; beat with whisk until light. Stir in cornstarch mixture until just mixed.

Heat oil in deep-fryer to 375°F or until small ball of flour mixed with water dropped into oil floats to top immediately. Dip chicken into egg mixture; drain slightly. Drop chicken, several cubes at a time, into oil. Fry until lightly browned; drain on paper toweling. Place chicken in individual serving dishes. Spoon sweet-and-sour sauce over chicken.

To make sauce, combine sugar, soy sauce, wine, vinegar, and catsup in saucepan; bring to boil. Dissolve cornstarch in water; add to sauce. Cook over low heat, stirring, until sauce has thickened. Makes 1 to 1¼ cups.

Fried Chicken Cantonese Style

CHINA — Yield: 3 to 4 servings

- 1 fryer/broiler, cut up (about 2½ pounds)
- ⅓ cup cornstarch
- 2 teaspoons paprika
- ¼ cup oil or shortening
- 14-ounce can sliced pineapple
- 1 cup celery, cut in 1-inch slices
- Brown sugar (small amount to taste)
- 2 tablespoons soy sauce

Shake chicken in bag with cornstarch and paprika. Save leftover cornstarch mixture. Sauté chicken in oil until lightly browned. This should take 15-20 minutes.

Drain pineapple (save juice). Put pineapple slices and celery under chicken. Cover and cook 5 minutes.

Combine 1 tablespoon leftover cornstarch mixture with brown sugar, soy sauce, and ¼ cup pineapple juice. Pour over chicken and blend with pan juices. Cover and cook 10 minutes. Serve on top of rice.

Japanese Fried Chicken

JAPAN — Yield: 4 servings

- 2½ to 3 pounds fryer, cut into pieces

Marinade

- 4 tablespoons soy sauce
- 2 teaspoons mirin or sherry
- Juice of 1 lemon
- Salt
- Paprika

4 tablespoons (approximately)
cornstarch
Oil for frying

After cutting up chicken, wash and pat it dry. Mix together soy sauce, mirin (if substituting sherry, add 1 teaspoon sugar), lemon juice, dash of salt, and dash of paprika. Marinate chicken pieces in marinade for at least 2 hours; drain off excess liquid. Sprinkle chicken thoroughly with cornstarch.

Fry in oil in medium temperature for about 15 to 20 minutes, or until chicken is nicely browned. Drain on paper towels.

Fried Chicken Balls

JAPAN   Yield: 4 servings

½ large onion, chopped
1 pound chicken, chopped finely
1 tablespoon sugar
1 tablespoon mirin (sweet rice wine)
2 tablespoons soy sauce
1 egg
2 tablespoons oil
3½ tablespoons water
1½ tablespoons sherry

Soak chopped onion in water, squeeze out moisture. Combine chicken and onion with sugar, mirin (or sherry mixed with sugar: 1 part sugar to 2 parts sherry), 1 tablespoon soy sauce, and egg. Stir until thoroughly mixed. Roll into bite-size balls.

Heat oil in pan; brown balls on all sides. Combine water, sherry, and remaining 1 tablespoon soy sauce. Add to pan; cook until liquid is almost evaporated.

Grilled Chicken

INDIA   Yield: 4 to 6 servings

1 2- to 3-pound chicken, halved or
    quartered, if you prefer
1 tablespoon salt
1 teaspoon curry powder
6 tablespoons butter
4 tablespoons bread crumbs

Wash chicken in cold water and dry with paper towels. Mix salt and curry together and rub mixture into chicken. Melt butter in a skillet. Roll chicken pieces into melted butter and then roll in bread crumbs. Broil in the oven at 500°F for 45 minutes. Baste frequently with remaining butter. Serve at once on a preheated platter.

Indian Boats

INDIA   Yield: 8 servings

½ cup flour
2 egg yolks
Generous pinch of salt
4 tablespoons butter
Extra butter for greasing molds
Flour for rolling dough

Filling

1 cup rice, cooked and drained
1 pound cooked, boned chicken meat

Sauce

3 tablespoons butter or margarine
1 small onion, peeled and finely
    chopped
2 tablespoons curry powder
3 tablespoons flour
2 cups hot chicken broth
Salt and white pepper to taste
Pinch of sugar
Juice of ½ lemon
Pinch of cayenne pepper
1 egg yolk
4 tablespoons cream
Green pepper, seeded and sliced in
    strips for garnish

To make the dough, place flour in a
bowl, making a hole in the center. Add egg
yolks and salt and cut in butter. Knead into
a smooth dough and form into a ball. Refrigerate for 30 minutes.

Grease the boat molds or individual oven
dishes. Roll out the dough to ¼ inch thick.
Line molds with the dough. Place on a
cookie sheet and bake at 300°F for 20 minutes. Remove from oven and invert molds on
a rack and allow to cool.

In the meantime, cook and drain the
rice. Cook and bone the chicken. Divide the
cooked chicken into 8 portions. Set aside.

In a saucepan, heat the butter for the
sauce. Add onion and cook until transparent. Dust with curry powder and cook for
2 minutes more. Add flour and cook for another 2 minutes. Gradually stir in the hot
chicken broth and boil for 5 minutes. Season
to taste with salt, pepper, sugar, lemon juice,
and cayenne pepper. In a small bowl, whisk
egg yolks and cream together. Gradually add
this mixture to the sauce. Mix half the sauce
with the cooked rice. Place rice mixture into
the bottom of the dough boats. Put a portion
of chicken on each and cover with remaining
sauce. Garnish with green peppers and serve
at once.

Indian-style Chicken

INDIA   Yield: About 6 servings

2 cups plain yogurt
2 cloves garlic, minced
2 teaspoons ground coriander
¼ teaspoon ground cloves
8 drops hot pepper sauce
½ teaspoon ground black pepper
1 teaspoon dry mustard
¼ teaspoon salt
½ teaspoon ground ginger
⅓ cup vinegar
2 tablespoons lemon juice
5 pounds leg quarters or whole chicken

Mix yogurt and other seasonings. Marinate chicken overnight, turning once. Bake
at 325°F for 2½ to 3 hours until tender and
juices run yellow when pierced with fork.
Baste with marinade about every half hour.

Japanese Chicken

JAPAN   Yield: 4 servings

4 chicken breasts, skinned and boned
4 tablespoons butter
1 tablespoon oil
1 clove garlic, crushed
½ cup brandy
½ cup port wine
¾ cup heavy cream

Stir-fry cut-up chicken breasts in butter, oil, and crushed garlic. When nearly done, pour a glass of brandy over it and light it. When the flames are at their height, extinguish with a glass of red port wine.

Cook a few minutes longer, reduce heat, and pour in warm cream, but do not boil. Serve immediately on rice.

Japanese Chicken Casserole

JAPAN   Yield: Approximately 4 servings

2 pounds chicken breasts
1 pound chicken livers
1½ teaspoons flour
Salt and pepper
3 tablespoons margarine or butter
1 pound small onions
1 green paprika
½ can bamboo shoots
3 to 4 slices of canned pineapple
1 teaspoon ginger
2 teaspoons brown sugar
2 teaspoons wine vinegar

Cut the chicken breasts into even pieces. Do the same with the livers. Coat breast and liver pieces in the flour combined with salt and pepper. Brown the pieces in a little more than half of the margarine or butter in a wok. Transfer to a casserole. Brown the onions in the rest of the melted fat, allowing the paprika to fry with the onions for a few minutes, then transfer to the casserole. Stir a small amount of water in the wok to get up drippings and pour into casserole. Add well-drained bamboo shoots, slices of pineapple, and seasonings. Simmer the dish, covered, for about 20 minutes. Meanwhile, boil rice to be served with the dish.

Korean Chicken

KOREA   Yield: 4 servings

1 frying chicken, cut in pieces
Salt and pepper
1 egg yolk
2 tablespoons honey
1 small clove garlic, crushed
2 tablespoons soy sauce
4 tablespoons butter

Cut skin off chicken; rinse and pat dry. Sprinkle lightly with salt and pepper. Mix together egg yolk, honey, garlic, and soy sauce in pie tin. Roll chicken in mixture and place in a buttered baking dish. Dot generously with butter. Cover and bake at 350°F until tender, 45 minutes to 1 hour. Serve with rice.

Korean Pupu Chicken

KOREA   Yield: 4 servings

8 broiler-fryer chicken thighs
⅓ cup flour
1 pint cooking oil (about)
½ cup soy sauce
6 tablespoons sugar
1 clove garlic, minced
1 stalk green onion, green and white
    part, chopped
1 small red chili pepper•

In shallow dish, place flour. Add chicken, turning to coat. In deep-fryer, place oil, filling utensil no more than ⅓ full. Heat to medium high temperature (about 360°F). Add chicken, a few pieces at a time, and cook about 15 minutes or until golden brown and fork can be inserted in test piece, which has been removed from oil.

In a bowl, make sauce by mixing together soy sauce, sugar, garlic, onion, and chili pepper. As soon as chicken is removed from deep-fryer, roll in sauce, turning over twice.

•If fresh chili pepper is not available, use ⅛ teaspoon dried chili pepper.

Paper-wrapped Chicken

CHINA   Yield: 4 servings

1 pound chicken meat, very thinly
    sliced
2 tablespoons soy sauce
1 tablespoon dry sherry (or dry white
    wine)
½ teaspoon brown sugar or honey
½ teaspoon salt
1 scallion, very thinly sliced
1 teaspoon fresh gingerroot, grated

16 pieces cellophane (cooking
    parchment) paper, 4 inches square
    (approximately)
2 cups vegetable oil for frying

Combine the chicken, soy sauce, sherry, brown sugar, salt, scallion, and ginger and marinate 20 to 30 minutes. Divide the chicken mixture into 16 portions and wrap each portion in a piece of cooking parchment and fasten well. Heat the oil in the wok to 375°F and deep-fry the packages a few at a time for 2 to 3 minutes. Drain on paper toweling and keep hot. Do not reheat. Serve wrapped to hold in the tasty juices. The diner unwraps each just before eating.

How to Wrap Paper-wrapped Chicken

1. Fold the paper around the chicken in the order shown:

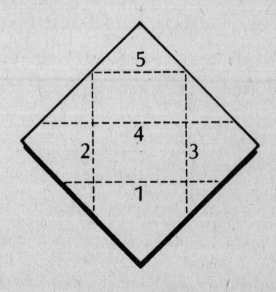

132

2. Tuck in the point of no. 5 securely:

Pineapple Chicken with Sweet-and-Sour Sauce

CHINA   Yield: 4 servings

2 tablespoons vegetable oil
1 green pepper, cut into ¼-inch strips
1 broiler-fryer chicken, skinned,
  boned, and cut into ½-inch cubes
1 8-ounce can pineapple rings, drained
  and cut into bite-size pieces

Sauce

½ cup chicken broth
¼ cup reserved syrup from canned
  pineapple
¼ cup dry sherry or white wine
1 tablespoon vinegar
1 tablespoon cornstarch in
  2 tablespoons cold water
2 tablespoons orange marmalade
1 tablespoon soy sauce
1 teaspoon gingerroot, grated

Heat oil in wok and stir-fry green pepper
1 to 2 minutes. Push aside. Stir-fry chicken 3
to 4 minutes, until done. Return green peppers to the chicken; add pineapple. Combine
sauce ingredients and add to the wok. Heat
and stir until sauce is thickened and clear.
Serve immediately with rice.

Roast Chicken Chinese Style

CHINA   Yield: 4 servings

4 scallions, chopped
2 small pieces fresh gingerroot
1 cup soy sauce
½ cup sherry
1 teaspoon sugar
¼ teaspoon salt
4 cups water
1 whole chicken, about 3 pounds
Scallions for garnish

Mix together chopped scallions, gingerroot, soy sauce, sherry, sugar, and salt. Add
water to stew pot. Mix in scallion mixture.
Bring to a boil. Wash chicken, place in pot,
cover, and simmer for 30 minutes.

Remove chicken from pot and place on
roasting rack in pan. Roast 45 minutes, or
until chicken is tender and browned, in
350°F oven. Split chicken in half, and cut
each half into 5 to 6 pieces. Arrange, skin-
side-up, on serving platter. Garnish with
scallions. Serve the broth as a dipping sauce.

Sesame Chicken

JAPAN   Yield: 3 to 4 servings

1 2½- to 3-pound chicken, cut-up
Flour mixed with salt and pepper
2 eggs, beaten
2 tablespoons milk
1 cup flour mixed with ½ cup sesame
  seeds, ½ teaspoon salt, and
  ¼ teaspoon pepper
Peanut oil for frying

Cream sauce

4 tablespoons butter, melted
4 tablespoons flour
½ cup half-and-half
1 cup chicken stock
½ cup whipping cream
½ teaspoon salt or onion salt,
  if desired

Wash chicken; pat dry. Dust with seasoned flour. Mix beaten eggs with milk. Dip chicken into this mixture, then roll it in the sesame-seed mixture. Fry in oil until light brown and tender.

To prepare the sauce, blend the flour into the butter over low heat, stirring constantly. Mix together the half-and-half, chicken stock, and whipping cream. Gradually add to the butter and flour, stirring constantly. When smooth, stir in the salt or onion salt. Serve sauce immediately with the chicken.

Shredded Chicken with Almonds

CHINA   Yield: 4 servings

2 tablespoons vegetable oil
¼ cup whole, blanched almonds
1 medium onion, chopped

1 teaspoon gingerroot, grated
4 chicken-breast halves, skinned,
  boned, and sliced into ½-inch strips
2 tablespoons soy sauce
1 tablespoon dry sherry
1 teaspoon sugar

Heat oil in the wok and stir-fry almonds 1 to 2 minutes, until golden. Remove from pan. Stir-fry onion and ginger 2 to 3 minutes. Add chicken and continue to stir-fry 3 to 4 minutes, until done. Return almonds to pan. Combine soy sauce, sherry, and sugar. Pour over chicken mixture. Heat and serve at once.

Skewered Chicken

INDONESIA   Yield: 6 or more servings

4 whole chicken breasts

Marinade

½ cup walnuts, chopped
Juice of 1 lemon
1 cup hot chicken broth
1 teaspoon salt
Generous dash of white pepper
1 onion, peeled and diced
1 clove garlic, peeled and crushed
2 tablespoons oil

½ cup cream
Parsley for garnish

Skin and bone the chicken. Cut meat into ½- to 1-inch wide strips.

Prepare the marinade by mixing walnuts, lemon juice, chicken broth, salt, and pepper in a bowl. Add onion, garlic, and oil to mixture. Set aside ⅓ of the marinade for later use. Place chicken strips in marinade and allow to sit for at least 3 hours.

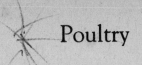

Drain chicken and place meat on 4 skewers. Put skewers on a flat pan and cook in broiler for 20 minutes, turning once. Mix reserved marinade with cream and serve separately. Remove chicken from skewers and put on preheated platter. Garnish with parsley and serve hot.

Skewered Chicken Pieces

JAPAN   Yield: 2 servings

  1½ to 2 pounds chicken meat, cut in cubes

Marinade
  1 cup soy sauce
  1 cup sake (rice wine) or sherry
  3 tablespoons sugar, or little less
  2 teaspoons freshly ground pepper

Mix together soy sauce, sake or sherry, sugar, and pepper; bring to a boil. Marinate the chicken in the marinade for 30 minutes; put chicken pieces on skewer and broil, or put them on a grill or hibachi. Brush with extra marinade during cooking, turning to brown well on all sides.

Steamed Chicken with Mushrooms

INDOCHINA   Yield: 4 servings

  6 dried Chinese mushrooms
  1 2-pound roasting chicken
  1 tablespoon ginger, finely shredded
  3 spring onions, sliced diagonally
  Ground black pepper, liberally used
  2 teaspoons fish sauce
  1 small clove garlic, peeled and crushed
  ¼ teaspoon salt
  1 teaspoon sesame oil

Soak mushrooms in hot water for at least 20 minutes. After cutting off and discarding stems, slice caps into thin slices. Divide the chicken in half. Set aside one half to be used at a later meal. Bone the chicken and cut flesh and skin into bite-size pieces. Place in a heat-proof bowl with all remaining ingredients. Mix well.

Bring water to a boil in large saucepan or deep frying pan. Place the bowl with chicken mixture into saucepan; cover and steam for 25 to 30 minutes. If water in saucepan cooks away, add more. When cooked and tender, serve chicken with your favorite rice or noodles.

Sweet and Pungent Chicken

CHINA   Yield: 4 servings

  2-3 boneless chicken breasts
  Bread crumbs
  2 eggs
  1 jar cherries
  1 small can pineapple chunks
  1 jar sweet-and-sour sauce
  Green pepper, optional
  Rice

Cube the chicken. Dip in eggs and bread crumbs and fry. Then to your taste, mix the cherries, pineapples, their juices, the sweet-and-sour sauce, and green pepper. Heat it. If you like crispy chicken, serve it by putting the sauce over the chicken and rice. Or you can simmer the chicken in the sauce.

Steamed Chicken with Tomatoes

INDOCHINA   Yield: 4 servings

1½ pounds breast and thigh pieces of
   chicken
3 ripe tomatoes, cut in wedges
3 spring onions, finely sliced
3 slices fresh ginger, cut into thin
   strips
2 tablespoons fish sauce
½ teaspoon salt
½ teaspoon sugar
Ground black pepper to taste
2 teaspoons sesame or vegetable oil

Prepare the chicken by boning and cutting the meat into bite-size pieces. Place chicken in a heat-proof bowl with tomatoes, onions, and ginger. Mix this thoroughly with fish sauce, salt, sugar, pepper, and oil.

In order to steam the chicken, place bowl in a pan filled with water halfway up the dish. Cover and steam on the stove for 25 to 30 minutes, or until the meat is fork tender. Add extra fish sauce if desired and serve with a bowl of white rice.

Stewed Chicken with Pork

CHINA   Yield: 3 to 4 servings

1 clove garlic
1 small slice fresh gingerroot
8 ounces pork, cut into 1-inch cubes
8 ounces chicken, cut into 1-inch
   cubes
2 tablespoons cooking oil
4 tablespoons soy sauce
3 teaspoons sugar
3 tablespoons dry sherry

Water—barely enough to cover
   ingredients
1 tablespoon cornstarch in 2 tablespoons cold water, optional

Brown the garlic, ginger, pork, and chicken in 2 tablespoons of cooking oil over medium-high heat. Add soy sauce, sugar, sherry, and sufficient water to cover meat.

Cover and simmer over low heat for about an hour or until meat is tender. Remove ginger and garlic clove. Serve meat hot with the sauce. If you wish, the sauce may be thickened by adding 1 tablespoon of cornstarch in 2 tablespoons of cold water to the sauce. Heat until the sauce thickens and is clear.

Sweet-and-Sour Chicken with Cucumbers and Cantaloupe

CHINA   Yield: 4 servings

4 chicken-breast halves, skinned,
   boned, and cut into bite-size cubes
1½ tablespoons soy sauce
1 tablespoon dry sherry
1 tablespoon cornstarch
2 tablespoons vegetable oil
1 cucumber, cut into bite-size cubes
   after the skin has been scored
   lengthwise with the tines of a
   fork (seeds may be removed)
¼ to ½ cantaloupe, seeded, rind removed, and cut into bite-size pieces
1 sweet red pepper (if available), cubed
2 ounces blanched, whole almonds

Sauce

3 tablespoons brown sugar
3 tablespoons vinegar
½ cup pineapple juice
1 teaspoon soy sauce
1 tablespoon cornstarch in 2 tablespoons cold water

Marinate the chicken cubes in the combined soy sauce, dry sherry, and cornstarch while remaining ingredients are being prepared. Heat the oil in the wok and stir-fry the chicken mixture for 3 to 4 minutes. Add the cucumber, cantaloupe, and red pepper (if used). Combine the ingredients for the sweet-and-sour sauce and add these to the wok. Stir gently and heat until the sauce boils and the cucumber and melon are heated through. Serve at once garnished with almonds.

Szechuan Chicken (Kang Pao Chicken)

CHINA   Yield: 4 servings

4 chicken-breast halves, skinned,
boned, and cubed into ¾-inch cubes
1 egg white
1 tablespoon cornstarch
2 tablespoons vegetable oil
1 cup unsalted peanuts or cashews
2 scallions, sliced
2 tablespoons dry sherry
2 tablespoons hoisin sauce
4 tablespoons black bean sauce
¼ to ½ teaspoon chili paste
1 tablespoon vinegar
1 teaspoon sugar

Combine the cubed chicken with the egg white and cornstarch. Refrigerate for ½ hour. Heat oil in the wok and stir-fry the chicken 3 to 4 minutes, until done. Add nuts, scallions, and remaining ingredients. Heat thoroughly and serve at once with rice.

Rumaki I

POLYNESIA   Yield: 24 appetizers

12 chicken livers, halved
12 water chestnuts, halved
1 cup brown sugar
12 bacon slices, halved
½ cup soy sauce

Soak livers in soy sauce for 4 hours. Drain and slit each piece of liver. Insert ½ water chestnut and dip in brown sugar. Wrap ½ slice bacon around each and fasten with a toothpick. Dip again in brown sugar. Place in shallow pan in 400°F oven and bake 20 to 30 minutes, turning occasionally until evenly brown and crisp.

Rumaki II

POLYNESIA   Yield: 12 appetizers

6 chicken livers, cut in half
4 water chestnuts, cut in thirds
½ cup soy sauce
6 slices bacon, cut in half

Marinate chicken livers and water chestnuts in soy sauce for one to four hours. Drain. Wrap a piece of chicken liver and water chestnut in each bacon slice. Secure with toothpick. Grill over medium flame, turning often, until bacon is crisp. Cook 15 to 20 minutes.

Chicken Livers with Eggs and Noodles

CHINA   Yield: 4 servings

4 eggs
¼ teaspoon salt
1 tablespoon vegetable oil
½ pound mushrooms, sliced into "T" shapes
2 scallions, sliced
1 pound chicken livers, cubed
2 tablespoons dry sherry
5 tablespoons soy sauce
½ pound thin spaghetti noodles
2 tablespoons parsley, chopped

Combine eggs and salt; pour into oiled skillet. Cook over moderate heat, without stirring, until eggs are set. Cut into ½-inch cubes.

Heat oil in wok. Stir-fry mushrooms and scallions 1 to 2 minutes. Push aside. Stir-fry chicken livers 1 to 2 minutes. Add sherry and 4 tablespoons soy sauce. Combine liver and vegetables; heat through. Add cubed eggs.

Prepare spaghetti according to package directions; drain well. Gently combine with 1 tablespoon soy sauce. Serve noodles on platter with liver mixture. Garnish with chopped parsley.

Livers with Rice Oriental

CHINA   Yield: 4 servings

1⅓ cups packaged pre-cooked rice
½ teaspoon salt
1⅓ cups boiling water
1 pound chicken livers
Soy sauce
¼ cup salad oil
½-1 cup drained pineapple chunks
½ cup blanched almonds, split
2 tablespoons cornstarch
⅔ cup pineapple juice
¼ cup vinegar
2 tablespoons sugar
½ teaspoon salt

Add packaged pre-cooked rice and ½ teaspoon salt to boiling water in saucepan. Mix just to moisten all rice. Cover, remove from heat, and let stand 5 minutes.

Meanwhile, cut chicken livers in halves. Dip in soy sauce and sauté in oil about 5 minutes, turning to brown. Add pineapple and almonds and heat about a minute. Make a paste of the cornstarch and about half of the pineapple juice. Then add remaining juice, vinegar, sugar, and ½ teaspoon salt.

Pour mixture over chicken livers. Cook and stir carefully until the sauce is slightly thickened. Then cover and simmer about 2 minutes. Serve over the rice.

Oriental Chicken Livers

CHINA   Yield: About 2 servings

8 ounces chicken livers, cut in half
⅓ cup soy sauce
½ cup flour
Oil for frying
1 small onion, sliced, or onion flakes

Marinate chicken livers overnight in soy sauce. Remove livers from marinade; dredge in flour. Heat small amount of oil in frying pan; fry livers and onions until browned.

Serve livers as an appetizer, or with rice as a main dish. Makes approximately 3 to 4 servings as an appetizer, or 2 servings as a main dish.

Simmered Chicken Livers

CHINA   Yield: 2 servings

1 pound chicken livers
1 cup soy sauce
3 tablespoons white wine
1½ cups water
3 tablespoons sugar
1 tablespoon freshly grated ginger or ½ tablespoon ground ginger
8 scallions, cut into 1-inch pieces

Cut the chicken livers in half. Mix together the soy sauce, wine, water, sugar, and ginger. Bring this mixture to a boil; add the livers to it. Boil slowly until most of the liquid is absorbed. Add scallions; cook for another 2 minutes.

Makes 4 servings as an appetizer, or 2 servings as a main dish.

Pineapple Duck

CHINA   Yield: 3 servings

1 duck, about 4 pounds
4 slices canned pineapple
1 large green pepper, cut into 1-inch squares
2 tablespoons oil
1 teaspoon salt
¼ teaspoon pepper
½ teaspoon MSG, optional
1 tablespoon soy sauce
1 tablespoon cornstarch mixed with 2 tablespoons cold water

Clean and quarter duck. Cover with boiling water and simmer genty until tender. Remove from broth and let duck drain. Reserve broth.

Cut each slice of pineapple into 8 pieces. Cut pepper into squares. Preheat skillet and add oil. Place pieces of duck in skillet, along with salt and pepper. Brown gently, turning frequently. When browned, add the pineapple and green pepper and stir-fry a few seconds. Add the broth, MSG, and soy sauce. Cover and simmer about 10 minutes. Thicken slightly with cornstarch mixture. Serve with rice.

Chinese Duck

CHINA   Yield: About 4 servings

2 cups sherry
½ cup honey
2 tablespoons soy sauce
2 tablespoons candied ginger, finely
    chopped
2 teaspoons powdered mustard
1 teaspoon sesame seeds
1 3- to 4-pound duck
Salt
2 tablespoons margarine

Orange sauce

6 oranges
1 piece of candied ginger, approxi-
    mately size of a walnut, chopped
2 to 3 tablespoons sugar
¼ cup sherry
1 teaspoon cornstarch
1 11-ounce can mandarin orange
    sections
1 banana

Garnish

1 orange, sliced
2 maraschino cherries
Parsley sprigs

Blend sherry, honey, soy sauce, finely chopped ginger, mustard, and sesame seeds thoroughly. Pour over duck in large bowl; cover and refrigerate for 3 hours, turning duck occasionally. Remove duck and drain well on paper toweling. Reserve marinade. Salt inside of duck lightly.

Heat margarine in large skillet or Dutch oven. Add duck and brown well on all sides. Place duck in preheated 350°F oven and cook for 1 hour and 10 minutes, basting occasionally with reserved marinade.

To prepare sauce, pare half an orange and cut rind into thin strips. Now squeeze oranges. Blend orange juice, sliced rind, and chopped ginger. Add sugar and half the sherry. Heat mixture in saucepan. Blend rest of sherry with cornstarch, and slowly add to orange sauce, stirring constantly until thick and bubbly. Drain mandarin orange sections and slice banana. Add half of the fruit to sauce. Place duck on preheated platter. Garnish with rest of mandarins, banana and orange slices, cherries, and parsley. Serve sauce separately.

Peking Duck

CHINA   Yield: Approximately 6 servings

4- to 5-pound duck
6 cups water
¼ cup honey
4 slices peeled fresh gingerroot, about 1
    inch in diameter and ⅛ inch thick
2 scallions, including the green tops,
    cut into 2-inch lengths

Sauce

¼ cup hoisin sauce
1 tablespoon water
1 teaspoon sesame seed oil
2 teaspoons sugar
12 scallion brushes
Mandarin pancakes

Wash the duck thoroughly with cold water, and dry. Tie a cord tightly around the neck skin and suspend the bird in an airy place to dry the skin (about 3 hours).

In a wok, bring water, honey, gingerroot, and cut scallions to a boil. Lower the duck by its string into the boiling liquid and use a spoon to moisten the duck's skin thoroughly.

Discard the liquid and suspend the duck by its cord until it is dry (2 to 3 hours).

Make the sauce by combining hoisin sauce, water, sesame seed oil, and sugar in a small pan, and stir until the sugar dissolves. Bring to a boil and then simmer, uncovered, for 3 minutes. Cool and save for later use.

Cut scallions to 3-inch lengths and trim off the roots. Standing each scallion on end, make 4 intersecting cuts 1-inch deep into its stalk. Repeat at other end. Place scallions in ice water and refrigerate until cut parts curl into brush-like fans.

Preheat oven to 375°F. Untie the duck and cut off any loose neck skin. Place duck, breast-side-up, on a rack and set in a roasting pan. Roast the duck for 1 hour. Lower the heat to 300°F, turn the duck on its breast, and roast for 30 minutes longer. Raise the heat to 375°F, return the duck to its back, and roast for a final 30 minutes. Transfer the duck to a carving board.

With a small, sharp knife and your fingers, remove the crisp skin from the breast, sides, and back of the duck. Cut the skin into 2- by 3-inch rectangles and arrange them in a single layer on a platter. Cut the wings and drumsticks from the duck and cut all the meat away from the breast and carcass. Slice the meat into pieces 2½ inches long and ½ inch wide, and arrange them on another platter.

Serve the duck with Mandarin pancakes, sauce, and the scallion brushes. Dip a scallion brush into the sauce and brush a pancake with it. The scallion is placed in the middle of the pancake with a piece of duck skin and a piece of meat. The pancake is rolled around the pieces and eaten like a sandwich.

Cantonese Turkey Pie

CHINA   Yield: 4 to 5 servings

½ cup onion, chopped
½ cup green pepper, chopped
1 10-ounce package frozen broccoli florets, thawed and halved lengthwise
1 13¾-ounce can chicken broth
¼ cup light cream or milk
1 30-ounce package stir-fry chow mein sauce
1 tablespoon soy sauce
1 teaspoon lemon juice
⅛ teaspoon pepper
Pinch nutmeg
2 cups cooked leftover turkey pieces
1 8-ounce package refrigerator crescent dinner rolls
1 egg yolk

In Dutch oven, heat oil and sauté onion and green pepper about 2 minutes. Add broccoli and stir-fry for 3 minutes. Add chicken broth, cream and chow mein sauce mix; heat just to boiling, stirring gently.

Remove from heat; season with soy sauce, lemon juice, and pepper. Drain chow mein vegetables; add with turkey to Dutch oven. Blend well and turn into lightly buttered 1½-quart baking dish.

Roll out crescent roll dough, combining sections and pinching closed the perforations, to conform to the shape of baking dish. To make a top crust, cut 7, ½-inch-wide strips for oblong dish or 8 strips for a round dish. Arrange 4 strips of pastry across filling, about 1 inch apart (crosswise for oblong dish). Lay remaining strips 1 inch apart at right angles to the first set. Trim strips at inner edge of baking dish.

Brush strips with egg yolk beaten with 2 teaspoons water. Bake in a preheated 375°F oven for 20 to 25 minutes or until pastry is golden brown and filling bubbly hot. Any remaining dough may be cut into small triangles, rolled, baked and served along with pie.

Poultry

Szechuan Duck

CHINA   Yield: Approximately 6 servings

4- to 5-pound duck
2 tablespoons salt
1 tablespoon whole Szechuan pep-
    percorns, crushed with a cleaver
    or with a pestle in a mortar
2 scallions, including the green tops,
    cut into 2-inch pieces
4 slices peeled fresh gingerroot, about 1
    inch in diameter and ¼ inch thick
2 tablespoons soy sauce
1 teaspoon 5-spice powder
3 cups peanut oil, or flavorless
    vegetable oil
¼ cup roasted salt and pepper

Wash the duck thoroughly with cold
water and dry. Mix the salt, crushed peppercorns, scallions, and ginger. Rub the duck
thoroughly with the mixture both inside and
out. Place the scallions and ginger inside the
duck and refrigerate overnight while covered
with plastic wrap or aluminum foil.

Mix the soy sauce and 5-spice powder
and rub it over the duck both inside and out.

Place the duck on its back on a platter
inside a bamboo steamer, add water to the
wok to within an inch of the steamer, and
steam for 2 hours. Turn off the heat and let
the duck rest in this position in the closed
steamer for another 30 minutes. Turn the
duck onto its breast, re-cover the steamer,
and let it rest for another 30 minutes. Remove the scallion and ginger pieces and let
the duck dry for 3 hours.

Pour 3 cups of oil into a wok and heat it
to 375°F. Carefully lower the duck into the
hot oil on its back and fry it for about 15
minutes. Move the duck periodically to pre-

vent it from sticking to the bottom of the
wok. Then turn the duck over on its breast
and deep-fry as before for another 15 minutes.

When the duck is a deep golden brown
on all sides, transfer it to a chopping board.
Cut off the wings, legs, and thighs of the
duck and chop them across the bone in
2-inch pieces. Cut away and discard the
backbone; chop the breast, bone and all,
into 2-inch squares. Serve the duck pieces,
attractively arranged, with roasted salt and
pepper. Steamed bun dough pancakes make
an excellent accompaniment.

Turkey Chow Mein

CHINA   Yield: 4 servings

2 cups turkey, thinly sliced
3 tablespoons salad oil
2 cups celery, cut in diagonal strips
2 onions, thinly sliced
½ pound mushrooms, sliced
1 cup turkey broth
1 tablespoon cornstarch
3 tablespoons soy sauce
1 5-ounce can water chestnuts, sliced
1 1-pound can bean sprouts, rinsed and
    drained
Chow mein noodles
Boiled rice

Cut turkey in thin strips; set aside. Heat
oil in a large skillet or wok; add celery and
onions. Stir-fry over a high heat until translucent. Add mushrooms and cook a minute
longer. Add broth and cornstarch mixed
with soy sauce. Cook until sauce is clear.
Add water chestnuts, bean sprouts, and turkey. Heat thoroughly and serve on Chinese
fried noodles or with boiled rice.

Meat

Beef and Rice Oriental

CHINA   Yield: 4 servings

1¼ cups cooked rice
1 pound ground beef
2 medium onions, sliced
2 cups fresh bean sprouts
1 package frozen cut green beans
1 cup beef bouillon
⅓ cup soy sauce
½ cup water
½ teaspoon powdered ginger

Preheat oven to 425°F. Mix all ingredients together in casserole dish. Bake covered for about 40 minutes.

Chinese Beef with Rice

CHINA   Yield: 6 servings

1½ pound ground beef
1 teaspoon salt
1 teaspoon sugar
¼ teaspoon ginger
3 tablespoons soy sauce
1 teaspoon Worcestershire sauce
6 stalks celery
8 green onions
1 green pepper
1 can beef consommé
2½ tablespoons cornstarch

Mix first 6 ingredients well and shape into 2-inch patties. Brown in skillet in 2 tablespoons hot shortening and move to one side. Cut celery, onions, and green pepper. Add to skillet; cook 5 minutes. Reserve some consommé and add rest to vegetables and heat. Combine reserved consommé with 2½ tablespoons cornstarch. Add and cook, stirring constantly, until thick. Serve over rice.

Beef with Chinese-style Vegetables

CHINA   Yield: 6 servings

1½ pounds beef chuck steak, boneless
2 tablespoons cornstarch
½ teaspoon salt
⅛ teaspoon garlic powder
¼ cup soy sauce
3 tablespoons Worcestershire sauce
1 cup water
1 cup green beans, cut in strips
1 cup carrots, thinly sliced
1 cup turnips, thinly sliced
1 cup cauliflower florets, thinly sliced
1 cup Chinese cabbage, cut in strips
1 cup boiling water
3 tablespoons oil

The day before, cut beef into strips, about 3 inches by ½ inch. Mix cornstarch, salt, garlic powder, soy sauce, Worcestershire sauce, and water. Pour mixture over beef strips. Let stand in refrigerator overnight.

The day of serving, simmer meat mixture for 1½ hours or until meat is tender.

Add vegetables to boiling water. Simmer for 5 minutes or until vegetables are tender but still crisp. Drain. Pour oil over drained vegetables. Serve meat sauce over vegetables.

Chinese Beef and Vegetables

CHINA   Yield: About 4 servings

> 1 pound round steak, sliced very thinly (3-inch lengths)
> 2 tablespoons soy sauce
> 3 tablespoons oil
> 5 tablespoons cornstarch
> 1 cup chicken broth
> 1½ teaspoons fresh ginger
> 3 tablespoons sherry
> 8 cups Chinese cabbage, cut-up and/or spinach

Mix meat with 4 teaspoons soy sauce and lightly brown in hot oil. Mix cornstarch with broth. Stir in remaining soy sauce, ginger, and sherry. Add greens to browned meat. Cook briefly until wilted. Then add broth and stir until broth thickens.

Japanese Vegetables and Flank Steak

JAPAN   Yield: About 6 servings

> 1½ pound flank steak
> Meat tenderizer
> Oil
> 2 packages frozen Japanese vegetables
> Soy sauce to taste

Tenderize flank steak according to directions on tenderizer. Cut steak into thin strips, about ½ × 2 inches. Brown steak quickly in hot oil. Remove from skillet and keep warm.

Cook vegetables in same skillet as used to brown meat, following package directions. Return meat to vegetables for simmering stage. Season with soy sauce to taste. Serve with hot rice.

Oriental Beef with Vegetables

CHINA   Yield: 3 to 4 servings

> ½ pound beef, thinly sliced
> ½ cup carrots, thinly sliced, cut at an angle
> 2 cloves garlic, crushed
> 2 tablespoons soy sauce
> 3 tablespoons sherry
> 2 tablespoons oil
> 4 scallions, cut into ½-inch pieces
> ½ cup celery, thinly sliced, cut at an angle
> ½ teaspoon powdered mustard
> 1 pound fresh spinach, chopped

Marinate beef, carrots, and garlic in a mixture of soy sauce and sherry, for at least 6 hours. Heat oil in wok. Remove meat from marinade and stir-fry for 1 minute. Add remaining ingredients and stir-fry only until vegetables are very bright in color, approximately 2 to 3 minutes. Serve with rice, if desired.

Beef Cantonese

CHINA   Yield: 4 to 6 servings

> 1 pound round steak, cut into small pieces
> 2 tablespoons salad oil
> 1 teaspoon salt
> Dash pepper
> 2 teaspoons onion, chopped
> 1 clove garlic, minced
> 1 can beef bouillon
> 2 3-ounce cans mushrooms, drained
> 2 tablespoons cornstarch
> 2 tablespoons soy sauce
> ¼ cup water

Sauté meat in hot oil; season with salt and pepper. Add onion and garlic and cook over low heat, stirring constantly for 20 minutes. Add bouillon and mushrooms. Cover and simmer for 30 minutes. Combine cornstarch, soy sauce, and water. Add to meat mixture, stirring until smooth. Continue to cook for 20 minutes longer. Serve over rice seasoned with lemon juice if desired.

Beef Chinese

CHINA   Yield: 4 to 6 servings

1 7-ounce package frozen Chinese pea pods
3 tablespoons oil
1 pound beef tenderloin tips, sliced thin across grain
½ cup onion, chopped
1 small clove garlic, finely minced
4 cups raw cauliflower florets, sliced
1 cup beef broth
2 tablespoons cornstarch
¼ cup soy sauce
½ cup water

Separate pea pods by pouring boiling water over them. Drain at once.

Heat 2 tablespoons oil in skillet. Add half the beef; brown quickly. Remove cooked beef, allow skillet to heat again, and brown rest of meat. Remove from skillet.

Add remaining tablespoon of oil; sauté onion and garlic 1 minute. Add cauliflower and beef broth. Cook just 3 minutes. Mix cornstarch, soy sauce, and water; stir into skillet. Add beef and pea pods; stir until sauce thickens. Serve at once over rice.

Chinese Beef

CHINA   Yield: 4 to 6 servings

½ cup dried Chinese mushrooms
1½ pounds flank steak
2 small tomatoes, peeled*
1 green pepper
2 tablespoons olive oil
1 clove garlic, crushed
1 teaspoon salt
Dash pepper
¼ teaspoon ginger
3 tablespoons soy sauce
2 tablespoons sherry
½ teaspoon sugar
1 1-pound can bean sprouts, drained
1 tablespoon cornstarch
3 tablespoons water

Soak Chinese mushrooms in water to cover for 20 minutes. Drain and halve large mushrooms. Cut flank steaks in strips across grain (about 2 × 1 × ¼ inches). Cut tomatoes in eighths. Cut green pepper in 1-inch cubes.

Heat the oil in a large skillet or wok. Add the flank steak strips, garlic, salt, pepper, and ginger. Sauté over high heat until the meat is evenly browned on all sides. Add the soy sauce, sherry, sugar, tomatoes, green pepper, mushrooms, and bean sprouts. Stir until well mixed, cover, and cook over medium heat for 5 minutes.

Make a paste of the cornstarch and water and add to the beef mixture. Cook, uncovered, stirring occasionally, until sauce thickens.

*Tomatoes can be peeled easily by dipping in boiling water for a few seconds or by holding directly over a flame for a few seconds. (If the second method is used, be sure fork used to hold tomato has a wooden handle.)

Chinese-style Beef

CHINA   Yield: 2 servings

     1 pound flank steak
     ¼ cup dry sherry
     1 green pepper
     ½ teaspoon salt
     Dash of pepper
     3 tablespoons soy sauce
     ½ teaspoon MSG, optional
     1 teaspoon sugar
     ½ cup water
     1 cup onions, sliced
     2 tomatoes, cut in eighths
     1½ teaspoons cornstarch
     3 tablespoons cold water

Slice flank steak across the grain into thin slices. Marinate meat in sherry.

Slice peppers into 1-inch squares. Mix salt, pepper, soy sauce, MSG, sugar, and water. In hot greased frying pan over high heat, cook onions and green pepper. Stir-fry for about 3 minutes. Add water mixture and cook covered for 10 minutes. Remove and set aside.

Heat and grease the pan again. Drain and stir-fry steak, until thoroughly brown, about 8 to 10 minutes. Add green pepper and onion mixture. When it comes to a boil, add tomatoes and cornstarch mixed with cold water, and cook for 20 minutes or until tomatoes are soft but not soggy. Serve with rice.

Beef Chow Mein

CHINA   Yield: 4 servings

     2 tablespoons oil
     ½ cup celery
     1 medium onion
     2 tablespoons soy sauce
     1 teaspoon sugar

     ½ cup beef broth
     1 cup cooked rice
     ½ cup bean sprouts
     1 cup cooked beef, shredded
     1 tablespoon cornstarch
     2 tablespoons cold water
     1 package chow mein noodles

Heat oil in a pan and stir-fry the celery and onion over high heat 2 to 3 minutes, separating the onion layers. Add soy sauce, sugar, and broth; bring to a boil. Add the bean sprouts and beef and stir to combine. Dissolve cornstarch in water and add gradually to sauce. Simmer gently until it thickens. Serve over noodles and rice.

Hamburger Chow Mein

CHINA   Yield: 4 servings

     1 pound hamburger
     1 onion, chopped
     ¼ cup butter
     2 teaspoons salt
     Dash of pepper
     2 cups celery, diced
     1½ cups water
     1 can mixed Chinese vegetables
     1 can bean sprouts
     1 small can mushrooms, sliced
     2 tablespoons cold water
     2 tablespoons cornstarch
     1 tablespoon soy sauce
     1 teaspoon sugar
     Chinese noodles

Cook hamburger and onion in butter until brown. Add salt, pepper, celery, and water. Bring to boil. Cover and simmer 20 minutes.

Add Chinese vegetables, drained, and bean sprouts, drained. Add mushrooms and heat. Combine cold water, cornstarch, soy sauce, and sugar. Add to meat mixture and heat. Serve with Chinese noodles.

Slivered Steak Chow Mein

CHINA   Yield: 4 servings

  3 large onions, diced
  3 large stalks celery, sliced
  1 tablespoon shortening
  1 pound thin shoulder steaks, slivered
  2 cups hot water
  2 bouillon cubes
  3 tablespoons soy sauce
  1 teaspoon sugar
  1 can bean sprouts, drained
  1 can chop suey vegetables, drained
  1⅓ cups instant rice
  3 tablespoons cornstarch in 2 table-
    spoons cold water

Brown onions and celery in shortening. Remove. Brown steak. Add hot water to the bouillon cubes and add it, the soy sauce, and the sugar to the steak. Cook until tender, about 1 hour.

Add browned onions and celery, bean sprouts, chop suey vegetables, and rice. Mix through. Add dissolved cornstarch in cold water to pot and stir thoroughly. Simmer 20 minutes, stirring frequently. Serve over noodles. Chicken can be substituted in place of steak.

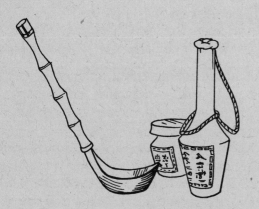

Beef Curry

BURMA   Yield: 4 to 6 servings

Marinate this beef overnight and then cook very slowly. Cooking time varies according to the tenderness of the meat.

  2½ pounds chuck steak, cut into
    1-inch cubes
  1 tablespoon shrimp-flavored soy sauce
  ½ teaspoon turmeric powder
  1 tablespoon malt or cider vinegar
  2 medium onions, peeled and pounded
  4 cloves garlic, peeled and crushed
  1-inch piece of fresh gingerroot, peeled
    and pounded
  1 teaspoon chili powder
  ¼ cup vegetable oil
  3 bay leaves
  2 pieces of cinnamon stick
  5 peppercorns
  Salt to taste

Marinate the beef in a bowl with soy sauce, turmeric, and vinegar.

Blend the onions, garlic, ginger, and chili powder. Heat oil in a deep heavy pan and stir-fry the onion mixture for about 10 minutes. When it begins to brown, it is done.

Place beef, bay leaves, cinnamon, peppercorns, and onion mixture in enough boiling water to half cover the beef. Cover and simmer for 45 minutes until meat is tender. Add water if necessary. Adjust seasonings, adding salt if needed at the end of the cooking time. Serve hot with rice or noodles.

Meat

Bobotee

INDIA   Yield: 8 servings

2 pounds ground beef
2 thick slices white bread
1 cup milk
3 onions, chopped
3 tablespoons curry powder (or paste)
½ tablespoon sugar
Salt
Juice of a lemon
10 almonds, slivered
3 eggs
1 tablespoon butter
¼ cup strong beef stock
2 bay leaves
½ cup chopped parsley

Grind the meat fairly coarsely. Soak the bread in some of the milk; squeeze until dry, retaining the milk.

Fry the chopped onions in butter. Add curry powder or paste, and fry for another minute. Add the meat, sugar, salt, lemon juice, and slivered almonds. Beat the eggs, and add half to the meat mixture. Whisk the other half into the milk. Now mix the soaked bread into the meat mixture thoroughly. Add stock.

Put the meat mixture into a buttered, fireproof dish and smooth top. Pour the egg and milk mixture over and add two bay leaves. Cook in oven for 30 minutes at 350°F or until set.

Remove from oven. Decorate top with chopped parsley and serve with plain boiled rice and chutney.

Beef and Potato Curry

BURMA   Yield: 4 to 6 servings

1½ pounds beef, cut into large squares
12 ounces potatoes, peeled, cut, and quartered
2 large onions, peeled and chopped
5 large cloves garlic, peeled and crushed
2 teaspoons fresh ginger, chopped
1 teaspoon ground turmeric
1 teaspoon chili powder
8 tablespoons light sesame oil or corn oil
½ teaspoon ground cumin
½ teaspoon ground coriander
1½ teaspoons salt
2 cups water

Purée and cook onions, garlic, ginger, turmeric, and chili powder in oil over low heat for at least 10 minutes. Stir with a wooden spoon to prevent sticking. Add the meat, cumin, and coriander and stir-fry for 5 minutes. Add salt, water, and potatoes. Reduce heat and simmer slowly until meat and potatoes are both fork tender. Serve from a warmed serving platter or in individual portions.

Beef Fuji

CHINA   Yield: 4 servings

2 tablespoons vegetable oil
1 pound beef steak (round, chuck blade, or flank steak), 1 to 1½ inches thick, cut into thin strips
½ pound fresh mushrooms, sliced into "T" shapes
1 small onion, sliced
½ cup chicken or beef broth
¼ cup soy sauce

1 tablespoon cornstarch in 2 tablespoons cold water
2 8-ounce can bamboo shoots, sliced
1 8-ounce can water chestnuts, sliced
3 scallions, cut into 1-inch lengths
1 6-ounce package frozen, defrosted
  pea pods
1 1-pound can sliced peaches, drained

Heat oil in the wok and stir-fry beef, mushrooms, and onion for 4 to 5 minutes. Add broth, soy sauce, and cornstarch mixture. Cook, stirring constantly, until sauce thickens. Add vegetables and peaches. Continue heating until the vegetables are heated through. Serve at once with rice.

Beef Oriental I

CHINA   Yield: 4 servings

1 pound beef, thinly sliced
1 tablespoon oil
1 can beef broth
1 or 2 teaspoons cornstarch
½ pound mushrooms
1 can water chestnuts
1 large can Oriental vegetables

Cut beef into thin strips and fry in oil for 2 or 3 minutes. Pour can of beef broth and cornstarch into pan and stir until sauce thickens. Add mushrooms, water chestnuts, and vegetables. Stir to mix well. Serve over cooked rice.

Beef Oriental II

CHINA   Yield: 4 servings

½ pound lean, tender beef, cut into
  strips
2 tablespoons peanut oil
1 clove garlic, chopped
1 onion, chopped
2 cups frozen green beans, French-style
1 cup celery, sliced

1 tablespoon cornstarch
1 tablespoon soy sauce
¾ cup liquid (1 tablespoon sherry,
  juice from canned mushrooms and
  water, or 1 tablespoon sherry and
  beef bouillon)
1 can sliced mushrooms, or 1 cup fresh
  mushrooms, sliced
Strips of pimiento for garnish
Cooked rice

Brown beef in oil, to which garlic is added. Add onion, beans, and celery. Cook 4 to 6 minutes, stirring frequently. Combine cornstarch and soy sauce with liquid. Add to meat mixture with mushrooms. Stir, cooking until liquid is glossy. Cover and cook until beans are tender but crisp. Garnish with pimiento and serve with rice.

Beef Strips Oriental

CHINA   Yield: 4 servings

1 pound round steak, ¾ inch thick
Cooking oil
1 cup water
2 tablespoons soy sauce
1 clove garlic, minced
1 cup carrot slices
1 cup celery slices
2 cups mushroom slices
¼ cup cold water
2 tablespoons cornstarch
½ cup Parmesan cheese, grated
Hot cooked rice

Cut meat into strips ¼ inch wide and 2-3 inches long. Brown meat in oil; drain. Add water, soy sauce, and garlic. Cover, simmer 45 minutes. Add vegetables; cover and cook 15 minutes. Combine cornstarch and water, stirring until well blended. Gradually add cornstarch mixture to hot meat and vegetables, stirring constantly until mixture boils and thickens. Remove from heat; stir in cheese. Serve over rice.

Meat

Oriental Beef and Peppers

CHINA   Yield: 4 to 6 servings

2 green peppers, sliced into rings
3 cups onions, thinly sliced
3 green onions, thinly sliced
1 tablespoon water
1 tablespoon dry vermouth
1½ pounds sirloin steak, sliced into
⅛-inch slivers
1 clove garlic, crushed
1½ teaspoons sugar
¼ cup sherry
½ teaspoon ginger
¾ cup beef bouillon
3 tablespoons cornstarch blended with
2 tablespoons water
½ cup water
2 tablespoons soy sauce

Sauté green peppers, onions, and green
onions in water and vermouth until onions
are soft. Add beef slivers and cook, stirring
over high heat, for 2 minutes. If necessary,
add 1 to 2 tablespoons water to keep meat
from sticking. Stir in garlic, sugar, sherry,
and ginger. Add bouillon and bring mixture
to a boil.

In a small bowl, combine cornstarch mixture, water, and soy sauce. Stir into beef
mixture and cook until sauce is thickened.
Serve on a bed of hot rice.

Oriental Beef and Pepper Crepes

CHINA   Yield: 6 servings

2 green peppers, sliced into rings
3 tablespoons vegetable oil
3 cups onions, thinly sliced
¾ teaspoon salt

1 clove garlic, crushed
3 green onions, thinly sliced
1½ pounds sirloin steak, sliced into
⅛-inch slivers
1½ teaspoons sugar
⅓ cup sherry
½ teaspoon ginger
¾ cup beef bouillon
3 tablespoons cornstarch
¾ cup water
2 tablespoons soy sauce
12 crepes

Heat oil in frying pan. Add green pepper
rings, onion slices, salt, garlic, and green
onions. Cook, stirring over high heat, for 3
minutes. Add beef slivers and cook, stirring
over high heat, for 2 minutes. Stir in sugar,
sherry, and ginger. Cook for 1 minute. Add
bouillon and bring mixture to a boil.

In a small bowl, combine cornstarch,
water, and soy sauce. Stir into beef mixture
and cook until sauce is thickened.

Divide mixture between warm crepes, roll
up, and serve. Pour any remaining juices
over tops.

Oriental Steak

CHINA   Yield: 6 servings

2 pounds chuck steak
Meat tenderizer
1 tablespoon salad oil
1 tablespoon bottled gravy sauce
1 teaspoon salt
2 teaspoons soy sauce
1 10½-ounce can consommé,
undiluted
1 large onion, thinly sliced
2 cups celery, in long strips
1 package Chinese pea pods, thawed

1 tablespoon cornstarch
2 tablespoons water
2 small red tomatoes
Hot fluffy rice
Snipped parsley

Tenderize steak, then cut diagonally across grain into thin slices. Brown meat in hot salad oil in a skillet. Add bottled gravy sauce. Now add salt, soy sauce, and consommé; simmer for 30 minutes.

Lay thinly sliced onion rings and celery on top of steak; then cook, covered, over medium heat for 5 minutes. Add thawed pea pods, then cook for 2 minutes. Blend cornstarch with water; stir into steak sauce to thicken. Add tomato cubes. Keep warm. Make rice. Add snipped parsley.

Steak Oriental

CHINA   Yield: 4 servings

1 small onion, chopped
1 clove garlic, minced
2 tablespoons soy sauce
1 scant teaspoon salt
Dash pepper
1 pound round steak, cut into pieces
2 tablespoons salad oil
1 small green pepper, chopped
1 4-ounce can mushrooms, chopped
1 4-ounce can slivered almonds, chopped

Combine onion, garlic, soy sauce, salt, and pepper. Pour over steak and set in refrigerator overnight to marinate. When ready to serve, drain meat and brown for 5 to 7 minutes in hot oil. Add green pepper, mushrooms, and almonds; cook for 5 minutes longer. Serve with fried rice or chow-mein noodles.

Beef Roll-ups

CHINA   Yield: 2 servings

Ground ginger
2 teaspoons soy sauce
8 ounces lean beef, thinly sliced
½ carrot
1 scallion
1 pimiento
2 fresh mushrooms
2 tablespoons oil
2 tablespoons soy sauce
2 tablespoons mirin (sweet rice wine)

Mix a small amount of ginger with 2 teaspoons of soy sauce. Put beef in the mixture; let stand for 20 minutes. Cut the carrot, scallion, and pimiento into thin slices. Thinly slice the mushrooms also. Lay the beef out flat and fill it with the vegetables. Roll up the beef; fasten it with toothpicks.

Heat oil in skillet. Fry the beef rolls, turning on all sides. Add 2 tablespoons soy sauce and the mirin; turn heat higher for 1 minute. Remove toothpicks and cut roll-ups into bite-size pieces. If desired, garnish with lettuce leaves.

If you do not have mirin, you can use sherry mixed with sugar: 1 part sugar to 2 parts sherry.

Meta

Beef Saté

MALAYSIA   Yield: 6 servings

1½ pounds steak
2 teaspoons ground turmeric
2 teaspoons ground cumin
2 teaspoons ground fennel
Finely grated rind of half a lemon
1½ teaspoons salt
1 tablespoon sugar
4 tablespoons thick coconut milk

Cube beef into 1-inch cubes, leaving a thin layer of fat where possible. Combine remaining ingredients in a bowl and stir until sugar is dissolved. Add beef and cover thoroughly with marinade. Let stand for at least 1 hour. The longer it marinates, the better the meat flavor.

Thread meat on skewers, about 5 pieces per skewer. Grill either on hot coals or in the broiler until meat is crisp, brown, and well done. Remove from skewers and serve at once with peanut sauce.

Beef Shreds with Carrots and Green Pepper

CHINA   Yield: 4 servings

2 tablespoons vegetable oil
2 thin slices of gingerroot
1 clove garlic, halved
1 large green pepper, cut into thin strips
2 carrots, shredded
1 onion, sliced
1½ cups bean sprouts
1 pound cooked beef, thinly sliced
2 tablespoons soy sauce
1 tablespoon cornstarch in ½ cup chicken broth or water

Heat oil in wok and brown the ginger slices and garlic clove. Remove and discard the ginger and garlic. Stir-fry the green pepper and carrots 2 to 3 minutes. Push aside. Stir-fry the onion 1 to 2 minutes. Push aside. Stir-fry the bean sprouts 1 minute. Push aside. Stir-fry the beef strips until heated. Return the vegetables to the beef in the wok. Stir the soy sauce into the cornstarch mixture and add to the wok. Heat until the sauce boils and thickens and the ingredients are heated through. Serve on a bed of boiled rice with shrimp crackers.

Shredded Beef with Vegetables

CHINA   Yield: 4 servings

1 pound beef (round or flank steak), sliced very thin and cut into strips 2 inches long
1 teaspoon sugar
1 tablespoon soy sauce
¼ teaspoon salt
2 tablespoons vegetable oil
1 carrot, cut into very fine 2-inch shreds
1 onion, sliced into ¼-inch slices
1 cup bean sprouts
1 tablespoon cornstarch in ½ cup chicken stock or water
1 tablespoon dry sherry

Marinate beef strips for 10 to 20 minutes in the combined sugar, soy sauce, and salt. Heat oil in wok and stir-fry the carrot shreds and onion rings 2 to 3 minutes. Push aside. Stir-fry the bean sprouts 1 to 2 minutes. Push aside. Stir-fry strips of beef 2 to 3 minutes. Return vegetables to the beef in the wok. Combine the cornstarch mixture and dry sherry. Add to the beef and vegetables and heat and stir until sauce is thickened. Serve at once with fried rice.

Beef Slices Peking

CHINA   Yield: 2 servings

Marinade

3 tablespoons soy sauce
1 tablespoon sherry

1 pound lean beef, sliced paper thin
1 cup oil
2 tablespoons flour
2 leeks, thinly sliced
2 cloves garlic, minced
½ teaspoon powdered ginger
2 tablespoons soy sauce
⅛ teaspoon ground anise
½ cup beef broth
1 teaspoon cornstarch

In a deep bowl, blend soy sauce and sherry. Add beef slices, coat well, cover, and let stand for 1 hour. Heat oil in a large skillet. Thoroughly drain beef slices on paper toweling. Sprinkle with flour, add to hot oil, and deep-fry for 3 minutes. Remove meat slices with slotted spoon and drain; set aside and keep warm.

Take 4 tablespoons of hot oil and pour into another skillet. Throw away rest of frying oil. Reheat oil; add leeks and garlic. Cook for 5 minutes while stirring. Add meat slices. Season with powdered ginger, soy sauce, and anise. Pour in beef broth. Cover and simmer over very low heat for 1 hour.

At end of cooking time, bring to a quick boil. Blend cornstarch with small amount of cold water; add it to skillet, stirring constantly until sauce is slightly thickened and bubbly. Correct seasoning, if necessary, and serve immediately.

Sliced Beef in Sweet Sauce

KOREA   Yield: 4 servings

This is made in a special pan in Korea, but it works quite well in a heavy skillet. It's quick and easy to make, especially if the beef is partially frozen when sliced.

1½ pounds beef top round, sliced thin into 2-inch squares
1 small apple, peeled, cored, and grated
1 small hard pear, peeled, cored, and grated
2 tablespoons onions, chopped
¼ cup scallions, thinly sliced
¼ cup soy sauce
2 tablespoons sake
½ cup water
1 tablespoon garlic, chopped
2 tablespoons sesame-seed oil
2 teaspoons sesame seeds
1 teaspoon freshly ground black pepper
2 tablespoons sugar

Place thinly sliced meat in a large bowl. In another bowl, mix all the remaining ingredients, which will be used as a marinade. Pour this over the beef and allow to marinate for at least 3 hours. Overnight is even better.

Heat skillet until moderately hot. Add beef and marinade and stir-fry for 5 minutes, until beef is tender. Serve piping hot with pickled Chinese cabbage.

Meat

Sliced Beef

INDONESIA   Yield: 4 servings

1 pound lean steak, rump or round
1 onion, peeled and chopped
4 cloves garlic, peeled
1 teaspoon coarsely ground black
  pepper
3 tablespoons dark soy sauce
2 tablespoons palm sugar
2 tablespoons peanut oil
2 ripe tomatoes, chopped

Slice the meat thinly and beat with a mallet, being careful not to break the slices.

Make a smooth mixture (electric blender or food processor is good to use here) of onion, garlic, pepper, soy sauce, and sugar. Pour this over the meat slices and allow to marinate at room temperature for at least 1 hour.

Use a skillet or wok and heat oil. Add the drained meat slices and brown on both sides. Pour marinade and tomatoes into skillet and lower heat to medium. Stir frequently while this cooks for about 12 minutes. When meat is fork tender, serve piping hot.

Beef Stew

JAPAN   Yield: About 6 servings

8 cups beef stock
3 pounds beef stew meat, cut into bite-
  size pieces
4 turnips, quartered
2 carrots, cut into bite-size pieces
2 cans water chestnuts, sliced if desired
10 small potatoes, peeled and left
  whole
Salt to taste
Freshly ground black pepper to taste

2 tablespoons soy sauce
4 stalks celery, cut into 1-inch pieces
10 small white onions
4 scallions, cut into ½-inch pieces

Bring beef stock to a boil; add all ingredients except celery, white onions, and scallions. Simmer for 30 minutes, add celery and onions, and continue simmering until meat is tender. Add scallions; simmer for 2 minutes more. Serve stew with rice, if desired.

Beef with Asparagus and Hoisin Sauce

CHINA   Yield: 4 servings

1 tablespoon soy sauce
1 tablespoon dry sherry
1 teaspoon cornstarch
1 teaspoon grated garlic
1 pound flank steak, thinly sliced with
  the knife held at 45° angle
  to the board
2 tablespoons vegetable oil
2 scallions, cut into ¼-inch diagonal
  slices
1 pound asparagus, cut diagonally into
  ¼-inch slices
3 tablespoons hoisin sauce
½ cup roasted peanuts

Combine the soy sauce, dry sherry, cornstarch, and grated garlic. Add the beef and marinate it for 20 to 30 minutes. Heat the oil in the wok and stir-fry the scallions for 1 to 2 minutes. Push aside. Stir-fry the asparagus for 2 to 3 minutes. Push aside. Stir-fry the beef 3 to 4 minutes, until done. Return the vegetables to the beef. Stir in the hoisin sauce and peanuts and serve at once.

Beef with Bamboo Shoots

INDOCHINA   Yield: 3 to 4 servings

¾ pound sirloin steak
4 tablespoons peanut oil
1 large can bamboo shoots, sliced
6 spring onions, sliced
1 tablespoon fish sauce
½ teaspoon salt
1 clove garlic, peeled and crushed
4 tablespoons sesame seeds, toasted and
    crushed

Slice beef very thinly into 2-inch strips. Use a wok or heavy skillet to heat 2 tablespoons of the peanut oil and stir-fry beef for 1 minute. Remove meat while it is still pink. Set aside.

Heat remaining oil in pan and stir-fry bamboo shoots and onions for 2 minutes. Add fish sauce and salt and continue frying for 5 minutes more. Add crushed garlic for 1 more minute. Return meat and stir-fry for 1 minute. Add sesame seeds. When well mixed, serve at once. (Do not double this recipe for a larger quantity. Rather, make it in 2 separate batches for best flavor and texture.)

Beef with Bamboo Shoots and Peppers

CHINA   Yield: 4 servings

1 pound beef (round or flank), cut into
    thin strips
2 tablespoons soy sauce
2 tablespoons dry sherry
1 tablespoon cornstarch
½ teaspoon sugar
1 clove garlic, halved
2 tablespoons vegetable oil
1 green pepper, cut into ½-inch strips
1 red pepper (a green one that has
    vine-ripened), if available, cut into
    ½-inch slices

2 scallions, cut into ½-inch slices
1 8-ounce can bamboo shoots, sliced
½ cup chicken or beef broth

Marinate the beef strips in the combined soy sauce, sherry, cornstarch, and sugar for 20 to 30 minutes. Brown the garlic in the vegetable oil. Remove and discard the garlic. Stir-fry the pepper strips 2 to 3 minutes. Push up the sides. Stir-fry the scallions and bamboo shoots 1 to 2 minutes. Push up the sides. Stir-fry the beef 3 to 4 minutes. Return the vegetables to the beef in the wok and add the broth. Stir and heat until the sauce boils. Serve at once with rice.

Beef with Hot Salad

THAILAND   Yield: 4 servings

1 pound fillet steak
1 large onion, peeled and sliced into
    rings
2 fresh chilies
2 cloves garlic, peeled and crushed
½ teaspoon sugar
1 teaspoon salt
½ teaspoon soy sauce
Juice of 1 lime or lemon
1 teaspoon mint, chopped
Fresh seasonal vegetables (cucumber,
    tomatoes, bok choy, bean sprouts,
    etc.), chopped

Slice the beef into strips measuring 2½ inches long, 1 inch wide, and ½ inch thick. Set aside.

Place onions and chilies on a skewer and broil until soft; then remove and finely mash them.

Broil the beef; mix cooked beef with onion and chilies. Add all remaining ingredients, except the vegetables, and mix.

Arrange chopped vegetables around the edge of a warm serving dish. Place beef mixture in center and quickly toss vegetables and beef together. Serve at once.

Beef with Bean Sprouts and Mushrooms

CHINA   Yield: 4 servings

    2 tablespoons vegetable oil
    ¼ pound mushrooms, cut into "T"
      shapes
    1 teaspoon fresh gingerroot, grated
    1 pound beef (round, chuck, flank),
      finely sliced
    2 tablespoons soy sauce
    2 tablespoons dry sherry
    ½ cup chicken broth or water
    1 tablespoon cornstarch in 2 table-
      spoons water
    1 or 2 cups bean sprouts
    2 stalks celery, cut into small cubes

Heat the oil in the wok and stir-fry mushrooms and grated ginger for 1 to 2 minutes. Push aside. Stir-fry the beef for 3 to 4 minutes. Return the mushrooms to the beef in the wok. Combine the soy sauce, sherry, broth, and cornstarch mixture. Stir and add to the beef and mushrooms. Heat until sauce thickens. Add the bean sprouts and continue heating just until they are heated through. Garnish with cubed celery and serve at once with rice.

Beef with Celery and Celery Cabbage

CHINA   Yield: 4 servings

    1 pound beef (chuck or round), cut
      into 1-inch cubes
    3 tablespoons soy sauce
    1 tablespoon dry sherry
    1 teaspoon sugar
    2 tablespoons vegetable oil

    1 cup celery cabbage (or bok choy),
      sliced diagonally across the stalks
      into ¼-inch slices
    1 cup celery, sliced diagonally across
      the stalks into ¼-inch slices
      (leaves may be left on)
    ¼ pound mushrooms, sliced into "T"
      shapes
    1 tablespoon cornstarch in 2 table-
      spoons water
    1 cup chicken broth or water

Marinate the beef for 20 to 30 minutes in the combined soy sauce, sherry, and sugar. Heat oil in the wok and stir-fry the celery cabbage and celery for 1 to 2 minutes or until the light-green color intensifies. Push aside. Stir-fry the mushrooms for 1 to 2 minutes. Push aside. Stir-fry the beef 3 to 4 minutes. Return the vegetables to the beef in the wok. Add the cornstarch mixture and broth to the beef and vegetables. Heat and stir until sauce is thickened and clear. Serve at once with rice.

Beef with Oyster Sauce

CHINA   Yield: 4 servings

    2 tablespoons soy sauce
    1 tablespoon dry sherry
    1 tablespoon cornstarch
    1 teaspoon sugar
    1 pound beef (chuck or round), cut
      into ¼-inch strips
    2 tablespoons vegetable oil
    1 green pepper, cut into ¼-inch strips
    8 canned water chestnuts, sliced
    2½ tablespoons bottled oyster sauce

Combine the soy sauce, dry sherry, cornstarch, and sugar in a small bowl. Add beef and marinate 20 to 30 minutes. Heat oil in the wok and stir-fry the green pepper strips and water chestnuts 1 to 2 minutes. Push aside and stir-fry the beef 2 to 3 minutes. Return the green pepper and water chestnuts to the beef in the wok. Gently stir in the oyster sauce. Heat through and serve at once garnished with nuts, if desired.

Beef with Sesame Sauce

INDOCHINA   Yield: 3 to 4 servings

½ pound round steak, shredded into
   thin strips
½ teaspoon salt
¼ teaspoon baking soda
2 tablespoons hot water
1 tablespoon soy sauce
1 clove garlic, peeled and crushed
3 tablespoons peanut oil
½ cup beef stock
3 teaspoons cornstarch
2 tablespoons cold water
2 teaspoons sesame paste
1 to 2 teaspoons Chinese chili sauce

Set shredded meat aside. Mix salt and baking soda with hot water and soy sauce. Pour over meat and squeeze meat with hands until liquid is absorbed. Allow to stand for 2 hours or refrigerate overnight.

Heat peanut oil in a wok or skillet. Stir-fry garlic and meat until meat is browned, about 2 minutes. Add stock and bring to a boil. Mix cornstarch with cold water and add to the boiling liquid. Stir until liquid has thickened. Turn off heat. Stir in sesame paste and chili sauce and serve at once.

Beef with Snow Peas

CHINA   Yield: 2 to 3 servings

½ pound beef, thinly sliced

Marinade

1 teaspoon cornstarch
1 teaspoon soy sauce
2 teaspoons sherry
¼ teaspoon sugar
¼ teaspoon oil

½ pound snow peas, with strings
   removed
2 teaspoons cornstarch mixed with 2
   teaspoons cold water
⅛ teaspoon freshly ground black
   pepper
½ teaspoon sugar
¼ teaspoon MSG
2 tablespoons oil, divided
¼ teaspoon salt
1 teaspoon fresh gingerroot, grated
½ cup chicken stock

Slice beef and set aside. Mix marinade ingredients and marinate beef while preparing rest of ingredients.

Remove string from snow peas. Mix together cornstarch and water. Add pepper, sugar, and MSG. Heat skillet or wok to medium-high. Add 1 tablespoon oil, salt, and gingerroot. Add snow peas, stir, and add the chicken stock. Cover for 10 seconds. Uncover, stir, and remove from pan. Reheat pan and add remaining 1 tablespoon oil. When pan is hot, add beef and stir-fry only about 45 seconds, until beef is almost cooked. Then add snow peas and cornstarch mixture. Stir until sauce is thickened.

Beef with Snow Pea Pods and Cashews

CHINA   Yield: 4 servings

1 pound beef (top of the round steak), sliced into ¼-inch strips
2 tablespoons black bean sauce
2 tablespoons soy sauce
1 clove garlic, grated
2 tablespoons vegetable oil
12 to 16 snow pea pods, strings removed
1 tablespoon cornstarch in ½ cup cold broth or water
½ cup cashews
1 cup bean sprouts, optional

Marinate the beef in a combined mixture of bean sauce, soy sauce, and grated garlic in a small bowl for 20 to 30 minutes. Heat oil in the wok and stir-fry the snow pea pods 1 to 2 minutes, until their green color brightens. Push aside. Stir-fry the beef 2 to 3 minutes. Return the snow pea pods to the beef in the wok and stir in the cornstarch and broth mixture. Heat until sauce boils and is clear. Add cashews and serve at once. (Bean sprouts may be added just before the cornstarch mixture is added, if desired.)

Beef with Snow Pea Pods and Mushrooms

CHINA   Yield: 4 servings

2 tablespoons vegetable oil
1 teaspoon fresh gingerroot, grated
1 clove garlic, grated
½ pound mushrooms, sliced into "T" shapes
14 to 16 snow pea pods, strings removed

1 pound flank steak, cut into thin slices
½ cup chicken broth or water
1 tablespoon cornstarch in 2 tablespoons water
3 tablespoons soy sauce
¼ cup cashews or peanuts

Heat oil in the wok and stir-fry the ginger, garlic, and mushrooms 1 to 2 minutes. Push aside. Stir-fry the pea pods 1 to 2 minutes or until they become bright green. Push aside. Stir-fry the beef 2 to 3 minutes. Return the vegetables to the meat. Add the broth, cornstarch mixture, and soy sauce and heat until sauce boils and is thickened and beef and vegetables are heated through. Add nuts and serve at once with rice.

Beef with Snow Pea Pods and Water Chestnuts

CHINA   Yield: 4 servings

2 tablespoons soy sauce
2 tablespoons dry sherry
1 pound beef (top of the round), sliced very thin
2 tablespoons vegetable oil
12 to 16 snow pea pods, strings removed
6 to 8 water chestnuts, sliced
½ cup chicken broth or stock
1 tablespoon cornstarch in 2 tablespoons cold water
Walnuts, optional

Combine 1 tablespoon soy sauce and 1 tablespoon dry sherry in a small bowl. Add sliced beef and let stand 20 to 30 minutes. Heat oil in wok and stir-fry the pea pods 1 to 2 minutes or just until their green color brightens. Push aside. Stir-fry the water chestnuts 1 minute. Push aside. Stir-fry the beef 3 to 4 minutes. Return the pea pods and water chestnuts to the beef in the wok. Add the broth, remaining 1 tablespoon soy sauce, remaining 1 tablespoon dry sherry, and the cornstarch mixture. Heat until the sauce boils and is thickened and clear. Garnish with walnuts if you wish. Serve at once with rice.

Beef with Spinach

CHINA   Yield: 2 servings

½ pound beef, thinly sliced

Marinade

2 tablespoons rice wine or sherry
½ teaspoon salt
Freshly ground black pepper to taste
1 egg white
1 tablespoon leek, chopped (onion may be substituted)
½ teaspoon gingerroot, grated
1 teaspoon chili powder
1 teaspoon garlic, grated
1 tablespoon cornstarch

Oil for cooking
1 tablespoon soy sauce
1 teaspoon vinegar
1¼ teaspoons sugar
1 10-ounce package spinach, washed and torn into bite-size pieces
Salt to taste

Cut beef into bite-size pieces. Mix marinade ingredients and marinate beef for 30 minutes. Heat oil in skillet or wok and sauté beef over medium-high heat for approximately 3 to 4 minutes. Add soy sauce, vinegar, and 1 teaspoon sugar. Stir well and remove meat mixture to serving platter. Heat

more oil if necessary and sauté spinach over high heat just until tender, 1 to 2 minutes. Add salt to taste and ¼ teaspoon sugar, and place on serving platter with beef.

Braised Meat with Onions

KOREA   Yield: 4 to 6 servings

1½ pounds lean round steak
24 spring onions, using only the white part, sliced
3 tablespoons toasted sesame seeds
1 clove garlic, peeled and quartered
½ teaspoon fresh ginger, finely chopped
¼ cup light soy sauce
½ teaspoon chili powder or cayenne pepper
2 tablespoons vegetable oil
6 dried mushrooms, soaked and sliced

Slice and cut meat into bite-size pieces. Then beat the meat with a mallet until very thin. Slice onions and set aside. In a large bowl, combine sesame seeds, garlic, ginger, soy sauce, and chili powder with the beef. Use your hand to rub seasonings into beef.

Heat oil in a skillet and stir-fry beef and mushrooms, using high heat, until beef is done. Remove beef and mushrooms with a slotted spoon and set aside. Add just enough oil needed to stir-fry the onions. Spoon onions over waiting meat and serve at once with white rice.

Meat

Chinese Casserole

CHINA   Yield: 4 servings

    1 pound lean beef, ground
    1 green pepper, chopped
    1 onion, chopped
    1 can Chinese mixed vegetables
    ¼ cup Parmesan cheese, grated
    1 can tomato soup
    ¾ package thin spaghetti, cooked
    ½ teaspoon salt

Brown meat in a skillet, stirring occasionally. Remove meat to a large casserole, leaving as much fat in the skillet as possible. Brown green pepper and onion in remaining fat. When brown, add to meat. Stir in the remaining ingredients and bake at 350°F for 45 minutes. Serve with soy sauce.

Chop Suey

CHINA   Yield: 4 to 6 servings

    3 tablespoons oil
    1½ pounds beef, cubed
    2 tablespoons soy sauce
    3 cups celery, diced
    2 cups onions, chopped
    1½ cups beef bouillon
    1 can Chinese vegetables
    1 can bean sprouts
    1 can water chestnuts, sliced and
      drained
    1 tablespoon bead molasses
    3 tablespoons cornstarch
    ⅔ cup water

Heat 3 tablespoons oil in skillet almost to a boil. Cook meat alone until nearly done. Add 1 tablespoon of the soy sauce, celery,

onions, and bouillon and sauté 10 minutes. Add Chinese vegetables, bean sprouts, and water chestnuts. Cook 5 minutes.

Add gravy, made out of molasses, 1 tablespoon soy sauce, cornstarch, and water. Season to taste. Mix all ingredients and simmer at least 30 minutes. Serve with rice and Chinese noodles.

Ground Beef Chop Suey

CHINA   Yield: 6 servings

    2 cups celery, cut into thin, 1-inch
      strips
    ½ cup onion, sliced
    1 pound ground beef
    1 tablespoon fat or oil
    2 tablespoons cornstarch
    1½ cups water
    1 beef bouillon cube
    ¼ cup soy sauce
    ½ teaspoon salt
    4 cups cabbage, chopped
    4 cups rice, cooked (about 1⅓ cups
      uncooked rice)

Cook celery, onion, and ground beef in hot fat in a large frying pan about 5 minutes until meat begins to brown.

Blend cornstarch with water and stir into beef mixture. Add bouillon cube, soy sauce, and salt. Cook, stirring constantly, until sauce is thickened and clear.

Stir in cabbage. Cook, covered, about 3 minutes until cabbage is tender but still firm. Serve on rice.

Note: In place of cabbage, a 16-ounce can of bean sprouts may be used. Drain and use the liquid in place of part of the water. Heat only to serving temperature after adding bean sprouts.

Deep-fried Beef Cubes

CHINA   Yield: Approximately 4 servings

Cooking oil
Slice of raw potato
2 pounds beef tenderloin or sirloin, cut
  in ¾-inch cubes
Meat tenderizer
Currant-Chutney Sauce (see Index)
Deviled Roquefort Butter (see Index)
Curry Sauce (see Index)
Chopped onions

Pour oil into an electric wok to ⅔ full. Use part olive or part peanut oil for flavor. Set to 425°F. Place a slice of raw potato in bottom of the pot to prevent oil from sputtering.

Have beef at room temperature and trim well of all fat. If you use sirloin, sprinkle with meat tenderizer, following label instructions.

Arrange the meat in the center of dinner plates with the sauces arranged in individual bowls so each guest can help himself. Provide guests with chopsticks or long-handled forks. Each guest picks up a piece of beef with chopsticks or fork and cooks it in the oil until the desired degree of doneness is reached. Dip the meat into one or more sauces or into the chopped onions.

Deep-fried Beef with Scallions

CHINA   Yield: 4 servings

1 pound beef (flank or round), cut into
  ¼ × 3-inch strips

Frying batter

1 large egg
1 cup sifted all-purpose flour
¾ cup water
2 cups oil for frying

8 scallions, sliced into ½-inch slices
1 clove garlic, minced
1 teaspoon gingerroot, grated
2 tablespoons vegetable oil
½ teaspoon salt
¼ cup dry white wine
1 to 2 tablespoons soy sauce
2 tablespoons black bean sauce

Combine batter ingredients. Let stand for 1 hour. Dip beef strips, a few at a time, into the batter and deep-fry in oil at 400°F. Drain on paper towels and keep warm.

Combine remaining ingredients and simmer, covered, for 20 minutes. Place scallion mixture on a serving platter and top with deep-fried beef. Serve with boiled rice.

Fried Beef and Horapa

THAILAND   Yield: 4 servings

Horapa is a spice used in Thailand. If unavailable, sweet basil may be used as a substitute.

2 tablespoons plus 1 teaspoon vegetable
  oil
1½ pounds chuck steak, thinly sliced
2 onions, peeled and sliced
3 cloves garlic, peeled and finely
  chopped
3 tablespoons horapa leaves, freshly
  chopped
3 fresh chilies, sliced
Nam pla to taste
Chopped scallions for garnish

Heat 1 teaspoon oil in a skillet or wok. Fry the beef until the juices are extracted. Stir twice and cook for about 3 minutes. Remove beef and set aside.

Add remaining oil to skillet and fry onions and garlic until brown. Stir in horapa. Return beef to the pan and add chilies. Stir-fry for 1 minute. Add nam pla to taste. Place meat on a serving dish and garnish with scallions.

Meat

Foil-wrapped Beef

CHINA   Yield: 4 servings

1 pound beef (top of the round or
   chuck blade steak or roast), very
   thinly sliced (partial freezing
   may make this step easier)
2 tablespoons hoisin sauce
1 tablespoon soy sauce
1 tablespoon dry sherry
1 tablespoon cornstarch
4 12-inch aluminum foil squares
1 scallion, finely sliced
Parsley leaves

Combine the beef, hoisin sauce, soy
sauce, dry sherry, and cornstarch. Place one-
fourth of this mixture in a single layer in the
center of each foil square. Top each with
sliced scallion and parsley leaves. (You can
divide the mixture into smaller portions and
make 6 to 8 squares.) Fold as for Paper-
Wrapped Chicken (see Index) into flat packages about 5 inches square. Keeping the
seams up to prevent the escape of juices,
bake at 450°F for 6 minutes. Serve still
wrapped so the diner can release the flavorful
juices at the moment of eating. (It is impor-
tant to wrap in a single layer in a flat package or the beef will not be uniformly
cooked.)

Tasty Fondue

JAPAN   Yield: 4 servings

Bouillon

6 cups chicken bouillon
2 carrots
1 leek
1 stalk celery
2 tablespoons parsley, coarsely chopped

Sauce tartare

5 tablespoons mayonnaise
2 tablespoons capers
2 tablespoons chives, finely chopped
2 dill pickles, finely chopped
2 teaspoons lemon juice
2 tablespoons evaporated milk
Salt
Pinch of sugar
White pepper

Catsup sauce

5 tablespoons mayonnaise
2 tablespoons tomato catsup
1 teaspoon Worcestershire sauce
1 teaspoon (or less) curry powder
Pinch of sugar
Salt

2 to 2½ pounds very lean beef
2 cups boiling water

Bring chicken bouillon to a boil either in
pot placed on the burner or in fondue pot.
Chop carrots, leek, and celery; add to broth
together with chopped parsley. Cook for 20
minutes.

To prepare sauces, stir listed ingredients
together until well blended. Season to taste.

Thoroughly dry meat with paper towels.
Cut into thin strips.

Place chicken-vegetable broth on top of
burner; make sure it continues to simmer (or
leave in fondue pot over low heat). Since
the liquid will evaporate, it is necessary to
add some of the hot water from time to time.

Each person places a piece of meat on a
fondue fork, puts it in simmering broth for 1
to 2 minutes, and dunks it in sauce. Each
person should have a separate bowl for each
of the sauces. Serve with rice.

Fried Cucumbers with Beef

KOREA   Yield: 4 servings

½ pound lean sirloin
2 teaspoons sesame oil
1 tablespoon light soy sauce
½ teaspoon salt
½ teaspoon sugar
¼ teaspoon cayenne pepper
2 large green cucumbers
1 tablespoon vegetable oil
2 tablespoons toasted, crushed sesame
   seeds

Cut beef into paper thin slices, 2 inches long. (It's easier to slice thin if it is partially frozen.) Place beef in a bowl with sesame oil, soy sauce, salt, sugar, and cayenne. Mix well to be sure the flavors penetrate the meat.

Peel cucumbers, leaving strips of green at intervals. Cut in half the long way and scoop out seeds. Cut the cucumbers crossways into medium slices.

Cover the bottom of a skillet or wok with oil, and heat. Stir-fry beef on high heat for 1 minute. Add the cucumbers, tossing lightly to blend flavors. Reduce heat and allow to simmer a few minutes until cucumber is tender but still crisp. Place in a serving bowl and garnish with sesame seeds.

Fried Steak with Chili

INDONESIA   Yield: 4 servings

1¼ pounds New York sirloin or round
   steak
2 teaspoons coriander powder
2 tablespoons tamarind water
1 teaspoon brown sugar
1 or more teaspoons salt to taste
Freshly ground black pepper to taste
8 red chilies, seeded and chopped

4 shallots, peeled and chopped
2 cloves garlic, peeled and chopped
6 tablespoons vegetable oil
1 teaspoon lemon juice

Slice the meat into thin strips; then cut into 2-inch squares. Arrange squares on plate singly and sprinkle with coriander, tamarind water, brown sugar, salt, and pepper. Use your fingers to press the spice mixture into the meat. Allow to stand for 2 to 3 hours.

Pound the chilies, shallots, and garlic until just broken into pieces. Set aside.

Heat oil in a skillet; brown the meat evenly on both sides until cooked through. Remove from pan. Add the pounded mixture to the oil and cook for 2 minutes. Return the meat to the skillet and coat with spices. Sprinkle with lemon juice and add more salt if needed. Serve hot at once.

Grilled Steaks

JAPAN   Yield: 4 servings

Marinade

½ cup soy sauce
4 tablespoons onions, minced
2 cloves garlic, minced
1 tablespoon (or less) sugar
1 tablespoon fresh gingerroot, minced
¼ cup rice wine, or dry white wine

4 small steaks of your choice, boneless
Cherry tomatoes for garnish

Mix marinade ingredients together. Pour marinade over steaks. Refrigerate overnight or let sit at room temperature for 3 to 4 hours. Broil steaks in the oven or on a grill or hibachi. Baste steaks with marinade while they are grilling. When steaks are almost done, grill tomatoes and use for garnish.

Meat

Chinese Ginger Beef

CHINA   Yield: 4 servings

1 pound lean boneless beef chuck
1½ tablespoons soy sauce
2 tablespoons cooking sherry
2 tablespoons cooking oil
¼ cup gingerroot, peeled and sliced very thin
¼ cup green onion, chopped
¼ cup beef broth
1 tablespoon cornstarch
1 tablespoon water

Partially freeze beef, then slice as thinly as possible. Combine soy sauce and sherry and toss with the sliced meat. Marinate for 1 hour.

Heat oil until very hot. Add beef, ginger, and onion to oil and cook for five minutes, stirring constantly, until meat is browned. Add broth and cook until meat is tender. Mix cornstarch and water until smooth. Add to meat mixture and cook, stirring until thickened. Serve over rice.

If you wish, you can add 1 box of frozen snow peas or frozen mixed Chinese vegetables to the beef when you add the broth. Do not overcook the vegetables; they should be tender-crisp.

Ginger Beef

CHINA   Yield: 6 to 8 servings

1 cup onions, minced
2 cloves garlic, pressed
2 teaspoons turmeric
2 teaspoons ginger
1 teaspoon chili powder
1 teaspoon salt
3 pounds of lean beef, cut into cubes

8 fresh tomatoes, peeled and cut into large pieces
½ cup peanut oil
4 cups beef bouillon
Boiled rice
Strips of red sweet pepper for garnish

Combine onions, garlic, turmeric, ginger, chili powder, and salt in a bowl. Mix well. Prepare the beef and place in a shallow dish. Sprinkle with the onion-garlic mixture and refrigerate for 3 hours, stirring occasionally. Prepare the tomatoes.

In a large skillet, heat the oil. Stir-fry the beef until browned on all sides. Place beef in a casserole and add skillet drippings, tomatoes, and bouillon. Bake, covered, in a 325°F oven for about 2 hours or until the beef is tender. Serve with boiled rice and garnish with strips of red sweet pepper.

Spiced Ground Beef Dumplings

INDIA   Yield: About 48 dumplings

1 large onion, chopped
2 tablespoons vegetable oil
1 pound lean ground beef
1 tablespoon curry powder
1 teaspoon paprika
½ teaspoon chili powder (or 1 teaspoon red pepper flakes if you like hot foods)
¼ teaspoon black pepper
½ teaspoon garlic salt
2 fresh medium tomatoes, diced
Salt to taste
1 8½-ounce can of peas
1 egg, lightly beaten
2 to 3 cups of oil for frying
Mustard Sauce or Curry Powder (see Index)

Sauté the onion in the oil in the wok until golden brown. Mix the beef, spices, tomatoes, salt, and peas thoroughly, using some of the liquid from the can. Add the sautéed onion and mix. Place a spoonful of the mixture into the center of a dough circle and fold for frying. Seal with the beaten egg and set on oiled waxed paper until ready to cook. Heat the 2 to 3 cups of oil to 350°F. Deep-fry the dumplings for 2 or 3 minutes, until golden brown; drain and serve hot with Mustard Sauce or Curry Powder.

Ground Beef Oriental

CHINA   Yield: 3 to 4 servings

1 tablespoon vegetable oil
1 pound ground chuck or ground round
1 small onion or 2 scallions, chopped
1 clove garlic, crushed
½ teaspoon salt
¼ teaspoon pepper
¾ cup beef bouillon
½ green pepper, cut in thin strips
1 fresh tomato, cut in eighths
¼ cup bamboo shoots, thinly sliced
1½ tablespoons soy sauce
½ teaspoon cornstarch

Heat vegetable oil in a wok. When hot, add the ground beef, onion, garlic, salt, and pepper. Stir with a fork, breaking up beef into small pieces, and sauté until beef is browned and onion soft. Pour off any fat that accumulates.

Pour in bouillon and add green pepper, tomato, and bamboo shoots. Bring mixture to a boil. Mix soy sauce and cornstarch together and add. Cook over low heat, stirring occasionally, until sauce thickens.

Ground Beef with Fresh Peas

INDIA   Yield: 4 to 6 servings

2 tablespoons ghee
1 large onion, peeled and finely sliced
2 cloves garlic, peeled and crushed
½ teaspoon fresh ginger, finely grated
1 teaspoon ground turmeric
½ teaspoon chili powder
1 pound ground meat
½ cup yogurt
1 cup fresh green peas
1 teaspoon garam masala
1½ teaspoons salt
2 tablespoons fresh coriander leaves, finely chopped
1 fresh red chili, finely sliced

Fry onions in heated ghee until soft. Add garlic and ginger and continue to fry until onions are golden brown. Add turmeric and chili powder, stir briefly, and add meat.

Continue to stir meat, breaking up large lumps, until it is browned. Then add yogurt and peas and lower the heat. Cover and cook for 15 minutes. Stir in garam masala and continue cooking until meat and peas are tender. Garnish with coriander leaves and chili.

Chinese Hamburgers

CHINA   Yield: 8 patties

    2 pounds ground meat, lean
    2 tablespoons soy sauce
    1 medium onion, finely chopped
    1 medium green pepper, finely chopped
    4 water chestnuts, finely chopped
    ¼ teaspoon MSG
    Salt to taste
    Pepper to taste
    2 eggs, lightly beaten

Combine all ingredients and mix thoroughly. Form into patties and broil in oven or cook on hibachi or grill, approximately 5 minutes on each side.

Oriental Hamburgers

CHINA   Yield: 8 servings

    ½ cup each soy sauce and water
    1 clove garlic, minced or mashed
    2 teaspoons fresh ginger, grated
    2 tablespoons Worcestershire sauce
    6 tablespoons firmly packed brown
      sugar
    3 pounds lean ground beef
    8 rectangular French rolls
    Thinly sliced tomatoes
    Green pepper rings

Combine soy sauce, water, garlic, ginger, Worcestershire, and brown sugar. Shape ground beef into 8 log-shaped meat patties (to fit the long French rolls). Pour soy sauce mixture over the meat and marinate for 1 to 1½ hours.

Lift patties from marinade, drain briefly, and grill about 4 inches above hot coals or broil 4 inches from heat, 4 to 5 minutes on each side for medium-rare or until done to

your liking. Baste several times with the marinade. Split rolls and toast them on the grill or under the broiler. Fill rolls with the meat patties, sliced tomatoes, and green pepper rings.

Marinated Flank Steak

JAPAN   Yield: 2 to 3 servings

    1 flank steak, approximately 2 pounds

Marinade
    4 tablespoons lemon juice
    ¼ cup soy sauce
    3 tablespoons honey
    3 scallions, finely chopped
    2 tablespoons sesame oil

Score steak on each side. Combine marinade ingredients and place steak in mixture and refrigerate overnight, turning occasionally. Broil steak on preheated broiler pan about 4 minutes on each side, basting frequently with marinade. Cut steak on angle into very thin slices.

Marinated Steak

JAPAN   Yield: About 4 servings

    1 to 1½ pounds filet mignon or round
      steak

Marinade
    4 tablespoons sherry
    4 tablespoons soy sauce
    1½ heaping tablespoons cornstarch
    Salt
    Pinch of sugar
    Pinch of white pepper

    4 tablespoons oil

Cut filet mignon into thin slices.

Prepare marinade by stirring sherry, soy sauce, cornstarch, a little salt, and a pinch each of sugar and white pepper thoroughly until well blended. Pour marinade over meat slices; marinate for 1 hour.

Heat oil in heavy skillet until very hot. Add meat, including marinade; cook for 5 minutes, stirring constantly. Serve steak immediately.

Chinese Meatballs

CHINA   Yield: 4 servings

1 pound ground beef
1½ cups cabbage, finely grated
1 large onion, finely grated
½ teaspoon ginger
2 teaspoons soy sauce
½ teaspoon salt
2 tablespoons shortening
½ cup water
1 teaspoon soy sauce

The night before you plan to serve them, mix ground beef, cabbage, onion, ginger, soy sauce, and salt in a large bowl. When thoroughly mixed, form into balls. Cover and set in the refrigerator. (While this can be done when preparing the meal, the flavors blend more fully under refrigeration.)

Heat shortening in pressure cooker and brown the meatballs. Add water and soy sauce and close cover securely. Put pressure control in place. When pressure is reached, cook for 5 minutes. Cool at once under running water.

Serve meatballs with your favorite sweet-and-sour sauce or as is.

Meatballs Chinese Style

CHINA   Yield: About 50 meatballs

Meatballs

2 pounds ground beef
1 egg
2 tablespoons onion, chopped
1 tablespoon cornstarch
1 teaspoon salt
Freshly ground black pepper to taste
Peanut oil

Sauce

1 cup pineapple juice
1 tablespoon oil
3 tablespoons cornstarch
1 tablespoon soy sauce
3 tablespoons vinegar
6 tablespoons water
½ cup sugar
1 green pepper, cut into small chunks
1 small can pineapple chunks, drained

Combine all ingredients for meatballs and shape into 1-inch balls. Brown in small amount of peanut oil. Drain.

In large saucepan, combine pineapple juice and oil. Set aside. Mix together cornstarch, soy sauce, vinegar, water, and sugar. Add to pineapple juice and oil. Bring to boil and simmer 1 minute. Add green pepper and pineapple chunks. Add meatballs.

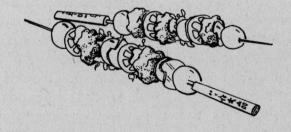

Hong Kong Meatballs I

CHINA   Yield: 4 servings

1 pound ground beef
¼ cup fine dry bread crumbs
¼ teaspoon salt
Dash pepper
1 tablespoon salad oil
1 small can sliced mushrooms; drain
  and reserve liquid
1 package onion soup mix
3 cups water
1 cup rice
2 tablespoons soy sauce
1 cup celery, sliced

Combine beef, bread crumbs, mushroom liquid, salt and pepper. Shape into tiny meatballs, about 30. Brown meatballs in oil. Pour off fat. Add remaining ingredients except celery. Cover and bake at 200°F for 15 minutes. Add celery, cover and bake for an additional 15 minutes.

Hong Kong Meatballs II

CHINA   Yield: 6 servings

1½ pounds ground beef
½ cup celery, very finely chopped
1 teaspoon seasoned salt
3 teaspoons soy sauce
1 tablespoon vegetable oil
¼ cup bamboo shoots, thinly sliced
1 1-pound can mixed Chinese
  vegetables or bean sprouts, drained,
  with liquid reserved
1 green pepper, seeded and cut in
  julienne strips

1 carrot, peeled and shredded
1 5-ounce can water chestnuts, drained
  and thinly sliced
1½ tablespoons cornstarch
2 teaspoons sherry
¼ cup blanched, slivered almonds

Mix ground beef with celery, seasoned salt, and 1 teaspoon of the soy sauce. Mix thoroughly to blend all ingredients, then shape into 1-inch-diameter meatballs.

Heat the vegetable oil in a large skillet or wok, and sauté the meatballs over high heat until browned on all sides. Stir in the bamboo shoots; cover and simmer 5 minutes, stirring occasionally. At the end of the cooking time, pour off any accumulated fat.

Add the drained Chinese vegetables, green pepper strips, shredded carrot, and water chestnuts. Stir well. In a 2-cup measure, mix the cornstarch, 2 teaspoons soy sauce, and sherry until a thin paste is formed. Add the liquid from the Chinese vegetables and enough water to make 2 cups in all. Add to the meatballs and cook uncovered for 5 to 10 minutes, stirring occasionally, until sauce is thickened. Sprinkle on the almonds before serving.

Oriental Meatballs

JAPAN   Yield: 6 servings

2 pounds lean ground beef
2½ teaspoons salt
⅛ teaspoon freshly ground black
  pepper
1 egg, beaten
2 tablespoons flour
Small amount freshly ground black
  pepper
½ cup oil

12 ounces canned chicken broth
3 tablespoons cornstarch
2 to 3 teaspoons soy sauce
½ cup vinegar
½ cup light corn syrup
5 medium green peppers, cut in sixths
8 slices canned pineapple, quartered or
    cut into chunks
10 maraschino cherries, optional

Combine beef, 1 teaspoon of the salt, and ⅛ teaspoon pepper. Shape into small meatballs. Combine egg, flour, ½ teaspoon salt, and a small amount of pepper. Beat until smooth. Heat oil and remaining 1 teaspoon salt in large frying pan.

Gently place meatballs in batter, 1 or 2 at a time, and fry in the hot oil, browning well on all sides. Remove meatballs from pan. Drain off remaining oil.

Blend ½ cup of the chicken broth with cornstarch. Add remaining chicken broth, soy sauce, vinegar, and corn syrup; cook over medium heat, stirring constantly, until thick and clear. Add green peppers, pineapple, and cherries. Lower heat; cook slowly for about 10 minutes. Pour over meatballs. Serve with rice.

Sweet-and-Sour Meatballs I

CHINA   Yield: 4 servings

1 pound extra-lean ground beef
¾ teaspoon salt
½ teaspoon pepper
½ teaspoon fresh gingerroot, grated
2 tablespoons vegetable oil
1 green pepper, cut into ¼-inch cubes
1 onion, chopped
1 carrot, grated
2 tablespoons vinegar
2 tablespoons brown sugar
1 teaspoon soy sauce
1 teaspoon dry sherry
1 tablespoon cornstarch, stirred into
    ½ cup cold chicken or beef broth

Blend together the ground beef, salt, pepper, and ginger. Shape into 1-inch meatballs. Heat oil in the wok and brown the meatballs on all sides for about 2 minutes. Add all remaining ingredients. Cook over moderate heat, stirring constantly, until mixture thickens. Cook an additional 5 minutes. Serve at once with rice.

Sweet-and-Sour Meatballs II

CHINA   Yield: 6 servings

1½ pounds ground beef
2 eggs
3 tablespoons flour
½ teaspoon salt
Freshly ground black pepper
¾ cup oil
1½ cups chicken bouillon
3 large green peppers, diced
6 slices canned pineapple, diced
8 to 10 sweet pickle chips
2 tablespoons cornstarch
2 tablespoons soy sauce
1 teaspoon MSG, optional
¾ cup vinegar
¾ cup pineapple juice
¾ cup sugar

Shape ground beef into 18 balls. Combine eggs, flour, salt, and pepper. Dip meatballs in batter and fry in oil until brown. Remove meatballs and keep hot.

Pour out all but 1 tablespoon oil from skillet. Add ½ cup bouillon, green peppers, pineapple, and pickles. Cover and cook over medium heat for 10 minutes. Mix remaining ingredients and add. Cook, stirring constantly, until mixture comes to a boil and thickens. Add meatballs and simmer for 15 minutes. Makes 18 hors d'oeuvres or serves 6

Sweet-and-Sour Meatballs III

CHINA   Yield: 4 servings

1 pound lean ground beef
1 egg, beaten
1 teaspoon (scant) salt
Pepper to taste, freshly ground
1 tablespoon onion flakes
1 tablespoon cornstarch
Oil for frying
1 13½-ounce can pineapple tidbits,
   drained (reserve liquid)
1 cup water
1 package sweet-and-sour sauce mix
½ cup green pepper, thinly sliced

Combine beef, beaten egg, salt, and pepper to taste. Mix in onion and cornstarch. Shape into small-size meatballs.

Brown meatballs in small amount of oil in frying pan or wok. Drain on paper towels. Discard pan drippings. In same pan, combine reserved pineapple liquid, water, and sweet-sour mix. Stir constantly until mixture boils. Add green pepper, meatballs, and pineapple. Bring to a boil; turn heat down; simmer for 5 minutes, stirring occasionally.

Serve meatballs on hot rice.

Teriyaki Meatballs

JAPAN   Yield: 4 servings

1 pound lean ground beef
2 tablespoons parsley, chopped
2 tablespoons chives, chopped
Leaves from 2 stalks of celery, finely
   chopped
1 egg
3 tablespoons bread crumbs

Salt
White pepper
Butter or margarine for frying

Sauce

½ cup soy sauce
Salt
White pepper
Sugar
⅛ teaspoon allspice
Ground ginger
1 sugared ginger

Mix ground beef thoroughly with chopped parsley, chives, and celery leaves. Stir in egg and bread crumbs. Season to taste with salt and pepper. Shape into balls about 1½ to 2 inches in diameter. Heat butter or margarine in heavy skillet. Add meatballs; fry for about 5 minutes or until browned on all sides.

While meatballs are frying, prepare the sauce. In a small saucepan, heat soy sauce over low heat. Season with salt, pepper, sugar, allspice, and ground ginger. Dice sugared ginger; add to sauce. Pour hot sauce over meatballs; let stand for 5 minutes, so flavors can blend.

Serve meatballs in preheated bowl.

Moo-Goo-Ngow

CHINA   Yield: 6 servings

1 clove garlic
3 tablespoons cooking oil
1½ pounds round steak (cut
   in ⅛-inch slices)
3 tablespoons onion, diced
½ pound fresh mushrooms, sliced
1½ cups bouillon
3 tablespoons cornstarch

1 tablespoon soy sauce
Water
1 can Chinese vegetables

Cook garlic in oil in heavy skillet for about 2 minutes, then remove garlic. Add the seasoned steak slices and onion, cooking gently until meat is browned. Stir frequently. Add bouillon and sliced mushrooms. Cover pan and cook for about 45 minutes.

Add soy sauce to cornstarch and enough water to make thin paste. Pour into broth and cook gently until thickened. Add Chinese vegetables and, when thoroughly heated, serve on hot boiled rice. Vegetables may be served separately.

Pearl Balls

CHINA   Yield: About 20 pearl balls

1 cup glutinous rice (available in
   Oriental food stores)
1 teaspoon ginger, grated
1 egg
1 tablespoon soy sauce
½ teaspoon salt
1 tablespoon cornstarch
1 pound ground beef

Cover the glutinous rice with water and set aside for 2 hours. Combine the remaining ingredients with the ground beef and shape it into balls the size of small walnuts. Drain the rice well. Roll each meatball in the rice firmly so the rice will adhere. Place on a dish lined with a paper towel. Set the dish on a rack inside the wok. Fill the wok with water to just below the rack. Cover and steam for 20 minutes.

Serve hot as appetizers with hot mustard sauce and soy sauce. The glutinous rice swells, when steamed, to resemble small pearls.

Pepper Steak

JAPAN   Yield: 4 servings

1 pound round steak
¼ cup oil
½ teaspoon salt
Pepper to taste
½ cup scallion, chopped
2 cloves garlic, finely chopped
4 green peppers, cut into bite-size
   pieces
1 cup celery, sliced
1½ cups beef bouillon
2 tablespoons cornstarch
¼ cup cold water
1 tablespoon soy sauce
Cooked rice

Cut steak into thin slices, then into 2-inch pieces. To make slicing easier, partially freeze the meat. Heat oil in large skillet. Add salt and pepper. Cook meat over medium to high heat until brown, stirring frequently. Add scallion and garlic. Add green peppers and celery; stir. Add bouillon; cover and cook until vegetables are tender but still crisp. Do not overcook.

Meanwhile, combine cornstarch and water. Blend in soy sauce until it makes a smooth paste. Slowly add paste to meat mixture, stirring constantly until liquid is thickened. Serve with rice.

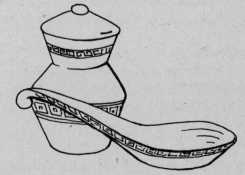

Meat

Chinese Pepper Steak I

CHINA   Yield: 6 servings

- 1½ pounds of ¼-inch thick round steak, cut into strips and browned in oil
- Seasoning to taste
- Chopped celery, onion, green pepper, and pimiento
- 1 can beef consommé
- 1 can Chinese vegetables
- 1 can mushrooms
- 1 tablespoon soy sauce
- ¼ cup water
- 2 tablespoons cornstarch

Combine last 3 ingredients and add to meat and vegetables. Simmer about 30 minutes or until meat is done. Serve over rice.

Chinese Pepper Steak II

CHINA   Yield: 2 servings

- 8 ounces flank steak
- 2 tablespoons shortening
- Salt
- Pepper
- 2 tablespoons onion, diced
- ½ clove garlic, minced
- 2 green peppers, cut up
- ½ cup celery, cut in chunks
- ½ cup beef bouillon
- 1 tablespoon cornstarch
- 2 tablespoons water
- 1 teaspoon soy sauce

Cut flank steak against the grain in ⅛-inch thick slivers and brown in heavy skillet in the shortening. Add salt and pepper to taste.

Add onion, garlic, green peppers, and celery. Add bouillon, cover pan tightly, and cook over moderate heat until meat and vegetables are tender but not limp (about 10 minutes).

Blend together the cornstarch, water, and soy sauce. Add to meat. Cook a few more minutes until juice thickens, stirring constantly. Serve at once with hot rice.

Chinese Pepper Steak III

CHINA   Yield: 6 servings

- 1½ pounds shoulder or sirloin steak
- Salt and pepper
- 2 tablespoons oil
- 1 medium onion, chopped
- 1 clove garlic, minced
- 2 green peppers, diced
- 1 cup bouillon
- 1 or 2 tomatoes
- 1½ tablespoons cornstarch
- 2 teaspoons soy sauce
- ¼ cup cold water

Season meat and brown in salad oil with onion and garlic. When browned, add bouillon and green peppers. Simmer covered for 15 minutes. Add tomatoes and simmer another 10 minutes. Mix cornstarch, soy sauce, and cold water and add to meat. Cook, stirring, until mixture is thickened and serve with rice.

Green Pepper Steak I

CHINA   Yield: 4 servings

- 1 pound flank steak, thinly sliced diagonally across grain with knife tilted at a 45° angle to the cutting board
- 3 tablespoons soy sauce
- ¼ teaspoon sugar
- 2 tablespoons vegetable oil

172

1 or 2 green peppers, cut into ¼-inch
strips
2 tablespoons cornstarch in 2 tablespoons cold water
1 cup chicken broth or water
2 or 3 firm tomatoes, cut into wedges
(peeled, if desired)

Marinate the steak in the soy sauce and
sugar for 20 to 30 minutes. Heat oil in the
wok and stir-fry the green peppers 1 to 2
minutes or until their green color brightens.
Push aside. Stir-fry steak 3 to 4 minutes. Return the green peppers to the steak in the
wok. Add the cornstarch mixture and broth
to the steak and peppers. Add the tomato
wedges and heat, stirring gently, until the
sauce is thickened and clear and the tomatoes are heated through. Serve at once with
rice.

Green Pepper Steak II

CHINA   Yield: 4 servings

2 tablespoons vegetable oil
1 or 2 green peppers, cut into ¼-inch
strips
1 pound flank steak, thinly sliced
directly across the grain with the
knife tilted at a 45° angle
to the cutting board
2 tablespoons cornstarch in 2 tablespoons cold water
1 cup chicken broth or water
3 tablespoons soy sauce (more, if
desired)
2 or 3 firm tomatoes, cut into wedges
(peeled, if desired)

Heat oil in the wok and stir-fry the green
peppers 1 to 2 minutes or until their green
color brightens. Push aside. Stir-fry the steak
3 to 4 minutes. Return the green peppers to

the steak in the wok. Stir the cornstarch
mixture, broth, and soy sauce into the steak
and peppers. Add the tomato wedges and
continue heating until the sauce is thickened
and clear and the tomatoes are heated
through. Serve at once with rice.

Pepper Steak Cantonese

CHINA   Yield: 2 gallons

10 green peppers, chopped
6 whole onions, chopped
4 pounds beef, cut into chips
1 gallon water
½ cup beef base or flavoring
Cornstarch
Flour
Water
1 cup soy sauce or to taste
Salt and pepper to taste

Sauté green peppers, onions, and chips of
beef. Combine with water and beef base.
Bring to boil. Thicken with mixture of ¾
part cornstarch, ¼ part flour, and water.
Add soy sauce and salt and white pepper to
taste.

Roast Beef with Horseradish

JAPAN   Yield: 2 servings

Horseradish, freshly grated or bottled
Water
4 slices roast beef, each about ⅛ inch
thick

Mix horseradish with small amount of
water until of spreading consistency. Spread
beef with horseradish; roll it up. Serve as an
appetizer.

Picadillo

PHILIPPINES   Yield: 6 servings

1 tablespoon lard
4 cloves garlic, peeled and finely
  chopped
1 medium onion, peeled and finely
  chopped
1 pound lean ground beef
2 tomatoes, peeled and chopped
2 cups beef stock
1 teaspoon salt
¼ teaspoon ground black pepper
1 pound potatoes, peeled and cubed

Cook garlic and onions in lard until both
are soft and golden. Add beef and stir until
meat is browned. Put in tomatoes and cook
until soft. Add stock, salt, and pepper and
bring to a boil. Reduce heat to medium,
cover the pot, and cook for 20 minutes. Add
the potatoes and cook 25 minutes more or
until potatoes are done. Serve at once.

Red-Stewed Beef I

CHINA   Yield: 6 servings

Red-stewing is the Chinese method of
preparing less-tender cuts of meat.

3 pounds lean pot roast (chuck, round,
  rump, or sirloin tip)
½ cup soy sauce
¼ cup sherry
4 slices fresh gingerroot
3 scallions
1 clove garlic
2 tablespoons brown sugar
½ teaspoon anise seeds
1 cup water

Place pot roast in a slow cooker and add
remaining ingredients. Cover and cook on

low about 10 hours. Slice meat and cover
with cooking sauce as it is served.

Red-Stewed Beef II

CHINA   Yield: About 4 servings

1½ pounds beef
Water to cover meat
1 tablespoon oil
1 clove garlic
4½ tablespoons soy sauce
1 tablespoon sugar
1 tablespoon wine
2 slices ginger the size of a penny

Cut the beef into cubes 1 × 1 inch and
simmer in a wok with enough water to barely
cover for 15 minutes. Drain beef and brown
it at medium temperature, using 1 tablespoon
oil and 1 clove of garlic. Add soy sauce,
sugar, wine, and ginger. Add the drained
juice; simmer at low heat until tender. During the stewing process you may add potatoes, turnips, Brussels sprouts, or carrots.

Red-Stewed Shin of Beef

CHINA   Yield: Approximately 4 servings

2 tablespoons cooking oil
2 pounds shin of beef
⅛ teaspoon pepper
2 slices fresh gingerroot
1 clove garlic
1 scallion, halved
1 teaspoon salt
2 teaspoons sugar
¼ cup soy sauce
1 teaspoon sesame seed oil
1 teaspoon sherry
Water to cover the meat

Heat the oil in a wok; when it is hot, add the meat and brown on both sides. Add the pepper, gingerroot, garlic, and scallion. Add the salt and sugar and pour the soy sauce, sesame seed oil, and sherry over it. Add enough boiling water to cover meat. Bring liquid to a boil, cover, and turn down heat. Simmer slowly for 2½ hours. Remove meat and cut into slices ¼ inch thick; arrange on a shallow dish. Pour gravy over it and serve at once.

Shining Beef

CHINA   Yield: 2 servings

2 ounces bean threads
2 tablespoons peanut oil
¾ cup Spanish onion, cut into thin strips
½ pound mushrooms, thinly sliced (about 2½ cups)
3 medium scallions, thinly sliced diagonally
1 clove garlic, minced
1 cup (scant) thin strips tender beef
¼ cup bottled teriyaki sauce

Cover the bean threads generously with boiling water and let stand off heat until soft—about 20 minutes; drain and with a scissors snip into about 3-inch lengths. In a wok, over high heat, heat the oil. Add the onion and mushrooms and toss constantly with a spatula just long enough to cook the onion slightly but not brown it. Add the scallions, garlic, and beef and toss constantly, separating the beef strips, until the meat loses its red color. Add the teriyaki sauce and the bean threads and heat, stirring constantly. Serve at once.

Note: The bean threads are available in Oriental and other markets; they are made from mung bean starch, protein, and water. For the beef you can use a boneless short loin steak that weighs a scant ¾ pound; remove all the fat before cutting the meat in strips.

Spiced Beef in Yogurt

INDIA   Yield: 4 servings

1 pound beef, thinly sliced
1 teaspoon salt
1¼ cups unflavored yogurt
¾ cup ghee
1 large onion, peeled and sliced
3 cloves garlic, peeled and sliced
1½ teaspoons ginger powder
2 teaspoons coriander powder
2 teaspoons chili powder
½ teaspoon cumin powder
1½ teaspoons turmeric powder
1 teaspoon garam masala

Tenderize beef slices with a mallet; rub with salt and place in a bowl. Cover with yogurt and allow to marinate overnight.

Melt ghee in a heavy skillet. Fry onion and garlic gently until soft. Add spices and stir-fry for 3 minutes. Add beef and marinade to pan. Stir to blend and cover. Reduce heat and simmer for 1½ hours or until meat is tender. Serve at once.

Short Ribs in Teriyaki Sauce

JAPAN   Yield: 4 servings

2 pounds short ribs
Teriyaki sauce to cover the ribs
½ cup water

Marinate the short ribs in teriyaki sauce for at least 1 hour.

Place the ribs and marinade in a pressure cooker, adding the water. Close the cover of the cooker and place control on. When pressure is reached, cook for 25 minutes. Allow this to cool naturally. Serve.

Spareribs of Beef

INDONESIA   Yield: 4 to 6 servings

3 pounds beef spareribs, cut into
    individual ribs and short lengths
3 cloves garlic, peeled and finely
    chopped
1 teaspoon fresh ginger, finely grated
1 teaspoon salt
3 tablespoons peanut oil
¼ cup dark soy sauce
½ cup water
2 tablespoons dry sherry
½ teaspoon five-spice powder
¼ teaspoon ground black pepper
1 tablespoon palm sugar or honey

Rub prepared ribs with garlic, ginger, and salt. Heat oil in a skillet or wok and stir-fry ribs on high heat until they are browned. Combine remaining ingredients, except the sugar or honey, in a bowl and pour over the ribs. Bring to a boil, then reduce heat to simmer. Cover and cook until meat is tender and liquid absorbed. Then uncover. Stir in sugar or honey and stir until dissolved. Serve hot.

If you prefer ribs with a heavier glaze, place in a moderately hot oven for a few minutes more.

Steak Encore

CHINA

This is an excellent "leftover" recipe. Chicken, roast, or any other meat may be used. Try various combinations of vegetables until you hit on the right combination for your family. Use any amount of meat to any amount of vegetables. Some prefer less meat and more vegetables, and others prefer more meat and fewer vegetables. You can use this recipe with any amount of leftover meat.

Steak, leftover cooked
Scallions or onions, chopped
Vegetables:
    Celery
    Green pepper
    Cauliflower
    Broccoli
    Water chestnuts
    Bamboo shoots
    Peas
    Pea pods
Salt to taste
Freshly ground pepper to taste
Soy sauce to taste

Slice leftover steak very thin. Set aside. Chop scallions or onions; add to the meat. Sauté any or all of the above vegetables in heated oil in skillet until just tender. (Pick the vegetables your family is fond of, or other vegetables you have on hand.) When the vegetables are almost done, add the meat and scallions or onions. Just before serving, season to taste with salt, pepper, and soy sauce.

Chinese Steak Fry

CHINA   Yield: 6 servings

1½ pounds boneless sirloin steak, cut into 1½-inch cubes
2 cloves garlic, minced
2 tablespoons soy sauce
2½ tablespoons dry sherry
2 teaspoons sugar
¼ teaspoon pepper
2 teaspoons cornstarch
¼ pound fresh mushrooms, sliced
½ cup drained bamboo shoots
6 ounces Chinese pea pods, thawed and patted dry
2 green onions, cut into 2-inch lengths
½ cup oil

Pound steak cubes lightly with blunt edge of kitchen knife. Combine soy sauce, 1 tablespoon sherry, 1 teaspoon sugar, pepper, and cornstarch. Pour over meat and mix well. Set aside for about 1 hour, mixing occasionally. Heat oil in wok or large skillet. Add steak cubes, cooking and stirring over high heat about 2-3 minutes. Remove steak and drain in a strainer. Pour off all but 3 tablespoons of the oil.

Heat oil remaining in pan. Add vegetables and cook 1 minute, stirring constantly. Add remaining 1 teaspoon of sugar and cook 1 more minute, stirring constantly. Add remaining 1½ tablespoons sherry and the steak. Continue to cook and stir about 2 more minutes.

Steak Japanese

JAPAN   Yield: 2 servings

2 filet mignon steaks, about 12 ounces each
2½ tablespoons soy sauce
1 can bean sprouts, or 8 ounces fresh
3 tablespoons butter
2 tablespoons lemon juice
Sugar
Black pepper
4 ounces mandarin oranges (canned)
4 tablespoons oil

Sprinkle 2 tablespoons of the soy sauce over steaks. Rub in; let steaks marinate for 1 hour. Meanwhile, drain bean sprouts; or, if using fresh bean sprouts, blanch them, rinse with cold water, then drain. Heat 2 tablespoons of the butter in a saucepan. Add bean sprouts; season with lemon juice, sugar, pepper, and ½ tablespoon soy sauce. Simmer for 5 minutes, then keep them warm.

In another small saucepan, heat remaining 1 tablespoon butter, add drained mandarin oranges, and heat through, about 2 minutes. Keep them warm.

In heavy skillet, heat oil over high heat until a light haze forms above it. Add steaks; quickly brown them on each side for about ½ minute. Lower heat; continue cooking steaks for about 10 minutes on each side.

Arrange steaks on preheated platter. Garnish with bean sprouts and mandarin oranges. Serve immediately.

Steak Kew

CHINA   Yield: 4 servings

14 ounces New York strip steak
1 tablespoon oil
2 cups bok choy, sliced
⅛ cup water chestnuts, sliced
⅛ cup bamboo shoots, sliced
½ cup Chinese black mushrooms
¼ pound snow pea pods, whole
1 teaspoon cooking sherry
⅛ teaspoon garlic, minced
1½ cups meat stock
½ teaspoon salt
1 teaspoon soy sauce
2 tablespoons cornstarch mixed with 2
   tablespoons cold water

Broil steak until it is ¾ done. Cut into bite-size pieces; set aside. Place oil in frying pan, stir in all vegetables with cooking sherry, minced garlic, and meat stock. Simmer for 4 minutes. Add steak, salt, and soy sauce. Stir in cornstarch mixture.

Chinese Stir-fried Beef and Mushrooms

CHINA   Yield: 6 to 8 servings

½ pound dried Chinese mushrooms
3 pounds lean steak, cut into thin
   strips
¼ cup flour
1 tablespoon sugar
½ cup sherry
½ cup soy sauce
¾ cup oil, divided
1 2-inch slice fresh gingerroot, minced
1 cup onions, chopped
2 cups beef bouillon
Salt to taste

Soak the mushrooms in water for 30 minutes. Drain well and set aside. Cut the steak into strips. In a bowl, combine flour, sugar, sherry, and soy sauce. Add the beef and marinate for 30 minutes, stirring frequently.

Heat ½ cup of the oil in a wok. Stir-fry the gingerroot for 1 minute. Add the beef with the marinade and stir-fry until the beef changes color. Remove the beef from the wok. Add the remaining oil to wok. Add the onions and stir-fry until almost tender. Add the mushrooms and stir-fry until soft. Place the beef in the wok and stir-fry for about 2 minutes. Add the bouillon, bring to a boil, and reduce heat. Add salt, cover, and cook for 2 minutes.

Stir-fried Beef Tenderloin with Vegetables

CHINA   Yield: 2 to 4 servings

4 dried Chinese mushrooms
¼ cup fresh snow peas (may use
   frozen)
1 teaspoon sugar
2 tablespoons soy sauce
1 tablespoon Chinese rice wine or pale
   dry sherry
2 teaspoons cornstarch
1 pound beef tenderloin, cut into
   1-inch cubes
3 tablespoons peanut oil or flavorless
   vegetable oil
6 water chestnuts, sliced ¼ inch thick
½ teaspoon salt
4 slices fresh gingerroot, about 1 inch
   in diameter and ⅛ inch thick

Soak mushrooms for 30 minutes in ½ cup of warm water. Cut the caps into quarters. Snap off the tips of fresh snow peas and blanch them in 1 quart of boiling water for 1 minute. Drain and run cold water over them. (Frozen snow peas need only be defrosted.)

Combine the sugar, soy sauce, wine, and cornstarch. Add the beef cubes and mix. Heat 1 tablespoon oil in wok. Add the mushrooms, snow peas, and water chestnuts and stir-fry for 2 minutes. Add salt. Remove the vegetables and set aside.

Pour remaining 2 tablespoons of oil in wok. Add the ginger and turn heat to high. Stir-fry the beef 2 to 3 minutes or until lightly browned. Discard the ginger. Return the vegetables to the wok and cook about 10 seconds. Serve at once.

Sukiyaki I

JAPAN   Yield: 4 servings

    1 pound rice
    1½ to 2 pounds beef tenderloin
    2 tablespoons bacon drippings
    ½ pound transparent or silver noodles
    8 dried mushrooms
    4 small onions
    4 leeks
    ¼ head white cabbage (about ½ pound)
    ½ pound fresh spinach
    1 pound canned bamboo shoots
    ½ pound bean sprouts

Sauce

    1 cup soy sauce
    6 tablespoons rice wine or sherry
    2 teaspoons sugar

    4 egg yolks

Cook rice according to directions; keep it warm.

Beef tenderloin must be cut into paper-thin slices. To achieve this, place meat in freezer for about 2 hours, or until partially frozen. You will then be easily able to slice it thin. Or, have the butcher slice it for you. Arrange meat slices on round platter, slightly overlapping. Place 2 tablespoons of bacon drippings (unmelted) into the middle, cover with aluminum foil, and refrigerate.

Place noodles and mushrooms into separate bowls. Cover with boiling water; soak for 20 minutes. Repeat procedure two more times. Drain; arrange in separate bowls.

Cut onions and leeks into thin slices. Place in separate bowls. Core cabbage, separate into individual leaves, and tear into bite-size pieces. Clean spinach; remove stems from leaves. Drain bamboo shoots, reserving liquid. Drain bean sprouts, if canned. If fresh, blanch, then rinse with cold water, and drain them.

To prepare sauce, bring soy sauce, rice wine or sherry, and sugar to a boil. Pour into sauce dish.

Place electric wok (or use frying pan on top of burner) in the middle of your table. Spoon rice into 4 individual bowls. Place slightly beaten egg yolks into 4 other small bowls. Now arrange all ingredients around the wok. Prepare the meal in portions; place one-fourth of bacon drippings into wok and heat, add one-fourth of meat slices and brown quickly. Push aside and pour some of the sauce over the meat. Add one-fourth of each of the vegetables and noodles and simmer for 3 minutes, while stirring constantly.

Each guest is given part of the cooked ingredients and starts eating while the second portion is being prepared. Cooked vegetables are dipped into raw egg yolk before being placed on plates. Sukiyaki is seasoned with sauce according to each individual's taste.

Sukiyaki II

JAPAN   Yield: 4 to 6 servings

3 tablespoons cooking oil
2 pounds sirloin steak, thinly sliced
  (1 inch × 2 inches)
2 tablespoons sugar
½ cup soy sauce
⅓ cup water
8-ounce can sliced bamboo shoots or
  Chinese mixed vegetables
1 cup celery, sliced
1 cup onion, thinly sliced
½ cup canned mushroom stems and
  pieces
11 ounces bean curd, cut in 1-inch
  cubes
¾ cup green onions and tops, cut in
  1-inch lengths
¾ cup watercress, sliced in 1-inch
  lengths

Preheat frying pan to 340°F. Add oil when hot. Add meat and brown lightly. Stir frequently (about 10 minutes). Combine sugar, soy sauce, and water. Add to meat, then blend. Bring to boil, cover, and then simmer 40 minutes or until meat is tender.

Add remaining ingredients, except green onions and watercress. Use liquid from canned vegetables. Over moderate heat (300°F), bring liquid to a boil, cover, and cook 5 minutes. Add green onions and watercress. Cook uncovered 1 minute longer, stirring. Serve at once, while vegetables are still crisp, over hot cooked rice.

Sukiyaki III

JAPAN   Yield: 2 servings

1 pound flank steak, thinly sliced
3 tablespoons oil

1 package fresh spinach
1 cup celery, diced
1 onion, thinly sliced
6 scallions
1 can water chestnuts
1 can mushrooms
1 can bean sprouts
⅓ cup soy sauce
Beef bouillon cube, in 1 cup water
2 tablespoons sugar

Brown meat in oil. Add all the vegetables and the soy sauce and cook 5 minutes. Add bouillon water. Simmer 15 minutes. Serve over cooked rice.

Sukiyaki IV

JAPAN   Yield: 5 to 6 servings

1½ pounds lean tender steak
Oil
2 large onions, peeled and sliced very
  thinly
2 cloves garlic, crushed
2 carrots, peeled and thinly sliced
6-8 leeks, cut into strips
1 can sliced bamboo shoots
1 small cabbage, very finely shredded
1 cup mushrooms, sliced

Sauce

4 tablespoons soy sauce
4 tablespoons dry sherry
2 teaspoons sugar
½ cup water

Heat all the sauce ingredients together in a small pan.

Slice the meat into very thin strips, about 1 inch wide and 2 inches long. Heat a little oil in a pan and just sear the meat on both sides.

Heat some more oil in a large pan, add onions and garlic, then carrots and leeks, and stir over high heat until the vegetables are well coated with the oil and beginning to soften. Add bamboo shoots, cabbage, and mushrooms, and cook for about 2 minutes stirring all the time.

Stir a little of the sauce into the vegetables, arrange the meat on top, and cook until the vegetables are tender, about 8-10 minutes.

Sukiyaki V

JAPAN   Yield: 4 servings

- 1½ to 2 pounds boneless beef sirloin (or top round)
- 2 tablespoons salad oil
- 2 medium carrots, cut diagonally into ⅛-inch slices
- ½ pound fresh mushrooms, washed, trimmed, and thinly sliced
- 8 green onions, cut into ⅛-inch pieces
- 3 large onions, thinly sliced
- 2 cups celery, cut diagonally into ¼-inch slices
- Water chestnuts, sliced
- 1 teaspoon instant beef bouillon
- 2 tablespoons sugar
- ⅓ cup soy sauce
- 6 cups frozen French-style green beans, thawed
- 3-4 cups hot cooked rice

Cut beef sirloin across the grain into ¼-inch slices, then into 2-inch strips. In large skillet, brown meat in hot oil. Push meat to one side. Place carrots, mushrooms, onions, celery, and water chestnuts in center of pan. Dissolve bouillon in water to make

about 2 cups, stir in sugar and soy sauce, and pour into skillet. Simmer uncovered 10 minutes, turning vegetables carefully.

Push vegetables and meat away from center of pan, add string beans, and simmer 5 minutes longer, turning vegetables occasionally. Serve with hot rice and, if desired, additional soy sauce.

Sukiyaki VI

JAPAN   Yield: 6 servings

- ½ cup bottled soy sauce
- 3 tablespoons sugar
- ¾ cup chicken broth, fresh, canned, or cubes
- ½ head Chinese cabbage or celery (approximately)
- ½ pound spinach (approximately)
- 1 bunch scallions
- 1 large onion
- ¼ pound fresh mushrooms
- 1 can water chestnuts
- 1 can bean sprouts
- 2 tablespoons salad oil
- 1 pound or more beef sirloin steak or tenderloin, thinly sliced

Combine soy sauce, sugar and broth. Cut cabbage in ½-inch diagonal slices. Cut up 3 cups of spinach. Cut scallions into 2-inch lengths. Cut onion into ¼-inch slices. Slice mushrooms and water chestnuts. Rinse bean sprouts with cold water.

Heat oil in large skillet; add all vegetables except spinach. Pour on sauce. Cook over medium heat for about 8 minutes. Put spinach and meat into mixture. Simmer together for 2 minutes. Then push down into sauce and cook from 5 to 10 minutes until meat is done. Serve over rice.

Meat

Sukiyaki VII

JAPAN   Yield: 4 servings

To cook sukiyaki outdoors, fill a hibachi with coals; let coals get red-hot before preparing your meal.

2 pounds beef tenderloin
½ pound transparent noodles
1 cup fresh mushrooms, sliced
4 small onions, thinly sliced
6 spring onions, thinly sliced
½ pound cabbage, chopped into bite-size pieces
½ pound spinach leaves, chopped
1 cup canned bamboo shoots, drained
2 cups canned bean sprouts, drained

Sauce

1 cup soy sauce
⅓ cup rice wine
1 tablespoon sugar
4 egg yolks
4 cups cooked rice
2 tablespoons bacon drippings

Cut beef tenderloin into paper-thin slices (beef is easier to cut when partially frozen). Place on serving platter. Cover; refrigerate.

Cover noodles with boiling water; soak 25 minutes. Repeat process 2 more times. Drain. Place in serving bowl. Arrange vegetables in serving bowls. Combine sauce ingredients; bring to boil. Pour into serving dish. Divide egg yolks into 4 serving bowls. Divide rice into 4 serving dishes.

Place hibachi with hot coals in center of picnic table. Place frying pan on top of hot coals. Arrange ingredients around wok, being sure each guest has a bowl of rice and a bowl of egg yolk.

Prepare meal in portions. Place ¼ of bacon drippings into pan; heat. Add ¼ of meat slices; brown quickly. Push to one side; pour a small amount of sauce over meat. Add ¼ of each vegetable; cook quickly, stirring constantly, about 4 minutes.

Dip cooked vegetables in egg yolk before serving to guests. Cook remaining food in same manner, serving each guest a portion of cooked food each time.

Sukiyaki VIII

JAPAN   Yield: 6 to 8 servings

3 pounds sirloin steak
¾ cup soy sauce
¾ cup beef broth
¼ cup dry sherry or sake
2 tablespoons sugar
¼ teaspoon freshly ground pepper
1 teaspoon MSG
Salt to taste
½ cup vegetable oil
1½ cups onions, sliced
¾ cup celery, sliced
1 cup bamboo shoots, sliced
1 cup fresh mushrooms, sliced
¾ cup green onions, sliced

Cut the steak into thin diagonal strips. Combine the soy sauce, broth, sherry, sugar, pepper, MSG, and salt in a small mixing bowl.

Heat the oil in a wok or deep skillet. Add the steak and stir-fry until browned. Push the steak to one side of the wok, then pour ½ cup of the soy sauce mixture over the steak. Add the sliced onions, celery, bamboo shoots, and mushrooms to the wok and stir-fry for 3 minutes. Pour the remaining soy sauce mixture over the celery mixture. Add the green onions and stir-fry for 3 minutes longer. The vegetables should be crisp-tender. Stir the steak into the vegetable mixture. Serve the Sukiyaki with thin, cooked noodles.

Thin strips of carrot and Chinese cabbage may be included in the celery mixture, if desired.

Beef Sukiyaki

JAPAN   Yield: 3 to 4 servings

2 pounds beef sirloin, cut into strips
1 large Bermuda onion
3 stalks celery
¼ pound fresh mushrooms
12 scallions
5 ounces canned water chestnuts
¼ pound fresh spinach
1 tablespoon oil
¾ cup beef bouillon
½ cup soy sauce
¼ cup vermouth
1 tablespoon sugar

Have the butcher cut the sirloin into thin strips, or, if you are cutting it, partially freeze it to make it easier to slice. Slice onion; put aside. Slice the celery at an angle into thin slices. Set aside. Thinly slice mushrooms; set aside. Slice scallions into approximately 1½-inch pieces. Drain the water chestnuts; slice in half. Wash the spinach; tear it into pieces. Arrange meat and vegetables on large platter.

Put oil into extra-large skillet or wok. Brown the meat; push to side of pan. Add all vegetables except spinach; stir in bouillon, soy sauce, vermouth, and sugar. Let sizzle for 5 minutes. Add spinach, cover, and cook 2 minutes more.

Serve sukiyaki with rice.

Stuffed Rolled Beef

PHILIPPINES   Yield: 6 to 8 servings

1 3-pound flank steak, in 1 piece
1½ teaspoons salt
½ teaspoon ground black pepper
2 tablespoons lemon juice
2 cloves garlic, peeled and crushed
2 sweet gherkin pickles
2 chorizo sausages
2 thick slices cooked ham
2 hard-boiled eggs, cut into quarters
2 tablespoons lard
2 tablespoons vinegar
3 ripe tomatoes, peeled and chopped
2 cups water

Begin at the thickest edge of the steak and make cuts in the meat, being careful not to cut all the way through. This will flatten the meat and almost double the size. Season this with salt, pepper, and lemon juice, and rub crushed garlic into the meat.

Slice pickles and chorizos the long way and slice the ham into strips. Arrange all of these ingredients plus the quartered eggs on top of the meat. Roll the meat around the ingredients and tie with a string.

In a large frying pan, heat the lard. Brown the meat on all of its outer surfaces, turning with tongs. If there is excess fat, drain. Add remaining ingredients and bring to a boil. Cover the pan, reduce heat, and simmer for 1¼ hours, until meat is tender. Lift out meat and place on a cutting board. Thicken sauce by bringing it to a rapid boil. Remove string from meat and slice into serving pieces. Serve with its own gravy.

Meat

Szechuan Beef

CHINA   Yield: 4 servings

 2 tablespoons vegetable oil
 1 or 2 green peppers, cut into ⅛-inch
   strips
 1 or 2 carrots, finely shredded into
   ⅛-inch, matchstick-size strips
   (sliced lengthwise, stack slices,
   slice lengthwise through stack)
 1 scallion, quartered lengthwise, then
   into 3-inch-long strips
 1 pound beef (round or chuck), cut
   into fine slivers or strips, ⅛ inch
   by 2 to 3 inches long
 2 tablespoons dry sherry
 2 tablespoons hoisin sauce
 1 tablespoon black bean sauce
 1 tablespoon vinegar
 1 teaspoon sugar
 ¼ to ½ teaspoon chili paste

Heat oil in the wok and stir-fry the green peppers, carrots, and scallion for 1 to 2 minutes. Push aside. Stir-fry the slivers of beef for 1 to 2 minutes and combine with the vegetables. Add the remaining ingredients. Stir and heat thoroughly. Serve at once with boiled rice.

Teriyaki I

JAPAN   Yield: 4 to 6 servings

 2 pounds sirloin steak ¼-inch thick
 1 tablespoon finely chopped fresh ginger or 2 teaspoons powdered ginger
 2 cloves garlic, finely chopped
 1 medium onion, finely chopped
 2 tablespoons sugar
 1 cup soy sauce
 ½ cup sherry

Cut the steak into thin slices or strips. Combine the ginger, garlic, onion, sugar, soy sauce, and sherry and pour the mixture over the meat. Let stand one to two hours.

Thread the meat on skewers and broil quickly on both sides over charcoal or in a preheated broiler. Serve hot.

Teriyaki II

JAPAN   Yield: 6 to 8 skewers

 2½-3 pounds sirloin steak, cut about
   ½-inch thick
 1 cup soy sauce
 ⅓ cup dry sherry
 4 tablespoons brown sugar
 1½ teaspoons ground ginger
 2 teaspoons onion, grated
 1 clove garlic, crushed
 18 chunks canned pineapple
 18 small mushroom caps
 2 tablespoons pineapple juice
 1 tablespoon cornstarch

Cut the steak into 1-inch squares. Mix together the soy sauce, sherry, sugar, ginger, onion, and garlic. Put in the meat and marinate for 3 hours.

Place the steak, pineapple, and mushrooms on the skewers, starting and finishing with a piece of meat. Cook for about 4-5 minutes or until the meat is cooked to your taste, turning once or twice to brown evenly.

Mix the pineapple juice slowly into the cornstarch, add the marinade, and cook, stirring constantly until the sauce thickens. Serve with the kabobs.

Teriyaki III

JAPAN   Yield: 4 to 6 servings

Teriyaki sauce

1 cup *mirin* (sweet sake) or 1 cup less
  2 tablespoons pale dry sherry
1 cup Japanese soy sauce
1 cup chicken stock

Teriyaki glaze

1¼ cup Teriyaki sauce
1 tablespoon sugar
2 teaspoons cornstarch mixed with 1
  tablespoon cold water

1½ pounds lean boneless beef, preferably tenderloin or boneless sirloin,
  cut in 12 slices, ¼ inch thick
4 teaspoons powdered mustard, mixed
  with just enough water to make a
  thick paste and set aside for 15
  minutes
12 sprigs fresh parsley

To make the sauce, warm the *mirin* or sherry in a 1½- to 2-quart enameled or stainless-steel saucepan over moderate heat. Take off the heat, ignite the *mirin* with a match, and shake the pan back and forth until the flame dies out. Then stir in the soy sauce and chicken stock, and bring to a boil. Pour the sauce into a bowl and cool to room temperature.

To make the glaze, combine ¼ cup of the Teriyaki sauce and 1 tablespoon of sugar in an enameled or stainless-steel saucepan. Bring almost to a boil over moderate heat, then reduce the heat to low. Stir the combined cornstarch and water into the sauce. Cook, stirring constantly, until it thickens to a clear syrupy glaze. Immediately pour into a dish and set aside.

Preheat the broiler to its highest point, or light a hibachi or charcoal grill. Dip the beef, 1 slice at a time, into the teriyaki sauce. Broil 2 inches from the heat for 1 minute on each side, or until lightly brown. For well-done meat, broil an additional minute.

To serve, slice the meat into strips 1-inch wide and place them on individual serving plates. Spoon a little of the glaze over each serving, and garnish each plate with a dab of the mustard and a sprig of parsley. If you prefer, mix the mustard into the glaze before pouring it over the meat.

Note: Any leftover Teriyaki sauce may be stored in tightly closed jars and refrigerated for as long as 1 month.

Teriyaki Kabobs

JAPAN   Yield: 6 servings

2 pounds round or chuck steak, cut
  ¾-inch thick
3 tablespoons Italian dressing
½ cup soy sauce
3 tablespoons white wine
2 tablespoons honey
½ teaspoon ground ginger
16 chunks of canned pineapple
8 kumquats, halved
8 mushrooms, halved
8 water chestnuts, halved

Cut steak into ¾-inch cubes and place in bowl or plastic bag. Combine Italian dressing, soy sauce, wine, honey, and ginger in saucepan. Simmer 10 minutes, stirring occasionally; cool. Pour over beef cubes, cover bowl or tie bag securely, and marinate in refrigerator 3 to 4 hours.

Remove cubes from marinade and thread on skewers, alternating each cube with a piece of pineapple, kumquat, mushroom, or water chestnut. Place kabobs on grill 3 to 4 inches from heat and broil, turning and brushing with marinade ocasionally 12 to 18 minutes to desired degree of doneness.

Meat

Teriyaki Beef Bites

JAPAN   Yield: About 3 dozen

1 pound beef tenderloin or filet, 1 inch
  thick
¼ cup sherry
¼ cup honey
¼ cup soy sauce
2 teaspoons lemon juice

Cut tenderloin into 1-inch cubes. Combine sherry, honey, soy sauce, and lemon
juice in deep bowl. Add meat and stir to
coat well. Marinate at least ½ hour. Spread
meat pieces apart in 12 × 8 × 2-inch baking
pan. Bake in 475°F oven 6 to 8 minutes.
Serve with wooden picks.

Steak Teriyaki

JAPAN   Yield: 4 servings

1½ pounds meat cubes (the cheaper
   the cut, the longer you marinate it)
½ cup brown sugar
½ cup soy sauce
½ teaspoon cinnamon
1 clove garlic, crushed
1 small can pineapple chunks, drained

Marinate meat in sugar, soy sauce, cinnamon, and garlic. Remove from sauce and
broil. While meat is broiling, add drained
pineapple chunks to sauce and cook. Return
meat to sauce and serve in chafing dish.

Teriyaki Steak I

JAPAN   Yield: 4 servings

4 boneless steaks, about ½ pound each

Marinade

1 clove garlic, finely minced
1 sugared or candied ginger, finely
  minced
1 tablespoon brown sugar
Salt
Pepper, freshly ground
½ cup rice wine or sherry
6 tablespoons soy sauce
½ cup white wine
Juice of half a lemon

Stuffed-tomato garnish

4 medium tomatoes
Salt
White pepper
4 tablespoons bean sprouts, canned or
  fresh (if using fresh bean sprouts,
  blanch, then rinse them with cold
  water before using)
1 tablespoon tomato catsup

Combine marinade ingredients in shallow
dish large enough to hold the steaks. Stir until well blended. Add steaks to marinade;
coat well. Marinate for 12 hours, turning
steaks frequently.

Drain steak; arrange on broiler pan. Place
under preheated broiler. Broil 4 minutes on
each side.

Meanwhile, remove stems from tomatoes;
cut off approximately ½-inch slices from bottoms. Scoop out seeds; discard. Sprinkle insides of tomatoes with salt and pepper. Place
bean sprouts and catsup into a small skillet.
Heat for 5 minutes. Spoon into tomatoes.

Arrange steaks on preheated serving platter. Garnish with stuffed tomatoes.

Teriyaki Steak II

JAPAN   Yield: 4 servings

¼ cup soy sauce
2 tablespoons onion flakes
1½ teaspoons liquid sweetener (equals ¼ cup sugar)
2 tablespoons vinegar
1 large clove garlic, quartered
2 teaspoons ginger
2 pounds steak, London broil, flank, or sirloin

In suitable container, combine all ingredients except steak to make marinade. Pour over steak and marinate at least 6 hours, turning occasionally. (Can also pour over frozen steak while defrosting in refrigerator). Cover tightly with plastic wrap. When ready to cook steak, broil in oven or over hot coals to desired degree of doneness.

Serve with rice and broccoli.

Teriyaki Tenderloin

JAPAN   Yield: 6 to 8 servings

½ cup dry sherry
¼ cup soy sauce
2 tablespoons dry onion soup
2 tablespoons brown sugar
3 pounds beef tenderloin
2 tablespoons water

Combine sherry, soy sauce, dry soup, and sugar. Place beef tenderloin in plastic bag with marinade, then in deep bowl. Chill 8 to 24 hours, occasionally pressing bag to side of meat to distribute marinade. Place meat in roasting pan and bake at 425°F for 1 hour and 15 minutes. Baste occasionally. Bring rest of marinade to boil with water. Serve over sliced beef.

Tomato Beef

CHINA   Yield: 2 to 3 servings

2 tablespoons cornstarch
1 tablespoon soy sauce
1 tablespoon brandy
½ pound flank steak, sliced ⅛ inch thick
2 tablespoons peanut oil
¼ cup onion, chopped
¼ cup celery, sliced diagonally
1 small green pepper, cut into 1-inch squares
2 tomatoes, each cut into 8 sections
¼ cup water chestnuts, sliced
1 cup chicken broth, heated
1½ teaspoons catsup
½ (scant) teaspoon salt
1 teaspoon sugar
1 tablespoon cornstarch mixed with about 3 tablespoons cold water

Mix together cornstarch, soy sauce, and brandy. Place sliced flank steak in mixture and marinate about 15 minutes. Heat oil in wok or pan. Add steak and stir-fry until golden brown. Remove from pan and set aside.

Sauté onion and celery for about 20 seconds, then add green pepper, tomatoes, and water chestnuts. Toss several times. Add broth, cover and let steam for 1 minute. Remove cover, add beef and mix well. Cover and steam for about 20 seconds. Add catsup, salt, and sugar; mix well. Thicken with cornstarch mixture. Don't let the sauce get too thick.

Tokyo Steak

JAPAN   Yield: 4 servings

Delicious with rice and stir-fried bean sprouts.

    Salt
    Ground ginger to taste
    Pepper to taste, freshly ground
    2 tablespoons rice wine or sherry
    4 filet mignon steaks, about 6 ounces
        each
    1½ tablespoons butter
    1 11-ounce can mandarin oranges
    1 tablespoon capers
    1 tablespoon butter, cut into small
        pieces

Combine salt, ginger, pepper, and rice wine (or sherry); blend well. Rub mixture onto steaks.

Heat 1½ tablespoons butter in heavy skillet. Add steaks; sauté 2 minutes on each side. Arrange mandarin oranges and capers on top of steaks; dot with remaining 1 tablespoon butter. Place skillet under preheated broiler; broil for 3 minutes. Serve steaks immediately on preheated plates.

Unusual Beef

CHINA   Yield: 2 servings

Marinade

    1 tablespoon sherry
    2 tablespoons soy sauce
    1 teaspoon cornstarch

    ½ pound lean beef, sliced and cut into
        bite-size pieces
    4 tablespoons oil
    3 cups potato chips
    1 cup snow peas, tips broken off
    Sprinkles of sherry

Blend marinade ingredients and marinate beef in mixture for 15 minutes. Heat oil to medium-high heat and stir-fry beef just until color changes. Add potato chips and snow peas and stir just until heated through, about 30 seconds. Sprinkle with sherry to taste and serve immediately.

Unusual Hamburgers

CHINA   Yield: 2 servings

    1 pound ground beef
    1 egg, beaten
    ¼ cup water chestnuts, finely chopped
    2 tablespoons onions, minced
    3 tablespoons mushrooms, minced
    ½ teaspoon MSG, optional
    ⅛ teaspoon freshly ground black
        pepper
    1 tablespoon oyster sauce

Mix ground beef with remaining ingredients. Shape into 2 patties, about ¾ inch thick. Broil about 4 inches from heat, for about 5 minutes. Turn and broil other side 4 to 5 minutes.

Wok Surprise

CHINA   Yield: 4 servings

    Oil for cooking
    1 cup green pepper, sliced
    1 cup celery, sliced diagonally
    1 cup zucchini, sliced
    2 cups leftover cooked roast beef,
        thinly sliced
    Beef gravy, beef broth, or chicken
        broth
    ½ cup fresh mushrooms, sliced
    2 cups fresh bean sprouts

2 cups fresh spinach, torn into bite-size
    pieces
Freshly ground black pepper to taste
Soy sauce to taste
Cornstarch mixed with cold water

Put small amount of oil in wok and heat to medium-high. Add green pepper and celery. Stir-fry for 1 minute. Add zucchini and stir-fry for 2 more minutes, or until the vegetables are bright in color and still crisp. Push vegetables up sides of wok (or remove) and place roast beef and a little gravy, beef broth, or chicken broth in wok, and toss meat until hot. Push meat up sides of wok and place mushrooms and bean sprouts in wok and stir-fry for 1 minute.

Add previously cooked vegetables, beef, spinach, pepper, and soy sauce. If desired, you may add a little cornstarch mixed with cold water to thicken the gravy. Serve with rice, if desired.

Calves Liver with Bean Sprouts

CHINA   Yield: 4 servings

3 tablespoons dry sherry
1 teaspoon gingerroot, grated
1 pound calves liver, cubed into bite-
    size pieces
2 tablespoons vegetable oil
¼ cup blanched, whole almonds
2 medium onions, finely chopped
¼ pound mushrooms, cut into cubes
1 cup fresh or frozen, defrosted peas
½ cup chicken or beef broth
2 tablespoons soy sauce
1 cup bean sprouts
1 tablespoon cornstarch in 2 table-
    spoons cold water

Combine the sherry and grated ginger in small bowl and add the cubed liver. Marinate for 20 to 30 minutes.

Heat the oil in the wok and stir-fry the almonds for 2 to 3 minutes, until browned. Remove from pan. Stir-fry the onions with the mushrooms 2 to 3 minutes. More oil may be necessary. Push aside. Stir-fry the peas 1 to 3 minutes. Push aside. Stir-fry the liver 2 to 3 minutes. Return the vegetables and almonds to the wok. Add the broth, soy sauce, and bean sprouts. Stir in the cornstarch mixture and heat until sauce becomes thick and clean and bean sprouts are heated through. Serve at once with rice.

Mandarin Liver

CHINA   Yield: 4 servings

1 pound liver (pork, baby beef, or
    calves)
2½ tablespoons flour
5 tablespoons safflower oil
Salt to taste
Pepper to taste
3 tablespoons soy sauce
2 tablespoons Chinese rice wine or
    sherry
2 large onions, thinly sliced
1 cup beef bouillon (from cubes)
1 red pepper, cut into strips
1 green pepper, cut into strips
½ pound savoy cabbage, cut into strips
6 ounces fresh bean sprouts
1 small can bamboo shoots (ap-
    proximately 6 ounces)

Pat liver dry with paper towels; cut into thin slices. Coat with flour. Heat oil in a heavy skillet. Add liver; brown on all sides; remove. Season to taste with salt and pepper. Set aside; keep warm.

Add soy sauce, wine, and onions to pan drippings; simmer 5 minutes. Pour in beef bouillon. Add red and green peppers and cabbage; simmer 10 minutes. Vegetables should still be crisp. Add bean sprouts, bamboo shoots, and

Spiced Braised Liver

MALAYSIA   Yield: 4 servings

 1 pound calves' liver
 3 tablespoons oil
 1 medium onion, peeled and finely
    sliced
 2 cloves garlic, peeled and finely
    chopped
 1 teaspoon fresh ginger, finely grated
 1½ teaspoons ground coriander
 ½ teaspoon ground cumin
 ½ teaspoon salt
 ¼ teaspoon ground black pepper
 2 tablespoons dark soy sauce
 ⅓ cup water

Use a sharp knife to slice the liver very
thin. Drain on paper towels and set aside.

Using a heavy skillet, heat the oil. Fry
the onion, garlic, and ginger on medium
heat for 5 minutes, until golden. Add liver
slices in single layers. Sprinkle with
coriander, cumin, salt, and pepper. Fry each
side of liver for 2 minutes. Last, add soy
sauce and water and simmer for about 5
minutes, until liver is cooked but not hard.
Remove to heated platter and serve at once.

Apricot Tongue

CHINA   Yield: 4 servings

 1 beef tongue
 Water
 ¼ cup soy sauce
 2 cloves garlic, cut

Sauce

 ⅔ cup brown sugar
 ¾ cup catsup

 ¼ teaspoon fresh gingerroot, grated, or
 ½ teaspoon powdered ginger
 1 tablespoon soy sauce
 1 package dried apricots

Place tongue in large pot. Add water to
cover. Mix in ¼ cup soy sauce and garlic.
Bring to boil and simmer until tongue is
tender.

To make sauce, combine all ingredients
in saucepan and simmer slowly until apricots
are soft. Pour sauce over sliced tongue.

Red-Stewed Beef Tongue

CHINA   Yield: About 4 servings

 1 beef tongue
 Boiling water to cover meat
 ½ clove garlic
 1 tablespoon oil
 2 tablespoons cooking wine
 2 tablespoons dark soy sauce per pound
    of meat
 1 teaspoon sugar per pound of meat

Immerse the tongue completely in boiling
water, turn off the heat, and let soak for 1
minute. Remove the tongue from the water
and use a blunt knife to peel off the skin.

Brown the garlic in oil in a wok, then
brown the tongue on both sides. Lower the
heat and add the cooking wine. For each
pound of tongue, add 2 tablespoons dark soy
sauce. Cook over low heat for 1½ to 2
hours. Turn the tongue at 20-minute intervals. Add water to maintain the quantity of
cooking liquid at 6 to 8 tablespoons. During
the last 20 minutes, add 1 teaspoon of sugar
per pound and serve.

Meat

Beef and Pork Balls

PHILIPPINES   Yield: 4 servings

½ pound ground pork
½ pound ground beef
1 teaspoon salt
¼ teaspoon pepper
1 small egg, beaten
1½ tablespoons oil
2 cloves garlic, peeled and finely
  chopped
1 medium onion, peeled and finely
  chopped
2 ripe tomatoes, diced
4 cups broth
2 teaspoons soy sauce

Mix meats, salt, pepper, and egg in a bowl. Roll into small balls about 1½ inches in diameter.

In a deep pan, heat oil and fry garlic and onion until golden. Add tomatoes and stir-fry until soft. Add broth and bring to a boil. Put in meatballs one at a time and let them simmer slowly until cooked through. Add soy sauce and serve at once.

Beef and Pork with Bean Sprouts

CHINA   Yield: 4 servings

½ pound beef (chuck or round), finely
  chopped
½ pound pork (butt or shoulder),
  finely chopped
2 tablespoons soy sauce
1 tablespoon vinegar
1 clove garlic, peeled and grated
1 teaspoon gingerroot, grated
2 tablespoons vegetable oil

¼ to ½ cup green beans, cut into
  1-inch pieces
¼ pound mushrooms, sliced into "T"
  shapes
1 cup bean sprouts
½ tablespoon cornstarch in ½ cup
  chicken or beef broth

Marinate beef and pork in combined soy sauce, vinegar, garlic, and gingerroot for 20 to 30 minutes.

Heat oil in wok or skillet. Stir-fry beans 2 to 3 minutes; push up to sides. Stir-fry mushrooms 2 to 3 minutes; push up to sides. Additional vegetable oil may be needed. Stir-fry sprouts 1 to 2 minutes; push up to sides. Stir-fry beef and pork 3 to 4 minutes, until well done. Return vegetables to center of the pan with the meat. Add cornstarch mixture; heat until the sauce is thickened and clear. Serve at once with rice.

Chinese Rolls

CHINA   Yield: Approximately 4 servings

1 pound lean pork shoulder, ham, or
  beef, cut into slices
1 teaspoon salt
¼ teaspoon pepper
½ to 1 tablespoon aniseed
2 tablespoons butter or margarine for
  frying
Juice from 1 large orange
1 tablespoon soy sauce
3 to 4 tablespoons chili sauce

Flatten the meat slices on a cutting board and season them with salt, pepper, and aniseed. Roll up the slices with a toothpick. Brown the rolls all around in browned butter or margarine and transfer them to a wok. Boil a few tablespoons of water in the frying pan and pour the gravy over the rolls. Add orange juice and soy sauce, bring to a boil, and let rolls simmer under cover for 25 to 30 minutes. Add the chili sauce toward the end of the cooking period. Serve with boiled rice.

191

Chop Suey I

CHINA   Yield: 4 servings

3 cups cooked meat
3 cups rich broth
3 cups cabbage, cut into large chunks
1 cup celery
1 cup onion
2 tablespoons brown gravy sauce
2 tablespoons soy sauce
2 cans drained chop suey vegetables
½ teaspoon salt and pepper
½ teaspoon celery salt
2 tablespoons flour, (for thickening)
1 large can chow mein noodles

Put meat, broth, cabbage, celery, onion, and brown gravy sauce into large pot and steam until vegetables are tender. Add soy sauce, chop suey vegetables, salt, pepper, and celery salt. Thicken with flour. Serve over fried rice or white rice. Sprinkle with chow mein noodles.

Chop Suey II

CHINA   Yield: 4 to 6 servings

¼ cup oil
1 cup onions, cubed
1 cup Chinese celery, cubed
1 teaspoon salt
⅛ teaspoon pepper
1 cup water
2 cans bean sprouts, drained in cold
    water
4 cups leftover beef, chicken, turkey,
    veal, pork, or 1½ pounds cooked
    shrimp
2 tablespoons cornstarch
2 tablespoons soy sauce
1 teaspoon sugar

Combine oil, celery, onions, salt, pepper, and a cup of hot water in large pan and cook for about 5 minutes. Add bean sprouts and beef. Dissolve cornstarch in ⅓ cup cold water, and add remaining ingredients. Mix well. Simmer for about 10 minutes. Serve over chow mein noodles and rice.

Cold Beef or Lamb Curry with Mayonnaise

INDIA   Yield: 4 servings

4 cups cooked cold rice
4 eggs, hard boiled
2-3 cups cold meat curry with sauce
4 tomatoes
2 boiled cold potatoes
Any leftover peas, beans, carrots, or
    other vegetables
1 lemon

Quick Mayonnaise

¾ teaspoon salt
¼ teaspoon pepper
1 teaspoon dry mustard
1½ teaspoons sugar
1 egg
1 cup salad oil
2 teaspoons lemon juice
2 teaspoons wine vinegar
1-2 tablespoons boiling water

Put rice into a deep dish. Cut eggs into quarters and arrange on the rice. Spoon over half of the curry. Make a layer on top with sliced tomatoes and potatoes and leftover vegetables, and spoon over remaining curry.

Make mayonnaise: Put salt, pepper, mustard, and sugar in blender. Add egg and mix thoroughly at a low speed. Add a few drops of oil and mix in well. Then add the rest of the oil in a steady stream until it has been absorbed and the mayonnaise is very thick. Add lemon juice, vinegar, and lastly boiling water, which thins it and helps to make it keep, if not to be used immediately. Let cool.

Pour mayonnaise over cold curry and serve with slices of lemon.

Fried Meatballs

THAILAND   Yield: About 30 small balls

¼ pound chopped beef
¼ pound chopped pork
¼ teaspoon ground black pepper
½ teaspoon ground nutmeg
2 tablespoons fresh coriander leaves, finely chopped
4 cloves garlic, peeled and crushed
½ teaspoon salt
1 spring onion, finely chopped
2 teaspoons fish sauce
1 tablespoon beaten egg
½ cup or more flour
Lard for frying

Mix beef and pork in a bowl. If pork is lean, add 1 tablespoon finely diced pork fat. Mix the meat with all ingredients except the flour and lard. Form into small balls, rolling between your palms. Roll each ball in flour generously. Heat fat on medium heat. Fry meatballs for about 5 minutes or until golden brown and cooked through. Drain on paper towels and serve.

Kabobs Kati

INDIA   Yield: 4 to 6 servings

Marinade

2 cups yogurt
Juice of 1 lemon
2 onions, peeled and grated
1 clove garlic, peeled and finely chopped
Salt to taste
2 fresh pepper pods, finely chopped
1 teaspoon curry
½ teaspoon ground ginger
1 pound beef fillet
1 pound lamb
3 tablespoons oil
Parsley for garnish

Mix yogurt and lemon juice in a large bowl. Add onion, garlic, salt, and pepper pods. Stir in the curry and ginger and mix well.

Notch the meat deeply—but do not cut through—into cubes. Place meat in yogurt mixture, cover and let stand for 1 hour. Remove meat and allow to drain. Cut into cubes. Place on four skewers and brush with oil. Put skewers into rotating mechanism or place them on grill so that handles can be turned to brown meat on all sides. Grill for 30 minutes. Place meat on platter. Garnish with parsley and serve.

Japanese Fondue

JAPAN   Yield: 4 servings

1 pound beef, cut into cubes
8 ounces hot dogs
4 pimientos
½ pound mushrooms
4 small onions
Oil for deep-frying

Sauces

Worcestershire sauce
Lemon juice
Mayonnaise
Catsup

Cut beef into cubes; set aside. Cut hot dogs into bite-size pieces; set aside. Cut pimientos into 2 or 3 pieces. Leave mushrooms whole. Slice onions into wide rings. Arrange all ingredients on platter.

Heat oil in fondue pot or wok set on table. Using fondue forks, pick up one ingredient at a time; deep-fry until done. Eat beef with any of the above sauces.

Cantonese Casserole

CHINA   Yield: 4 servings

1 10-ounce package frozen French-cut green beans
1 tablespoon butter
1 tablespoon flour
¾ cup milk
2 tablespoons soy sauce
1 cup sour cream
2 cups cooked ham, diced
1 5-ounce can water chestnuts, sliced
½ cup buttered bread crumbs

Cook beans briefly (they should remain crisp.) Melt butter; blend flour. Stir in milk and soy sauce and simmer until thick. Add sour cream, ham, green beans, and water chestnuts. Pour into baking dish and sprinkle with crumbs and paprika. Bake at 350°F until hot and bubbly.

Ham-Chicken Kabobs

JAPAN   Yield: 4 servings

½ pound chicken fillets
   (1 boneless, skinless breast)
½ pound ready-to-eat, cured ham steak
2 fresh zucchini
1 cup unsweetened pineapple chunks, drained (reserve juice)
¾ cup pineapple juice (from canned pineapple)
3 tablespoons Japanese soy sauce
1 tablespoon salad oil
1 teaspoon cornstarch

Cut chicken and ham into 1½-inch cubes. Quarter each zucchini lengthwise and cut into 1-inch chunks. Alternate ham, chicken, zucchini, and pineapple on skewers.

Combine remaining ingredients in a jar. Cover and shake up. Pour over skewers in a shallow pan. Rotate skewers to coat food. Broil 5 minutes each side, basting often with the soy mixture in the pan.

Cantonese Kabobs

CHINA   Yield: 4 servings

½ cup soy sauce
½ cup maraschino cherry juice
½ cup red wine
¼ cup apple-blossom honey

1 teaspoon ginger
2 teaspoons garlic powder
¼ cup olive oil
4 pounds lamb riblets

Combine all ingredients except lamb. Pour over lamb; marinate 24 hours.

Drain riblets; place on skewers. Grill over hot coals 45 to 60 minutes, turning and basting frequently during cooking period.

Chinese-style Lamb

CHINA   Yield: About 4 servings

2-pound boneless leg of lamb
Salt and pepper
2 tablespoons vegetable oil
1 small, sliced onion
2 large carrots, sliced
1 tablespoon corn syrup
3 tablespoons tomato catsup
1 tablespoon soy sauce or Worcestershire sauce
1 tablespoon juice from pineapple rings
8-ounce can pineapple rings
1 bunch spring onions

Remove and discard excess fat from the meat. Cut the meat into 1-inch cubes. Season well with salt and pepper.

Heat the oil in a wok. Gently fry the lamb, onion, and sliced carrots until golden. Add the syrup, catsup, soy or Worcestershire sauce, and 1 tablespoon of juice from the pineapple rings.

Drain the pineapple rings and cut them in half. Wash the spring onions and cut off some of the green part.

Cover pan with tightly fitting lid and simmer very gently for 45 minutes or until the lamb is very tender. Add the pineapple and spring onions about 5 minutes before the

end of cooking time. Serve with boiled rice, mixed with peas and, if you like, bean sprouts.

Hot Spicy Lamb with Peppers Szechuan Style

CHINA   Yield: 4 servings

1 pound lean lamb, cut from leg
    (lean pork or beef may be used)
3 tablespoons soy sauce
¼ cup dry sherry or other white wine
1 clove garlic, minced, optional
¾ cup pineapple juice, unsweetened
2 bell peppers (1 green, 1 red)
4 small onions, or 1 large Spanish onion
1 cup tomato juice
1 to 2 tablespoons liquid hot pepper sauce
¾ cup cold water, divided
1 tablespoon cornstarch

Trim fat and bone from lamb and cut the meat into 1-inch cubes. Combine with soy sauce, sherry, garlic, and pineapple juice in a nonmetallic bowl. Cover and refrigerate all day or overnight.

At dinner time, seed peppers and cut into 1-inch squares. Peel onions and cut in half. Cut each half into quarters, then separate. (Or peel and slice 1 large onion into chunks.)

Drain lamb and reserve marinade. Spray a large nonstick skillet or electric frying pan with cooking spray for no-fat frying. Sauté lamb cubes with no fat added until lightly browned. When brown, drain fat, if any, add reserved marinade, tomato juice, hot pepper sauce, and onions.

Cover and simmer 4 to 5 minutes, until lamb is cooked through and vegetables are tender-crisp. Combine cornstarch with remaining water and stir into pan. Cook and stir until sauce is thick.

Indian Curried Lamb Chops

INDIA   Yield: 4 servings

8 rib lamb chops
6 tablespoons butter
1 cup long-grain rice
1 small can clear consommé
1 tablespoon plus ½ teaspoon gelatin
2 onions
1 tablespoon curry powder (or paste)
1 tablespoon flour
2 cups stock
1 teaspoon shredded coconut
1 teaspoon red currant jelly
A little lemon juice
1 lemon
1 tomato
1 hard-boiled egg, optional
1 cucumber

Trim the bones of the chops and scrape clean. Melt 3 tablespoons of butter and fry the chops for about 4 minutes on each side. Lay out on a dish, put a baking sheet on top with a weight, and let cool. Cook the rice and let cool. Dissolve ½ teaspoon of the gelatin in the consommé and let cool.

Melt 3 tablespoons of butter and cook sliced onions until soft and golden. Add curry powder and cook for 1 minute. Add flour, cook 1 minute; add stock and bring to boil. Add coconut and simmer for 15 minutes. Now add jelly and lemon juice, and cook for a few minutes. Strain sauce, return to pan, and add remaining gelatin. Dissolve it adding salt and pepper to taste and let cool.

Place cold chops on a wire cake rack and spoon the setting curry sauce over one side of the chops. Leave to set. At this stage the chops can be decorated with pieces of lemon and tomato (or cold hard-boiled egg whites cut into shapes). The decorations are kept in place by the consommé, which is now spooned over each chop. Let set.

Arrange the cold rice in the center of a dish, stand the chops around, bones upwards. These can be decorated with paper frills if available. Chop any remaining jellied consommé and arrange around the edge. Decorate the dish with slices of lemon, tomato, and cucumber.

Kabobs

INDIA   Yield: 4 to 6 servings

2 quarts salted water
1 pound lamb, ground
2 small potatoes, cooked in jackets, peeled and mashed
1 onion, peeled and grated
1 small green pepper pod, finely chopped
½ bunch parsley, chopped
1 teaspoon mustard
1 teaspoon curry
1 teaspoon salt
4 tablespoons rice flour
Oil for frying

When salted water has come to a boil, place ground lamb in a kitchen strainer and submerge the meat in the water for 2 minutes. Drain and place in a mixing bowl.

Add mashed potatoes to meat with onion, pepper, and parsley. Season with mustard, curry, and salt. Mix well.

Run cold water over your hands and then roll the meat mixture into small balls. Put each ball into rice flour, then fry in heated oil for 5 to 7 minutes. Remove from the pan and drain on paper towels, then serve.

Lamb and Cabbage Oriental Style

CHINA   Yield: 4 servings

1 pound lean lamb, cut from leg (lean pork or beef may be substituted)
¼ cup soy sauce
2 tablespoons dry sherry or other white wine
1 small head of cabbage, about 1 pound
1½ cups tomato juice
2 tablespoons catsup
1 cup water
1 tablespoon cornstarch

Trim fat and bone from lamb. Cut the meat into thin strips, about 2 inches long. Combine the meat in a bowl with soy sauce and wine. Cover and refrigerate all day.

At dinner time, drain the meat and reserve the marinade. Quarter the cabbage and remove the core. Slice cabbage into thick shreds, about half-inch wide. Then, slice shreds in the opposite direction, so the cabbage is in 2-inch strips.

Spray a large nonstick skillet or electric frying pan with cooking spray for no-fat frying. Sauté the lamb strips over high heat with no fat added, until lightly browned.

When brown, add the cabbage, tomato juice, catsup, reserved marinade, and ½ cup water. Cover and cook 4 to 5 minutes, until lamb is cooked through and cabbage is tender crunchy. Stir cornstarch and reserved half cupful of water together until blended, then stir into the skillet. Cook and stir over moderate heat until sauce simmers and thickens. Serve immediately.

Lamb Curry I

INDIA   Yield: 4 servings

1½ pounds lean lamb
3 tablespoons oil
1 large onion, finely sliced
2 stalks of celery, finely sliced
1½ tablespoons curry powder
2 teaspoons curry paste
1½ tablespoons flour
1 cup stock, warmed
1 apple, peeled and diced
2 tablespoons sultana raisins
2 tablespoons chutney
Salt to taste
1 bay leaf
2 tablespoons shredded coconut
Juice of ½ lemon
1 dessert spoon jam or jelly

Cut the meat into cubes and brown quickly all over in oil. Put into a casserole and keep warm. Cook the onion and celery in the hot oil for 2-4 minutes. Add curry powder and paste, and cook for 2 minutes. Add flour and cook for 1 minute. Stir in the warmed stock and stir until smooth. Bring to a boil and cook for 2-3 minutes. Add apple, raisins, chutney, salt, and bay leaf. Pour over meat and cook over gentle heat for 1 hour, stirring occasionally. By this time the meat should be tender.

While meat is cooking, pour ¼ cup of boiling water over the coconut and let stand for 30 minutes. When the meat has been cooking for 50 minutes, add strained juice of coconut to the meat with the lemon juice and jam or jelly. Continue cooking for 10 minutes.

When cooked, serve with plenty of plain boiled rice, chutney, quartered lemon, shredded coconut, sliced bananas, and grated cucumber in yogurt.

Lamb Curry II

INDIA   Yield: 8 servings

3 pounds lean lamb, cut in cubes
Burgundy wine
½ cup flour
1 tablespoon hot curry powder
2 teaspoons sea salt
⅓ teaspoon black pepper
1 cup onions, diced
3 cloves garlic, minced
2 red apples, peeled, cored, and sliced
2 red apples, unpeeled, cored, and
  chopped
1 cup raisins
1 14-ounce can beef broth

Dampen lamb cubes with Burgundy. Mix flour and curry powder in bowl. Coat meat with flour mixture and place in bottom of crock pot. Sprinkle with salt and pepper. Pour mixture of onions, garlic, apples, and raisins over meat. Pour broth over mixture and stir to mix. Cover and cook on low setting 8 to 12 hours. Serve over white rice with chutney on the side.

Lamb Stew

INDONESIA   Yield: 6 to 8 servings

Although very meaty, this is fairly liquid stew and should be served over rice.

4 kemiri, chopped
1 small onion, peeled and chopped
3 cloves garlic, peeled and chopped
2 teaspoons coriander powder
1 teaspoon ginger powder
½ teaspoon turmeric powder
Pinch of white pepper
Pinch of cayenne pepper
Pinch of chili powder

Pinch of laos powder
2 tablespoons vegetable oil
2 pounds boneless leg or shoulder of
  lamb, cubed small
1 teaspoon brown sugar
¼ cup tamarind water
Salt to taste
1 sereh stalk, bruised
1 small cinnamon stick
3 whole cloves
1 salam leaf, optional
2 cups water
2 cups thick santen (coconut milk)

Make a smooth paste of kemiri, onion, and garlic. Add spices in order given and mix well.

Heat oil in a heavy pan. Stirring constantly, fry the spice paste for 1 minute. Add the lamb and stir-fry for 2 minutes. Stir in brown sugar, tamarind water, and salt to taste. Cover and simmer for 4 minutes.

Add all remaining ingredients except the santen. Simmer, covered, for 20 minutes. Last, pour in the santen, cover, and simmer for 25 minutes more, stirring occasionally. Remove the sereh, cinnamon, cloves, and salam leaf. Pour the stew into a deep serving dish and serve at once.

Lamb with Saffron Rice

INDIA   Yield: 4 to 6 servings

4 cups water
1 cup long-grain rice
1 teaspoon salt
3 tablespoons boiling water
¼ teaspoon saffron threads
6 tablespoons oil
2 onions, peeled and finely chopped
½ teaspoon chopped caraway
¼ teaspoon yellow ginger

1 pound lean ground lamb
Salt to taste
1 bunch parsley, chopped
¼ teaspoon fennel seed
1 cup chicken broth

Bring water to a boil. Add salt and stir in rice. Boil uncovered for 10 minutes. Drain.

Meanwhile, pour 3 tablespoons boiling water over saffron threads in a cup. Let sit for 10 minutes.

Heat 3 tablespoons oil in a skillet. Fry onions for 3 minutes. Sprinkle with caraway and ginger. Stir for 1 minute more. Add ground lamb and season with salt. Fry for 10 minutes, stirring to prevent sticking. Remove from the range. Mix chopped parsley into it.

Heat remaining oil in a fire-proof casserole. Stir in fennel and drained rice. Cook for 2 minutes. Add saffron threads with their liquid and mix well. Remove from heat.

Remove ⅔ of saffron rice mixture from casserole. Spread the remaining evenly on the bottom. Cover with half the ground lamb. Add a layer of rice, the remaining meat, and then the remaining rice. Carefully pour chicken broth over all. Return to stove and allow to come to a boil. Then remove and cover casserole. Place in a 350°F oven for 25 minutes. When rice is soft and liquid absorbed, remove from oven. Fluff the surface with a fork and serve at once.

Lamb with Spinach

INDIA   Yield: 6 servings

3 onions, thinly sliced
3 pounds lean lamb, cut into 2½-inch squares
1½ teaspoons turmeric
1 tablespoon whole coriander
4 teaspoons powdered ginger

1½ pounds spinach, finely shredded
3 tablespoons yogurt
¼ teaspoon thyme
4 teaspoons mustard seeds
1 teaspoon salt
¼ cup water

Sauté onions in butter. Add meat, turmeric, coriander, and ginger. Mix well and cook over medium heat 10-12 minutes. Add spinach, yogurt, thyme, mustard seeds, and salt. Mix well, cover, and cook for 30 minutes, shaking the pan several times. After first 15 minutes of cooking, add ¼ cup water. Spinach should be a thick puree completely mixed with the meat. Finished dish should have no moisture.

Marinated and Broiled Lamb Chops

JAPAN   Yield: 4 servings

4 lamb chops, each about 1½ inches thick

Marinade

½ cup soy sauce
½ cup water
2 cloves garlic, minced
1 tablespoon freshly grated gingerroot or 1½ teaspoons ground ginger

Put lamb chops in a dish large enough to hold them and the marinade. Mix together soy sauce, water, garlic, and ginger. Blend well. Pour marinade over chops. Marinate overnight in refrigerator.

Let chops come to room temperature, place on broiler pan, and brush with marinade. Broil about 5 minutes, then turn and brush with additional marinade; broil for about 3 more minutes or until desired brownness is reached.

Boil and strain the remainder of the marinade. Serve it with the chops, along with rice, if desired. This can also be cooked on grill or hibachi.

Meat

Skewered Lamb

INDIA   Yield: 6 servings

 2 pounds lamb, preferably from the leg,
  cubed
 1 teaspoon ground caraway
 1 teaspoon salt
 White pepper to taste
 Pinch of saffron
 ½ teaspoon ground ginger
 1 clove garlic, peeled and crushed
 ½ bunch parsley, chopped
 6 onions, peeled
 2 cups sour cream
 ¼ pound bacon
 1 tablespoon ground caraway
 1 tablespoon ground black pepper

In a bowl, put 1 teaspoon caraway, salt, pepper, saffron, ginger, garlic and parsley. Finely chop 1 onion and add to the spices with the sour cream. Mix well. Add the meat and cover. Refrigerate for at least 2 hours.

Quarter remaining onions and cut bacon into ½-inch pieces. Set aside.

When ready to cook, remove meat from marinade, reserving the liquid. Place meat on skewers, alternating with onion pieces and bacon. Grill for 45 minutes, turning frequently and basting with marinade. Dish on a preheated platter and sprinkle with caraway and pepper.

Almond-Sprinkled Pork Stew

CHINA   Yield: Approximately 4 servings

 1 pound sliced pork shoulder
 ½ teaspoon paprika powder
 1 teaspoon curry

 2 tablespoons flour
 2 cups bouillon
 2 onions
 1 green and 1 red paprika
 1 cup celery root, grated
 1 apple (not sweet), grated
 ½ cup almonds
 Soy sauce

Cut pork in fine strips and brown slightly in a frying pan or wok. Remove to casserole. Sprinkle paprika powder, curry, flour and hot bouillon over the pork while stirring briskly. Brown small wedges of onion, strips of paprika, celery, and apple in the frying pan and add to pork. Cook on slow heat or simmer tightly covered for about 25 minutes. Add liquid, if necessary, and season to taste. Halve the almonds and brown slightly in a small amount of oil. Serve with soy sauce over rice.

Oriental Pork Stew

CHINA   Yield: 4 servings

 1 pound cooked pork, cut into bite-size
  pieces
 1 leek or 2 scallions, sliced
 1 small head of cabbage, sliced into
  ¼-inch slices

Marinade

 2 tablespoons vegetable oil
 2 tablespoons soy sauce
 1 teaspoon ginger, grated
 ½ teaspoon garlic salt
 8- to 10-ounce can pineapple slices (4
  or 5 slices), cut into pieces
 Syrup from drained pineapple slices

Combine the ingredients for the marinade in a small bowl. Add pork, cover, and marinate a few hours in the refrigerator. Pour the meat and marinade into the wok or saucepan. Add the scallions and cabbage. Simmer for 30 minutes. Serve with boiled rice.

Baked Spring Rolls with Cabbage

CHINA   Yield: 4 to 6 servings

9 ounces white cabbage
2 tablespoons vegetable oil
1 tablespoon soy sauce
1 teaspoon salt
¼ teaspoon pepper
9 ounces pork, minced (about 1 cup)
1 green onion, minced
Batter for 12 to 16 crepes

Slice the cabbage into fine strips and fry in oil until partially soft. Add the soy sauce, salt, and pepper, and cook 2 minutes more. In a separate pan, fry the pork with the green onion until done. Mix with cabbage.

Fry crepes on one side only. When done, place filling on browned side of crepes. Wrap up like a parcel. Place crepes in a lightly greased ovenproof dish and brush with soy sauce and oil. Bake in oven at 400°F for about 15 minutes.

Spring Rolls Fried in Oil

CHINA   Yield: 4 servings

1 can bean sprouts
Vegetable oil for deep-fat frying
6 ounces pork, minced (about ¾ cup)
1 large onion, minced

1 can bamboo shoots, thinly sliced
1½ tablespoons soy sauce
1 teaspoon freshly ground black pepper
Batter for 16 crepes
1 egg white or 2 tablespoons flour and ¼ cup water

Rinse bean sprouts in cold water; drain well. Heat 1½ tablespoons vegetable oil in pan and fry pork and onion for about 4 minutes. Add bean sprouts, bamboo shoots, soy sauce, and pepper. Fry for 2 minutes while stirring.

Make crepes, frying on one side only. Distribute the filling on the fried side of the crepes. Fold in sides and roll up like small parcels. Seal with egg white or with flour stirred in a small amount of water. Deep-fat fry in oil at 400°F until golden brown. Drain on paper towels. Serve immediately with soy sauce and a large green salad.

Boiled Pork

KOREA   Yield: 4 to 6 servings

2 pounds pork
3½ cups boiling water
2 teaspoons salt
¼ cup soy sauce

Vinegar soy sauce

½ cup soy sauce
1 tablespoon sugar
3 tablespoons vinegar

Place pork and salt in a pot with boiling water. Simmer until almost tender, at least 1 hour. Add the soy sauce and simmer for another 20 minutes. Remove pork from broth and allow to cool. Then slice thin and serve with vinegar soy sauce.

To make the sauce, combine ingredients listed above in a bowl, stirring until all sugar has dissolved. Adjust sugar and vinegar to your personal taste.

Cantonese Pork

CHINA   Yield: 4 servings

1 pound lean pork
1 cup flour
1 cup cornstarch
⅓ teaspoon baking powder
2½ teaspoons salt
1 tablespoon plus 1 teaspoon catsup
Cooking oil
1 green pepper, sliced
1 cup pineapple chunks
1 cup onion, sliced
6 tablespoons sugar
½ cup vinegar
1 cup water
1 cup celery, sliced
Cornstarch

Cut pork into small strips about ½ inch by ¼ inch by ½ inches. Mix batter of flour, 1 cup cornstarch, baking powder, ½ teaspoon salt, and 1 teaspoon catsup with enough water to make it the proper consistency.

Dip pork strips in batter and fry in oil heated to 350°F for 6 or 7 minutes. Place fried pork in saucepan, add all the remaining ingredients except the cornstarch, and cook over a hot flame until the mixture boils briskly. Then add a little cornstarch slowly, stirring until the liquid thickens to the consistency of gravy.

Cantonese Steamed Pork Dumplings

CHINA   Yield: About 48 dumplings

2 stalks bok choy (or Chinese celery cabbage)
1 pound boneless pork shoulder, finely ground

1 tablespoon Chinese rice wine or pale dry sherry
1 tablespoon soy sauce
2 teaspoons salt
1 teaspoon sugar
1 tablespoon cornstarch
¼ cup canned bamboo shoots, finely chopped

With a cleaver or heavy, sharp knife, trim the wilted leaves and root ends from the bok choy. Wash the stalks under cold running water, drain, and chop finely. Squeeze the chopped cabbage in a kitchen towel or double layer of cheesecloth to extract as much of its moisture as possible.

Combine the pork, wine, soy sauce, salt, sugar, and cornstarch and, with a large spoon, mix them thoroughly together. Stir in the cabbage and bamboo shoots. Place a spoonful of filling in the center of a dough circle and fold into a dumpling suitable for steaming.

Pour enough water into the base of the wok to come within an inch of the bamboo steamer and bring to a boil. Place the dumplings into as many steamer racks as are needed to hold them and steam for 30 minutes. Add water as needed. Serve the dumplings directly on the steamer plate set on a platter.

Northern-style Pork Dumplings

CHINA   Yield: About 48 dumplings

½ pound bok choy (or Chinese celery cabbage)
1 pound lean boneless pork, finely ground
1 teaspoon fresh gingerroot, grated

1 tablespoon Chinese rice wine or
    pale dry sherry
1 tablespoon soy sauce
1 teaspoon salt
1 tablespoon sesame seed oil
2 tablespoons peanut or vegetable oil
1 cup chicken broth, fresh or canned
¼ cup soy sauce combined with 2
    tablespoons white vinegar (to be
    used as a dip or sauce)

With a cleaver or heavy, sharp knife,
trim the wilted leaves and root ends from the
bok choy and separate the cabbage into
stalks. Wash the stalks under cold running
water, drain, and chop finely. Squeeze the
chopped cabbage in a kitchen towel or
double layer of cheesecloth to extract as
much of its moisture as possible.

Combine the ground pork, chopped gingerroot, wine, soy sauce, salt, and sesame
seed oil, and then add the chopped cabbage.
Mix with your hands or a large spoon until
the ingredients are thoroughly blended. This
mixture can then be used as a filling for
dumplings, folded and sealed for boiling or
frying.

To boil: Bring 2 quarts of water to boiling in your wok and drop in the dumplings.
Stir to make sure the dumplings are not
sticking together. Boil for 10 to 15 minutes,
adding additional water as needed. Serve the
dumplings hot with the soy sauce and vinegar dip.

To fry: Place 2 tablespoons of oil into the
wok and swirl it about. Place the dumplings,
pleated side up, into the wok and cook until
the bottoms brown lightly (about 2 minutes
at low heat). Add the chicken broth, cover

tightly, and cook until it has been absorbed
(about 10 minutes). Add the remaining 1
tablespoon of oil and fry each dumpling at
least another 2 minutes. Serve the fried
dumplings hot with the soy sauce and vinegar dip.

Pork Chop Suey

CHINA   Yield: 4 to 6 servings

3 cups cooked pork
½ cup celery
½ cup spring onions
1 cup mushrooms
1 green pepper
1 pound can bean sprouts
2 tablespoons oil
1 cup chicken bouillon
1 tablespoon cornstarch
1 tablespoon soy sauce

Cut pork into thick strips. Cut celery
into slices and spring onions into lengths.
Slice mushrooms. Seed and chop the green
pepper and cook for 5 minutes in boiling
water. Drain. Rinse bean sprouts in cold
water and drain.

Heat oil and cook celery and onions for
2-3 minutes. Add mushrooms and pork, and
cook for 2 minutes. Add chopped pepper and
bean sprouts, and cook for 2 minutes, stirring
all the time.

Add stock with cornstarch dissolved in it.
Bring to boil and simmer for 5 minutes. Add
soy sauce, season, and serve with plain
boiled rice or fried noodles.

Chop Suey

CHINA   Yield: About 3 servings

1 pound lean pork, cut into thin slices
2 tablespoons sherry
2 tablespoons soy sauce
Salt to taste
Freshly ground pepper to taste
Pinch of powdered ginger
2 ounces transparent noodles, broken
    into small pieces
1 stalk celery, cut into thin slices
4 tablespoons dried Chinese mush-
    rooms, soaked in water for 30
minutes
8 tablespoons oil
2 medium onions, thinly sliced
¼ cup bamboo shoots, thinly sliced
1 cup fresh bean sprouts
½ pound fresh mushrooms, sliced
3 tablespoons soy sauce
1 teaspoon sugar
1 tablespoon cornstarch
2 jiggers sherry
Cooked rice

Cut pork into thin slices and mix with 2 tablespoons sherry, 2 tablespoons soy sauce, salt, pepper, and ginger. Place in glass or ceramic bowl. Press down meat and cover. Let marinate for 1 hour.

Break noodles into small pieces and boil in salted water for 5 minutes. Drain and set aside. Cut celery in thin slices; blanch for 5 minutes. Drain and set aside. Slice Chinese mushrooms into bite-size pieces.

Heat oil in skillet until very hot. Add marinated pork and fry for 2 minutes. Remove and keep warm. Add onions, bamboo shoots, bean sprouts, and fresh mushrooms. Simmer for 3 minutes. Fold in meat, celery, and noodles. Season with 3 tablespoons soy sauce and sugar. Stirring carefully, cook for an additional 3 minutes. Blend cornstarch with 2 jiggers sherry and slowly stir it into the sauce until sauce is thick and bubbly. Correct seasonings if necessary and serve immediately with rice.

Chow Mein

CHINA   Yield: 6 servings

3 cups pork, cooked and cut in
    julienne strips
1½ cups celery, cut into thin 1-inch
    strips
1 cup onion, sliced
1 tablespoon fat or oil
2 tablespoons cornstarch
1½ cups bean sprout liquid plus water
½ teaspoon salt
Few grains pepper
3 tablespoons soy sauce
16-ounce can bean sprouts, drained
Chow mein noodles

Cook pork with celery and onion in the fat in a large frying pan until mixture begins to brown. Mix cornstarch with a little of the bean sprout liquid. Add to meat mixture with remaining liquid, salt, pepper, and soy sauce. Stir until well mixed. Cook until thickened, stirring as needed.

Add bean sprouts and heat to serving temperature. Serve over chow mein noodles.

Note: If preferred, start with 1½ pounds lean raw pork cut into julienne strips. Brown the meat in the fat. Add ½ cup water and simmer, covered, until the meat is almost tender, about 45 minutes. Add celery and onion and cook until the vegetables are tender. Add cornstarch-liquid mixture and continue as directed in recipe.

Curried Pork with Shrimp

CHINA   Yield: 4 servings

½ pound pork (shoulder or butt),
    shredded into thin strips
2 tablespoons soy sauce
2 tablespoons vegetable oil
2 teaspoons curry powder
1 small onion, minced
3 celery stalks, cut into ¼-inch slices
2 scallions, cut into ⅛-inch slices
½ tablespoon cornstarch in ½ cup
    water or chicken broth
½ pound whole cooked shrimp

Marinate pork in soy sauce for 20
minutes. Heat oil in wok and brown curry
powder and onion until the aroma becomes
strong. Stir-fry the pork for about 4 minutes
or until well done. Push aside. Combine celery and scallions and stir-fry 1 to 2 minutes.
Return pork and add cornstarch mixture.
Heat until sauce is clear and thickened and
shrimp are heated through. Serve with
noodles.

Dry Pork Curry

BURMA   Yield: 4 servings

1 pound pork, cut into 2-inch pieces
    with some fat left on meat
1 large onion, peeled and chopped
3 cloves garlic, peeled and crushed
1 teaspoon fresh ginger, finely grated
½ teaspoon chili powder
½ teaspoon ground turmeric
3 tablespoons light sesame oil
1 stalk lemon grass or 2 strips lemon
    rind
2 tablespoons tamarind liquid
1 tablespoon fish sauce

When meat is prepared, set it aside.
Purée and cook onion, garlic, ginger, chili,
and turmeric in oil over low heat for at least
10 minutes, stirring with a wooden spoon to
prevent sticking to the pan. Add pork and
allow all to simmer until meat is tender.
Finely chop the lemon grass and add it to
the meat along with the tamarind liquid and
fish sauce. When the water has evaporated
and the oil separates from the gravy, the
meat is done. Serve at once.

Fresh Vegetables with Pork

CHINA   Yield: 6 servings

2 tablespoons vegetable oil
6 stalks celery, sliced diagonally
½ pound mushrooms, halved
1 medium green pepper, sliced
1 medium red pepper, sliced
1 medium onion, sliced
1 pound boneless pork, cut into
    ½-inch cubes
1 cup chicken broth
1 tablespoon soy sauce
1 tablespoon cornstarch
½ teaspoon ginger
¼ teaspoon pepper

Heat oil in wok or frying pan. Stir-fry
celery about 4 minutes. Add mushrooms,
peppers, and onion; stir-fry 5 minutes. Remove vegetables; reserve. Add pork to pan;
stir-fry 5 minutes. Add broth; stir in vegetables. Simmer 5 minutes.

Meanwhile, blend soy sauce with cornstarch, ginger, and pepper. Stir into pork
and vegetable mixture; cook, stirring constantly, about 3 minutes or until heated and
thickened.

Serve mixture over rice.

Deep-fried Pork with Sweet-and-Sour Sauce

CHINA　　　　　　　　Yield: 4 servings

1 pound pork, cut into ¼-inch strips
2 tablespoons vegetable oil
3 tablespoons soy sauce

Frying batter

1 egg
¾ cup milk
1 cup sifted all-purpose flour
2 teaspoons baking powder
½ teaspoon salt
2 cups oil for frying

Sweet-and-sour sauce

½ cup brown sugar
½ cup vinegar
½ cup pineapple juice
½ cup water or chicken broth
1½ tablespoons soy sauce

Stir-fry pork in oil 3 to 4 minutes or until well done. Allow to marinate in soy sauce for 20 to 30 minutes.

Combine ingredients for the frying batter and beat until smooth. Allow to stand for 1 hour. (Flour absorbs some of the liquid.)

Dip pork strips in batter and deep-fry in oil at 400°F a few strips at a time until light, golden brown. Remove pork with a slotted spoon and drain on paper towels. Keep warm.

In a small saucepan, combine the ingredients for the sweet-and-sour sauce. Bring to a boil over moderate heat, stirring continuously. Arrange pork in a serving bowl and pour sauce over immediately before serving.

Fried Pork

CHINA　　　　　　　　Yield: 4 servings

1 medium red pepper
2 tablespoons scallions, chopped
2 tablespoons ground sesame seeds
3 tablespoons soy sauce
2 tablespoons rice wine or sherry
1 pound sliced pork, ¼ inch thick
2 tablespoons oil
2 ounces transparent noodles or very thin spaghetti
1 medium cucumber, cut into thin strips
1 medium tomato, cut into thin strips

Sauce

2 tablespoons vinegar
1 teaspoon freshly ground black pepper
1 tablespoon sugar

Remove seeds from pepper; dice it fine. Mix with scallions, sesame seeds, soy sauce, and rice wine or sherry. Marinate pork in this mixture for at least 1 hour.

Heat oil in frying pan. Drain pork; brown well on both sides in hot oil. Cut into smaller pieces, if desired.

Prepare noodles or thin spaghetti. Combine with cucumber and tomato strips. Place on platter along with the pork. Prepare sauce by blending the vinegar, black pepper, and sugar. Spoon sauce over the pork.

Javanese Spiced Pork

INDONESIA　　　　　　Yield: 6 servings

1½ pounds boneless pork
2 large yellow onions
1 teaspoon coriander
1 teaspoon curry

1 teaspoon salt
½ teaspoon freshly ground black
   pepper
2 medium cloves garlic, pressed
1 tablespoon soy sauce
¾ cup shelled and deveined shrimp
3 eggs

Sauce

4 tablespoons peanut butter
3 tablespoons milk
2 tablespoons soy sauce
½ to 1½ teaspoons Tabasco sauce
1 teaspoon corn syrup

Cut the pork into very thin slices. Peel and finely chop the onions. Brown the pork and onion in some oil in the wok, cover, and continue to fry on very low heat for 10 minutes. Add the coriander, curry, salt, black pepper, garlic, and soy sauce. Mix thoroughly. Let fry slowly for another 10 minutes. Add the shrimp and let them get warm. Meanwhile, beat the eggs and stir them into the wok. Let simmer for 1 minute and remove from the heat. Serve with boiled rice and the special sauce.

To make the sauce, beat the peanut butter rapidly with the milk and soy sauce. Keep these ingredients cold. Add the Tabasco sauce and the corn syrup. Beer makes an excellent companion beverage.

Meat Platter Szechuan

CHINA   Yield: 4 servings

7 tablespoons oil
6 ounces fresh mushrooms, sliced
½ pound tomatoes, peeled, sliced
½ pound green peppers, cut in half,
   seeds removed, cut into julienne
   strips

1½ pounds lean pork, cut into 2-inch-
   long julienne strips
Salt
¼ teaspoon ground ginger
½ pound onions, minced
1 clove garlic, minced
2 tablespoons sherry
1 cup hot beef broth (made from cubes)
1 tablespoon soy sauce
2 tablespoons cornstarch
4 tablespoons water

Heat 4 tablespoons oil in skillet. Add mushrooms, tomatoes, and green peppers. Cook 5 minutes; set aside.

Heat 3 tablespoons oil in another skillet. Add meat strips. Season to taste with salt and ginger, stirring constantly. Brown 10 minutes. Add onions and garlic; cook 5 minutes. Pour in sherry. After 1 minute, pour in broth and soy sauce. Add vegetable mixture. Cover; cook over medium heat 25 minutes.

Blend cornstarch with water; stir in. Cook until thickened and bubbly. Serve immediately on preheated platter.

Oriental-style Pork Roast

CHINA   Yield: About 6 servings

4½ pounds blade pork roast
1 teaspoon soy sauce
½ cup sherry
½ teaspoon garlic powder
½ teaspoon onion powder
1 teaspoon ground ginger

Trim excess fat from roast. Mix liquids and seasonings. Baste the roast thoroughly with sauce. Roast at 325°F for 3½ hours, or until meat thermometer reads 180°. Baste with more sherry or chicken broth if meat seems dry. Save leftovers for chop suey or an Oriental stir-fry dish.

Mu Zhi Pork

CHINA   Yield: 4 servings

½ pound boneless pork loin
1 tablespoon sherry
1 tablespoon plus 1 teaspoon soy sauce
1 teaspoon cornstarch
½ teaspoon sugar
4 tablespoons peanut oil
3 eggs, well beaten
¼ teaspoon ginger
1 cup cabbage, firmly packed and shredded
½ cup water chestnuts, sliced
⅓ cup scallions, finely chopped
1 teaspoon sesame seeds
2 cups hot cooked rice

Thinly slice pork; then cut into very fine strips 1½ inches long. Combine pork with sherry, soy sauce, cornstarch, and sugar. Mix well and set aside.

Heat 2 tablespoons peanut oil in a wok. Add eggs and scramble until very dry. Break eggs into small pieces with a spoon. Remove from wok and set aside. Heat remaining 2 tablespoons peanut oil in the same wok.

Add the prepared pork mixture and ginger, stir-frying until the pork begins to turn color and separates into shreds. Add the cabbage and water chestnuts. Stir to mix well and cook over high heat for two minutes, stirring constantly. Add the scrambled eggs, scallions, and sesame seeds. Stir and cook for 1 minute. Serve hot with rice.

Oriental Pork Loin

CHINA   Yield: About 4 servings

2 pounds pork loin
1 red and 1 green pepper
½ teaspoon curry powder
½ teaspoon paprika powder
3 tablespoons vegetable oil
3 tablespoons flour
1 cup bouillon
½ cup milk
½ cup cream
1 small can of vegetable juice
Salt
Garlic powder
1 tablespoon mango chutney
2 tablespoons dry white wine (if desired)

Cut the meat into strips and the peppers into small pieces. Brown the curry and paprika in the vegetable oil until pungent. Add, while stirring in the wok, the flour, bouillon, milk, and cream. Add the juice, meat, and the diced peppers. Simmer for about 5 minutes. Add water, if needed, spices, mango, and wine. Serve with almonds and rice.

Cantonese Pork Roast

CHINA   Yield: 4 to 6 servings

2½ to 3 pounds boneless pork roast
1 tablespoon soy sauce
2 tablespoons chicken broth
1 tablespoon honey
1 tablespoon sugar
Salt to taste
2 tablespoons sesame-seed oil

Rinse pork and pat dry with paper toweling. Blend next five ingredients and spoon over meat and rub in thoroughly. Place roast in bowl, cover, and let stand for 1 hour. Remove and drain, reserving any marinade. Brush meat with oil and place in ovenproof dish. Brush with reserved marinade. Place in preheated 325°F oven and roast for approximately 1½ hours.

Pepper Pork

CHINA   Yield: 4 servings

¼ cup peanut oil
1 medium (¾-pound) Spanish onion, cut in thin strips
2 large sweet red peppers, seeded and cut in thin strips
1 cup roast pork, cut in thin strips
¼ cup bottled teriyaki sauce

In a wok, heat the oil. Add the onion and peppers; over high heat, toss constantly until slightly cooked—a few minutes. Add the pork and teriyaki sauce; mix well and heat rapidly, tossing as you do so. Serve with rice.

Polynesian Pork

POLYNESIA   Yield: 4 servings

2 tablespoons shortening
1½ pounds pork, cut into bite-size cubes
1 medium onion, sliced
1 cup pineapple juice
¼ cup vinegar
¼ cup brown sugar
1 teaspoon salt
1 green pepper, diced
1 1-pound 4-ounce can pineapple chunks, drained
1 cut-up orange
1 tablespoon soy sauce
3 tablespoons cornstarch
¼ cup water

Heat shortening in a pressure cooker and brown the pork with the onion. Add pineapple juice, vinegar, brown sugar, and salt. Close cover of cooker and put pressure control in place. When pressure is reached, cook for 12 minutes. Reduce pressure under faucet. Open cooker. Add green pepper, pineapple chunks, orange, and soy sauce.

Mix cornstarch with water and pour into cooker. Stir constantly until slightly thickened. Serve pork over rice or noodles.

Pork in Soy Sauce

MALAYSIA   Yield: 4 servings

4 cloves garlic, peeled and crushed
2 tablespoons all-purpose flour
1 tablespoon light soy sauce
1½ pounds pork loin, cubed
3 ounces dried Chinese mushrooms, soaked in warm water for 30 minutes or 1 cup button mushrooms, sliced
7 tablespoons vegetable oil or melted pork fat
1 teaspoon ginger powder
5 scallions, thinly sliced
Freshly ground black pepper to taste
3 tablespoons dark soy sauce
1 teaspoon white vinegar
2 tablespoons rice wine

Mix 2 cloves garlic, flour, and light soy sauce and use this to thoroughly coat the pieces of pork. Allow to stand for 30 minutes. If using Chinese mushrooms, discard the stalks and cut the caps into 4 pieces.

Heat the oil in a skillet or wok and fry half of the meat for 6 to 8 minutes, turning frequently; remove meat and drain on paper towels. Repeat process for the remaining meat.

Reduce fat in skillet to 3 tablespoons. Fry mushrooms in this for 3 minutes. Add remaining garlic to pan with ginger. Stirring to mix, add meat, scallions, dark soy sauce, and vinegar. Stir-fry for 2 minutes; add rice wine at the end. Serve piping hot.

Pork Adobo

PHILIPPINES   Yield: 6 servings

6 pork loin chops or leg chops, about 2
   pounds
8 to 10 cloves garlic, peeled
1 cup white vinegar
1 cup water
1½ teaspoons salt
2 bay leaves
½ teaspoon ground black pepper
Lard or oil for frying

Cut chops into serving pieces. In a deep saucepan, marinate the meat in all the listed ingredients except the lard. Allow to stand for 1 hour. Bring this to a boil, then reduce the heat and simmer until pork is tender—40 minutes to 1 hour. Lift the meat out of the pan.

Allow the liquid to boil by itself until it is reduced and thickened. Strain this into a small bowl. Allow to stand until fat rises to the top. Take off the fat and put it in a frying pan. Add enough fat to cover the bottom of the pan. Fry the pork until it is crisp and brown on both sides. Arrange on a serving platter and pour gravy over all. Serve with white rice.

Pork and Spring Onions

CHINA   Yield: 2 servings

2 tablespoons vegetable oil
½ pound pork (butt or shoulder),
   trimmed and cut into thin strips
   across the grain
½ cup chicken broth
2 tablespoons tomato paste
1 teaspoon sugar
1 teaspoon chili sauce
8 scallions, cut in quarters lengthwise,
   then into 4-inch lengths

Heat oil in wok and stir-fry pork strips 5 to 10 minutes, until crisp and golden. Combine remaining ingredients and add to pork. Simmer for 1 to 2 minutes. Serve at once.

Pork Cooked with Sugar

INDOCHINA   Yield: 6 to 8 servings

2 to 2½ pounds fresh pork or loin,
   cubed
2 tablespoons oil
3 spring onions, finely chopped
2 teaspoons sugar
½ teaspoon salt
¼ teaspoon ground black pepper
4 cups water
2 tablespoons fish sauce

When cubing pork, let fat remain. Set aside meat. Use a large saucepan to heat oil. Fry spring onions until golden. Add pork and fry until meat loses its pink color. Stir constantly. Add sugar, salt, and pepper, continuing to stir until meat is brown. Add water and allow to simmer uncovered for 1 hour. Stir occasionally as liquid will become absorbed.

Add fish sauce and stir. This dish is done when meat is almost dry. Serve with plain white rice.

Pork Vindaloo

INDIA   Yield: 4 to 6 servings

Vindaloo mixtures can be purchased in many specialty food stores. Use only if you prefer a hot curry. Vindaloo is used dry or mixed into a paste with vinegar, according to the needs of the recipe.

3 tablespoons onions, peeled and
  chopped
½ teaspoon garlic, peeled and chopped
½ cup butter or fat
3 tablespoons vindaloo, made into
  paste with vinegar
2 pounds pork, cut into cubes
1 teaspoon salt

In a large heavy skillet, heat butter and
sauté onions and garlic until onions are
golden. Add the vindaloo mixture and cook,
stirring constantly, for 3 minutes, using low
heat. Add pork and salt. Cover and simmer
over low heat until pork is tender and
cooked through. Add water if needed to
make a thick gravy. Stir frequently, as this
dish can burn quickly. Serve hot.

Pork and Peas

JAPAN   Yield: About 4 servings

12 ounces lean pork or tenderloin

Marinade

2 tablespoons soy sauce
2 teaspoons rice wine or sherry
1 egg white
1 teaspoon cornstarch
Salt
White pepper

4 ounces frozen peas
8 tablespoons oil
½ cup hot beef broth
Salt
Sugar
1 leek
1 clove garlic
1 sugared or candied ginger

4 ounces canned sliced mushrooms
4 ounces canned bamboo shoots
1 tablespoon rice wine or sherry
1 tablespoon cornstarch
2 tablespoons oyster sauce
2 teaspoons soy sauce
White pepper
Pinch of ground ginger

Cut pork or tenderloin crosswise into
thin strips. Prepare marinade by stirring soy
sauce, rice wine (or sherry), egg white, and
cornstarch together until well blended.
Season to taste with salt and white pepper.
Pour marinade over meat, cover, and refrigerate for 30 minutes.

In the meantime, let peas thaw for 5
minutes. Heat 2 tablespoons of the oil in a
small saucepan. Add peas. Pour in beef
broth; season to taste with salt and sugar.
Cook for 5 minutes. Drain peas, reserving
cooking liquid. Set peas aside; keep them
warm.

Thoroughly clean the leek; cut it into
long, thin strips. Mince the garlic. Cut sugared ginger into slices. Drain mushrooms
and bamboo shoots. Heat 3 tablespoons of
the oil in a large saucepan. Add all the vegetables and garlic; cook for 5 minutes, stirring constantly. Set aside; keep them warm.

Heat remaining oil (3 tablespoons) in
skillet. Add meat strips and marinade; cook
for 3 minutes, stirring constantly. Add meat
and reserved peas to vegetables. Pour in rice
wine (or sherry) and cooking liquid from
peas. Bring to a boil.

Blend together cornstarch, oyster sauce,
and soy sauce. Pour into meat-vegetable mixture; stir until smooth and bubbly. Correct
seasoning, if necessary, with salt, pepper,
ground ginger, and sugar. Serve immediately.

Pork Loaf

INDOCHINA   Yield: 4 to 6 servings

8 to 10 dried Chinese mushrooms
1½ pounds ground pork
6 spring onions, finely chopped
4 eggs, beaten
1 tablespoon fish sauce
½ teaspoon salt
¼ teaspoon ground black pepper

Prepare mushrooms by soaking in hot water for 30 minutes. Squeeze out moisture. Cut off and discard stems and finely chop the caps. Use a mixing bowl to blend pork, mushrooms, and spring onions.

In another bowl, mix eggs, fish sauce, and salt and pepper. Add this to the pork mixture and mix well. Place mixture in a well-greased loaf tin, 9 × 5 × 2 inches. Cover with foil. Allow to steam over high heat for 1 hour or longer. (Pork must always be well cooked.)

When meat is done, allow it to cool in loaf pan slightly. Turn out and and slice; put on serving platter.

Pork with Oyster Sauce

CHINA   Yield: 4 servings

1 pound lean pork, cut into 1-inch cubes
3 scallions, cut into ½-inch slices
½ cup chicken broth
2 tablespoons soy sauce
2 tablespoons oyster sauce
1 tablespoon sherry
½ teaspoon salt
1 tablespoon brown sugar
1 clove garlic, crushed
1 slice fresh gingerroot

Combine all the ingredients in a wok. Cover and simmer for 15 minutes or until pork is done. Uncover and boil away excess liquid until only ½ cup remains. Remove the ginger slice. Serve with a stir-fried vegetable and boiled rice.

Pork with Peppers and Cashews

CHINA   Yield: 4 servings

1 pound pork, cut into ¾-inch cubes
2 tablespoons soy sauce
½ teaspoon sugar
2 tablespoons vegetable oil
1 small onion, cut into ¾-inch cubes
1 large green pepper, cut into ¾-inch cubes
1 large red (vine-ripened green) pepper, cut into ¾-inch cubes
1 tablespoon soy sauce
1 tablespoon cornstarch in ½ cup cold water or chicken broth
4 ounces cashews

Combine pork, 1 tablespoon soy sauce, and sugar; let sit while vegetables are prepared.

Heat oil in wok; stir-fry pork mixture 4 to 5 minutes, until pork is well done. Push aside. Stir-fry onion 1 to 2 minutes; add green peppers. Stir-fry for 2 to 3 minutes. Return pork; add combined 1 tablespoon soy sauce and cornstarch mixture. Heat and stir gently until sauce is thickened and clear. Add cashews; allow to heat through. Serve at once with rice.

Pork with Peppers and Tomatoes

CHINA   Yield: 4 servings

1½ pounds lean pork
½ pound green peppers
5 ounces fresh mushrooms
½ pound tomatoes, peeled
7 tablespoons oil
Salt
¼ teaspoon ground ginger
½ pound onions
1 clove garlic
2 tablespoons sherry
1 cup hot beef broth
1 tablespoon cornstarch
4 tablespoons cold water

Cut pork and green peppers into long, thin strips. Cut mushrooms and peeled tomatoes into thin slices. Heat 4 tablespoons of the oil in skillet. Add green peppers, mushrooms, and tomatoes; cook for 5 minutes. Set aside.

In second skillet, heat remaining 3 tablespoons oil. Add meat; sprinkle with salt and ginger; brown, stirring constantly, for about 10 minutes. Chop onions finely; mince garlic. Add to meat; continue cooking for another 5 minutes. Pour in sherry, beef broth, and soy sauce. Add vegetable mixture to meat; cover, and simmer for 25 minutes over medium heat.

Blend cornstarch and water; stir into skillet until smooth and bubbly. Serve pork immediately on preheated platter.

Red Pork

BURMA   Yield: 4 to 6 servings

This dish takes its name from the color of the chili powder and is very rich and flavorful.

2 pounds boneless pork, cubed into
   1-inch pieces
3 tablespoons soy sauce
1 teaspoon freshly ground black pepper
2-inch piece of fresh gingerroot,
   peeled
3 medium onions, peeled and pounded
3 cloves garlic, peeled and crushed
1 cup boiling water
1 teaspoon chili powder
⅓ cup vegetable oil

Mix the pork with 2 tablespoons soy sauce and pepper. Set aside.

Pound half the ginger and mix with onions and garlic. Stir in all but 1 tablespoon of the boiling water. Strain and save both the liquid and the ingredients.

Stir chili powder into reserved boiling water. Slice remaining ginger into strips. Heat oil in large skillet and fry ginger until just sizzling. Add pork and stir-fry until brown. Pour in reserved liquid, cover the pan, and simmer for 10 minutes, until liquid has been absorbed. Add chili water, remaining soy sauce, and reserved mixture. Reduce heat and cook for 40 minutes covered, stirring occasionally. If needed, add a small amount of extra water during cooking time to prevent sticking.

Meat

Sesame Pork with Sweet-and-Sour Vegetables

CHINA   Yield: 4 servings

1 pound lean pork, cut into ¾-inch
  pieces
⅓ cup soy sauce
⅓ cup dry sherry
1 clove garlic, crushed

Frying batter

1 egg
¼ cup flour
¼ cup cornstarch
½ cup water
2 cups oil for frying

Sauce

1 cup chicken broth
½ cup reserved syrup from pineapple
  chunks
½ cup vinegar
½ cup brown sugar
2 teaspoons soy sauce
2 tablespoons cornstarch in ¼ cup
  water
1 8-ounce can water chestnuts, drained
  and sliced
1 15¼-ounce can pineapple chunks,
  drained
2 green peppers, cut into ½-inch cubes
2 cooked carrots, quartered lengthwise
  and cut into 2-inch lengths
1 tablespoon toasted sesame seeds

Combine the pork, soy sauce, sherry, and garlic. Marinate for 2 hours in the refrigerator. Drain. Combine the batter ingredients and beat just until smooth. Let stand for 1 hour. Dip pork a few pieces at a time into the batter. Drain. Deep-fry at 375°F until pork is done and the batter coating is a light, golden brown. Drain on paper toweling and keep warm. (If you wish, you may precook the pork.)

Combine the broth, reserved pineapple syrup, vinegar, brown sugar, and soy sauce. Heat until the sugar dissolves. Add the cornstarch mixture and cook until the mixture thickens. Add the pork, water chestnuts, pineapple, peppers, and carrots. Heat until the ingredients are heated through. Serve on chow mein noodles immediately, before the crisp batter on the pork softens. Garnish with sesame seeds.

Skewered Pork and Vegetables

CHINA   Yield: 4 servings

8 ounces pork
Salt and pepper to taste
Lima beans
Celery, cut into 1-inch pieces
Small green peppers, cut into cubes
Small onions, quartered
Fresh mushrooms, halved
Flour
Eggs, beaten
Bread crumbs
Oil for frying

Sauce

2 tablespoons Worcestershire sauce
1½ tablespoons catsup

Cut meat into 1-inch chunks. Season with salt and pepper. Prepare vegetables, using as much as is needed. Dip meat and vegetables into flour, beaten eggs, and bread crumbs in that order, again using as much as is needed. Put meat and vegetables on skewers; fry pork over medium heat until done. Fry vegetables over high heat until browned.

Serve with sauce made from Worcestershire sauce and catsup.

Skewered Pork

JAPAN   Yield: 2 to 3 servings

> 1 pound pork, cut into bite-size pieces,
>   ½ inch thick
> 1 small eggplant, cut into bite-size
>   cubes
> 4 or 5 scallions, cut into 1½-inch
>   lengths
> 2 green peppers, cut into chunks
> Flour for dredging
> Oil for frying

Skewer pork, eggplant, scallions, and peppers on skewers. Dredge in flour; fry in oil for about 4 minutes, or until browned. Remove from oil and, if desired, brush with soy sauce. Serve with rice.

Barbecued Spareribs

INDOCHINA   Yield: 4 servings

> 5 shallots, peeled
> 2 cloves garlic, peeled
> 2 tablespoons sugar
> ¼ cup fish sauce
> ¼ teaspoon freshly ground black
>   pepper
> 1½ pounds pork spareribs

Use a mortar and pestle to pound the shallots, garlic, and sugar together. When a paste has formed, add fish sauce and pepper and stir well. Put spareribs in a roasting pan and pour mixture over them, turning the ribs to coat both sides. Allow ribs to marinate for at least 1 hour.

Preheat oven to 350°F. Roast spareribs for 45 minutes until they are well browned. Cut ribs into separate pieces and serve hot with a dish of Nuoc Cham (see Index) beside them.

Cantonese Spareribs

CHINA   Yield: 2 to 3 servings

> 2½ pounds baby ribs
> 1 teaspoon salt
> ¼ cup sugar

> **Sauce**
> ½ cup soy sauce
> 3 tablespoons brown sugar
> ½ cup catsup
> 1 egg-size piece gingerroot, grated
> 1 teaspoon MSG, optional

Buy baby ribs or have large ribs cut in half. Let ribs stand in salt and sugar mixture 2 hours.

Make the sauce the night before using. Brush ribs with sauce about 1 hour before baking. Place on rack in shallow pan. Bake at 450°F for 15 to 20 minutes. Pour off fat. Turn heat to 350°F and bake for 1 hour longer. Turn and baste with the sauce several times during the cooking.

Baked Spareribs

CHINA   Yield: 4 to 6 servings

> 3-4 pounds pork spareribs
> ½ clove garlic
> ¼ cup soy sauce
> ¼ cup sherry
> 3 tablespoons honey
> ¼ teaspoon ginger

Crush garlic, mix ingredients together, add seasoning. Pour mixture over spareribs. Leave to marinate overnight or longer, turning as often as possible.

Bake spareribs in a 350°F oven for 1¼-1½ hours, basting every 15 minutes with marinade. The ribs should be well browned and meat tender. Serve with rice and salad.

Meat

Spareribs with Fresh Peppers

CHINA   Yield: 4 to 5 servings

4 pounds spareribs, cut into serving
 pieces
Salt to taste
⅔ cup brown sugar
3 tablespoons cornstarch
1 teaspoon powdered ginger
1 teaspoon powdered mustard
2 cups fresh orange juice
⅓ cup fresh lemon juice
⅓ cup soy sauce
3 tablespoons butter or margarine
½ pound fresh mushrooms, sliced if
 large
1 medium onion, chopped
1 green sweet pepper, cut into squares
1 red sweet pepper, cut into squares
1 large can pineapple chunks

Cut the spareribs into serving pieces.
Place in roasting pan bone-side-down and
sprinkle with salt to taste. Bake in a 350°F
oven for 1 hour. Drain off excess fat.

In saucepan combine brown sugar, cornstarch, ginger, and mustard. Stir in orange
juice, lemon juice, and soy sauce. Bring to a
boil and cook and stir until thickened. Set
aside.

Melt the butter or margarine in skillet.
Sauté mushrooms for 5 minutes. Pour sauce
over spareribs. Add the onion, green and red
peppers, pineapple, and mushrooms. Bake for
30 minutes, basting occasionally.

Spareribs Chinese Style

CHINA   Yield: 4 servings

4 pounds spareribs
¼ cup water
4 teaspoons sugar
2 cloves garlic, crushed
2 teaspoons soy sauce

Cook ribs in a 400°F oven until tender.
Drain off fat and pour the remaining ingredients, combined, over them and allow to
bake about 10 minutes longer.

Lime Spareribs

CHINA   Yield: 6 to 8 servings

4 pounds spareribs, cut into serving
 pieces
¼ cup olive oil
1 cup onions, chopped
1 cup fresh mushrooms, sliced
1 clove garlic, minced
½ cup chili sauce
2 tablespoons red wine vinegar
¼ cup lime juice
2 tablespoons prepared mustard
¼ cup soy sauce
⅔ cup water
2 tablespoons honey
1 teaspoon salt
Freshly ground pepper to taste

Cut spareribs into serving pieces and
place in baking pan. Heat oil in saucepan.
Sauté onions, mushrooms, and garlic until
tender. Add chili sauce, vinegar, lime juice,
mustard, soy sauce, water, honey, salt, and
pepper, and mix thoroughly. Pour sauce over
the spareribs. Bake in a 325°F oven for 1
hour, or until the spareribs are tender. Baste
frequently.

Spareribs with Black Beans

CHINA   Yield: 2 to 3 servings

1 pound pork spareribs cut into 2-inch-
    long pieces
4 tablespoons black beans (dow see),
    mashed or minced
1 to 2 cloves garlic, grated
2 scallions, finely sliced
2 tablespoons vinegar
1 tablespoon sherry
1 tablespoon sesame oil
3 tablespoons sugar or honey
½ teaspoon cornstarch
1 teaspoon salt

Boil the spareribs for 4 to 5 minutes to remove the excess fat. Rinse and drain. Combine all the remaining ingredients in a bowl that will fit in a steamer (or in the wok on a rack above boiling water). Add spareribs to the bowl and coat well with the bean mixture. Place the bowl in a bamboo steamer (or on a rack set 1 to 2 inches above the water level) and steam for 30 to 45 minutes or until ribs are tender. Serve at once.

Spicy Chunking Pork

CHINA   Yield: 4 servings

1 slice gingerroot
2 tablespoons vegetable oil
1 pound pork, boiled 1 hour and very
    thinly sliced
1 8-ounce can bamboo shoots, thinly
    sliced
10 to 12 water chestnuts, sliced
6 to 8 Chinese black mushrooms,
    soaked 30 minutes in water and
    thinly sliced

3 tablespoons dry sherry
3 tablespoons hoisin sauce
1 cup sliced almonds or whole cashews

Brown the ginger slice in the hot oil. Remove and discard the slice. Add pork and stir-fry 2 minutes. Add bamboo shoots, water chestnuts, and mushrooms. Stir-fry 2 minutes. Add sherry and hoisin sauce. Stir and heat well. Add nuts. Serve at once with rice.

Sweet-and-Sour Pork I

CHINA   Yield: 6 servings

Oil for deep-fat fryer
1 egg, beaten
½ cup unsifted flour
½ teaspoon salt
1 teaspoon soy sauce
¼ cup water
1½ pounds pork shoulder, cut in
    ½-inch cubes
2 tablespoons cornstarch
¼ cup sugar
⅓ cup vinegar
¾ cup water
1 tablespoon soy sauce
½ cup green pepper, cut in squares
13-ounce can pineapple chunks
½ cup sweet mixed pickles, drained

Heat oil to 375°F in deep-fat fryer or heavy saucepan.

Mix egg, flour, salt, 1 teaspoon soy sauce, and ¼ cup water. Coat pork pieces with egg mixture. Fry in hot fat until brown, about 5 minutes. Drain on absorbent paper.

Mix cornstarch and sugar in saucepan. Add vinegar, ¾ cup water, 1 tablespoon soy sauce, green pepper, pineapple, and pickles. Cook, stirring constantly, until mixture is thickened and clear. Stir in meat. Heat to serving temperature.

Sweet-and-Sour Pork II

CHINA   Yield: 4 servings

1½ pounds lean pork, cut into 1-inch cubes
3 tablespoons dry white wine
3 tablespoons soy sauce
2 medium carrots, in julienne strips
1 large red sweet pepper, cut into rings
4 tablespoons olive oil
1 slice ginger, minced
1 medium onion, chopped
¼ pound fresh mushrooms, sliced
½ cup beef broth
Salt to taste
1 cup your favorite sweet-and-sour sauce

Place pork in shallow dish. Combine wine and soy sauce; pour over pork, turning to coat all sides. Marinate at least 15 minutes, stirring frequently. Prepare carrots and pepper.

Heat 2 tablespoons oil to medium heat; stir in ginger. Add pork; stir-fry about 5 minutes. Remove pork; set aside.

Add remaining oil to pan. Add carrots, pepper, onion, and mushrooms. Stir-fry for 5 minutes. When carrots and pepper are crisp-tender, add pork; stir-fry for 5 minutes more. Add broth and salt; mix well. Stir in sweet-and-sour sauce, and bring to boil. Reduce heat; cover pan. Cook for 2 minutes more. Serve pork with rice.

Sweet and Sour Pork III

CHINA   Yield: 4 servings

1½ pounds lean pork, cut in small cubes
3 tablespoons oil
3 onions

2 carrots
3 tablespoons sweet pickle chutney
1 small can pineapple chunks, drained
½ cup pineapple juice
3 tablespoons soy sauce
½ cup stock
3 tablespoons sugar
3 tablespoons vinegar
2 tablespoons cornstarch
2 eggs
2 teaspoons flour
Oil for deep frying

Make sauce: Heat oil, fry sliced onion and carrots until golden brown, about 10 minutes. Add chutney, pineapple chunks and juice, soy sauce, stock, sugar, vinegar and salt. Cover pan and cook slowly for 15 minutes. Mix 2 teaspoons cornstarch with a little cold water. Add to sauce and heat again almost to boiling point, stirring all the time for 5-6 minutes. Season. Keep hot.

Heat oil and fry meat cubes until golden brown. This should take 3-4 minutes. Drain on paper towel.

Beat egg, add flour and remaining cornstarch and mix well. Reheat fat until it will cook a bread cube in 20 seconds. Coat the pork pieces with the egg mixture and fry until golden brown, 1-2 minutes.

Drain and serve with plain boiled rice, pouring sauce over top.

Sweet-and-Sour Pork IV

CHINA   Yield: 6 servings

2½ cups (1¼ pounds) lean pork shoulder, cut into 1-inch pieces
2 tablespoons fat or oil
1 teaspoon garlic salt
⅛ teaspoon pepper
1¾ cups water

1½ cups green pepper, cut into 1-inch
    pieces
½ cup raisins
3 tablespoons cornstarch
⅓ cup sugar
⅓ cup vinegar
¼ cup soy sauce
3 cups (about 1 cup uncooked) cooked
    rice

Brown meat in hot fat or oil. Add garlic salt, pepper, and water. Cover and simmer about 40 minutes until meat is tender. Add green pepper and continue cooking until it is tender.

Mix remaining ingredients, except rice, and stir into meat mixture. Cook, uncovered, until broth is clear and thickened. Stir just enough to prevent sticking. Serve on rice.

Sweet Pork

THAILAND   Yield: About 4 servings

While some cooks use sweet pork as an ingredient in other dishes, some serve it by itself with a hot chili sauce and rice.

1 pound loin of pork
3 cups water
½ cup palm sugar
½ cup fish sauce

Cut rind from the pork but save it. Slice the pork into thin slices. In a medium-size saucepan, cook both pork and rind, water, sugar, and fish sauce over medium heat. When mixture comes to a boil, skim off the top. Cover. Reduce heat and cook for 40 minutes. Continue cooking uncovered until the pork is quite tender to the fork. Allow to cool. Use as a main dish or in Pork and Chicken Soup (see Index).

Tasty Kabobs

INDIA   Yield: 4 to 6 servings

Marinade

2 medium onions, peeled and grated
2 tablespoons currant jelly
10 pimiento corns, crushed
Generous dash of ground ginger

1½ pounds pork fillet, cubed
4 tablespoons butter
2 tablespoons water
2 tablespoons peanut butter
½ teaspoon ground cinnamon
Pinch of ground cloves
2 teaspoons cornstarch
3 tablespoons yogurt

In a large bowl, mix onions with currant jelly. Add pimientos and ginger to onion mixture. Place meat cubes in this and allow to stand for 2 hours. Stir from time to time. Remove meat and scrape off any remnant of the marinade with a knife. Put cubes on skewers.

Heat butter and water in a pot. Stir in peanut butter until a creamy mass forms. Season with cinnamon and cloves. In a cup, mix cornstarch with yogurt, then add to bowl. Mix well. Place skewers of meat on rotating mechanism of grill. Brush with peanut butter mixture. Grill meat for 50 minutes, turning and brushing several times. Serve hot.

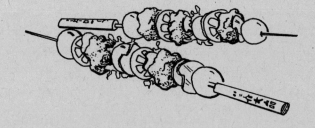

Twice-cooked Szechuan Pork

CHINA   Yield: 4 servings

1 pound lean pork
2 tablespoons vegetable oil
1 large green pepper, cut into ¼-inch
   strips
1 scallion, sliced
1 teaspoon gingerroot, grated
1 clove garlic, grated
1 tablespoon black bean sauce
2 tablespoons water
2 tablespoons hoisin sauce
1 tablespoon dry sherry
¼ to ½ teaspoon chili paste
1 teaspoon sugar
½ teaspoon salt

Cover pork with water and simmer, covered, for 1 hour, until done. Cool and slice into ¼-inch slices. Heat oil in wok and stir-fry green pepper for 1 minute. Add pork and scallion and continue to stir-fry for 1 minute. Combine remaining ingredients and add to pork-and-green pepper mixture. Heat thoroughly and serve at once with boiled or fried rice.

Hum Gok

CHINA   Yield: 18 hum goks

10 black mushrooms
7 water chestnuts
2 cups glutinous rice flour
⅔ cup hot water
2 teaspoons vegetable oil
1 tablespoon scallions, chopped
½ cup shrimp, diced
½ cup cooked pork
½ teaspoon sugar
½ teaspoon salt

Wash mushrooms; soak in warm water until soft (10 to 15 minutes); drain. Dice mushrooms and water chestnuts. Mix glutinous rice flour and hot water thoroughly. Divide into 18 balls. Using hand, flatten each ball as thin as possible. After flattening each ball, you may work dough thinner with fingers.

Heat oil. Stir-fry chopped scallions for about a minute or less; add mushrooms. Stir-fry for about a minute. Add diced shrimp and pork; stir-fry another minute. Add water chestnuts, sugar, and salt. Cook all together for about 2 minutes. Remove to bowl.

As you flatten each ball into a thin piece of circular dough, place 1 tablespoon filling on one side of dough; fold dough into half-moon shape. Press along edge. After all 18 hum goks are ready, fry in deep fat until golden brown. Remove and place in napkin-lined receptacle.

Mandarin Combination

CHINA   Yield: 4 servings

2 tablespoons oil
1 medium onion, chopped
2 cloves garlic, minced
1 green pepper, cut into ¼ × 1-inch
   strips
¼ pound cooked pork or chicken,
   shredded
2 cups cold, boiled rice
1½ tablespoons soy sauce
¼ pound whole shrimp, cooked
1 cucumber, sliced lengthwise,
   unpeeled
2-egg omelette, cut into ½-inch strips

Heat the oil in the wok and add onion, garlic, and green pepper. Stir-fry 1 to 2 minutes. Add cooked meat and stir-fry 1 to 2 utes. Add cooked meat and stir-fry 1 to 2 minutes. Add rice, soy sauce, and shrimp. Continue to stir-fry until all ingredients are thoroughly heated. Cut the lengthwise cucumber slices crosswise every ¼-inch but not all the way through. They will hang together like a comb. Insert them here and there in the dish. Garnish with strips of egg omelette.

Chinese Sweet Bones

CHINA   Yield: 6 servings

- 2 pounds sausage
- 4 tablespoons flour
- 1 egg
- 4 tablespoons butter
- ½ cup onion, thinly sliced
- 1½ cups celery, thinly sliced
- 2 cups water
- 1 medium-sized cucumber, peeled and finely diced
- 1 teaspoon salt
- ½ teaspoon pepper
- 1 tablespoon lemon juice
- 2 pimientos
- ½ cup toasted almonds

Cut sausage into strips four inches long and ¼ inch thick. Roll in flour, dip in slightly beaten egg and then in flour. Place butter in frying pan and, when hot, but not smoking, brown sausage all over. Add onion and celery and cover with 1 cup water and simmer gently 20 minutes. Remove sausage and vegetables.

Add cucumber, seasonings, and lemon juice with remaining cup of water to frying pan. Cover and cook 15 minutes. Add meat and vegetables to the cucumber, reheat, turn onto serving platter, and garnish with pimientos and toasted almonds.

Sub Gum

CHINA   Yield: 4 servings

- 2 tablespoons vegetable oil
- ½ pound pork, cut into thin strips
- 2 cloves garlic, crushed
- 2 chicken-breast halves, skinned, boned, and cut into thin slices
- ½ pound boiled ham, cut into thin slices
- ½ pound shrimp, shelled and deveined
- 1 small can bamboo shoots, sliced
- 4 or 5 water chestnuts, sliced
- 2 cups bean sprouts

Sauce

- 5 tablespoons soy sauce
- 3 tablespoons dry sherry
- 2 tablespoons water
- 1½ tablespoons cornstarch
- 1 teaspoon sugar
- ¼ teaspoon pepper

Heat oil in the wok and stir-fry the pork for 6 minutes. Add garlic, chicken, and ham. Stir-fry 3 minutes. Add shrimp, bamboo shoots, and water chestnuts. Heat for 3 minutes. Combine the sauce ingredients and add to the wok. Heat until sauce is thickened. Add bean sprouts and continue heating 1 to 2 minutes, until they appear wilted. Serve at once.

Oriental Firepot

CHINA   Yield: Approximately 4 servings

1 pound sirloin or flank steak, sliced
   paper thin across the grain (slice
   flank steak on the diagonal)
2 chicken breasts, skinned, boned, and
   sliced very thin across the grain
½ pound red snapper fillet, or sole or
   haddock, thinly sliced
½ pound chicken livers, sliced
½ pound small spinach leaves, washed
   and trimmed of stems
¾ pound mushrooms, wiped and
   quartered
2 cups cubed bean curd or peeled and
   cubed eggplant
1 10-ounce package frozen snow pea
   pods or frozen Italian-style beans,
   thawed
2 cups cherry tomatoes
1 bunch scallions, trimmed and cut
   into 2-inch lengths
Chicken broth or stock
¼ teaspoon ginger
Pungent Sweet-and-Sour Sauce (see
   Index)
Ginger-Soy Sauce (See Index)
Mustard Cream Sauce (see Index)
Hot cooked rice

Prepare the foods as indicated in the ingredient list. This may be done several hours
before serving time. The sauces should be
prepared well in advance so that the flavors
blend well. Keep food and sauces covered
and refrigerated.

Shortly before serving time arrange meat,
chicken, fish, chicken livers, and vegetables
in small dishes or on plates. Set out the
sauces and provide the guests with chopsticks
or long-handled forks.

If using the Mongolian cooker, place 6 to
8 charcoal briquettes in the bottom section
of the cooker, add charcoal starter, and
light. On the range, heat enough chicken
broth with the ginger added to fill the
Mongolian cooker ⅔ full. Pour into cooker
when hot. Cover and continue to heat until
broth is just bubbling. Or, fill the electric
wok ⅔ full with chicken broth. Add ginger.
Cover and bring to boiling point. Adjust
heat until broth is just bubbling.

Each guest spoons some of each sauce
onto his plate, then picks up desired foods
with chopsticks or fork, and lowers them
into broth to cook. When food is cooked, he
lifts it out with a wire ladle and dips each
piece into one of the sauces. Do not try to
cook too much food in the broth at one
time, as the broth must always be bubbling
slightly. Serve with fluffly hot rice. Add
noodles to the remaining broth and, when
they are done, ladle the soup into soup bowls
for each guest.

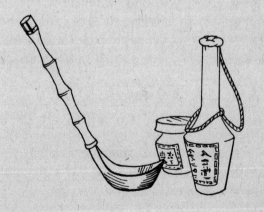

Dips, Gravies & Sauces

Chinese-style Dip

CHINA   Yield: 1¼ cups

1 cup yogurt
2 tablespoons soy sauce
2 scallions, very thinly sliced

Combine all ingredients.
Serve dip with Japanese crackers.

Hot Mustard Dip

CHINA   Yield: 2 to 4 tablespoons

2 to 4 tablespoons dry mustard
Sufficient vinegar to make a paste

Combine the dry mustard with vinegar. This makes a very hot dip. Only a small amount should be used on foods.

Soy-Sesame Oil Dip

JAPAN   Yield: ¾ cup

½ cup soy sauce
¼ cup sesame seed oil
1 teaspoon sugar
2 tablespoons dry sherry

Mix all the ingredients together. Serve in dipping bowls. Recipe may be halved, as sauce is thin and small amounts adhere to the food.

Sweet-and-Sour Dip

CHINA   Yield: Approximately 2½ cups

2 tablespoons cornstarch
¾ cup pineapple juice
½ cup brown sugar
½ cup vinegar
1 tablespoon catsup
1 teaspoon salt
Cup crushed pineapple

Combine cornstarch and pineapple juice in a saucepan. Add remaining ingredients and stir over medium heat until the sauce boils and is thickened.

Chinese Gravy

CHINA   Yield: About 1 cup

1 tablespoon cornstarch
¼ teaspoon salt
1 teaspoon sugar
1 teaspoon MSG
1 cup liquid (drained from Chinese
     vegetables plus water to make 1 cup)
1 tablespoon soy sauce

In a small saucepan, mix cornstarch, salt, sugar, and MSG. Gradually stir in 1 cup juice, keeping smooth. Cook and stir constantly over medium high heat until clear and thickened. Stir in soy sauce to taste.

Bar B Q Sauce I

CHINA   Yield: About 2 cups

1 cup catsup
1 cup water
1 teaspoon paprika
3 tablespoons Worcestershire sauce
1 teaspoon lemon juice

Mix all of the ingredients together.

Bar B Q Sauce II

CHINA   Yield: About 3 cups

1 medium onion, chopped
1 tablespoon margarine
1 small bottle chili sauce
Water
1 cup catsup
2 tablespoons vinegar
3 tablespoons sugar
Pinch of garlic powder
1 tablespoon lemon juice

Sauté onion in margarine until golden. Add chili sauce; then fill chili sauce bottle with water and add water. Add catsup, vinegar, sugar, garlic, and lemon juice. Simmer over low heat for 15 minutes.

Bar B Q Sauce III

CHINA   Yield: About 4 cups

1 bottle barbecue sauce
1 bottle orange marmalade

Mix the barbecue sauce and the marmalade. Makes a delicious sauce.

Barbecue Sauce

JAPAN   Yield: 5 cups

1½ cups peanut oil
¾ cup Japanese soy sauce
½ cup mirin (Japanese sweet rice wine) or dry sherry
2 tablespoons dark molasses
¼ cup Worcestershire sauce
2 tablespoons dry mustard
3 tablespoons salt
1 tablespoon black pepper
½ cup wine vinegar
2 teaspoons parsley flakes
3 cloves garlic, crushed
¼ cup lemon juice
2 tablespoons grated orange peel

Mix all ingredients thoroughly. Marinade may be stored in tightly covered jar in refrigerator as long as five days or indefinitely in freezer. If kept in freezer, separate into one cup measure for convenience. To make sauce less sweet, eliminate molasses. Use as marinade, or basting or serving sauce for lamb, pork, poultry, or fish.

Chili Sauce

MALAYSIA   Yield: 4 to 6 servings

3 tablespoons dark soy sauce
2 shallots, peeled and finely sliced
1 clove garlic, peeled and crushed
1 green chili, finely chopped, or ¼ teaspoon chili powder
Juice of ½ lemon
1 teaspoon olive oil, optional
½ teaspoon brown sugar

This chili sauce does not have to be cooked. Place all the ingredients in a bowl and mix thoroughly. When all flavors are blended, put it in a serving bowl to accompany your main dish.

Currant-Chutney Sauce

INDIA   Yield: About 1 cup

  ¾ cup red currant jelly
  ⅓ cup chutney, chopped
  Juice of ½ lemon
  Pinch of salt

Combine all ingredients in a saucepan and heat, stirring occasionally. Serve warm.

Curry Sauce

INDIA   Yield: About 1½ cups

  1 onion, chopped
  1 tablespoon butter or margarine
  1 tablespoon flour
  2 to 3 teaspoons curry powder
  1 tomato, peeled and chopped
  ¼ cup apple, chopped
  1 tablespoon brown sugar
  1 cup chicken broth

Sauté onion in butter or margarine until golden. Add flour and curry powder and stir until smooth and blended. Add tomato, apple, brown sugar, and chicken broth and stir until smooth and thickened, about 15 minutes. Flavor is improved by making this ahead and reheating just before serving.

Curry Powder I

INDIA   Yield: 1¼ cups

  ½ cup ground coriander
  ¼ cup ground cumin
  ¼ cup ground turmeric
  ¼ cup ground ginger

Mix well and bottle tightly.

Curry Powder II

INDIA   Yield: ½ cup

  ¼ cup coriander seed
  2 tablespoons saffron threads
  1 tablespoon cumin seed
  1 tablespoon mustard seed
  ½ tablespoon crushed red pepper
  1 tablespoon poppy seed

Grind together in a pepper mill, mix well, and bottle tightly.

Far Eastern Curry Sauce

CHINA   Yield: About 1½ cups

  ¼ cup butter
  ⅔ cup onion, finely chopped
  ¼ cup all-purpose flour
  4 teaspoons curry powder
  2 teaspoons sugar
  1 teaspoon salt
  ¼ teaspoon ginger
  ⅛ teaspoon white pepper
  2 cups milk
  2 teaspoons lemon juice

Melt the butter in a medium saucepan over low heat. Add the onion and sauté, stirring occasionally, for about 5 minutes or until golden. Remove from heat. Combine the flour, curry powder, sugar, salt, ginger, and pepper, and stir into the onion mixture.

Return to heat and add the milk gradually, stirring constantly. Cook over medium heat, stirring constantly, until mixture comes to a boil. Reduce heat and simmer until thick, then stir in the lemon juice. This sauce may be served with poultry, rice, or potatoes.

Deviled Roquefort Butter

CHINA   Yield: 1 cup

¼ pound soft Roquefort cheese
½ cup soft butter or margarine
1 tablespoon prepared mustard
1 small clove garlic, crushed
3 drops Angostura bitters

Combine all ingredients and whip until light and fluffy. Cover and refrigerate several hours to blend flavors. Let stand at room temperature to soften. Whip with a fork to fluff before serving.

Beef Gravy Sauce

CHINA   Yield: About 2 cups

1 onion, chopped
1 clove garlic, crushed
¼ cup butter or margarine
½ cup red wine
1 10-ounce can beef gravy with
    mushrooms
1 tablespoon Worcestershire sauce
1 tablespoon lemon juice
1½ teaspoons dry mustard
1 teaspoon salt
1 teaspoon pepper

Sauté onion and garlic in butter or margarine until golden. Add remaining ingredients. Simmer for 15 minutes, stirring occasionally. This may be prepared ahead and reheated just before serving.

Duck Sauce I

CHINA   Yield: 4 servings

1 cup plum jelly
½ cup chutney, finely chopped
1 tablespoon white vinegar
1 tablespoon sugar
Dash ground ginger

Mix all ingredients until they are smooth. Use with beef or pork or use with Chinese mustard sauce. Can be stored one week in refrigerator or in freezer indefinitely.

Duck Sauce II

CHINA   Yield: 2 cups

1 cup red plum jam
1 cup chutney
6 tablespoons dry mustard
¼ cup Sauterne

Combine the jam and the chutney in a small bowl and blend thoroughly. The sauce may be served hot or cold. Place the dry mustard in a small bowl and stir in a small amount of the Sauterne until smooth. Add the remaining Sauterne gradually and blend thoroughly. Serve the sauce and hot mustard separately in small individual bowls.

Garlic, Chili, and Fish Sauce

INDOCHINA   Yield: 4 servings

Since this is used in small quantities, it goes a long way. Serve it with any Indonesian main dish.

2 ripe red chilies
1 clove garlic, peeled
1 teaspoon sugar
1 lemon
1 tablespoon vinegar
1 tablespoon water
4 tablespoons fish sauce

Remove stalks from chilies and cut the chilies down the center. Remove seeds and center membrane and discard. Cut chilies into pieces; add the garlic and grind to a paste with a mortar and pestle. Add the sugar and a peeled, seeded lemon gradually, continuing to pound to a pulp. Last, stir in vinegar, water, and fish sauce. Place in a small serving bowl.

If an electric blender is used, the mixture will be frothy. While the taste will be the same, it will look slightly different.

Garlic and Vinegar Sauce

THAILAND   Yield: 4 servings

2 or 3 fresh red chilies
3 cloves garlic
2 tablespoons sugar
4 tablespoons vinegar
Salt to taste

Finely chop or crush the chilies and garlic. Add the remaining ingredients and mix thoroughly. This sauce is best made several hours before using and left to blend at room temperature. If a blender is used, the sauce must be made well ahead of time.

Ginger-Soy Dipping Sauce

JAPAN   Yield: ¾ cup

¼ cup soy sauce
1 teaspoon sugar
1 teaspoon powdered ginger
½ cup dashi (fish broth) or chicken bouillon

Combine all the ingredients in a small saucepan. Warm and place in dipping bowls.

Ginger-Soy Sauce

CHINA   Yield: About 1½ cups

½ cup soy sauce
1 cup water
2 tablespoons white wine, optional
2 teaspoons sugar
1 teaspoon powdered ginger

Mix together all ingredients and heat gently. Serve warm.

Fluffy Horseradish Sauce

JAPAN   Yield: About 1½ cups

1 cup sour cream
¼ cup prepared horseradish, drained
1 tablespoon lemon juice
1 tablespoon sugar
1 tablespoon chives, minced

Mix together all ingredients in a bowl. Cover and refrigerate several hours to blend flavors. Stir before serving.

Lemon Dipping Sauce

JAPAN   Yield: 1½ cups

1 cup cold chicken broth
2 tablespoons cornstarch
3 tablespoons lemon juice
½ teaspoon ginger, grated
2 tablespoons soy sauce
1 tablespoon honey or sugar
2 teaspoons grated lemon rind

Combine all the ingredients in a sauce-pan. Stir constantly and bring to a boil. Serve in dipping bowls garnished with a lemon slice.

Hot Mustard Sauce

CHINA   Yield: ½ cup

3 to 4 tablespoons vinegar
    (approximately)
½ cup dry mustard

Add sufficient vinegar to mix the mustard into a paste the consistency of mayonnaise. This sauce is very hot.

Mustard Cream Sauce

CHINA   Yield: About ¾ cup

¼ cup prepared mustard
1 tablespoon minced chives
1 teaspoon lemon juice
¼ cup sour cream
¼ cup mayonnaise

Blend together all ingredients and let stand several hours before using.

Mustard Sauce I

CHINA   Yield: About ¼ cup

2 tablespoons mustard
4 tablespoons cold water
½ teaspoon vinegar
¼ teaspoon salt
¼ teaspoon brown sugar

In a small bowl, combine mustard with half the water. Stir to a smooth paste. Stir in the vinegar, salt, brown sugar, and, finally, in a thin stream, the remaining water. Store in the refrigerator.

Mustard Sauce II

CHINA   Yield: Varies

Dry mustard
Water or stale beer
Turmeric

Mix the dry mustard with water; color with turmeric. If you like it hotter, mix it with stale beer instead of water. Cover and refrigerate. Serve with egg rolls, pork strips, or ribs.

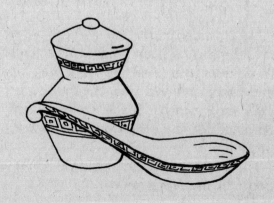

Nuoc Cham

INDONESIA   Yield: 4 servings

This hot, tangy sauce can be safely kept in the refrigerator for a week.

2 cloves garlic, peeled
4 dried red chilies or 1 fresh red chili
5 teaspoons sugar
Juice and pulp of ¼ lime
¼ cup fish sauce
⅓ cup water

Use a mortar and pestle to pound the garlic, chilies, and sugar. Add the juice and pulp of the lime; then add fish sauce and water. Mix well to combine all the ingredients.

Peanut Sauce I

INDONESIA   Yield: About 1 cup

6 tablespoons peanut butter (smooth or crunchy)
1 cup water
¾ teaspoon garlic salt
2 teaspoons palm sugar or substitute
2 tablespoons dark soy sauce
Lemon juice to taste
½ teaspoon shrimp paste
Coconut milk or water for thinning

Place peanut butter and water in a saucepan and stir constantly. When well blended, remove from heat. Add the remaining ingredients and blend well until the sauce is a paste consistency but is able to be poured. Add more salt and lemon juice to taste if desired.

This sauce will keep for several weeks in a bottle in the refrigerator.

Peanut Sauce II

MALAYSIA   Yield: 4 to 6 servings

5 tablespoons vegetable oil
4 ounces whole shelled peanuts
3 shallots, peeled and chopped
1 clove garlic, peeled and chopped
1 slice trasi (shrimp paste)
Pinch of chili powder
Salt to taste
1 tablespoon peanut oil
1½ pints water
1 tablespoon tamarind water
1 teaspoon brown sugar

Heat the vegetable oil in a skillet. Fry the peanuts for about 5 minutes or until lightly browned, shaking the pan to prevent sticking. Remove; allow to cool. Using an electric blender, food processor, or mortar and pestle, grind peanuts to a powder.

Pound shallots, garlic, and trasi to a smooth paste. Add chili powder and salt and mix well.

Heat the peanut oil; add the spice paste and fry gently for 30 seconds, stirring constantly. Add water to the spice paste and bring to a boil. Put in ground peanuts, tamarind water, and brown sugar. Stir and check seasonings, adding more salt if needed. Continue cooking until the sauce thickens, stirring all the while. Serve at once.

Plum Sauce

CHINA   Yield: 1½ cups

1 cup plum, peach, or apricot preserves
½ cup chopped chutney or Indian relish
1 tablespoon sugar
1 tablespoon vinegar

Combine the ingredients and refrigerate for 1 to 2 hours. Serve in dipping bowls.

Dips, Gravies & Sauces

Sweet-and-Sour Plum Sauce

CHINA   Yield: About 1½ cups

    ½ cup water
    1 cup plum jelly
    2 tablespoons catsup
    2 tablespoons vinegar

Place ingredients in saucepan and stir. Bring to boil. Serve warm.

Sambal Tomat

INDONESIA   Yield: 4 servings

This spicy hot tomato sauce is particularly tasty served cold over fish, shrimp, or chicken.

    2 tablespoons crushed red peppers
    1 tablespoon water
    2 tablespoons fresh tomatoes, chopped
    1 teaspoon shrimp or anchovy paste
    ½ teaspoon salt

After you have crushed the peppers, soak them for 10 minutes in water. Add the remaining ingredients and mash them together until all flavors have blended. You can do this with your electric blender, food processor, or mortar and pestle.

Sesame-Seed Sauce

KOREA   Yield: 4 servings

This is a delicious dipping sauce for cooked or raw vegetables—and it can be made several days in advance.

    ½ cup sesame seeds
    1 tablespoon sugar

    3 tablespoons vinegar
    4 tablespoons light soy sauce

Place sesame seeds in a dry frying pan over medium heat and stir constantly until toasted. After about 5 minutes, they will be brown in color. Crush the seeds with a mortar and pestle or in an electric blender or food processor. Mix the toasted and ground sesame seeds with sugar, vinegar, and light soy sauce. Store in a bottle, shaking well before serving.

Shrimp Sauce

THAILAND   Yield: About 1 generous cup

This can be used as a dip or over white rice as a main course.

    2 tablespoons dried shrimp
    Hot water
    1 teaspoon dried shrimp paste (kapi)
    4 cloves garlic, peeled and quartered
    2 teaspoons ground chilies or 2 fresh
      red chilies
    2 teaspoons palm sugar or substitute
    2 tablespoons lemon juice
    1½ tablespoons soy sauce
    3 tablespoons water

Soak washed shrimp in hot water for 20 minutes. Rinse thoroughly. Wrap shrimp paste in foil and grill for 3 minutes on each side.

Place shrimp, shrimp paste, garlic, chilies, sugar, lemon juice, soy sauce, and water in blender. Cover and blend until smooth. If blender is unavailable, use mortar and pestle to pound these ingredients into the needed texture.

Soy Sauce

KOREA   Yield: 4 servings

This enriched soy sauce can be used as a dip with many kinds of Oriental food.

3 tablespoons soy sauce
1 tablespoon scallions, chopped
1 teaspoon sesame seeds
1 teaspoon sesame-seed oil
1 teaspoon garlic, peeled and crushed
½ teaspoon sugar
1 teaspoon vinegar
Pinch of chili powder

Mix these ingredients together and let stand for an hour until the flavors blend. Serve in individual shallow dishes as a side accompaniment to other foods.

Pungent Sweet-and-Sour Sauce

CHINA   Yield: About 1 cup

1 cup bottled sweet-and-sour sauce
2 tablespoons catsup
2 teaspoons prepared mustard

Mix ingredients together and heat gently. Serve warm.

Sweet-and-Sour Sauce I

CHINA   Yield: About ½ cup

1 tablespoon cornstarch
3 tablespoons water
2 tablespoons soy sauce
3 tablespoons sugar
2 tablespoons vinegar
1 tablespoon catsup

Mix cornstarch and water in a custard cup. Mix soy sauce, sugar, vinegar, and catsup in a small saucepan and bring to a simmer. Add cornstarch mixture and simmer until it thickens and clears, stirring constantly. If too thick, thin with water.

Sweet-and-Sour Sauce II

CHINA   Yield: About 1½ cups

½ cup chutney
½ cup plum jam
¼ cup cold water
1 tablespoon sugar
1 tablespoon vinegar

Combine ingredients in a small saucepan; simmer 1 minute. Cool; store in refrigerator.

Sweet-and-Sour Sauce III

CHINA   Yield: About 1¼ cups

4 tablespoons catsup
¼ cup brown sugar
2 tablespoons soy sauce
3 tablespoons wine vinegar
2 tablespoons dry white wine
2 tablespoons cornstarch, dissolved in
   ½ cup cold water

Combine catsup, sugar, soy sauce, vinegar, and wine in saucepan. Bring to a boil. Add the cornstarch dissolved in water to the sauce. Cook over low heat, stirring constantly, until sauce has thickened. Serve this with chicken, beef, pork, or seafood.

Sweet-and-Sour Sauce IV

CHINA   Yield: About 2 cups

1 tablespoon oil
1 medium onion, finely sliced
1 medium carrot, sliced
½ green pepper, diced
½ red pepper, diced
1 15-ounce can pineapple chunks
1 small cucumber, peeled and diced
1 tablespoon cornstarch
2 teaspoons fresh ginger, grated
½ cup white vinegar
2 teaspoons sugar
3 teaspoons tomato sauce
2 teaspoons soy sauce
1 cup liquid (juice from pineapple
     chunks plus chicken stock)
Salt and pepper to taste
2 shallots or spring onions

Heat oil; sauté onion, carrot, and pepper 2 to 3 minutes. Drain pineapple, reserving liquid. Add pineapple chunks and cucumber to pan. Stir to combine vegetables; remove; set aside.

Blend cornstarch and ginger with vinegar, sugar, tomato sauce, and soy sauce. Combine this with the liquid; add to pan. Stir constantly until sauce boils and thickens. Season with salt and pepper. Return vegetables to pan; reheat thoroughly. Last, add sliced shallots to sauce. Cook for 2 minutes more.

Tempura Dipping Sauce I

JAPAN   Yield: About 3 to 4 servings

2 teaspoons soy sauce
¼ teaspoon salt
½ teaspoon sugar

½ cup white radish, grated
2 cups dashi (broth made from dried
     bonito and seaweed)
1 tablespoon scallions, chopped

Mix soy sauce, salt, sugar, and grated radish together. Blend in dashi; then add scallions. This sauce can be used with any food that has been fried in a tempura batter.

Tempura Dipping Sauce II

JAPAN   Yield: About 1½ cups

1 cup basic mayonnaise
⅓ cup chili sauce
3 tablespoons prepared horseradish

Combine the mayonnaise, chili sauce, and horseradish in a small bowl and mix well. Chill before serving.

Tempura Dipping Sauce III (Green Mayonnaise Sauce)

JAPAN   Yield: About 1½ cups

½ cup frozen spinach, thawed
1 tablespoon fresh parsley, chopped
2 tablespoons chives, chopped
1 teaspoon dried dillweed, crumbled
1 cup mayonnaise

Drain the spinach well, then squeeze out any remaining moisture. Place the spinach, parsley, chives, and dillweed in a blender container and process until pureed. Combine the puree and mayonnaise in a small bowl and mix well. Chill before serving.

Tempura Dipping Sauce IV

JAPAN   Yield: About 1 cup

1 cup yogurt
2 tablespoons green onion, finely
   minced
2 teaspoons curry powder
Salt to taste

Combine the yogurt, onion, curry powder, and salt in a small bowl and blend well. Chill well before serving.

Tempura Sauce for Chicken

JAPAN   Yield: 1 cup

½ cup chicken broth
4 tablespoons soy sauce
4 tablespoons sherry

Combine all ingredients and warm in a saucepan. Serve in dipping bowls.

Tempura Sauce for Seafood

JAPAN   Yield: ¾ cup

½ cup dashi (fish broth) or chicken
   broth
2 tablespoons soy sauce
2 teaspoons sugar
1 tablespoon horseradish sauce

Combine all ingredients and serve warm in dipping bowls.

Tempura Sweet-and-Sour Sauce

JAPAN   Yield: 2 cups

1 tablespoon butter
1 cup water
½ cup cider vinegar
3 tablespoons soy sauce
¼ cup sugar
1 tablespoon cornstarch
3 tablespoons sherry

Melt the butter in a saucepan over medium heat. Blend in water, vinegar, soy sauce, and sugar. Bring to a boil. Lower heat; simmer for 10 minutes.

Make a paste of the cornstarch and sherry; slowly blend it into the rest of ingredients, stirring constantly until thickened.

Teriyaki Sauce for Steak

JAPAN   Yield: 2 cups

1 cup soy sauce
1 cup brown sugar
1½ teaspoons cinnamon
2 ounces gin
1 clove garlic, minced
Dash of pepper

Mix ingredients. Marinate steak 5 minutes each side. Brush with sauce before serving. Spoon remaining sauce *sparingly* over rice and serve with meat.

Salads & Vegetables

Japanese Egg Salad

JAPAN   Yield: 4 servings

7½ ounces canned tuna fish
1 can mandarin oranges, approximately
   11 ounces
16 stuffed olives
4 hard-boiled eggs

Salad dressing

2 tablespoons oil
2 scant tablespoons lemon juice
2 tablespoons soy sauce
Salt
Pepper
Pinch of sugar

Parsley sprigs for garnish

Drain tuna fish; tear into bite-size pieces with a fork. Drain mandarin oranges and olives. Slice olives and hard-boiled eggs. Toss all ingredients lightly.

To prepare dressing, combine oil, lemon juice, soy sauce, salt, pepper, and sugar; stir until well blended.

Pour dressing over salad. Refrigerate for 10 minutes or longer. Divide among 4 individual glass bowls and garnish with parsley sprigs.

Raw Fish Salad

INDOCHINA   Yield: 4 to 6 servings

2 pounds fresh fish, boned and finely
   chopped
1 teaspoon salt
½ cup water
Juice of 5 or 6 lemons
5 medium onions, peeled and finely
   chopped
5 cloves garlic, peeled and finely
   chopped

3 or 4 fresh pimientos, finely chopped
2 tablespoons fennel or shallots, finely
   chopped
Lettuce leaves

Place minced fish in a large bowl. In another bowl, mix salt, water, and lemon juice. Pour liquid over fish and allow to stand for at least 15 minutes. Press out the water from the fish; bring water to boil and put in saucepan. Set aside the water to cool. Add cooled water to fish, followed by onions, garlic, pimientos, and fennel. Mix well. Serve on a bed of lettuce with your favorite green salad.

Apple Salad

THAILAND   Yield: 6 servings

3 tart, green cooking apples, peeled
   and thinly sliced
1 teaspoon salt
1 tablespoon peanut oil
4 cloves garlic, peeled and thinly sliced
6 spring onions, sliced
½ pound pork finely shredded
1 tablespoon dried shrimp powder
1 tablespoon fish sauce
2 tablespoons roasted peanuts, crushed
1 teaspoon palm sugar
Pepper to taste
Red chili, finely chopped, for garnish

Sprinkle prepared apples with salt in a large bowl.

Heat oil and fry garlic. Remove from pan and fry spring onions. Set aside. In the same pan, stir-fry pork. When cooked, add shrimp powder, fish sauce, peanuts, and sugar. Remove from heat.

When ready to serve, mix everything together and season with pepper to taste. Garnish with chilies and serve.

Mandarin-Orange Gelatin

CHINA   Yield: 6 servings

1 11-ounce can mandarin oranges,
  drained; reserve ½ cup liquid
3 tablespoons sauterne
2 3-ounce packages orange-flavored
  gelatin
1 envelope unflavored gelatin
2 cups hot water
1 cup cold water

Combine oranges with 2 tablespoons sauterne.

Combine orange-flavored and unflavored gelatins in a large bowl; mix well. Add hot water; stir until gelatin is dissolved. Stir in 1 tablespoon sauterne, reserved mandarin-orange liquid, and cold water. Chill until gelatin is thick and syrupy.

Pour about ½ cup gelatin into 1½-quart mold rinsed in cold water. Arrange orange segments petal-fashion in gelatin. Chill until set. Spoon about a 1-inch layer of thickened gelatin over the oranges. Arrange a layer of orange segments around edge of mold. Chill until set. Spoon another layer of gelatin over the oranges. Repeat layers. Chill until set.

Papaya Salad

PHILIPPINES   Yield: 6 servings

1 medium, firm papaya (pawpaw),
  peeled
1 small ripe pineapple, peeled and
  diced
2 spring onions, finely sliced
1 cooking apple, peeled and diced
½ cup celery, thinly sliced
½ cup prepared salad dressing or
  mayonnaise
Salt and pepper to taste

Cut the papaya in half and scoop out the seeds. Dice the fruit into a serving bowl. Add all of the other ingredients in the order given and toss gently. Cover the bowl and chill the salad for at least 1 hour before serving.

Fruit Salad I

CHINA   Yield: About 12 servings

All the fruits in this recipe are available at Oriental food stores. Some may be available at your supermarket.

1 4-ounce jar ginger in syrup, drained
1 11-ounce can lichees in syrup,
  drained
1 8-ounce can kumquats, drained
1 20-ounce can longans, drained
1 12-ounce can water-lily roots,
  drained
1 16-ounce can mangos, drained
1 round watermelon, chilled, cut in
  half, meat and seeds removed, meat
  cut into balls or cubes
1 18-ounce can white nuts
1 lemon, sliced

Place ginger, lichees, kumquats, longans, lily roots, and mangos in a large bowl; mix well. Chill until cold.

Cut slice off base of each watermelon half; place each half on serving dish. Place melon balls or cubes back into shells. Spoon mixed fruit on watermelon balls. Serve with nuts and lemon.

Fruit Salad II

KOREA   Yield: 4 to 6 servings

½ cup water
6 tablespoons sugar
1 tablespoon white wine
2 oranges
2 pears
2 peaches
1 cup morello cherries
3 tablespoons lime juice
2 tablespoons peeled pistachio nuts

In a pot, bring water, sugar, and wine to a boil. Allow to cool.

Peel, seed, and dice the oranges. Peel, core, and halve the pears. Peel, seed, and dice the peaches. Remove seeds from cherries. Place all fruit in a serving bowl. Add lime juice to the cooled liquid and pour over the fruit. Cover and refrigerate at least 30 minutes. When ready to serve, mix fruit with slotted spoon. Sprinkle nuts on top and serve.

Fruit Salad III

INDONESIA   Yield: 4 to 6 servings

This can be served with the main course or as a dessert.

2 cups honey
2 tablespoons peanut butter
1 teaspoon vinegar
1 teaspoon salt
1 teaspoon red pepper
4 cups shredded carrots, apples, pears, and cucumbers

Combine honey, peanut butter, vinegar, salt, and pepper and stir until well mixed.

Last, put in the shredded vegetables and fruit. Mix again so that the flavors blend; refrigerate for at least 1 hour. Serve chilled.

Spiced Fruit Salad I

MALAYSIA   Yield: 4 to 6 servings

In Malaysia, this is made with native fruits, such as kedondong and jeruk bali. Here, fruits that are available in the West are substituted.

1 underripe mango
2 crisp dessert apples
½ fresh pineapple
½ teaspoon salt
1 pink meat grapefruit
¼ cucumber, peeled and sliced

Seasonings

¼ teaspoon chili powder
1 slice trasi, broiled, optional
⅔ cup palm sugar
Pinch of salt
1 tablespoon tamarind water

Peel and slice the mango into a bowl. Peel, core, and slice the apples into the same bowl. Peel pineapple and cut into chunks as well. Add enough cold water to cover and stir in the salt. Peel the grapefruit and divide it into segments, keeping it separate from the other fruit for the time being.

Blend the seasonings, using a mortar and pestle, until very smooth. Add salt and tamarind water and stir to mix. Drain the water from the fruit; place it in a serving bowl and add grapefruit and cucumber. Pour the seasonings on top and stir the fruit gently to mix well. Chill until ready to serve.

Spiced Fruit Salad II

INDIA   Yield: About 4 servings

2 oranges
2 bananas
2 pears
1 apple
2 guavas, optional
Juice of 1 lemon
2 teaspoons chili powder
1 teaspoon ginger powder
1 teaspoon garam masala
1 teaspoon salt
½ teaspoon freshly ground black
  pepper

Peel the oranges and bananas and cut into pieces. Core the pears and apple, leaving skin on for color and texture. Chop pears and apple with guavas, including the guava seeds.

Place prepared fruit in a bowl and sprinkle lemon juice over all. Mix the spices and seasonings and sprinkle them over the fruit. Toss gently to cover the fruit with the spices. Refrigerate for at least 2 hours before serving.

Pork Skin Salad

THAILAND   Yield: 4 servings

½ cup boiled pork skin, finely sliced
½ cup boiled lean pork, finely
  chopped
1 cup fresh mint leaves
½ teaspoon lemon rind, grated
3 tablespoons dried shrimp powder
1 tablespoon fresh coriander leaves,
  chopped
1 tablespoon spring onions, chopped
2 to 3 tablespoons coconut cream
1 tablespoon nam prik (shrimp sauce)
1 tablespoon lime juice
1 tablespoon fish sauce
1 to 2 tablespoons sugar
Greens for garnish

Slice the fat away from the boiled pork skin, leaving only the jelly-like skin.

Mix all the rest of the ingredients together just before serving. Toss with pork and pork skin. Garnish with your choice of greens.

Chicken and Shrimp Salad

INDIA   Yield: 4 to 6 servings

½ pound dark meat of chicken,
  cooked and diced
½ cup cooked rice
1 leek, cut in half lengthwise and
  finely chopped
¼ pound shrimp, cooked, deveined,
  and cut in half
1 small onion, peeled and finely
  chopped

Marinade

2 tablespoons each of mango chutney,
  oil, and lemon juice
1 teaspoon vinegar
½ teaspoon Worcestershire sauce
Pinch of curry
Salt and white pepper to taste

Garnish

Lettuce leaves, washed and drained dry
1 banana, peeled and sliced

Prepare chicken and rice. Add the chopped leek to the rice during the last 5 minutes of cooking. When the rice has cooled, put chicken, shrimp, and onion in a bowl with the rice. Mix well.

In a small bowl, mix ingredients for the marinade and stir well or blend with a whisk. Pour this mixture over the salad and toss all together gently. Line serving dish with lettuce leaves. Make a mound of the salad and garnish with slices of bananas. Allow to chill for 30 minutes before serving.

Chicken Salad with Lichees

CHINA   Yield: 5 to 6 servings

3 cups cooked chicken, diced
2 or 3 stalks celery, chopped
1 green pepper, chopped
Salt and pepper
¾ cup French dressing
Salad greens
1 can lichees
1 small can mandarin oranges

Curry salad dressing

¾ cup mayonnaise
¼ cup sour cream
2 teaspoons curry powder
2 tablespoons onions, grated
2 tablespoons parsley, chopped

Combine chicken, celery, and green pepper. Add salt, pepper, and French dressing; toss lightly. Chill about ½ hour.

Arrange salad greens around large platter. Pile chicken mixture in center.

Drain lichees and oranges. Place orange segment in each lichee; arrange around edge of platter.

Blend all dressing ingredients together; chill well. Serve dressing separately.

Curried Chicken Salad

INDIA   Yield: 6 servings

3 tablespoons instant minced onions
3 tablespoons water
2 tablespoons butter
1¼ teaspoons curry powder
⅓ cup mayonnaise
1 tablespoon lemon juice
½ teaspoon salt

Dash of cayenne pepper
3 cups cooked chicken, diced
1 (1-pound, 4-ounce) can pineapple chunks, drained
½ cup nuts, coarsely chopped
⅓ cup golden raisins
1 red apple, cored, diced
Lettuce
2 tablespoons shredded coconut

Combine onion and water in small bowl; let stand 10 minutes.

Melt butter in small skillet over medium heat; stir in onion and curry powder. Sauté, stirring constantly, 3 to 5 minutes; cool. Combine curry mixture with mayonnaise, lemon juice, salt, and cayenne; blend thoroughly.

Combine chicken, pineapple, nuts, raisins, and apple in large bowl. Add curry dressing; toss gently until mixed. Line salad bowl with lettuce. Add salad; sprinkle with coconut.

Chinese Turkey Salad

CHINA   Yield: 6 servings

1 small head lettuce, shredded
4 green onions, chopped
2 cups cooked turkey (or chicken), shredded
2 ribs celery, shredded

Dressing

¼ cup sugar
1 teaspoon salt
1 teaspoon pepper
½ cup oil (half peanut oil)
6 tablespoons wine vinegar
1 clove garlic, crushed

1 cup slivered almonds, toasted
2 cups chow mein noodles

In a salad bowl, combine lettuce, green onions, turkey, and celery and toss.

Combine sugar, salt, pepper, oil, vinegar, and garlic until well mixed. Pour over salad; top with almonds and chow mein noodles.

Asparagus Salad

CHINA   Yield: About 4 to 5 servings

  1 tablespoon soy sauce
  ½ teaspoon red-wine vinegar
  2 teaspoons sesame oil
  1 teaspoon sugar
  1 pound asparagus, tough ends broken
    off, sliced into 2-inch lengths

Combine soy sauce, vinegar, oil, and sugar; stir until sugar dissolves. Bring pot of water to boil. Drop asparagus into water; cook 1 minute. Drain; rinse with cold water. Toss asparagus with soy sauce mixture; chill.

Cole Slaw with Sesame Dressing

CHINA   Yield: 4 servings

  3 cups cabbage, shredded
  2 medium carrots, shredded
  ½ medium onion, grated

Sesame dressing

  ¼ cup sesame seeds, toasted
  1½ tablespoons lemon juice
  1½ tablespoons vinegar
  1 teaspoon sugar
  1 tablespoon soy sauce
  ¼ teaspoon MSG, optional
  ¼ cup peanut oil

Combine cabbage, carrots, and onion.

Place sesame seeds in ungreased skillet over low heat and stir until lightly browned. Grind toasted seeds in blender. Add lemon juice, vinegar, sugar, soy sauce, and MSG, and blend into smooth paste. Combine mixture with peanut oil and blend well. Mix thoroughly with cabbage mixture.

Cauliflower Salad

JAPAN   Yield: 4 servings

  1 small cauliflower
  3 tablespoons peanut butter
  Water
  Pinch of salt
  Chopped peanuts

Boil cauliflower; separate into florets. Mix peanut butter with water until thin. Season with salt. Mix in with the cauliflower. Sprinkle a little chopped peanuts over the top.

Cucumber Salad I

THAILAND   Yield: 4 servings

  2 green cucumbers
  1 small onion
  2 tablespoons dried shrimp powder
  1 or 2 fresh red chilies, seeded and
    chopped
  2 tablespoons fish sauce
  Lemon juice to taste

Peel, seed, and grate cucumbers coarsely. Peel and grate the onion. Mix all ingredients in a bowl until well blended, adding lemon juice at the end to taste. Serve slightly chilled.

Salads & Vegetables

Cucumber Salad II

JAPAN   Yield: 6 servings

3 medium cucumbers

Marinade

⅓ cup white-rice vinegar
4 teaspoons sugar
1 teaspoon salt
Fresh gingerroot to taste, finely
    chopped

Peel (optional) cucumbers; cut them in half lengthwise. Remove large seeds; slice crosswise into thin slices.

Mix together vinegar, sugar, salt, and ginger. Chill cucumber slices in vinegar marinade for at least 2 hours.
Note: White vinegar can be substituted for the rice vinegar, but you might want to dilute it with a little water.

Wilted Lettuce Salad

JAPAN   Yield: 6 servings

8 strips bacon
¼ cup vinegar
2 tablespoons water
2 tablespoons sugar
½ teaspoon salt
2 quarts torn leaf lettuce
¼ cup chopped green onions
2 hard-cooked eggs, chopped

Cook bacon in 10-inch skillet over medium heat until crisp, about 6 minutes. Remove bacon and drain on paper towels. Crumble bacon and set aside. Pour off all but 3 tablespoons bacon drippings. Combine vinegar, water, sugar, and salt with the 3 tablespoons bacon drippings. Bring mixture to a boil, stirring to dissolve sugar, about 2 minutes.

Combine lettuce, onions, and bacon in large serving bowl. Add hot vinegar mixture and toss to coat lettuce. Garnish with hard-cooked eggs and serve at once.

Indian Potato Salad

INDIA   Yield: 4 servings

3 or 4 medium new potatoes, boiled,
    chilled, and cubed
¾ cup plain yogurt
⅛ teaspoon curry powder
¼ teaspoon chili powder
1 roasted green chili, chopped (available canned in Mexican food section
    of your supermarket)
4 large fresh mint leaves, minced
½ teaspoon salt

Combine all ingredients; serve at once. Seasonings may be increased for a stronger curry-chili flavor.

White Radish Salad

KOREA   Yield: 4 servings

2 giant white radishes, peeled and cut
    into matchstick strips
1 or 2 crisp cooking apples, peeled,
    cored, and cut into thin strips
Juice of half lemon
3 spring onions, including green tops,
    very finely sliced

Dressing

3 tablespoons light soy sauce
1 tablespoon salad oil
2 teaspoons sesame oil
3 tablespoons mild vinegar
3 teaspoons sugar

1 teaspoon salt

1 tablespoon toasted, crushed sesame
seeds

1 fresh, hot red chili, seeded and finely
chopped

Prepare radishes and set aside. Prepare
apples and soak in cold water with lemon
juice to prevent discoloration. Slice onions
as directed.

Mix ingredients for the dressing in the
order given. Drain the apples and combine
with radishes, onions, and dressing in a large
bowl. Be sure vegetables are well coated with
the dressing. Serve chilled.

Fruited Rice Salads

JAPAN   Yield: 6 servings

2 tablespoons butter

½ cup celery, diced

¼ cup onion, minced

2 teaspoons grated orange rind

1 cup orange juice

1 cup water

½ teaspoon poultry seasoning

1 cup long-grain rice

⅓ cup golden raisins

6 orange shells

Heat the butter in medium-sized saucepan
and sauté the celery and onion until tender.
Stir in the orange rind, juice, water, poultry
seasoning, rice, and raisins. Bring to a boil.
Stir well, reduce heat, and cover. Simmer
until liquid is absorbed and rice is tender,
about 30 minutes. Remove from heat. When
cool, refrigerate for several hours. Serve in
orange shells.

Rice Salad I

CHINA   Yield: 6 to 8 servings

3 tablespoons oil

2 cups long-grain rice

3¾ cups chicken stock

1 teaspoon salt

1 pound shrimp, shelled, deveined,
and cooked

6 shallots or spring onions, chopped

½ green cucumber, chopped

1 small green pepper, diced

1 small red pepper, diced

2 sticks celery, sliced

⅓ cup French dressing

1 teaspoon soy sauce

Heat oil in a large saucepan. Add rice;
stir until golden brown. Add soup stock and
salt. Cover; simmer gently 12 minutes or until rice has absorbed all liquid. Turn out onto
a large tray; allow to cool. When rice has
cooled completely, add shrimp, shallots, cucumber, peppers, and celery. Mix gently.

Combine French dressing and soy sauce;
pour over salad. Toss gently to mix.

Rice Salad II

JAPAN   Yield: 4 servings

2 cups water
Salt
4 ounces long-grain rice
1 ounce dried mushrooms
8 ounces bean sprouts, canned or fresh
8 ounces canned bamboo shoots
4 ounces cooked ham
1 medium cucumber
4 tablespoons rice wine or brandy

Salad dressing

5 tablespoons oil
5 tablespoons lemon juice
3 tablespoons rice wine or sherry
2 tablespoons soy sauce
Salt

Garnish

1 small head Boston lettuce
1 lemon
Salt

Bring salted water to a boil. Add rice; cook for 15 minutes (or use your own method). Place rice in sieve. Pour cold water over it; drain thoroughly.

Chop mushrooms; place in small bowl. Cover with boiling water; let soak for 20 minutes. Drain bean sprouts, if canned. If using fresh bean sprouts, blanch, rinse with cold water, and drain them. Drain the bamboo shoots. Cut bamboo shoots into ¼-inch-wide strips. Cut ham into ¼-inch-wide, 2-inch-long strips. Cut unpeeled cucumber in half, then into thin slices lengthwise, and finally into 2-inch-long thin strips. Drain the mushrooms.

To prepare the salad dressing, combine oil, lemon juice, rice wine or sherry, soy sauce, and salt to taste; stir until well blended. Add rice, bean sprouts, bamboo shoots, ham, cucumber, and mushrooms to dressing; toss thoroughly. Cover; refrigerate for 30 minutes to let flavors blend.

Meanwhile, wash the lettuce and pat it dry. Tear it into large pieces and line a serving platter with it. Arrange rice salad on top.

Cut off both ends of a lemon until pulp is visible. Place on platter. Sprinkle top of lemon with salt. Heat rice wine or brandy; pour it over the lemon and ignite. Serve immediately. (Lemon is only a garnish, it is not eaten).

Rice Salad III

INDONESIA   Yield: 4 to 6 servings

2 cups water
1 teaspoon salt
½ cup long-grain rice
1 cup cooked chicken, cubed
1 apple, peeled, seeded, and quartered
1 orange, peeled, seeded, and quartered
1 banana, peeled and sliced
½ fennel bulb, coarsely chopped
1 red paprika pod, seeded and chopped
1 pepperoni, preserved in vinegar, seeded, and chopped
1 ginger plum from a jar, chopped
2 tablespoons oil
1 onion, peeled and chopped
2 heaping teaspoons curry powder

Marinade

Juice of 1 lemon
4 tablespoons catsup
1 to 2 teaspoons anise spirits
4 tablespoons mayonnaise
2 tablespoons sour cream

Garnish

¼ cup almond slices
1 orange, sliced
8 maraschino cherries

Bring water to a boil. Add salt. Stir in the rice and cook for 20 minutes. Strain; rinse with cold water and drain well. Prepare fruits, fennel, paprika, pepperoni, and ginger plum as directed.

Heat oil in a skillet and fry onion for 5 minutes. Remove from heat. Stir curry powder into rice and put in serving dish. Prepare the marinade by stirring lemon juice, catsup, anise spirits, mayonnaise, and sour cream together.

Mix chicken, fruit, vegetables, and marinade in a bowl. Allow to absorb flavors by setting aside for 1 hour. Taste and add more seasoning if needed.

Dry-roast almonds for 5 minutes in a skillet, stirring constantly.

Mix meat and vegetable mixture into rice, stirring gently. Garnish with almonds, orange slices, and cherries and serve at once. This refreshing cold salad is particularly good on a hot summer's day.

Spinach Raita Salad

INDIA   Yield: 4 servings

Popping mustard seeds sound like popping corn. The dressing is a bit unusual and very good.

    1 tablespoon vegetable oil
    2 teaspoons mustard seeds
    ½ teaspoon salt
    1 cup plain yogurt
    1 10-ounce bag fresh spinach, stems
      removed, washed and drained

Shake mustard seeds in hot oil in a covered pan over moderate heat until they pop (1 to 2 minutes). Cool. Combine oil and popped mustard seeds, salt, and yogurt. Add to well-drained spinach. Toss and serve at once.

Fresh-Spinach Salad

JAPAN   Yield: 4 servings

    10 ounces fresh spinach
    4 ounces fresh mushrooms
    ¼ cup scallion, chopped
    Small amount soy sauce
    Sesame seeds, optional

Thoroughly wash spinach and tear up larger pieces. Drain well. Slice mushrooms and add to spinach. Add chopped scallion and toss well. Sprinkle with the amount of soy sauce desired and toss lightly. Sprinkle each portion with sesame seeds.

Tomato Salad

BURMA   Yield: 4 servings

The flavor of the salad will be improved if you use tomatoes that are not fully ripe.

    ¼ cup vegetable oil
    1 medium onion, peeled and sliced
    4 tomatoes, thinly sliced
    1 tablespoon pounded, roasted, shelled
      peanuts
    3 tablespoons coriander leaves,
      chopped
    1 teaspoon shrimp-flavored soy sauce
    Juice of ½ lemon
    Coriander leaves for garnish

In a small skillet, heat 3 tablespoons of the oil. Fry the onion until crisp and golden. Use a slotted spoon and remove from pan. Drain on paper towels.

Place tomatoes in a bowl with peanuts, coriander, soy sauce, and remaining oil. Toss lightly. Spoon the tomato mixture onto a serving plate. Sprinkle with lemon juice and then put onions on top. Garnish with coriander and chill before serving.

Water Chestnut Salad

THAILAND   Yield: 4 to 6 servings

8 ounces fresh water chestnuts or 1
    small can, drained
1 tablespoon lard or oil
1 small onion, peeled and finely
    chopped
2 teaspoons garlic, peeled and finely
    chopped
2 tablespoons fish sauce
2 tablespoons lemon juice
1 tablespoon sugar
¼ cup cooked pork, diced
¼ cup cooked shrimp, chopped
¼ cup crab meat, flaked
2 tablespoons fresh coriander leaves,
    chopped
3 or 4 tender citrus leaves, chopped
2 fresh red chilies, seeded and chopped

Wash and peel water chestnuts; slice and
cut into strips. (If using canned, drain and
cut the same way.)

Heat fat and stir-fry onion and garlic over
medium heat for 2 minutes. In a bowl, make
a dressing of the fish sauce, lemon juice,
sugar, and onions and garlic. In a larger
bowl, combine chestnuts, pork, shrimp, and
crab meat. Pour the dressing over this mixture and toss gently. Garnish with citrus
leaves and chilies.

Assorted Vegetable Salad

BURMA   Yield: 6 to 8 servings

Although the vegetables in this salad are
cooked, the cooking time is short so that
they do not lose their crispness. The vegetables can be cooked ahead.

4 carrots, scraped
Saltwater, boiling
1½ cups string beans, topped and
    tailed
1 cup okra
2 cups fresh bean sprouts
2 large cauliflower florets
1 cup bamboo shoots, optional
5 tablespoons sesame seeds
2 tablespoons vegetable oil
1 medium onion, peeled and sliced

Cook carrots in boiling saltwater for 7
minutes. Remove and allow to cool. Cook
the remaining vegetables separately in the
same saltwater, for 3 minutes each. Allow to
cool.

Use a small skillet and fry sesame seeds
over dry heat until golden brown, shaking
pan constantly. Remove and set aside. Add
oil to pan. When hot, fry onion until
golden. Remove and drain on paper towels.
Reserve 1 tablespoon of oil, adding a pinch
of salt.

Slice carrots into thin strips. Slice beans
and okra into ½-inch pieces, diagonally. Arrange vegetables in separate piles on serving
dish. Sprinkle oil over vegetables, followed
by sesame seeds and onions. Chill and serve.

Chinese Vegetable Salad

CHINA   Yield: 8 servings

1 8½-ounce can peas
1 8½-ounce can water chestnuts,
    sliced
1 16-ounce can Chinese mixed
    vegetables
2 cups celery, diced
1 cup sugar
¼ cup tarragon vinegar
¾ cup vinegar

Drain canned vegetables and place these along with celery in a 2-quart casserole. Combine sugar and vinegars, stirring until sugar dissolves. Pour over vegetables making sure all vegetables are submerged. Refrigerate for 24 hours, occasionally stirring. At end of 24 hours, drain, then store in refrigerator until ready to serve. Keeps well refrigerated several days.

Cooked Salad with Coconut Dressing

INDONESIA   Yield: 4 servings

Use any combination of fresh vegetables that you choose but be careful not to overcook them. They should be crisp when served.

1 slice dried shrimp paste (trasi), broiled in foil for 5 minutes
2 cloves garlic, peeled and chopped
1 shallot, peeled and chopped
½ teaspoon chili powder
1 teaspoon brown sugar
1 tablespoon tamarind water
Salt to taste
2 cups white coconut flesh, grated
1½ cups cabbage
¼ pound string beans, topped and tailed
2 medium carrots, peeled and sliced
2 cups bean sprouts
Boiling water
Watercress for garnish
Cucumber slices for garnish

Pound shrimp paste, garlic, and shallots to a very thin paste. Add chili powder, sugar, tamarind water, and salt and mix very well. Put in the coconut and mix some more.

Cook vegetables separately in boiling water for just 3 minutes, so that they remain crisp. Drain.

When ready to serve, toss vegetables with coconut mixture until all are well coated. Put in serving bowl and garnish with watercress and cucumber slices.

Djakarta Salad

INDONESIA   Yield: 4 to 6 servings

4 cups water
1 teaspoon salt
½ cup long-grain rice
1½ pounds cooked chicken, boned and diced
1 red and 1 green pepper pod, cut into thin strips
2 bananas, peeled and sliced
1 cup yogurt
3 tablespoons mayonnaise
2 tablespoons catsup
1 tablespoon curry
¾ teaspoon ground ginger
Salt
White pepper
Cayenne pepper
Pinch of sugar

Bring water with salt to a boil. Add rice and cook on medium heat for 15 minutes. Drain well; rinse with cold water and allow to cool.

Add chicken and pepper pods to rice. Mix well. Gently stir in bananas.

In a separate bowl, combine yogurt, mayonnaise, catsup, curry, and ginger until well blended. Add remaining seasonings to taste. Pour this over the rice mixture. Cover and allow to marinate in refrigerator for at least 1 hour. Mound on a large platter when ready to serve.

Japanese Salad

JAPAN   Yield: 6 servings

1 large cucumber
2 carrots
1 large white radish
Salt
½ pound fresh mushrooms
10 ounces fresh shrimp
2 tablespoons parsley, chopped
1 tablespoon fresh dill, chopped

Salad dressing

2 eggs
Salt
Pinch of sugar
3 tablespoons melted butter
2 tablespoons wine vinegar
1 teaspoon paprika

Garnish

1 peach, sliced
1 mandarin orange or 1 tangerine,
  sectioned
½ orange, sliced

Grate unpeeled cucumber, carrots, and radish. Sprinkle with salt; let stand for 30 minutes. Drain off as much liquid as possible. Thinly slice mushrooms; mix with vegetables. Add shrimp and chopped fresh herbs. Toss; set aside for 15 minutes.

Meanwhile, prepare dressing by placing eggs, salt, sugar, and melted butter in top of double boiler. Beat over hot water until creamy. Remove from heat. Gradually add vinegar, beating constantly until dressing has cooled off. Season to taste with paprika.

Pour dressing over salad. Garnish with peach slices, mandarin orange or tangerine sections, and orange slices.

Mixed Salad

JAPAN   Yield: 6 servings

1 large cucumber
2 carrots
1 large white radish
Salt
½ pound fresh mushrooms
10 ounces fresh shrimp
2 tablespoons parsley, chopped
1 tablespoon fresh dill, chopped

Salad dressing

2 eggs
Salt
Pinch of sugar
3 tablespoons melted butter
2 tablespoons wine vinegar
1 teaspoon paprika

Garnish

1 peach, sliced
1 mandarin orange or 1 tangerine,
  sectioned
½ orange, sliced

Grate unpeeled cucumber, carrots, and radish. Sprinkle with salt; let stand for 30 minutes. Drain off as much liquid as possible. Thinly slice mushrooms; mix with vegetables. Add shrimp and chopped fresh herbs. Toss; set aside for 15 minutes.

Meanwhile, prepare the dressing by placing eggs, salt, sugar, and melted butter in top of double boiler. Beat over hot water until creamy. Remove from heat. Gradually add vinegar, beating constantly until dressing has cooled off. Season to taste with paprika.

Pour dressing over salad. Garnish with peach slices, mandarin orange or tangerine sections, and orange slices.

Oriental Salad

CHINA   Yield: 4 servings

2 pounds chicken breast, skinned and
   boned and cut in 1-inch wide strips
¼ cup soy sauce
⅔ cup salad oil
1 clove garlic, scored
1 teaspoon grated lemon peel
¼ cup lemon juice
10-ounce bag fresh spinach, washed
   and well drained
⅓ head iceberg lettuce
3 cups fresh bean sprouts
Salt to taste
¼ cup toasted sesame seeds

Mix together well the chicken, 1 tablespoon of the soy sauce, 2 tablespoons oil, the
garlic, and half the lemon peel; chill for several hours. Divide into 4 batches. Heat 2
more tablespoons oil in a large skillet; sauté
the chicken, one batch at a time, for 3 to 5
minutes or until cooked through and firm; do
not overcook. Discard garlic.

Mix chicken with the remaining oil, soy
sauce, and lemon peel. Add the lemon juice
and mix well; chill. When ready to serve,
sprinkle spinach, lettuce, and bean sprouts
with the salt and sesame seeds; toss with
chicken mixture and serve immediately.

Quick-and-Easy Salad

JAPAN   Yield: 2 servings

1 large cucumber, sliced
2 scallions, sliced in 1-inch pieces

Salad dressing

1½ teaspoons soy sauce
2½ tablespoons sugar
6 tablespoons vinegar

Slice cucumber (do not peel). Slice scallions; toss with cucumber.

Mix together soy sauce, sugar, and vinegar. You may want to adjust the amounts to
suit your taste. Pour dressing over vegetables.
Toss well; serve. If you desire, you can
sprinkle a few sesame seeds on top.

Yogurt Salad with Cucumber and Tomato

INDIA   Yield: 4 to 6 servings

1 large cucumber, peeled
4 shallots, peeled and finely chopped
1 teaspoon salt
2 tomatoes, cut in quarters, seeded,
   then diced
1 bunch parsley, chopped
4 cups yogurt
1 teaspoon ground caraway
Salt to taste
White pepper to taste
1 bunch dill, for garnish

Cut the peeled cucumber in half, lengthwise and crosswise. Scrape out and discard
the seeds; cut the cucumber into strips and
then into 1-inch pieces. Mix in a bowl with
tomatoes, shallots, and salt. Let stand for 15
minutes.

Mix parsley with cucumber mixture. Beat
yogurt with a whisk until it is light. Pour
over the vegetables. Add salt, caraway, and
pepper to taste. Refrigerate for 1 hour. Garnish with dill and serve at once.

Chinese Stir-fry Asparagus

CHINA   Yield: 4 to 6 servings

2½ pounds asparagus, trimmed and
   washed
1 scallion, diced
3 tablespoons peanut oil
1 teaspoon salt
½ teaspoon MSG, optional
1 5-ounce can water chestnuts, drained
   and sliced very thin

Cut the asparagus spears obliquely into
1½-inch lengths. Place, along with the scallion, in a large skillet in which the oil has
been heated to just below the smoking point.
Add salt and MSG and cook over high heat,
stirring frequently, 3 to 4 minutes, but do
not allow to brown.

Cover the pan, reduce heat to medium
and cook 3-5 minutes longer until asparagus
is cooked to desired doneness. It should remain crisp. Add chestnuts during the last
minutes of cooking.

Bean Curd and Bean Sprouts

MALAYSIA   Yield: 4 to 6 servings

2 squares yellow bean curd, cut in
   slices
½ pound fresh bean sprouts, washed,
   drained, and tails pinched off
2 cloves garlic, peeled and crushed
2 tablespoons oil
Salt and pepper to taste
Soy sauce to taste

Prepare bean curd and sprouts as directed
above. Heat oil in a skillet and fry the
crushed garlic until it turns golden. Add

bean curd and bean sprouts and stir-fry for 3
to 4 minutes. Add seasonings to taste and
serve at once.

Fried Bean Curd Peking Style

CHINA   Yield: About 4 servings

1 cup peanut oil
2 bean curds, each cut into 8 pieces
¼ cup soy sauce
2 tablespoons red-wine vinegar
1 tablespoon white vinegar
4 tablespoons scallions, chopped
1½ teaspoons hot oil

Heat peanut oil to 350°F. Cook bean
curds until golden brown.

Mix together soy sauce, red-wine vinegar,
white vinegar, scallions, and hot oil in bowl.
Serve sauce with bean curds.

Bean Sprouts with Celery and Mushrooms

CHINA   Yield: 4 servings

2 tablespoons oil
3 stalks celery, sliced diagonally
1 onion, chopped
¼ pound fresh mushrooms, sliced
½ cup chicken stock
1 tablespoon soy sauce
1 pound fresh bean sprouts
1 tablespoon cornstarch mixed with
   ¼ cup cold water

Add oil to a preheated pan. Sauté celery, onion, and mushrooms until onion is soft. Add chicken stock and soy sauce. Bring to a boil and add bean sprouts. Stir-fry only for about 30 seconds. Cover and simmer 3 seconds.

Thicken with the cornstarch mixture, adding it a little at a time. Serve immediately.

Frying-Pan Bean Sprouts

CHINA   Yield: 2 servings

>   2 cups fresh bean sprouts
>   Oil for frying, enough to cover bottom
>   of pan
>   Sprinkles of soy sauce

Blanch bean sprouts in colander, rinse them with cold water. Drain well. Heat oil in frying pan until hot. Place bean sprouts in pan; toss until heated through. Cook quickly on high heat. Remove bean sprouts to serving plate. Sprinkle with soy sauce to taste.

If desired, chopped scallion may be added when cooking.

Grow-Your-Own Bean Sprouts

CHINA

>   ¼ cup mung beans
>   Quart of water

There is nothing like growing your own bean sprouts to have them available when you desire and to know that they are fresh. It's a very simple procedure and takes very little time. All you need is a package of mung beans, a quart jar, water, and a strainer.

Soak the bean sprouts in a quart jar overnight. Pour off the water, using a strainer if desired, and place the jar in a dark place for 3 days, rinsing the beans 3 times a day and draining them thoroughly after each rinsing. At the end of 3 days, you will have ready-to-eat, home-grown bean sprouts. Refrigerate and use as needed.

Marinated Bean Sprouts

JAPAN   Yield: 4 servings

This is an excellent salad to serve with meat or fish. It has a unique flavor.

>   1 pound fresh bean sprouts

Marinade

>   3 tablespoons scallion (use green and
>   white parts), chopped
>   2 tablespoons sesame-seed oil
>   2 tablespoons soy sauce
>   1 tablespoon vodka
>   1 tablespoon vinegar

Place bean sprouts in colander; blanch. Immediately rinse them with cold water; drain well. Combine remaining ingredients in a large bowl. Add bean sprouts and marinate at room temperature for 1 hour. Refrigerate for at least 3 hours before serving.

Spiced French Beans

INDONESIA   Yield: 4 servings

2 tablespoons vegetable oil
3 shallots, peeled and finely sliced
1 garlic clove, peeled and crushed, optional
1 teaspoon ginger powder
Pinch of chili powder
Pinch of grated nutmeg
1 pound string beans, topped, tailed, and cut in half
Salt
Freshly ground black pepper
6 tablespoons strong-flavored chicken stock

Heat oil in deep frying pan and fry shallots and garlic gently for 1 minute. Stir in remaining ingredients, except for the chicken stock. Stir-fry this for 2 minutes.

Gradually stir in chicken stock and cover the pan. Simmer gently for 5 minutes. Cook uncovered 2 minutes more, stirring constantly. Adjust seasonings if needed and serve hot.

Chinese Green Beans

CHINA   Yield: 6 servings

1 quart fresh green beans
1 can cream of celery soup
½ cup celery, diced
1 cup mushrooms, sliced
1 can water chestnuts, sliced
1 tablespoon soy sauce
4 ounces pimientos
½ cup green onions, sliced
¾ cup chow mein noodles or 1 can French-fried onion rings

Boil fresh green beans; cool. Drain. Combine all ingredients except noodles and pour into beans. Preheat oven to 350°F. Pour everything into a casserole dish; bake 45 minutes. Top with noodles or onion rings. Bake for another 10 minutes.

Chinese-Mexican Green Beans

CHINA   Yield: 4 to 6 servings

1 pound fresh snap beans
¼ cup boiling water
¼ cup peanut oil
½ teaspoon sugar
1 teaspoon cider or white rice wine vinegar
2 tablespoons soy sauce
3 tablespoons bacon bits, from a 2½-ounce can
3 tablespoons minced Mexican-style hot pickles, from a 12-ounce jar
2 medium or 4 thin scallions, sliced thin crosswise

Tip beans; wash; with a knife or the wide shredding blade of an electric food processor, cut crosswise into ¼- to ½-inch lengths. In a 10-inch skillet rapidly heat the beans, water, and peanut oil; stir well. Cover tightly and simmer until the beans are tender-crisp and the liquid evaporates—5 to 8 minutes.

Stir together the sugar, vinegar, and soy sauce and add; mix well. Stir in the bacon bits and the hot pickles; heat rapidly, stirring. Turn into a heated serving dish; sprinkle with the scallions.

Green Beans Indonesian

INDONESIA   Yield: 6 servings

½ cup onion, chopped
1 clove garlic, minced
2 tablespoons lemon rind
½ teaspoon dried chili peppers
4 tablespoons peanut oil
1 pound green beans, preferably fresh
  or frozen-thawed
1 teaspoon salt
Pinch of sugar
1 bay leaf

Finely chop onions; add garlic, lemon rind, chili peppers. Heat oil; sauté mixture 3 minutes, stirring constantly. Add beans and seasonings; mix thoroughly. Cover and cook over low heat until barely tender, adding oil if necessary.

Green Beans with Shrimp

KOREA   Yield: 4 to 6 servings

1 pound small shrimp, shelled and
  deveined
1 pound tender green beans, topped
  and tailed
2 tablespoons vegetable oil
1 tablespoon sesame oil
1 medium onion, peeled and thinly
  sliced
3 tablespoons light soy sauce
1 teaspoon sugar
3 teaspoons toasted, crushed sesame
  seeds

Chop shrimp and set aside. Prepare beans and cut into thin diagonal slices.

Heat vegetable and sesame oil in a wok or skillet. Fry the onions and shrimp together for 2 minutes. Add beans and stir-fry for 3 minutes more. Put in seasonings and mix well; cover and simmer on low heat for 5 to 8 minutes. When beans are tender, serve at once.

Stir-fried Green Beans with Variations

CHINA   Yield: 4 servings

2 tablespoons vegetable oil
1 clove garlic
2 to 3 cups green beans, washed,
  stemmed, and cut into 1-inch pieces
½ cup chicken broth
½ teaspoon salt
½ teaspoon sugar
1 teaspoon cornstarch in 1 tablespoon
  cold water

Heat the oil in the wok. Brown and discard the garlic. Stir-fry the green beans for 3 minutes. Add the chicken broth, salt, and sugar. Cover and steam over moderate heat for 3 to 4 minutes, until beans are tender but still bright green and crisp. Stir the cornstarch mixture and add it to the wok. Cook, stirring, until the sauce is thickened. Serve at once.

Variations: Combine 1 tablespoon black bean sauce, 1 teaspoon dry sherry, and 1 teaspoon sugar; stir into the beans just before serving. Or add 8-10 water chestnuts, sliced, to the beans just before the stock is added.

Spicy Fried Beans

INDIA   Yield: 4 to 6 servings

1 pound tender green beans, topped
  and tailed and cut into bite-size
  pieces
1 tablespoon ghee
1 medium onion, peeled and finely
  chopped
½ teaspoon ginger, finely grated
1 teaspoon ground turmeric
1 teaspoon garam masala
½ teaspoon chili powder, optional
2 teaspoons salt
2 ripe tomatoes, chopped
1 or more teaspoons lemon juice to
  taste

Heat ghee in a saucepan. Using medium
heat, fry onion and ginger until onion is
golden. Add spices and stir-fry for 2 minutes.
Put in tomatoes and continue stirring until
tomatoes are cooked through and most of the
liquid is evaporated. Add the beans and stir
well. Partially cover the pan and allow beans
to steam until just tender. Stir in lemon
juice and serve at once.

String Beans
Chinese Style I

CHINA   Yield: 4 servings

2 cloves garlic, minced
1 medium onion, chopped
1 tablespoon oil
2 tablespoons soy sauce
1 pound fresh string beans
1 cup chicken broth

Mince garlic and chop onion. Heat oil in
skillet to medium-high. Sauté garlic and
onion until golden. Add soy sauce and string
beans. Pour in the chicken broth, turn temperature down, and let mixture simmer for
approximately 7 to 8 minutes, until beans are
tender, but still crisp.

String Beans Chinese
Style II

CHINA   Yield: 10 to 12 servings

3 packages French-style string beans
  (cooked as directed)
1 can bean sprouts
1 can cream of mushroom soup
1 can stems and pieces of mushrooms
Spring onions, cut-up
A dash of garlic and salt
1 can French-fried onions

Combine all ingredients except can of
fried onions. Bake for 20 minutes in 400°F
oven. Remove from oven and add 1 can
French-fried onions. Bake for another 10
minutes.

Beans and Sprouts

CHINA   Yield: 8 servings

1 pound snap beans, tipped and
  washed
¼ cup boiling water
2 tablespoons peanut oil
2 tablespoons bland, pale sesame oil
1 pound fresh mung bean sprouts
½ cup thin strips Spanish onion, cut
  into thin strips and loosely packed
Slice of fresh ginger, minced
1 large clove garlic, minced
3 tablespoons soy sauce mixed with 2
  teaspoons sugar

Cut the beans, with the wide slicing blade of a food processor or with a knife, into ¼- to ½-inch lengths. Turn into a wok with the water and oils; cover and simmer until the beans are tender-crisp and the water has evaporated—5 to 8 minutes. Add the bean sprouts, onion, ginger, garlic, and soy-sauce mixture; stir constantly over high heat to cook the bean sprouts and onion slightly—a minute or so.

Stir-fry Broccoli with Shoyu Ginger Sauce

CHINA   Yield: 4 servings

1 head fresh broccoli or 1 package frozen, defrosted broccoli
2 tablespoons vegetable oil

Sauce
½ tablespoon cornstarch
½ tablespoon soy sauce
⅛ teaspoon powdered ginger
½ cup chicken broth
½ teaspoon salt

Prepare the fresh broccoli for stir-frying by breaking off the branches from the main stem and slicing the branch stems very thin. Cut each floret into several bite-size pieces. Heat the oil in the wok and add broccoli. Stir-fry for 1 minute, cover, and steam for 3 minutes. Broccoli should still be bright green in color, crisp, but heated through.

Serve at once with the ginger sauce that has been prepared by combining the sauce ingredients and bringing them to a boil, stirring constantly. Sauce may be served separately or poured over the broccoli in the wok just before the broccoli is removed.

Sweet Broccoli with Pork and Dried Mushrooms

CHINA   Yield: 6 servings

¼ pound dried mushrooms
½ cup brown sugar
¼ teaspoon MSG
1 teaspoon salt
¼ cup soy sauce
½ cup dry sherry
2 tablespoons cornstarch
⅓ cup vegetable oil
2 slices ginger, shredded
1 clove garlic, shredded
1 pound lean, sliced pork
1 bunch fresh broccoli, sliced

Soak the dried mushrooms in lukewarm water to cover for 20 minutes or until soft. Drain and dry thoroughly. Mix together the brown sugar, MSG, salt, soy sauce, sherry, and cornstarch.

Heat the dry wok until hot. Add ½ of the vegetable oil. Over a medium heat, stir-fry the garlic and ginger until they have turned a golden brown. Add the pork, turn heat to high, and stir-fry until the pork has lost its raw color and is just about cooked through. Remove to a dish.

Add the rest of the oil and allow that to become hot. Add the broccoli and the drained and dried mushrooms, stir-frying long enough for the broccoli to have turned bright, deep green (2 to 3 minutes) and the mushrooms to have cooked. Return the pork to the wok.

Add the brown sugar, soy sauce/sherry mixture, and allow the liquid to come up to the boil. Cover the wok and take it off the heat. Let stand for 2 minutes so that the sauce and the wine have a chance to penetrate the food. Serve immediately.

Salads & Vegetables

Cabbage and Mushrooms

CHINA   Yield: 4 servings

> 1 pound cabbage
> 2 tablespoons oil
> 2 cloves garlic, crushed
> ½ cup fresh mushrooms, sliced
> ½ teaspoon sugar
> ½ teaspoon soy sauce

Cut cabbage into bite-size pieces and set aside. Heat oil in skillet to medium-high heat and sauté garlic approximately 3 minutes. Discard garlic. Add cabbage and sauté for 2 minutes. Add mushrooms, sugar, and soy sauce and mix well to heat through. Serve immediately.

Cabbage with Sesame Seeds

CHINA   Yield: About 4 servings

> 1 head cabbage
> 1 tablespoon sesame seeds, toasted
> Soy sauce
> Sugar
> Pepper

Shred cabbage. Place in pot with small amount of water, cook until just tender. Drain well. Toss with sesame seeds, soy sauce to taste, pinch of sugar, and pepper to taste.

Cooked Cabbage

CHINA   Yield: 4 servings

> 1 head cabbage
> Oil for cooking
> Soy sauce

Cut cabbage into cubes. Heat oil to medium high; toss cabbage in oil until completely stirred. Lower heat; let cabbage cook until tender. Sprinkle cabbage with soy sauce to taste; serve it hot.

Fried Cabbage

INDIA   Yield: 6 servings

> Half a large head cabbage, shredded
>   coarsely
> 4 tablespoons oil
> 1 large onion, peeled and finely sliced
> 2 or 3 fresh green or red chilies, seeded
>   and sliced
> 2 cloves garlic, peeled and finely grated
> 1 teaspoon fresh ginger, finely grated
> 1 teaspoon ground turmeric
> 1½ teaspoons salt
> 2 tablespoons desiccated (dehydrated)
>   coconut

Using a large saucepan, heat the oil. Fry onions and chilies until soft. Add garlic and ginger and stir until golden. Last, put in turmeric and cabbage, stirring until all of the ingredients are well blended. Cover and cook over low heat for 10 minutes. Cabbage should be tender but not mushy. Sprinkle with salt and coconut and mix well. Uncover and continue cooking over medium heat until all liquid is absorbed. Serve hot.

Indian Cabbage

INDIA   Yield: 4 servings

> 3 tablespoons peanut oil
> 1 teaspoon turmeric
> 1 teaspoon mustard seed
> ½ teaspoon salt
> 1 head cabbage

Heat oil; add turmeric, mustard seed, and salt. Simmer until mustard seed pops. Then add 4 cups finely chopped cabbage. Stir briskly over heat.

Spiced Cabbage in Coconut Milk

INDONESIA   Yield: 6 or more servings

1 pound cabbage, coarsely shredded
2 onions, peeled and chopped
2 cloves garlic, peeled and chopped
2 fresh red chilies, seeded and
    chopped, or 1 teaspoon chili powder
1 teaspoon dried shrimp paste (trasi)
1 daun salam or 3 curry leaves
2 tablespoons peanut oil
2 strips lemon rind
1½ cups thick coconut milk
1 teaspoon salt
3 tablespoons tamarind liquid

After shredding the cabbage, blend onions, garlic, and chilies into a fine paste. Use either electric blender, food processor, or mortar and pestle. Wrap the dried shrimp paste in foil and broil for 5 minutes, turning once.

In a large saucepan or wok, fry the curry leaves in hot oil for 1 minute. Add the onion paste mixture and the dried shrimp paste and stir-fry until mixture darkens in color. Add lemon rind, coconut milk, and salt and reduce heat to a simmer. At this point, put in the cabbage and simmer uncovered for about 3 minutes or until cabbage is cooked but still crisp. Last, stir in the tamarind liquid; then serve.

Steamed Celery Cabbage

CHINA   Yield: 4 servings

1 small head celery cabbage, sliced
    diagonally into ¼-inch slices
1 tablespoon soy sauce
1 teaspoon sugar

Place the cabbage in a bowl and season with the soy sauce and sugar. Set the bowl on a rack inside the wok. Add water to the wok to a level below the rack. Cover and steam 15 to 20 minutes. Serve at once.

Other vegetables are prepared in the same manner. Adjust the steaming time for other vegetables.

Stir-fried Chinese Celery Cabbage

CHINA   Yield: 4 servings

2 tablespoons vegetable oil
1 slice fresh gingerroot
1 pound Chinese celery cabbage (bok
    choy), cut diagonally into ¼-inch
    slices
3 stalks celery, cut diagonally into
    ¼-inch slices
½ teaspoon salt
½ teaspoon sugar
3 tablespoons chicken broth
1 teaspoon sesame oil

Heat oil in the wok. Brown and discard the ginger slice. Stir-fry the bok choy and celery for 2 to 3 minutes. Add the salt, sugar, and chicken broth. Cover and heat for 1 minute. Serve at once sprinkled with a little sesame oil.

Baked Chinese Cabbage

CHINA   Yield: 4 servings

2 heads Chinese cabbage
4 cups beef bouillon
1 small onion, coarsely chopped
Margarine to grease ovenproof baking
  dish
6 tablespoons grated cheese,
  Emmenthal or Gruyère
2 tablespoons butter or margarine

Sauce

½ cup sour cream
2 tablespoons parsley, chopped
1 small onion, chopped
Salt to taste
White pepper to taste
1½ tablespoons grated cheese,
  Emmenthal or Gruyère

Remove outer wilted leaves from cabbage and cut cabbage in half lengthwise. Cut each half into 3 or 4 pieces. Wash thoroughly and pat dry. Bring beef bouillon to boil, add onion and cabbage, and simmer for 20 minutes. Remove cabbage with slotted spoon and drain. Grease ovenproof baking dish with margarine. Place ⅓ of cabbage in dish, sprinkle with ⅓ of cheese, and dot with ⅓ of butter or margarine. Repeat this until cabbage, cheese, and butter are used.

Prepare sauce by combining and stirring thoroughly sour cream, parsley, onion, salt, and pepper. Pour over cabbage. Sprinkle with 1½ tablespoons grated cheese. Bake in preheated 375°F oven until cheese melts completely, approximately 10 to 15 minutes.

Chinese Cabbage with Mushrooms

CHINA   Yield: 4 to 6 servings

1 medium head Chinese cabbage,
  washed and cut into 1½-inch pieces
½ pound fresh mushrooms, diced
1 teaspoon salt
½ cup water
4 tablespoons melted butter

Place cabbage, mushrooms, salt, and water in a pressure cooker. Close cover and set pressure control in place. When pressure is reached and control jiggles gently, cook for 3 minutes. Cool cooker at once under running water.

Put vegetables in serving dish and pour melted butter on top.

Chow Choy

CHINA   Yield: About 4 servings

¾ cup olive oil
½ to 1 teaspoon cayenne pepper
1 clove garlic, pressed
Salt to taste
4 cups Chinese cabbage or chopped
  celery
2 tablespoons soy sauce
2 tablespoons red wine vinegar
1 teaspoon MSG, optional
1 teaspoon sugar
3 green onions or scallions, chopped
1 tablespoon cornstarch

Heat the oil in a large skillet over medium heat. Stir in the cayenne pepper, garlic, and salt. Add the cabbage and soy sauce and stir-fry for 2 minutes. Add the vinegar, MSG, sugar and onions and stir-fry for 1 minute. Mix the cornstarch with 2 table-spoons water until smooth, then stir into the cabbage mixture. Stir-fry for 3 minutes longer or until the cabbage mixture is lightly browned.

Delicious Chinese Cabbage

CHINA   Yield: 4 servings

1 Chinese cabbage
½ cup water
1 tablespoon salt
1 tablespoon sesame oil
½ cup carrot, shredded
2 tablespoons gingerroot, shredded
1 tablespoon sugar
½ teaspoon salt
2 tablespoons vinegar
Few drops Tabasco

Slice cabbage, sprinkle with water and salt, and let stand overnight. Squeeze water from cabbage and arrange on serving platter.

Heat oil in skillet or wok to medium-high heat and sauté carrot and ginger for approximately 3 minutes. Add sugar, salt, vinegar, and a few drops Tabasco. Bring to a boil. Pour over cabbage. Let stand at least 15 minutes before serving.

Fried Chinese Cabbage

CHINA   Yield: 6 servings

½ cup water
1 teaspoon soy sauce
½ teaspoon crushed ginger
1 teaspoon sugar
1 teaspoon cornstarch
1 teaspoon sherry, optional

1½ tablespoons oil
1 clove garlic, minced
Salt to taste
1 pound Chinese cabbage

Mix water, soy sauce, ginger, sugar, cornstarch, and sherry. Stir well. Put oil in a very hot skillet. Add garlic and salt. Cut cabbage leaves into 1-inch sections with the stem slanting about 45°. Put white stems in and stir-fry 2 minutes. Add green leaves and fry another minute. Add prepared mixture. Stir for 1 minute. Cover and cook for 2 minutes.

Kim Chee

KOREA   Yield: About 8 servings

2 pounds Chinese cabbage
½ cup salt
1 quart water
1½ tablespoons hot red peppers
1 clove garlic, minced
1 teaspoon fresh ginger, minced
1 tablespoon sugar

Wash cabbage; cut into 1½-inch pieces. Sprinkle with salt. Add water and let stand overnight. Rinse cabbage and drain. Make a paste of the rest of the ingredients and rub into cabbage slices. Pack into quart jar and cover with plastic bag to prevent odor. Ready in 4-5 days.

Pickled Chinese Cabbage

KOREA   Yield: 4 to 6 servings

1 head bok choy, chopped
3 tablespoons salt
2 teaspoons hot chili powder
2 teaspoons crushed garlic
4 scallions, finely chopped
1 tablespoon sugar
1 hard pear, peeled, cored, and grated

Use a large bowl to hold the bok choy. Sprinkle with salt and stir well. Allow to stand overnight.

When ready to prepare, rinse the cabbage under cold running water. Drain and pat dry with paper towels. Put it in a large jar. Mix the remaining ingredients together and add to the cabbage. Stir well. Cover with a heavy weight, such as a heavy can. Allow the spices to mingle this way for 1 or 2 days before using.

This may be stored refrigerated for as long as 3 weeks.

Stir-fried Spiced Chinese Cabbage

CHINA   Yield: 4 servings

1 pound Chinese cabbage
2 tablespoons sugar
2 tablespoons white vinegar
1 tablespoon soy sauce
1 teaspoon salt
¼ teaspoon cayenne pepper
1 tablespoon oil

With a cleaver or sharp knife, trim the top leaves off the cabbage and the root ends. Separate the stalks and wash them under cold running water. Cut each stalk, leaves

and all, into 1 inch × 1½ inch pieces. In a small bowl, combine the sugar, vinegar, soy sauce, salt, and cayenne pepper, and mix thoroughly. Have the oil within easy reach.

To cook: Set a 12-inch wok or 10-inch skillet over high heat for about 30 seconds. Pour in the oil, swirl it about the pan, and heat for about 30 seconds, then turn heat down to moderate. Immediately add the cabbage and stir-fry for 2 to 3 minutes. Make sure all the cabbage is coated with the oil. Remove the pan from the heat and stir in the soy-vinegar mixture. Transfer the cabbage to a platter and let it cool to lukewarm before serving. Or if you prefer, serve it chilled.

Carrots Chinese

CHINA   Yield: 4 servings

5 or 6 medium carrots
¾ teaspoon salt
2 tablespoons butter
Parsley

Coarsely shred the carrots. Sprinkle with salt. Cover and cook in butter for 5 to 7 minutes. Top, when serving, with snippets of parsley.

Sweet-and-Sour Carrots

CHINA   Yield: 4 servings

2 tablespoons vegetable oil
1 slice fresh gingerroot
1 pound carrots, cleaned and roll-cut into 1-inch pieces
½ teaspoon salt
½ cup chicken broth

1 tablespoon vinegar
½ tablespoon brown sugar
2 teaspoons cornstarch in 2 tablespoons
  cold water
½ cup canned pineapple chunks,
  optional

Heat the oil in the wok. Brown and discard the ginger slice. Stir-fry the carrots for 1 minute. Add the salt and chicken broth. Cover and steam over moderate heat for 5 minutes. Stir in the vinegar, brown sugar, cornstarch mixture, and pineapple chunks (if desired). Heat until sauce thickens. Serve at once.

Carrots and Cauliflower

INDONESIA   Yield: 4 servings

6 carrots, peeled and sliced diagonally
3 large cauliflower florets
Boiling water
2 tablespoons vegetable oil or melted
  butter
1 clove garlic, peeled and crushed
1 slice dried shrimp paste (trasi),
  crushed, optional
4 scallions, cut into ½-inch lengths
1 tablespoon light soy sauce
Pinch of chili powder
Pinch of ginger powder
Salt to taste

Boil the carrots and cauliflower in a saucepan for 3 minutes. Drain.

Use a wok or deep frying pan to heat the oil or butter. Fry the garlic and trasi for just a few seconds. Stir in scallions and soy sauce; then stir in the carrots and cauliflower. Add chili and ginger powders and salt to taste. Stir constantly for 2 minutes. Serve at once.

Cauliflower Chinese Style

CHINA   Yield: About 4 servings

1 small cauliflower
2 tablespoons oil
¼ pound fresh mushrooms, sliced
1 cup chicken broth, warmed
2 tablespoons soy sauce
½ teaspoon MSG
1 tablespoon cornstarch mixed with ¼
  cup cold water

Trim cauliflower, wash, and separate into florets. Slice large florets. Pour oil into preheated pan. Add cauliflower and sauté lightly. Add mushrooms and sauté a few seconds longer. Add chicken broth, soy sauce, and MSG. Bring to a boil, cover, and simmer until cauliflower is done, but still crisp. Thicken with cornstarch mixture, adding it slowly.

Chili-fried Cauliflower

MALAYSIA   Yield: 6 servings

3 tablespoons peanut oil
4 fresh red chilies, finely chopped, or 2
  teaspoons sambal ulek
1 large onion, peeled and finely
  chopped
2 cloves garlic, peeled and finely
  chopped
1 teaspoon dried shrimp paste
1 teaspoon salt
1 pound cauliflower, washed and sliced
2 tablespoons hot water

Using a wok or skillet, heat the oil. On low heat, fry chilies, onion, and garlic until onion is soft, stirring constantly. Add shrimp paste and crush with back of spoon. Fry for 1 minute. Add salt and cauliflower and stir constantly, coating the vegetable with the fried onion and chili mixture. Sprinkle with hot water; cover and cook for 10 minutes. Serve at once.

Cauliflower with Water Chestnuts and Mushrooms

JAPAN   Yield: 4 servings

1 small cauliflower
2 tablespoons oil
8 mushrooms, sliced
1 cup hot chicken broth
¼ cup water chestnuts, sliced
2 tablespoons soy sauce
Salt to taste
1 tablespoon cornstarch mixed with
  cold water

Trim and wash cauliflower. Break into florets. If florets are large, slice them.

Heat oil in pan; gently sauté cauliflower. Add sliced mushrooms; sauté for about 30 seconds. Add chicken broth, sliced water chestnuts, soy sauce, and seasonings. Bring mixture to a boil, cover, and simmer until cauliflower is just tender, i.e., still crunchy.

Mix cornstarch with enough cold water to make a smooth paste; slowly add to cauliflower mixture, stirring constantly until thickened.

Cauliflower with Noodles

CHINA   Yield: 4 servings

1 small head of cauliflower
2 tablespoons oil
½ pound beef, thinly sliced
Salt to taste
1 small onion, chopped
2 tablespoons soy sauce
1 cup beef bouillon
1 teaspoon cornstarch
½ teaspoon cold water
½ pound egg noodles

Clean cauliflower and divide into small florets. Heat 1 tablespoon oil in heavy skillet. Add cauliflower and beef slices and cook until lightly browned. Season with salt. Add chopped onion and soy sauce and cook for 5 minutes. Pour in beef bouillon and simmer for 35 minutes. Blend cornstarch with cold water. Stir into cauliflower mixture until slightly thick and bubbly.

Cook egg noodles in 3 quarts of salted water for 10 minutes. Drain. Heat other tablespoon of oil in skillet; add noodles and fry until golden. Mix noodles with cauliflower. Heat through and serve.

Celery and Mushrooms

CHINA   Yield: 4 servings

2 tablespoons vegetable oil
½ pound mushrooms, cut into "T"
  shapes
1 small bunch celery, sliced diagonally
  into ½-inch slices
1 teaspoon sugar
2 teaspoons soy sauce

Heat oil in the wok and stir-fry the mushrooms 1 minute. Add celery, sugar, and soy sauce. Stir-fry 2 to 3 minutes or just until the celery becomes a brighter green. Serve at once.

Stir-fried Celery and Bean Sprouts

CHINA   Yield: 2 servings

2 cups celery, sliced diagonally
Oil
4 cups fresh bean sprouts
Sprinkles of soy sauce

Slice celery and set aside. Heat oil in skillet and stir-fry celery for about 2 minutes, until bright green and tender but still crisp. Add bean sprouts and stir-fry for 1 minute, or until bean sprouts are heated through. Sprinkle with soy sauce to taste and serve immediately.

Corn Fritters

MALAYSIA   Yield: 4 servings

This is really an all-purpose dish—it may be served hot or cold, for a vegetable with a meal, or as a between-meal snack.

    6 ears corn-on-the-cob, or 1 12-ounce
        can corn, drained
    2 medium shrimp, shelled, optional
    4 shallots, peeled
    2 cloves garlic, peeled, optional
    ½ teaspoon chili powder
    1 teaspoon coriander powder
    1 teaspoon or more salt to taste
    1 large egg, beaten
    Vegetable oil

Cut corn kernels from the cob. Grind shrimp, shallots, and garlic. Mix with corn. Add chili powder, coriander, and salt. Last, put in a beaten egg and mix thoroughly.

Heat enough oil in a skillet to cover the bottom of the pan. Drop batter by heaping tablespoons into skillet. Flatten fritters with a spatula. Cook about 5 at a time. Fry about 2 minutes on one side, and then turn to brown the other side. Remove and drain on paper towels. Add oil to pan if needed and continue to fry fritters until all the batter is used. Serve hot or cold.

Cucumber Raita

INDIA   Yield: 4 to 6 servings

    2 medium cucumbers, pared and thinly
        sliced
    2 teaspoons salt
    10 ounces unflavored yogurt
    ½ teaspoon sugar
    ¼ teaspoon powdered cumin
    ½ medium onion, finely chopped

Sprinkle 1 teaspoon of the salt over the cucumbers and let them stand for at least 1 hour. Drain thoroughly.

In another bowl, whisk together the yogurt, remaining 1 teaspoon salt, the sugar, and the cumin until the yogurt is smooth. Stir in the cucumbers and the onion. Chill.

If you wish, you may garnish the raita with 2 tablespoons finely chopped fresh coriander leaves.

Japanese Pickles

JAPAN   Yield: About 4 servings

    2 large cucumbers
    ⅛ cup soy sauce
    ¼ cup vinegar
    ¼ cup sugar

Peel cucumbers; slice them very thin. Mix together soy sauce, vinegar, and sugar. Pour this over the cucumber slices; mix well, gently. Refrigerate for at least 2 hours before serving.

Fried Eggplant

BURMA   Yield: 4 servings

1 large eggplant
2 tablespoons vegetable oil
1 medium onion, peeled and sliced
1 clove garlic, peeled and crushed
½-inch piece fresh gingerroot, peeled
    and pounded
½ teaspoon salt
2 scallions, including greens, chopped
    for garnish

Bake eggplant on lightly oiled sheet at 425°F for about 1 hour or until soft to the touch. Remove from oven and allow to cool.

Heat oil in a skillet and fry onion and garlic gently until lightly browned. Peel skin from eggplant. Scoop out flesh and mash with a fork. Add this to the skillet with ginger and salt, and stir-fry for 5 to 10 minutes. Transfer to a warmed serving dish and garnish with spring onions. This may be served hot or cold.

Pickled Eggplant

JAPAN   Yield: About 4 servings

1 large eggplant
Salt
4 tablespoons oil
4 tablespoons soy sauce
4 tablespoons sugar
4 tablespoons vinegar

Peel eggplant; slice it thin. Salt it lightly; let stand 20 minutes. Combine oil, soy sauce, sugar, and vinegar in a saucepan; heat to boiling. Drain thoroughly. Pour over eggplant; refrigerate for at least 3 hours before serving.

This can also be served as an appetizer. Serve it cold. Makes approximately 8 servings as an appetizer.

Stuffed Eggplant I

JAPAN   Yield: 4 to 6 servings

6 eggplants, small size

Stuffing

½ onion, chopped
Oil, butter, or margarine
8 ounces ground chicken
½ to ¾ cup bread crumbs
½ teaspoon salt
1 tablespoon water (a little more, if
    necessary)
4 tablespoons grated cheese

Cornstarch
Oil for frying
Grated gingerroot
Soy sauce for dipping

Remove stem part of eggplants. Make a cut lengthwise in half, but not all the way through. Soak eggplants in salted water.

Sauté onion in a small amount of oil, butter, or margarine just until soft. Combine with chicken, bread crumbs, salt, and water. Gently mix in cheese. Divide into 6 parts.

Wipe eggplants dry. Sprinkle cut surfaces with cornstarch. Place a layer of meat mixture inside the eggplant. Sprinkle a small amount of cornstarch on the meat.

Heat oil in a deep frying pan; cook over medium heat until meat is well done. Serve with grated ginger and soy sauce.

Stuffed Eggplant II

PHILIPPINES   Yield: 4 servings

  2 medium eggplants, peeled and halved
     lengthwise
  Lightly salted water
  1 tablespoon oil
  3 cloves garlic, peeled and finely
     chopped
  1 medium onion, peeled and finely
     chopped
  ½ pound ground pork
  1 large ripe tomato, chopped
  1 teaspoon salt
  ½ teaspoon black pepper
  1 cup soft, fresh breadcrumbs
  1 egg, beaten
  Dry breadcrumbs for coating
  Oil for frying

Place eggplants in lightly salted boiled water and cook for 5 minutes. Remove from water and drain, cut side down. Scoop out a thin layer of the pulp, being sure to leave a firm shell.

Using a large skillet, heat the oil. Fry the garlic and onion until golden; then add the pork and fry until it browns all through. Add tomato, salt, and pepper and lower the heat for 15 minutes, stirring from time to time. Chop pulp taken from the eggplant and add it to the skillet, cooking until most of the moisture has disappeared. Remove from heat. Mix in the soft breadcrumbs and add extra seasoning if needed.

Divide the mixture and spoon it into eggplant halves. Brush the top with beaten eggs and coat with dried breadcrumbs.

Heat oil in a skillet and fry the eggplant halves, first on one side, then on the other. When golden brown, serve at once. (If preferred, eliminate the last frying by putting eggplants into a 400°F oven for 15 minutes, until tops of eggplants are golden brown.)

Chinese Greens

CHINA   Yield: 4 servings

  1 small bunch bok choy (or Chinese
     cabbage, spinach, Swiss chard, other
     greens)
  1 onion, chopped
  1 tablespoon fat or oil
  ⅓ cup tender beef, thinly sliced or
     ground
  2 tablespoons soy sauce
  2 teaspoons cornstarch
  ½ cup water

Separate greens from stems. Cut each in 1-inch pieces. Fry onion in fat or oil for 2 minutes. Add meat and cook until the bright red is gone. Add stems of vegetables; cook and stir about 2 minutes. Mix and add soy sauce, cornstarch, and water. Add leaves of greens. Cook covered until leaves are just limp. Serve over rice.

Note: Cooked or canned meat or poultry may be used in place of beef in this recipe.

Oriental Greens

Instead of your usual salad greens, make this switch. Toss together young spinach leaves, a handful of fresh bean sprouts, sliced mushrooms, strips of cooked ham or crumbled crisply-cooked bacon, sliced celery, chopped green onion and plenty of coarsely broken walnuts to step up the taste and texture. Drizzle lightly with a dressing made of salad oil blended with half as much cider vinegar, and seasoned with a little granulated sugar, soy sauce, crushed garlic and freshly ground black pepper. What you have is an appealingly different green salad with "chop suey" vegetable overtones. As a spring menu picker-upper, it's tops.

Leeks in Egg Shirts

KOREA   Yield: 4 servings

8 thin leeks
1 quart water
1 teaspoon salt
1 tablespoon oil
Ground nutmeg
4 tablespoons flour
1 egg, beaten
6 tablespoons oil

Sauce

2 tablespoons soy sauce
1 tablespoon lemon juice
Salt and white pepper to taste
Pinch of sugar

Clean the leeks, removing dark green leaves. Cut the leeks diagonally into 2-inch-long pieces. In a pot, bring water, salt, and 1 tablespoon of oil to a boil. Add leeks. Cover and cook over medium heat for 10 minutes. Remove and drain leeks. Then sprinkle with nutmeg.

Place the flour on one plate, the egg on a second plate. Roll the leeks first in flour and then in egg. Immediately, put them in hot oil and fry for 2 minutes until golden brown and crisp. Drain on paper towels and keep warm.

Combine remaining ingredients for dip sauce and serve with the fried leeks.

Mushrooms and Bamboo Shoots with Hoisin Sauce

CHINA   Yield: 4 servings

2 tablespoons vegetable oil
½ pound fresh mushrooms, cut into "T" shapes

4 ounces bamboo shoots, sliced
   (½ small can)
½ teaspoon salt
1 teaspoon cornstarch in 1 tablespoon
   cold water
2 tablespoons hoisin sauce

Heat the oil in the wok. Stir-fry mushrooms for 2 to 3 minutes. Add bamboo shoots and stir-fry 1 minute longer. Combine the remaining ingredients and add to the vegetables. Heat and stir gently until the sauce thickens and the vegetables are coated. Serve at once.

Chinese-style Mushrooms

CHINA   Yield: 6 servings

1 pound fresh mushrooms
2 tablespoons vegetable oil
2 tablespoons soy sauce
2 tablespoons water
1 teaspoon sugar
1 tablespoon cornstarch

Wash mushrooms and cut vertically into thin slices. Cook mushrooms in hot oil in frying pan for 3 minutes, stirring as needed.

Combine other ingredients and stir into mushrooms. Cook for 2 minutes more until the juice is translucent.

Sautéed Mushrooms

CHINA   Yield: 3 to 4 servings

1 pound fresh mushrooms
1 medium onion, chopped
Oil or butter
Freshly ground pepper
Soy sauce

Slice mushrooms. Chop onion; sauté with the mushrooms in oil or butter for about 4 minutes. Add pepper to taste, sprinkle with soy sauce, toss, and serve.

Braised Okra

INDIA   Yield: 4 servings

¼ cup ghee
1 large onion, peeled and sliced
3 cloves garlic, peeled and sliced
1-inch piece of fresh gingerroot, finely chopped
2 green chilies, finely chopped
½ teaspoon chili powder
1 pound okra, topped and tailed
1 cup water
Salt
2 teaspoons coconut, shredded

Using a heavy pan, melt the ghee. Gently fry the onion, garlic, ginger, chilies, and chili powder for 5 minutes, until soft. Stir occasionally. Put in okra, water, and salt to taste and bring to boil. Reduce heat, cover, and simmer for 5 minutes until the okra is tender. Just before serving, stir in the coconut.

Indian Okra

INDIA   Yield: 2 to 4 servings

1 pound okra
4 tablespoons oil
2 teaspoons cumin
1 teaspoon salt
1 teaspoon turmeric
½ teaspoon cayenne
1 teaspoon ground corinader

Cut okra into thin slices. Heat oil; add cumin, salt, turmeric, and cayenne. Throw in okra, and stir like mad until covered with oil. Cover and cook over low heat for 5 minutes. Don't add water; stir again. Cook 10 minutes more, add coriander, and serve.

Fried Onions or Leeks

INDIA   Yield: 4 to 6 servings

5 or 6 large leeks or 3 large onions
2 tablespoons ghee
1 teaspoon cumin seeds
1 teaspoon ground turmeric
1 teaspoon fresh ginger, finely grated
1 teaspoon garam masala
1 teaspoon salt

Wash leeks well at least twice or peel the onions. Cut them into fairly thick slices. Heat ghee in large saucepan and stir-fry the cumin for 2 minutes. Add turmeric and ginger and fry for 1 minute more. Add leeks or onions and stir well to cover with the seasonings. Fry for 5 minutes. Sprinkle with garam masala and salt, and cover. Cook until vegetables are tender, stirring occasionally.

Onion Casserole

CHINA   Yield: 4 servings

    8 medium onions, peeled
    1 tablespoon sherry
    2 cups chicken stock
    1 teaspoon Chinese brown gravy sauce
    4 teaspoons cornstarch

Place the onions in a casserole. Combine the sherry, stock, and brown gravy sauce and mix well. Pour over onions; cover. Bake at 350°F for 2 hours or until onions are tender. Remove from oven. Remove the onions from casserole with slotted spoon and place in serving bowl.

Place the cornstarch in a small bowl; stir in a small amount of the onion liquor to make a smooth liquid. Add the cornstarch mixture to remaining liquor and cook over low heat until thickened and transparent. Pour over onions and serve steaming hot.

Onions and Seafood in Miso Sauce

JAPAN   Yield: 2 servings

    1 pound small onions
    1 cup small clams or scallops
    Vinegar for soaking clams

Miso sauce

    2 tablespoons sugar
    2 tablespoons dashi
    4 tablespoons miso
    2 tablespoons vinegar

Slice the onions; boil until just tender. Soak the clams in a small amount of vinegar while onions are boiling. If using scallops, lightly salt them before soaking in the vinegar.

Add sugar and dashi to the miso; blend very well. Stir in the vinegar. Drain the clams or scallops; add, along with the onions, to the sauce. Serve seafood immediately.

Pea-pod Casserole

CHINA   Yield: 4 servings

    1 package frozen pea pods, boiled
    1 can water chestnuts, sliced
    2 cups fresh bean sprouts, or 1 can
      bean sprouts
    1 can cream of mushroom soup
    1 can onion rings, optional

Boil pea pods for 2 minutes. Drain and place in casserole dish. Place sliced water chestnuts on top of pea pods.

Next, add a layer of bean sprouts. If fresh sprouts are used, first blanch, then rinse with cold water and drain well. If canned bean sprouts are used, drain, rinse with cold water, and drain well.

Cover with cream of mushroom soup. Bake for 15 minutes at 350°F. Place onion rings on top and heat again for about 2 or 3 minutes.

Chinese Peas

CHINA   Yield: 6 to 8 servings

    ½ cup onions, thinly sliced
    1 6-ounce can sliced mushrooms,
      drained
    ¼ cup butter

1 package frozen peas, partially
   defrosted
1 can bean sprouts, drained
1 can water chestnuts, sliced
1 can cream of mushroom soup
⅓ cup milk
1 teaspoon salt
Dash of pepper

Sauté onions and mushrooms in butter until onion is soft. Add peas, which have been broken apart, bean sprouts, and water chestnuts. Blend together the soup, milk, salt, and pepper. Pour over vegetable mixture and mix carefully. Place in ½ quart shallow casserole. Edge casserole with noodles. Bake in 350°F oven about 30 to 40 minutes.

This recipe can be prepared early and baked later.

Fresh Green Peas

CHINA   Yield: 4 servings

2 cups fresh green peas
2 cups boiling water
¼ teaspoon salt
6 tablespoons sugar
1 teaspoon cornstarch
Soy sauce

Add peas to boiling water. Put in salt. Bring to a boil again, reduce heat, and simmer until soft. Add sugar, simmer for 15 minutes more. Cool. If desired, thicken with cornstarch.

Before serving, add soy sauce to taste.

Peas Oriental

CHINA   Yield: 4 servings

1 box frozen peas
1 can bean sprouts
1 can water chestnuts, sliced
½ pound fresh mushrooms
1 can French-fried onion rings

Cook and drain peas. Drain bean sprouts and water chestnuts. Sauté mushrooms. Mix together and put in buttered casserole and bake at 350°F for 30 minutes. Sprinkle onion rings on top and continue baking until onions are crisp, about 10 to 15 minutes.

Split Pea Fritters

BURMA   Yield: 4 to 6 servings

1 cup split peas, soaked in water
   overnight
2 medium onions, peeled and finely
   chopped
2 fresh red chilies, finely chopped, or
   ¼ teaspoon chili powder
½ teaspoon ground turmeric
½ teaspoon salt
Oil for deep frying
Sliced onion and lemon wedges for
   garnish

Drain the soaked peas and grind them to a paste, using either a blender, food processor, or a mortar and pestle. Mix in all of the ingredients, except for the oil. Roll into small balls about 1 inch in diameter and then flatten with the palm of your hand to ½-inch thick.

Heat oil in heavy skillet. Fry fritters, dropping into the oil one at a time. Do not crowd the skillet. When fritters are golden brown, remove and drain on paper towels. Garnish with raw onion and lemon wedges.

Salads & Vegetables

Sugar Snaps with Water Chestnuts

CHINA   Yield: 4 servings

½ pound sugar snap peas
⅓ cup whole water chestnuts
3 tablespoons vegetable oil
Salt to taste

Wash peas. Slice chestnuts into thin rounds. Heat oil in skillet or wok. Season with salt. Mix and cook about 3 minutes. Add chestnut slices and mix again. Serve.

Green-Pepper Sauté

CHINA   Yield: 2 to 3 servings

2 large green (or red) peppers, cut into
    chunks
Boiling water
Butter or oil
Pepper
Soy sauce

Cut peppers; cook them in boiling water for about 2 minutes. Drain; sauté in butter or oil until just beginning to turn brown. Sprinkle with pepper and soy sauce.

Potato Straws

INDIA   Yield: 4 to 6 servings

4 large potatoes
Ice water
Oil for frying
1 teaspoon salt
½ teaspoon chili powder
½ teaspoon ground cumin
½ teaspoon garam masala

Peel the potatoes and slice very thin. Then cut them into matchstick strips. Cover the straws with ice water. Drain and dry well on paper towels.

Heat the oil in a skillet and fry a few of the potatoes at a time until they are golden and crisp. Lift out with a slotted spoon and drain on paper towels. When all are fried, mix the salt and spices together and sprinkle over the potato straws. Gently shake to spread the spices all around.

Spiced Potatoes and Cauliflower

INDIA   Yield: 4 servings

¾ cup ghee
2 pounds potatoes, peeled and cut into
    1-inch pieces
2 large onions, peeled and sliced
4 cloves garlic, peeled and sliced
2 teaspoons chili powder
1 teaspoon turmeric powder
1 teaspoon coriander powder
2 teaspoons salt
½ teaspoon freshly ground black
    pepper
5 cups water
8 large cauliflower florets
2 teaspoons garam masala

Using a large saucepan, melt the ghee. Stir-fry the potatoes for about 1 minute. Remove them from the pan and set aside.

Put the onions and garlic in remaining ghee and fry gently until soft. Add chili powder, turmeric, coriander, salt, and pepper and stir-fry for 3 minutes more. Return potatoes to the pan along with the water. Bring to a boil; then lower the heat to simmer for

10 minutes. Place cauliflower in with potatoes and continue to simmer for 15 minutes. The dish is done when vegetables are tender and sauce has thickened. Add garam masala. Mix well and serve hot.

Sweet Potato Balls

INDONESIA   Yield: 4 to 6 servings

> 2 cups mashed, cooked sweet potatoes
> 1 tablespoon flour
> 1½ tablespoons sugar
> 1 egg
> Oil for deep frying
> Confectioners' sugar

Mix potatoes, flour, sugar, and egg in a bowl. The mixture should be stiff. If it is not stiff enough, add extra flour by teaspoons. Roll the mixture into 1-inch balls. Heat oil in a deep frying pan and fry the sweet potato balls until golden brown. Remove from pan and drain on paper towels.

These may be served hot or cold and should be sprinkled lightly with confectioners' sugar.

Boiled Pumpkin with Soy Sauce

CHINA   Yield: 4 servings

> 2-pound pumpkin
> Pinch sugar
> Soy sauce
> Sherry

Cut pumpkin in half; take out seeds and fibers. Cut pumpkin meat into bite-size pieces; boil until tender. When cooked, mash until smooth; add pinch of sugar and soy sauce and sherry to taste.

Radish Flowers

CHINA   Yield: 10 radish flowers

> 10 medium radishes
> 1 tablespoon sugar
> 2 teaspoons salt

Cut the tops and roots from the radishes, then wash and dry the radishes well. Cut 1/16-inch wide slashes across each radish ¾ of the way to the bottom, then cut the same number of slashes at right angles to the first slashes. Place the radishes in a jar. Mix the sugar and salt and pour over the radishes. Cover tightly with a lid, then shake the jar until all the radishes are coated. Chill for 24 hours, shaking the jar twice.

Remove radishes from the jar and place on a flat surface, cut-sides-up. Press down in the center of each radish with thumb to create a flower effect. The radishes may be cut and placed in ice water instead of salt mixture, for at least 2 hours or longer, if crispness is desired.

Marinated Radishes and Celery

CHINA   Yield: 6 servings

> 4 tablespoons soy sauce
> 6 tablespoons vinegar
> 1 tablespoon sesame oil
> 6-ounce bag radishes, cleaned
> 2 stalks celery, sliced diagonally into
>   1-inch pieces

Mix soy sauce, vinegar, and sesame oil in small bowl. Add radishes and celery. Cover and refrigerate 1 hour—no longer.

Cooked Spinach

CHINA   Yield: 2 servings

½ pound spinach
1 tablespoon oil
1 clove garlic, crushed
½ cup chicken stock, warmed
Salt to taste
Sugar to taste
1 teaspoon soy sauce
½ teaspoon cornstarch
2 teaspoons water

Wash spinach and tear into bite-size pieces. Drain well and set aside. Heat oil in skillet or wok and fry garlic until lightly browned. Discard garlic. Add spinach and stir-fry for 1 minute. Add chicken stock, salt, sugar, and soy sauce. Simmer for 2 minutes. Mix together cornstarch and water and slowly stir into spinach mixture. Simmer for 1 minute. Serve immediately.

Delicious Spinach

CHINA   Yield: 2 servings

1 pound fresh spinach, washed and cut
    into 2-inch pieces
2 tablespoons oil
Salt to taste
1 small can bamboo shoots
8 fresh mushrooms, sliced
¼ cup chicken broth

Wash and cut the spinach into pieces. Heat oil in wok or skillet. Add salt and spinach and stir-fry for 2 minutes. Add bamboo shoots, mushrooms, and chicken broth. Mix, cover, and simmer for about 2 minutes, or until heated through.

Spinach with Mushrooms and Bamboo Shoots

CHINA   Yield: 2 servings

1 pound fresh spinach, washed and cut
    into 2-inch pieces
2 tablespoons oil
Salt to taste
1 small can bamboo shoots
8 fresh mushrooms, sliced
¼ cup chicken broth

Wash and cut the spinach into pieces. Heat the oil in a wok or skillet. Add salt and spinach and stir-fry for 2 minutes. Add bamboo shoots, mushrooms, and chicken broth. Mix; cover and simmer for about 2 minutes, or until heated through.

Sweet Spinach with Garlic

KOREA   Yield: 4 servings

1½ pounds fresh, young spinach leaves
Boiling water
3 tablespoons soy sauce
1 tablespoon sesame seeds
1 tablespoon sesame-seed oil
1 tablespoon peeled, crushed garlic
2 tablespoons scallions, chopped
2 tablespoons sugar
Salt to taste
Carrot, boo, and parsley for garnish

Wash spinach twice and remove and discard stalks. To a large pan of boiling water, add spinach and cook for 3 minutes. Drain and then chop the spinach.

Place hot spinach on a serving platter and sprinkle with the remaining ingredients. Garnish as desired and serve at once.

Tossed Spinach with Peanuts

CHINA   Yield: 4 servings

1 pound fresh spinach, washed and
  stemmed
¼-cup peanuts (or more)
1 tablespoon vegetable oil
1 tablespoon soy sauce
Salt and pepper

Steam the spinach in a small amount of
boiling water for only 2 to 3 minutes. Drain
at once, pat dry, and cut into fine strips.
Crush half the peanuts with a rolling pin or
mince with a cleaver. Heat oil in the wok
and add the crushed peanuts, spinach, soy
sauce, and salt and pepper to taste. Stir-fry
for 1 to 2 minutes. Serve garnished with the
remaining peanuts.

Succotash Raita

INDIA   Yield: 4 servings

1 cup lima beans, cooked and chilled
1 cup corn, cooked and chilled
1 cup plain yogurt
½ teaspoon salt
¼ teaspoon curry powder
Chili powder

Combine all ingredients except the chili
powder. Garnish each serving with chili
powder when served.

Tomato Raita

INDIA   Yield: 4 servings

3 large chilled tomatoes, cubed
1 medium onion, coarsely grated

1 tablespoon fresh basil or coriander
  leaves, minced
1 roasted green chili, chopped (available canned in the Mexican food
  section of your local supermarket)
¾ cup (or more) plain yogurt
½ teaspoon salt

Combine all ingredients. Serve at once.

Watercress in Sweet Gravy

INDONESIA   Yield: 6 servings

The Indonesian vegetable used for this is
called kangkung, a dark green leaf. Substitutes for this are watercress, spinach, or
chicory.

1 pound kangkung or substitute
½ cup hot water
4 tablespoons dehydrated shrimp
1½ cups coconut milk
1 large onion, peeled and finely
  chopped
1 small clove garlic, peeled and
  crushed
1 teaspoon salt
1 teaspoon fresh ginger, finely grated
1 fresh red chili, seeded and sliced
2 tablespoons palm sugar
½ teaspoon laos powder

Wash greens 3 times in cold water and
drain; then slice coarsely. Soak shrimp for 5
minutes in hot water. If brown dried shrimp
are used, they will need to soak for 25
minutes.

Place coconut milk and all other ingredients in a large saucepan. Bring to a boil,
uncovered. Add shrimp, plus the water in
which they soaked, and green vegetables.
Cover pan and simmer for 20 minutes or until greens are tender. Serve hot.

Sweet-and-Sour Yams and Pineapple

CHINA   Yield: About 8 servings

1 20-ounce can sliced pineapple
1 tablespoon cornstarch
¼ teaspoon salt
3 tablespoons fresh lemon juice
2 1-pound cans of yams, drained
Oil
4 scallions, sliced
1 small green pepper, cut into small chunks
½ cup celery, sliced diagonally

Drain pineapple; reserve syrup. In a saucepan, combine the reserved syrup, cornstarch, and salt. Blend well. Bring to a boil over medium heat. Cook until thickened, stirring constantly. Stir in the lemon juice

Arrange the pineapple and yams in a casserole and pour the sauce over them. Bake, covered, in a 350°F oven for about 30 minutes or until hot.

In a small amount of oil in a skillet, sauté the scallions, green pepper chunks, and celery until just tender, but still crisp. Stir carefully into yam mixture. Serve immediately.

Hibachi Zucchini

JAPAN   Yield: 2 servings

1 medium zucchini
1 teaspoon oil
3 tablespoons Japanese-style soy sauce
1 teaspoon (instant) minced onion
Pinch of instant garlic

Cut zucchini into thick (half-inch) slices. Combine with remaining ingredients in a

plastic bag. Twist the bag closed, grasping tightly at the top to trap air and form a "balloon."

Shake vigorously, to coat zucchini slices evenly. Lay the slices in a single layer on a rack about 2 inches from the heat source.

Barbecue about 3 minutes each side. Turn with a spatula.

Stuffed Zucchini

CHINA   Yield: 2 servings

Zucchini, large size (½ zucchini per serving)

Stuffing

Meat for stuffing (ground beef, ground veal, or leftover ground meat)
Salt
Pepper
Ginger
Soy sauce

Cut zucchini in half; scoop out centers. Pat dry before filling. Mix fresh meat as for hamburgers; season well. If desired, you may add a little ground ginger and a small amount of soy sauce to meat mixture.

Fill zucchini with mixture of your choice; bake in shallow baking pan at 350°F about 45 minutes or until browned. Serve zucchini with tomato sauce. One pound of meat will probably fill 4 to 6 halves.

Zucchini Chinese Style

CHINA   Yield: About 6 servings

2 pounds zucchini, sliced in ¼-inch slices
½ pound fresh mushrooms, sliced
¼ cup oil

1 tablespoon soy sauce
½ cup chicken broth
2 tablespoons cornstarch mixed with 4
teaspoons cold water

Wash and slice zucchini, and set aside. Wash and slice mushrooms. Heat oil in skillet and sauté mushrooms for a few seconds. Add zucchini and stir-fry until zucchini is coated with oil. Add soy sauce and chicken broth. Bring to a boil, cover, and simmer until zucchini is bright green and just tender and still crisp. Thicken with cornstarch mixture and serve immediately.

Crispy Fried Vegetables

CHINA   Yield: 4 to 6 servings

Batter for frying
1 cup sifted all-purpose flour
1 egg
½ cup milk
Salt and pepper
Cut the following vegetables into
    matchstick size strips:
        2 carrots
        2 potatoes
        1 stick celery
        8 small cauliflower florets
        1 sliced onion
        2 cups oil for frying

Prepare the batter by combining the flour, egg, milk, and a little salt and pepper in a small bowl. Mix or whisk until the batter is smooth and lump-free. Batter should be thin. If it seems very thick, add more milk.

Thoroughly mix the cut-up vegetables into the batter. Let stand for ½ hour. Using a slotted spoon, lift out spoonfuls of mixed vegetables and drop gently into deep fat at 375°F. (Use an electric wok or a thermometer to maintain proper temperature of the fat.) Deep-fry for 2 to 3 minutes, a few spoonfuls at a time. Lift out and drain on paper towels. Serve as a vegetable at any meal.

Five Precious Oriental Vegetables

CHINA   Yield: 4 servings

5 to 6 Chinese dried black mushrooms
1 small head of Chinese celery cabbage
1 or 2 bamboo shoots
4 or 5 water chestnuts
2 tablespoons vegetable oil
1 cup bean sprouts
3 tablespoons chicken broth
1 teaspoon salt
2 teaspoons soy sauce
1 teaspoon sugar

Soak the mushrooms in warm water for 20 to 30 minutes; drain, remove and discard the tough stems, and cut the caps into strips. Wash the cabbage well, drain, and cut diagonally into ½-inch slices. Cut the bamboo shoots and water chestnuts into slices.

Heat oil in the wok. Stir-fry the cabbage 1 minute, then add mushrooms, bean sprouts, water chestnuts, and bamboo shoots. Sitr-fry all together for 3 to 4 minutes. Add broth with the remaining ingredients. Mix well and heat through. Vegetables should be tender but still crisp. Serve at once.

Fried Vegetables

CHINA   Yield: 2 servings

> Oil for cooking
> ½ cup celery, sliced diagonally
> 4 ounces bamboo shoots
> 4 ounces water chestnuts, sliced
> 3 scallions, sliced into 1-inch pieces
> ½ cup fresh mushrooms
> 1 cup bean sprouts, fresh or canned
> Soy sauce to taste

Heat the oil in a skillet or wok. Add celery, bamboo shoots, and water chestnuts. Stir-fry for 2 minutes. Add scallions, mushrooms, and bean sprouts and stir-fry for 1 minute or until heated through. Sprinkle with soy sauce to taste and serve immediately.

Lo Mein

CHINA   Yield: 4 to 6 servings

> 1 pound spaghetti noodles
> 3 tablespoons oil
> 3 cups Chinese cabbage, first cut into
>   2-inch lengths, then julienne sliced
>   lengthwise
> ½ cup carrots, julienne sliced
> 4 green onions, julienne cut
> 4 dried Chinese mushrooms, which
>   have been soaked for 20 minutes in
>   hot water, sliced, optional
> 2 teaspoons salt
> 3 tablespoons soy sauce

Prepare spaghetti noodles according to package instructions. Heat oil in wok or large skillet over high heat. Add cabbage, carrots, green onions, and mushrooms; stir-fry for 1 minute. Add salt and soy sauce;

stir-fry for another minute. Add drained spaghetti noodles, stirring constantly for about 2 minutes. Serve hot. If you wish, add between ½ and 1 cup shredded ham and/or shredded cooked chicken breast along with the salt and soy sauce.

Medley of Vegetables

INDIA   Yield: 4 to 6 servings

> 2 tablespoons butter or margarine
> 2 large onions, peeled and diced
> 4 cups hot water
> ½ head cabbage, sliced into thin strips
> 1 small cauliflower, cut in small florets
> 2 leeks, sliced
> 2 carrots, diced
> 1 bay leaf
> 2 teaspoons caraway seeds
> 4 teaspoons curry powder
> 2 cloves garlic, peeled and finely
>   chopped
> 2 tomatoes, diced
> 2 small eggplants, peeled and sliced
> ½ cup frozen green beans
> ½ cup frozen peas
> Salt to taste
> Sambal ulek to taste
> Tabasco sauce to taste

Heat butter or margarine in a large saucepan and cook onions until transparent. Add water and bring to a boil. Place cabbage, cauliflower, leeks, and carrots in the boiling liquid. Add bay leaf, caraway, curry, and garlic; cook at medium heat for 15 minutes. Add remaining vegetables and cook for 5 minutes more. Last, add seasonings to taste and serve.

Mixed Vegetables Chinese Style

CHINA   Yield: 2 servings

5 large dried Chinese mushrooms
1 cup lukewarm water
5 ounces green cabbage
4 ounces carrots
4 ounces cucumbers
5 ounces canned bamboo shoots
4 tablespoons sesame-seed oil
2 ounces frozen peas
½ cup hot chicken broth
2 tablespoons soy sauce
Salt
Pinch of sugar

Soak the mushrooms in water for 30 minutes. Shred the cabbage. Cut the carrots, cucumber, and bamboo shoots into julienne strips. Cube the mushrooms.

Heat oil in a skillet. Add cabbage; cook 2 minutes. Add mushrooms, cucumber, carrots, bamboo shoots, and peas. Pour in broth. Season with soy sauce, salt, and sugar. Simmer over low heat for 15 minutes. Serve at once.

Oriental Medley

CHINA   Yield: 6 servings

¼ pound fresh mushrooms, sliced
Butter
1 cup celery, sliced diagonally
1 cup green onions, finely slivered
3 cups fresh bean sprouts
2 tablespoons soy sauce
1 cube beef bouillon

Sauté mushrooms lightly in butter. Add celery and onions and cook for 3 to 4 minutes. Add bean sprouts and soy sauce.

Crumble bouillon cube over all. Cover and cook for 2 minutes. Be careful not to overcook; vegetables should still be crisp. Stir well and serve.

Sweet-and-Sour Vegetable Medley

CHINA   Yield: 4 servings

2 tablespoons vegetable oil
2 medium potatoes, peeled and very thinly sliced
2 medium carrots, sliced diagonally very thin
4 scallions, sliced
1 cup green beans
½ cucumber, unpeeled, sliced into ⅛-inch slices

Sauce

1 tablespoon cornstarch
1 tablespoon soy sauce
1 tablespoon vinegar
1 tablespoon tomato paste
1 tablespoon dry sherry
2 teaspoons sugar

Heat oil in the wok and stir-fry the potatoes 1 minute. Add carrots; stir-fry 1 minute. Add scallions and green beans and continue to stir-fry until vegetables are heated through. Stir together the ingredients for the sauce and add to the vegetables in the wok. Add the cucumber slices and gently stir the vegetables and sauce until the sauce thickens and the cucumbers are heated. Serve at once.

Salads & Vegetables

Oriental Vegetables

CHINA   Yield: 4 servings

1 tablespoon vegetable oil
¼ cup blanched almonds, slivered
2 green peppers, sliced into ½-inch
    strips
2 scallions, cut into thin strips about 2
    inches in length
1 onion, thinly sliced
1 8-ounce can bamboo shoots, sliced
Soy sauce to taste

Heat oil in frying pan (or wok if available). Stir-fry almonds 1 to 2 minutes or until lightly browned. Remove from pan and reserve. One at a time, stir-fry vegetables for 1 to 2 minutes each. Remove each vegetable when done. After all vegetables have been cooked, return vegetables to pan. Add soy sauce to taste. Return almonds to pan and serve.

Stir-fried Vegetables on the Grill

CHINA   Yield: 6 to 8 servings

¼ cup cooking oil
1 bunch green onions, cut in 1-inch
    lengths
1 green pepper, diced
4 stalks celery, sliced diagonally into
    ½-inch slices
½ pound fresh mushrooms, thinly
    sliced
1 16-ounce can bean sprouts, rinsed
    and drained
1 6-ounce package frozen Chinese pea
    pods
¼ cup soy sauce
1 tablespoon sugar

Place skillet or wok directly on hot briquets in grill. Add oil. When oil is hot, add onions, green pepper, and celery and cook, stirring constantly, until vegetables are softened. Add remaining ingredients and continue to cook and stir until vegetables are tender-crisp. Serve immediately.

Stir-fried Mixed Vegetables

INDOCHINA   Yield: 4 servings

6 dried Chinese mushrooms, soaked in
    hot water for 30 minutes
½ cup water
1 tablespoon dark soy sauce
1 teaspoon sesame oil
2 tablespoons sugar
3 stalks celery, sliced diagonally
¼ medium cabbage or white Chinese
    cabbage
Few leaves mustard cabbage, if
    available
1 small head lettuce
3 spring onions, cut into 1-inch pieces
1 tablespoon oil
1 clove garlic, peeled and finely grated
½ teaspoon fresh ginger, finely grated
1½ tablespoons light soy sauce
¼ cup water
1 teaspoon cornstarch

Cut off and discard the mushroom stems. Slice tops thin and simmer in ½ cup water with dark soy sauce, sesame oil, and sugar until the liquid is absorbed. Prepare celery and cut greens into bite-size pieces.

In a wok or skillet, heat the oil and fry the garlic and ginger for 30 seconds or less. Add vegetables and stir-fry for 2 minutes on high heat. Add the light soy sauce and prepared mushrooms and mix well. Add ¼ cup of water. Allow it to come to a boil, add cornstarch blended with 1 tablespoon cold water, and stir until it thickens. Serve at once.

Vegetable and Ham Rice Cake

CHINA   Yield: 4 servings

2 tablespoons vinegar
2 tablespoons sugar
½ teaspoon salt
3 cups cooked, cold rice
2 tablespoons vegetable oil
3 carrots, cut into matchstick-size shreds
2 ounces mushrooms, sliced
½ unpeeled cucumber, sliced
3 scallions, sliced
2 tablespoons soy sauce
2 teaspoons prepared horseradish sauce
2 tablespoons light cream
4 slices boiled ham, shredded

Combine vinegar, 1 tablespoon of the sugar, and salt together with the rice. Toss well. Heat oil in the wok. Add carrots and stir-fry 2 to 3 minutes. Add mushrooms, cucumber, and scallions and continue to stir-fry until all the vegetables are very tender. Stir in the remaining 1 tablespoon of sugar and the soy sauce. Set aside.

Grease an 8-inch springform pan (or use an 8-inch-square baking pan lined with plastic wrap extending well over the sides so the mixture can eventually be lifted out). Pack half of the rice in the bottom. Cover with ¾ of the prepared vegetables, then the remaining rice. Combine the horseradish sauce and cream and spread over the rice. Cover with the remaining ¼ of the vegetables and the ham shreds. Place a piece of waxed paper over the top and weight it down. Chill for 30 minutes. Remove weight and paper, then carefully remove cake from pan. Use a wet knife to cut cake into slices and arrange on a platter. Serve cold with a little soy sauce.

Vegetable Platter

INDOCHINA   Yield: 4 servings

1 head lettuce, washed and leaves separated
Mint leaves
Coriander leaves
2 cucumbers, partially peeled and halved, cut into half-moon shapes

Mound the lettuce leaves in center of serving platter. Surround the center with piles of the mint leaves, coriander leaves, and prepared cucumbers. Any arrangement that is pleasing to the eye will do. Serve chilled with your favorite dressing.

Vegetable Curry I

MALAYSIA   Yield: 4 servings

Fiddlehead ferns are used for this dish in Malaysia. A good substitute for the fern is curly kale.

    6 kemiri, chopped
    6 shallots, peeled and chopped
    3 cloves garlic, peeled and chopped
    2 red chilies, seeded and chopped, or
        ½ teaspoon chili powder
    2 teaspoons ginger powder
    1 teaspoon turmeric powder
    Pinch of laos powder
    Pinch of sereh powder
    Salt to taste
    2 cups thick coconut milk
    ¼ cup tamarind water
    3 sprigs mint
    1¼ pounds fiddlehead ferns or kale,
        cut into 2-inch lengths

Make a smooth paste of the kemiri, shallots, garlic, and chilies. Add the spices, salt, coconut milk, tamarind water, and mint and mix well.

In a saucepan, bring the mixture to a boil for 5 minutes. Add the kale and cover. Reduce the heat to a simmer and cook for 10 minutes. Bring back to a boil just long enough to reduce the sauce. Adjust seasonings and serve hot.

Vegetable Curry II

BURMA   Yield: 4 servings

The vegetables suggested here can be changed, depending on what is available seasonally.

    3 medium potatoes, peeled and cut
        into 1-inch cubes
    1 medium eggplant, cut into 1-inch
        slices
    4 carrots, peeled and diced
    1 medium cauliflower, divided into
        florets
    ½ pound okra, cut into 1-inch lengths
    ¼ cup vegetable oil
    1 medium onion, peeled and pounded
    3 cloves garlic, peeled and crushed
    ½-inch piece fresh gingerroot, peeled
        and pounded
    1 teaspoon chili powder
    ½ teaspoon turmeric powder
    3 tomatoes, roughly chopped
    3 tablespoons coriander leaves

Place potatoes, eggplant, carrots, cauliflower, and okra in a bowl. Cover with cold water and set aside.

Heat oil in deep-fat fryer or wok. Stir-fry onion, garlic, ginger, chili powder, and turmeric until quite fragrant. Stir in 1 tomato and the coriander. Add potatoes and enough water to cover. Bring to a boil; reduce heat and simmer for 10 minutes. Add eggplant and carrots and simmer for 5 minutes more. Add cauliflower and a little more water if needed. Bring back to a boil. Put in remaining tomatoes and simmer 5 minutes. Add okra and simmer for 5 minutes more. Most of the liquid will be absorbed. Serve piping hot.

Vegetables, Chinese Style

CHINA   Yield: 4 servings

    1 chicken bouillon cube, crushed
    1 clove garlic, chopped
    1 teaspoon sugar
    2 tablespoons soy sauce

2 tablespoons dry sherry
¼ teaspoon crushed red pepper, or to taste
3 tablespoons cooking oil
2 cups carrots in julienne strips
¼ pound medium mushrooms, cut in half
3 cups fresh broccoli flowerettes
2 cups celery, diagonally sliced
1 cup green onions, cut in 1-inch lengths
1 8-ounce can water chestnuts, drained and sliced
2 tablespoons toasted sesame seed

Combine bouillon cube, garlic, and sugar; mash together until smooth. Add soy sauce, sherry, and crushed red pepper. Let stand while preparing vegetables.

Heat oil in wok or large skillet over high heat. Add carrots; cook and stir 1 minute. Add mushrooms; cook and stir 1 minute. Add broccoli, celery, green onions, and water chestnuts; stir. Pour soy sauce mixture over vegetables. Cover and steam 3 to 4 minutes until vegetables are tender-crisp. Sprinkle with sesame seed. Serve immediately.

Vegetables with Pork

CHINA   Yield: 6 servings

4 tablespoons butter
4 cups celery, sliced diagonally
1 green pepper, sliced
1 red pepper, sliced
½ pound fresh mushrooms, sliced
½ cup onions, sliced
2 cups cooked pork, cubed
1¼ cups beef bouillon
1 tablespoon cornstarch
3 tablespoons soy sauce
½ teaspoon ginger
¼ teaspoon salt
Fresh ground pepper to taste
Boiled rice

Melt the butter in a wok or large skillet. Add celery; stir-fry for 5 minutes. Stir in green and red peppers, mushrooms, and onions; stir-fry for another 5 minutes. Add pork and bouillon; bring to boil. Reduce heat; simmer for 5 minutes.

Blend cornstarch with soy sauce, ginger, salt, and pepper. Stir into pork mixture. Cook, stirring constantly, just until heated through and thickened. Serve vegetables and pork on a bed of rice.

Vegetable Tempura

JAPAN   Yield: About 2 servings

Vegetables

Use a variety of the following, or whatever is available to you:
Eggplant
Green pepper
String beans
Mushrooms
Onion
Potato

Tempura batter

1 egg
½ cup ice water
1 cup sifted flour

Oil for deep-frying

Slice vegetables into thin strips, keeping them separate, and set aside.

To mix the batter, beat the egg; add cold water and sifted flour all at once. Blend thoroughly, but do not overmix.

Heat oil in a deep pan (or wok) until a drop of water dropped into the oil sizzles. Dip vegetables, a few at a time, in batter; then fry them until crisp, using tongs to turn them. Take them out of pan or wok with a slotted spoon. Drain on paper towels.

Dip vegetables in soy sauce before enjoying.

Eggs & Pancakes

Chicken and Mushrooms in Eggs

JAPAN   Yield: 4 servings

¼ pound chicken meat
¼ pound fresh mushrooms
2 onions

Sauce

½ cup chicken stock
4 tablespoons soy sauce
4 tablespoons rice wine or sherry

4 eggs
4 cups rice

Thinly slice chicken meat, mushrooms, and onions. Combine the chicken stock, soy sauce, and rice wine or sherry. Bring to boil. Add chicken, mushrooms, and onions to sauce. Cook this mixture slowly for about 15 minutes.

Place ¼ of the cooked mixture in a small frying pan. Pour a lightly beaten egg over this; cook until almost firm. Remove from pan and serve over rice. This is repeated 3 more times.

Curried Eggs

INDIA   Yield: 4 servings

1 medium-sized onion, peeled and chopped
2-3 tablespoons oil
2 tablespoons flour
1 tablespoon curry powder
Salt
2 cups stock or 1 bouillon cube and water
1 large apple, peeled, cored, and diced
1 tablespoon Worcestershire sauce
4 hard-boiled eggs
About 2 cups freshly cooked rice
Chutney

Sauté the onion in the oil until soft but not browned. Add flour, curry powder, and a little salt, and stir over low heat until the mixture forms a smooth paste. Add stock gradually, stir until boiling. Add apple and Worcestershire sauce, cover, and simmer gently for 15-20 minutes. Add eggs and heat through.

Put the rice on a large platter and arrange the eggs and sauce on top. Serve with chutney and a tossed green salad.

Curried Eggs with Mushrooms

INDIA   Yield: 3 or 4 servings

6 hard-cooked eggs, cut in half lengthwise
8 ounces mushrooms
1 large onion, peeled and finely chopped
2 tablespoons margarine or butter
1 teaspoon ground coriander
1 teaspoon salt
½ teaspoon ground turmeric
½ teaspoon ground ginger
½ teaspoon ground cumin
3 medium tomatoes, cut into wedges
¼ cup chicken broth
1 teaspoon lemon juice
3 cups hot cooked rice

In a medium-size skillet, stir mushrooms and onions in margarine for 5 minutes. Add coriander, salt, turmeric, ginger, and cumin. Stir-fry together for 1 minute. Put in tomatoes and chicken broth and bring to a boil.

Then reduce heat to a simmer, cooking uncovered for 5 minutes.

Place eggs gently in skillet and spoon the sauce over them. Simmer again without stirring, for 5 minutes. Sprinkle with lemon juice and serve eggs with sauce over rice.

Egg Curry

INDIA   Yield: 4 to 6 servings

6 hard-boiled eggs, cooled, shelled, halved, and set aside
2 tablespoons ghee or oil
2 medium onions, peeled and finely chopped
3 cloves garlic, peeled and finely chopped
2 teaspoons fresh ginger, finely grated
3 teaspoons ground coriander
2 teaspoons ground cumin
1 teaspoon ground turmeric
½ teaspoon chili powder
2 to 3 ripe tomatoes, diced
1 teaspoon salt
½ cup hot water
½ teaspoon garam masala

After the eggs are prepared and set aside, heat ghee in skillet. Stir-fry onions, garlic, and ginger until soft and light brown. Add coriander, cumin, turmeric, and chili and stir for a few seconds. Put in tomatoes and salt and cook until tomatoes are pulpy. Add hot water and then cover and simmer until gravy has thickened. Last, stir in garam masala and the egg halves, and mix well until all is hot and spicy. Serve at once with rice.

Egg Foo Yung I

CHINA   Yield: 6 servings

1 cup chicken broth
2 tablespoons soy sauce
1 tablespoon cornstarch
¼ cup water
6 eggs
½ cup cooked pork, diced
⅔ cup onions, thinly sliced
16-ounce can bean sprouts, drained
4-ounce can mushrooms, drained
2 tablespoons fat or oil

Combine broth and soy sauce. Heat to boiling. Blend cornstarch and water. Stir slowly into the broth. Cook and stir constantly until thickened. Keep warm while cooking egg mixture.

Beat eggs until very thick and light. Fold in the pork, onions, bean sprouts, and mushrooms. Heat fat in frying pan over moderate heat. Pour the egg mixture by ½ cupfuls into the pan. Cook until lightly browned on one side; turn and brown the other side.

Serve the sauce over the patties.

Egg Foo Yung II

CHINA   Yield: 4 to 6 servings

1 can Chinese vegetables
5 eggs, beaten
½ cup chicken or shrimp, diced
Peanut oil

Drain vegetables and mix with the beaten eggs and diced meat. Ladle into hot fat in skillet and fry until brown.

Egg Foo Yung III

CHINA					Yield: 4 servings

1 small onion
1 tomato
½ cup cooked chicken
¼ cup canned sliced water chestnuts
3 scallions, thinly sliced
2 tablespoons soy sauce
3 large mushrooms, sliced
2 eggs, slightly beaten
2 tablespoons vegetable oil
1 cup bean sprouts
2 teaspoons sugar
1½ teaspoons cornstarch
¾ cup water

Peel onion. Cut in half lengthwise; cut halves into ½-inch-wide lengthwise strips. Cut tomato in half and into thin lengthwise wedges. Place chicken in bowl. Add water chestnuts, scallions, 1 tablespoon soy sauce, mushrooms, and eggs; mix together lightly.

Heat 1 tablespoon oil in small, heavy frying pan. Spoon about ¼ of egg mixture into pan. Spread ¼ of sprouts, tomato slices, and ⅛ teaspoon sugar over egg mixture. Cook until "cake" is nicely browned on underside, about 3 minutes. Carefully turn with pancake turner; brown other side. Cook until edges are a little crisp. Remove cake; keep warm. Add more oil to pan as necessary. Cook remaining cakes.

While cakes are cooking, mix cornstarch and 1½ teaspoons sugar in small saucepan. Add water gradually; blend until smooth. Heat to boiling. Add 1 tablespoon soy sauce; simmer 1 minute. Serve hot sauce on egg foo yung.

Egg Foo Yung IV

CHINA					Yield: 2 to 4 servings

Oil to cover bottom of skillet
½ pound fresh mushrooms, sliced
½ cup celery, chopped
½ cup scallions, diced
1 cup fresh bean sprouts, rinsed and drained
1 cup leftover cooked chicken, beef, or shrimp, cut into small pieces
4 eggs
Salt and pepper to taste

Sauté mushrooms, celery, and scallions for 5 minutes. Cool. Add bean sprouts and chicken, beef, or shrimp to sautéed mixture. In large bowl, beat eggs well with salt and pepper. Combine other ingredients with eggs.

Drop by spoonfuls into greased skillet. Cook over medium-high heat until browned on both sides. You may use a wok, and drop mixture by spoonfuls just to cover bottom of wok.

Egg Foo Yung V

CHINA					Yield: 4 servings

2 tablespoons vegetable oil
½ cup scallions, thinly sliced
¼ cup celery, finely chopped
1 clove garlic, crushed
1 cup cooked shrimp or pork, diced
6 eggs
½ teaspoon salt
¼ teaspoon pepper
1 tablespoon soy sauce

Heat the oil in the wok. Add scallions, celery, and garlic, and stir-fry 2 to 3 minutes. Remove and discard the garlic. Add the shrimp and continue to stir-fry until shrimp are lightly browned. Beat the eggs with the salt, pepper, and soy sauce until frothy. Add to the shrimp mixture and stir until blended. Cook over low heat until the eggs set. Fold over and slide onto serving plate. Serve at once.

Egg Foo Yung VI

CHINA   Yield: 4 servings

½ cup scallions (green onion), white and green parts, thinly sliced
½ cup celery
¼-½ cup salad oil
6 large eggs
1 teaspoon salt
1 tablespoon parsley flakes
1 cup cooked chicken, diced (or 12-ounce can tuna fish)
1 1-pound can bean sprouts, well drained
½ of 5-ounce can water chestnuts, drained and thinly sliced

Sauté scallions and celery in 2 to 3 tablespoons oil until lightly browned. Add to egg mixture when cool. In medium mixing bowl, beat eggs, salt, and parsley flakes only enough to combine yolks and white. Stir in chicken, bean sprouts, water chestnuts, scallions, and celery.

In a 10-inch skillet, heat ¼ cup oil over moderately low heat until it bubbles. Add egg mixture; spread vegetables evenly. Cover tightly and adjust heat so bottom is browned and top is set in about 15 minutes (around 300°F). Cut into 4 wedges, serve brown-side-up with Chinese gravy.

Egg Foo Yung VII

CHINA   Yield: 4 servings

½ cup onion, chopped
½ cup celery, chopped
3 tablespoons oil
1 can bean sprouts, drained
6 eggs, beaten
1 tablespoon soy sauce
1 tablespoon cornstarch
1 teaspoon salt
⅛ teaspoon pepper

Sauce

½ cup water
2 teaspoons sherry
1 tablespoon soy sauce
2 teaspoons cornstarch

Sauté onion and celery in oil until limp. Add bean sprouts. Put in bowl. Add beaten eggs, soy sauce, cornstarch, salt, and pepper. Put 1 tablespoon mixture on greased skillet or griddle and brown. (This is appetizer size. For meal size, use ½ cup mixture). Turn and brown other side. Keep hot until all are cooked. Combine all sauce ingredients and cook until thickened. Pour sauce on top.

For variations, add any of the following to the above mixture: 1 cup crabmeat, 1 cup lobster meat, 1 cup shrimp, 1 cup diced chicken, 1 cup diced pork.

Egg Foo Yung VIII

CHINA   Yield: 4 to 6 servings

> 1 small can Chow Mein vegetables,
>   drained
> 1 tablespoon soy sauce
> Dash salt and pepper
> 6 eggs, beaten
> Oil

Mix all ingredients, except oil, together. Heat small amount of oil in 7-inch frying pan. Drop in enough mixture to cover the bottom. Fry until golden brown. Roll. Place in oven on rack pan to keep warm. Repeat above procedure until all the batter is used.

Egg Foo Yung IX

CHINA   Yield: 4 to 6 servings

> 1 or 2 medium onions, chopped
> 3 stalks celery
> 6 eggs
> 1 teaspoon salt
> 1 can bean sprouts
> 1 small can water chestnuts
> 1 stick butter
> 1 6-ounce can mushrooms

Sauce

> 1 can cream of mushroom soup
> Soy sauce to taste
> ½ reserved liquid from bean sprouts

Sauté onions and celery in butter until golden brown. Beat eggs with salt. Drain bean sprouts, reserving liquid. Drain water chestnuts, cut in thirds, and add to egg mixture. Take ⅛ stick butter and melt in a baking dish or loaf pan; swish around pan. Add remaining butter to mixture. Add cut-up mushrooms. Bake in a 350°F oven for 45 minutes. Combine sauce ingredients and serve with eggs.

Shrimp Egg Foo Yung

CHINA   Yield: 4 servings

> 1 cup fresh bean sprouts, chopped
> ¼ cup white onions, chopped
> ¼ cup fresh mushrooms, chopped
> ¼ cup cooked shrimp, finely chopped
> 1 teaspoon soy sauce
> Pinch of salt
> 4 eggs
> ¼ cup crisp noodles
> Oil for frying

Mix together sprouts, onions, mushrooms, shrimp, soy sauce, and salt. Add eggs; mix. Mix in noodles. Shape mixture into hamburger-size patties. Heat oil (small amount) in frying pan. Cook each patty about 2 minutes on each side. Can be served with Sweet-and-Sour Sauce (see Index).

Eggs in Fried Chili Sauce

INDONESIA   Yield: 4 servings

> 1 medium onion, peeled and sliced
> ½ cup oil
> 1 tablespoon ground chili
> 2 tomatoes, peeled and chopped
> 1 chicken stock cube
> 1 or more teaspoons salt
> 6 hard-boiled eggs, shelled

In a skillet, fry onions until they change color. Reduce heat. Add chili, tomatoes, crumbled chicken cube, and salt. Simmer for 5 minutes, stirring constantly. Add the shelled eggs and simmer for 5 minutes more.

Remove from heat and remove eggs from pan. Cut each egg in half and arrange on a prepared platter. Pour the sauce over eggs and serve at once.

Eggs in Coconut Milk Gravy

INDIA   Yield: 4 to 6 servings

6 hard-boiled eggs, shelled, halved, and set aside
1½ cups thick coconut milk
2 cups thin coconut milk
2 tablespoons ghee or oil
1 large onion, peeled and finely sliced
3 cloves garlic, peeled and finely chopped
2 teaspoons fresh ginger, finely grated
3 fresh green chilies, seeded and sliced
6 curry leaves
1 teaspoon ground turmeric
1 teaspoon salt
2 tablespoons lemon juice

Prepare coconut milk, keeping the thick milk separate from the thin.

Fry onions, garlic, ginger, chilies, and curry leaves in heated ghee. Cook only until onions are soft. Add turmeric and stir for 1 minute. Add thin coconut milk and simmer gently for 10 minutes. Add thick coconut milk and salt and stir constantly. When mixture has come to a soft simmer, put in egg halves and simmer for 6 to 7 minutes more. Remove from heat. Add lemon juice to taste and serve at once.

Eggs with Bean Sprouts

CHINA   Yield: 4 servings

2 tablespoons vegetable oil
2 scallions, cut into ¼-inch slices
2 ounces mushrooms, cut into "T" shapes
4 eggs
3 water chestnuts, cut into thin slices
3 ounces cooked chicken meat, shredded
1 tablespoon soy sauce
½ teaspoon sugar
½ teaspoon salt
½ tomato, cut into thin wedges
1 cup bean sprouts

Sauce

¾ cup water
1½ teaspoons cornstarch
1½ teaspoons sugar
1 tablespoon soy sauce

Heat the oil in the wok and stir-fry the scallions and mushrooms 1 to 2 minutes. Combine the eggs, water chestnuts, chicken, soy sauce, sugar, and salt. Add to the scallions and mushrooms in the wok and stir briefly. After the eggs have heated for about a minute, spread the tomato wedges and bean sprouts over the top. Continue cooking until the eggs are browned on the bottom. Do not stir. Carefully turn the eggs over and cook for another minute.

Slide the omelette out onto a hot dish and serve with the thickened soy sauce prepared by combining all ingredients and bringing to a boil, stirring continuously. Serve at once.

Fried Stuffed Eggs

THAILAND   Yield: 6 to 8 servings

4 large eggs, boiled slowly, shelled and
  halved lengthwise
½ cup raw prawns or shrimp, chopped
½ cup cooked crab meat
½ cup cooked pork, chopped
1 teaspoon fresh coriander leaves,
  chopped
Hearty dash of ground black pepper
½ teaspoon salt
1 tablespoon fish sauce
1 to 2 tablespoons thick coconut milk

Batter

½ cup flour
½ cup tepid water
2 teaspoons oil
¼ teaspoon salt

Oil for deep frying

After eggs are prepared, scoop out the
egg yolks into a bowl. Add all ingredients
except the coconut milk. When well mixed,
add enough of the coconut milk to make the
mixture hold together without getting too
moist. Divide this yolk mixture into 8 portions and stuff each egg.

Mix the batter in order given. Dip each
egg into the batter, then drop it stuffed-side-
down into heated oil for quick deep fry.
When golden brown, remove and drain on
paper towels. This can be served hot or cold.

Marbled Eggs

INDONESIA   Yield: 6 or more servings

10 eggs
3 tablespoons loose tea or 6 tea bags
2 stalks parsley

2 stalks shallots
2-inch piece fresh green ginger, thinly
  sliced
½ tablespoon salt
2 chicken cubes
2 tablespoons soy sauce

Make enough strong tea to cover 10 eggs.
Allow to stand for 10 minutes. Strain into a
large saucepan. Place all ingredients except
the eggs in the tea solution. Allow to come
to a boil. Lower the heat and add eggs one
by one. Simmer for 30 minutes.

Take the eggs out and rinse. Very gently,
crack the egg shells all over but do not remove the shells. Strain the liquid and return
to pan. Return eggs to the pan and continue
to simmer for 20 minutes more. Turn off the
heat but let eggs remain in the liquid for at
least 3 hours, and up to 24 hours. When the
eggs are peeled, the marbled effect will show
where the shell was cracked. Serve hot or
cold.

These may be made ahead and refrigerated for several days.

Scrambled Eggs I

JAPAN   Yield: 2 servings

4 fresh mushrooms, sliced
2 scallions, cut into ½-inch pieces
Butter or oil
4 eggs, lightly beaten
Few sprinkles of soy sauce

Slice mushrooms and scallions; sauté in
butter or oil for 2 minutes.

Beat eggs, add a few sprinkles of soy
sauce, and scramble in skillet with mushrooms and scallions until sufficiently cooked.
If desired, add ½ teaspoon sherry to the eggs
before cooking.

Scrambled Eggs II

INDIA   Yield: 4 to 6 servings

6 to 8 eggs, well beaten
4 tablespoons milk
¾ teaspoon salt
¼ teaspoon ground black pepper
2 tablespoons ghee
6 spring onions, finely chopped
2 to 3 fresh red or green chilies, seeded
    and chopped
1 teaspoon fresh ginger, finely grated
Dash of ground turmeric
2 tablespoons fresh coriander leaves,
    chopped
1 ripe tomato, diced, optional
½ teaspoon ground cumin
Tomato wedges to garnish
Fresh coriander leaves to garnish

When eggs are well beaten, add milk,
salt, and pepper. In a large skillet, heat ghee
and cook onions, chilies, and ginger until
soft. After you add turmeric, coriander
leaves, and tomato, fry for 1 minute.

Stir in egg mixture with ground cumin.
Cook over low heat. Stir the eggs as they
start to set. The eggs are finished when they
are of a creamy consistency, not dry. Place
on a serving plate and garnish with tomato
wedges and coriander.

Unusual Scrambled Eggs

CHINA   Yield: 2 servings

4 eggs
½ teaspoon salt
Freshly ground black pepper to taste
½ cup green pepper, finely chopped
Oil for cooking, enough to cover
    bottom of pan

Beat eggs with salt and pepper. Add
green pepper. Heat oil in skillet and cook
mixture over medium-high heat until desired
doneness. (Don't cook until dry.)

Scrambled Eggs with Shrimp

CHINA   Yield: 3 to 4 servings

½ pound shrimp, cooked
1 teaspoon rice wine or sherry
½ teaspoon cornstarch
Salt (about ½ teaspoon)
2 tablespoons oil
6 eggs, beaten lightly
Salt to taste

Marinate shrimp in mixture of wine or
sherry, cornstarch, and salt for 15 minutes.
Heat oil in large skillet and sauté shrimp
over medium-high heat for approximately 2
minutes. Remove from skillet. Add salt to
taste to beaten eggs and add shrimp to egg
mixture. Add more oil if necessary to skillet,
heat to medium-high. Pour in egg-shrimp
mixture and cook and stir until done to
taste.

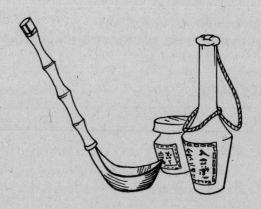

Son-in-Law Eggs

THAILAND   Yield: 4 servings

    2 tablespoons vegetable oil
    5 shallots, peeled and finely chopped
    4 hard-cooked eggs, shelled and
        quartered
    2 tablespoons tamarind water
    1 tablespoon water
    2 teaspoons brown sugar
    Nam pla to taste

Using a wok or deep skillet, heat oil. Fry shallots until brown. Remove from pan.

Add eggs and fry until crisp on the outside. Remove from pan with slotted spoon and set aside.

Place remaining ingredients in skillet; cook for 5 minutes, stirring constantly. Return eggs to pan and cook gently for 2 minutes more. Arrange egg mixture on a warm platter and garnish with the shallots. Serve at once.

Chinese Omelet

CHINA   Yield: 4 servings

Tomato sauce

    1 8-ounce can tomato sauce
    1 tablespoon olive oil
    1 clove garlic
    2 tablespoons soy sauce
    1 slice fresh gingerroot or ¼ teaspoon
        ground ginger

Omelette

    1 small leek, sliced
    2 small onions, sliced
    Several dark-green celery leaves
    3 tablespoons vegetable oil
    8 eggs, lightly beaten with a fork

    4 ounces canned lobster tails, coarsely
        chopped
    Salt and pepper to taste
    ½ cup cooked small peas

Simmer together the ingredients for the tomato sauce, about 10 minutes. Remove garlic clove and ginger slice before serving.

Stir-fry the leek, onions, and celery leaves in vegetable oil in a large skillet. Pour in eggs; add lobster, salt, and pepper. Cook over low heat without stirring. As eggs set on bottom, lift edges to allow uncooked mixture to run underneath. When omelet is set, serve at once. Garnish with peas and serve with tomato sauce.

Mushroom Omelet

CHINA   Yield: 4 servings

    2 tablespoons butter
    ¼ cup mushrooms, sliced
    ¼ cup onions, finely chopped
    6 eggs
    Salt and pepper
    Lettuce or parsley for garnish

Melt butter in wok, and, over a very low heat, stir-fry the mushrooms and onions. (Butter will burn if heated over 225°F.) Remove and set aside.

Beat eggs with salt and pepper. Pour into wok and heat slowly. Lift up edges of the eggs as they become set on the bottom and allow uncooked egg to run under. Cook until golden brown on bottom and creamy on top. Place mushrooms and onions in center and roll out on plate. Garnish with lettuce or parsley. Serve at once.

Crab Omelet

INDOCHINA   Yield: 3 to 4 servings

4 eggs
½ teaspoon salt
¼ teaspoon black pepper
4 ounces crab meat, fresh, frozen, or
   canned
2 spring onions, chopped
1 fresh red chili, optional
1 teaspoon fish sauce
Oil for frying

Put eggs in a small bowl; beat slightly
and season with salt and pepper. Pick over
crabmeat for bits of shell.

In a frying pan, sauté onions and chili in
oil for 1 minute. Add crabmeat and stir for
another minute. Sprinkle mixture with fish
sauce and remove to a small plate.

Add 1 teaspoon oil to frying pan if
needed and pour in seasoned, beaten eggs.
Draw the eggs from the sides of the pan until
they are set on the bottom. Spoon the crab
mixture in center of omelet and fold in half.
Cook for 1 minute more. Lift with a spatula
to a warm serving plate.

Fish Omelet

JAPAN   Yield: 4 servings

4 ounces white fish meat, finely
   minced
2½ tablespoons flour
½ teaspoon salt
6 eggs, beaten
3 tablespoons sugar
Oil for frying

Mix fish, flour, and salt together. Add
beaten eggs; mix well. When thoroughly
blended, add sugar.

Heat oil in pan; when hot, pour in egg
mixture. Cover; simmer for 15 minutes or
until bottom is browned. Turn; cook other
side. If desired, sprinkle with finely chopped
scallion.

Rolled Fish Omelet

JAPAN   Yield: 4 to 5 servings

6 ounces white fish, such as sole,
   flounder, etc.
6 eggs, lightly beaten
3 tablespoons soy sauce
3 tablespoons sugar
3 tablespoons water
3 tablespoons mirin or sherry
Salt
Dash freshly ground pepper
Oil

Chop fish finely; mix with eggs, soy
sauce, sugar, water, mirin (if sherry is substituted, add 1½ tablespoons more sugar),
salt to taste, and pepper. Cook half of this
mixture in pan on medium heat, turning to
cook both sides. Remove from pan; roll it up
like a jelly roll. Serve omelet hot.

Shredded Omelet

INDONESIA   Yield: 2 servings

3 eggs
½ teaspoon salt
Dash of pepper
3 tablespoons butter or margarine
¼ cup onion, peeled and chopped

Beat the eggs in a bowl, together with the salt and pepper. Melt, but do not brown, the butter in a medium-size skillet. Sauté the chopped onions for 2 minutes—just until they are transparent.

Pour the eggs into the pan so that they cover the onions and are spread evenly over the bottom of the skillet. When set and firm, turn with a spatula to brown the top side. Remove from the pan and cut into thin slices. Serve at once.

Watercress Omelet

CHINA   Yield: 2 servings

3 eggs
1 tablespoon water
½ teaspoon salt
2 tablespoons watercress, finely
    chopped
2 tablespoons melted butter or
    margarine
2 tablespoons Gruyère cheese, grated
2 tablespoons cooked bacon or ham,
    diced
3 tablespoons diced peeled tomato, or
    6 to 8 cherry tomatoes, halved
Freshly grated pepper
Watercress (garnish)

Mix eggs and water slightly. Stir in salt and chopped watercress. Place the wok over heat for a few minutes. Add butter or mar-garine; when it sizzles, add egg mixture and stir rapidly with a fork until mixture begins to set. Sprinkle cheese, bacon or ham, and tomatoes on top. Lower heat.

When omelet is set, loosen edges and fold over in half. Slide onto a warm plate. Sprinkle with pepper and garnish with watercress. Serve.

You can repeat this process at the table for any desired number of omelets. Have the egg mixture ready with bowls of grated cheese, bacon or ham, and tomato.

Zucchini and Mushroom Omelet

JAPAN   Yield: About 4 servings

1 zucchini, thinly sliced
12 fresh mushrooms, sliced
¼ cup onions, chopped
Butter or oil
Salt
Pepper
6 eggs, beaten

Slice zucchini; set it aside. Slice mush-rooms; set them aside. Chop onions; com-bine with zucchini. Heat butter or oil in skil-let; sauté the zucchini and onions until just tender. Add the mushrooms; cook for about 30 seconds more. Add salt and pepper to season.

Add beaten eggs to mixture in skillet. Cook on medium heat until bottom is browned. Carefully turn omelet, cover, and cook until browned on other side.

Crepes

CHINA   Yield: 4 servings

8 ounces lean pork or ham
1 tablespoon water
1 tablespoon dry vermouth
½ teaspoon curry
½ teaspoon paprika
2 scallions, minced
1 green pepper, chopped
1 red pepper, chopped
1 can bean sprouts, drained and heated
8 ounces small shrimp, peeled and
   deveined
2 tablespoons soy sauce
2 tablespoons white wine, optional
8 warm crepes
2 tablespoons grated Parmesan cheese
1 tablespoon polyunsaturated margarine

Cut meat into thin strips. Over high heat, cook meat slightly in water and vermouth. Sprinkle with curry and paprika. Add scallions and peppers; cook for 2 minutes longer. Add heated bean sprouts and shrimp. Season with soy sauce, and wine if desired.

Spread filling on crepes. Roll up; place seam-side-down on greased baking dish. Sprinkle with grated cheese, if desired, and dot with a few pats of margarine. Bake in preheated 400°F oven 10 to 15 minutes.

Bean Pancakes

KOREA   Yield: 20 pancakes

1 cup mung beans or dried split peas
1 cup water
2 eggs, beaten
4 ounces ground pork
1 small onion, peeled and finely
   chopped
1 spring onion, finely chopped
2 cloves garlic, peeled and crushed
1 teaspoon salt
¼ teaspoon ground black pepper
1 teaspoon fresh ginger, finely grated
½ cup fresh bean sprouts, chopped
½ cup kim chi or shredded white
   Chinese cabbage
2 tablespoons sesame oil

Wash beans and soak overnight in cold water. Drain well and then grind to a paste with 1 cup of water. (This is easiest done in a blender or food processor). When smooth, pour into a bowl large enough to hold all ingredients. Add remaining ingredients and mix well.

Use a griddle or heavy frying pan. Heat well and grease lightly. Drop the pancake mixture by spoonfuls onto the griddle. When bottom is lightly browned, turn and brown the other side. Remove to a waiting heated platter and continue cooking in this manner until all batter is used. These pancakes are frequently served cold as well as hot.

Bintatok

KOREA   Yield: 4 servings

This pancake would be delicious for a light supper or an evening snack.

> 1⅓ cups mung beans
> ¼ cup vegetable oil
> 1 large onion, peeled and finely chopped
> 4 scallions, greens only, finely chopped
> 1 carrot, peeled and finely chopped
> 1 small red pepper, cored, seeded, and thinly sliced
> ¼ cup ground beef
> Salt and freshly ground pepper to taste
> Korean soy sauce

Cover beans with warm water and allow to soak overnight. Work beans with their liquid to a smooth batter using either mortar and pestle, blender, or food processor.

Use a small 6-inch omelet pan to heat ¼ of oil. Add a quarter of the batter and tilt pan to spread batter evenly. Sprinkle with ¼ of all remaining ingredients. When edges begin to curl, lift the pancake and turn once. It should cook about 3 minutes a side. Lift out and place on a warmed platter. Repeat process until all batter is used.

Coconut Pancakes

MALAYSIA   Yield: 4 to 8 servings

Filling

> 1 cup brown palm sugar
> 1¼ cups water
> 4 cups white coconut flesh, freshly grated
> Pinch of ground cinnamon
> Pinch of grated nutmeg

> Pinch of salt
> 2 teaspoons lemon juice

Crepes

> 1 cup flour
> 1 egg, beaten
> 1¼ cups milk
> Oil for shallow frying

Melt the brown palm sugar in water. Place in a small saucepan and heat slowly until sugar has dissolved. Add remaining ingredients except lemon juice and stir. Simmer for just a few minutes, until coconut has absorbed all the water.

Sift flour into a bowl. Stir in beaten eggs and gradually add milk until batter is very smooth and even. Lightly grease a small frying pan and put on moderate heat. Pour in enough batter to coat the bottom of the pan. Tilt pan to spread batter. Cook for 1 minute on each side.

When all crepes are cooked, add lemon juice to the filling. Divide the filling between the crepes, roll up, and serve warm.

Crispy Pancake Rolls with Pork

CHINA   Yield: 8 rolls

> Pancake batter to make 8 thin, 5- to 6-inch pancakes
> 2 slices bacon, cut in small pieces
> 2 ounces pork, chopped
> 1 onion, chopped
> 2 tablespoons vegetable oil
> ¼ cup mushrooms, chopped
> 2 teaspoons cornstarch in 2 tablespoons cold water
> 1 tablespoon soy sauce
> 1 egg, beaten (for sealing)
> 2 cups vegetable oil for deep-fat frying

Prepare 8 thin pancakes, cooked on one side only. Combine bacon, pork, and onion and stir-fry in 2 tablespoons vegetable oil for 6 to 8 minutes. Combine the mushrooms, cornstarch mixture, and soy sauce. Add to pork and stir-fry for 2 to 4 minutes. Cool and place a spoonful on each pancake. Roll up and tuck ends in. Seal edges with beaten egg.

Heat oil to 400°F and deep-fry pancake rolls 2 to 3 minutes or until crisp and golden brown. Fry only 2 or 3 at a time or the temperature of the fat cannot be maintained. Drain on paper towels. Rolls are best served hot.

Dosas (Pancakes)

INDIA   Yield: 12 to 15 servings

These are particularly popular in southern India as breakfast snacks.

1 cup urhad dal (or lentils)
¼ cup rice
2½ cups water
½ teaspoon baking soda
1 teaspoon chili powder
½ teaspoon salt
Vegetable oil for shallow frying

Wash and drain dal and rice. Put them in a bowl with the water and allow to soak overnight. The next day, put this mixture in an electric blender or food processor and mix until smooth. Put in soda, chili powder, and salt and stir well.

Prepare a heavy frying pan or skillet with a light coating of oil. Pour in enough batter to cover the bottom of the pan. Fry until golden and then turn once. Remove from pan and roll up like a crepe. These can be

filled if you prefer, but are good as they are. Continue frying and rolling until all batter is used.

Rice Pancakes

INDIA   Yield: 25 to 30 pancakes

2 tablespoons shredded coconut
1 cup water
1 cup rice
½ teaspoon baking soda
½ teaspoon salt
2 tablespoons butter

Allow the coconut to soak in water for at least 4 hours. Meanwhile, with a mortar and pestle, blender, or food processor, grind the rice.

Strain the coconut water into the ground rice with baking soda and salt. Continue beating this until a smooth batter forms. Allow the rice to absorb the liquid by letting mixture stand for at least 12 hours. When ready to cook, beat the batter again to stir in air.

Use a hot frying pan greased lightly with butter. Pour in a little batter, tilting the pan to spread it all over the pan. Cook for just 30 seconds or until the center of the pancake is solid. Place on a warm platter. (Do not turn. Only 1 side is cooked.) Continue in the same way until all batter has been used, adding butter if needed.

Lacy Pancakes

MALAYSIA   Yield: About 12 pancakes

2 eggs
2¾ cups coconut milk or fresh milk
2 cups plain flour
½ teaspoon salt
2 tablespoons oil for frying

Beat eggs and milk together until well mixed and frothy. Place flour and salt into a large bowl. Make a well in the middle of the flour, adding liquid fairly rapidly. Stir with a wooden spoon; beat well until batter is smooth.

Lightly grease and heat a heavy skillet. Pour batter into pan. Use your ladle to make holes in the batter and give a lacy effect. Cook until both sides are pale and golden. Proceed in this way until all the batter is used.

If batter thickens on standing, add enough water to give needed consistency.

Mandarin Pancakes

CHINA   Yield: About 24 pancakes

2 cups sifted all-purpose flour
¾ cup boiling water
1 to 2 tablespoons sesame seed oil

Prepare a well in the sifted flour and pour the water into it. Mix and knead the dough for 10 minutes. Let it rest for 15 minutes under a damp kitchen towel. Roll to a thickness of about ¼ inch with a rolling pin. Stamp out circles 2½ inches in diameter with a cookie cutter or a glass.

Brush half of the circles lightly with the sesame seed oil. Place an unoiled circle on top of an oiled one and roll flat to a diameter of about 6 inches. Fry each pancake, 1 minute to a side, in an unoiled skillet. As each pancake is finished, gently separate the halves and stack them. These are traditionally served with Peking duck.

Pancakes with Chicken and Fruit Filling

INDIA   Yield: 4 to 6 servings

3 eggs
4 cups water
1 teaspoon salt
1 cup flour
2 teaspoons curry powder
¼ cup coconut oil
Oil for frying pancakes

Filling

1 cup boned chicken, cut in strips
3 tablespoons butter
2 teaspoons curry powder
¼ cup canned royal cherries
¼ cup canned green gage plums
¼ cup canned Mandarin orange slices
1 large banana
Lemon juice
¼ cup canned sliced pineapple
4 tablespoons slivered almonds

For the pancake, mix eggs, water, and salt in a bowl. Gradually blend in the flour. Last, add coconut oil very slowly. When all are blended into a fairly smooth batter, fry pancakes in oil on a hot griddle. Keep warm.

To make the filling, put butter in deep skillet and fry chicken pieces. Add 1 teaspoon curry powder. Then stir in cherries, plums, and orange slices. Lower heat so fruit does not burn. Peel and slice banana and sprinkle with lemon juice. Add banana and pineapple to other fruits. Add remaining curry powder to taste.

Fill each pancake with some of the meat and fruit mixture and roll up loosely. Sprinkle with almonds and serve at once.

Stuffed Pancakes

THAILAND   Yield: 4 servings

1 cup ground pork
2 tablespoons tung chai
1 teaspoon sugar
2 tablespoons soy sauce
2 onions, peeled and finely chopped
2 tablespoons vegetable oil
6 eggs, beaten well
Coriander leaves for garnish

In a large bowl, mix pork, tung chai, sugar, soy sauce, and onions until well blended. Heat 1 tablespoon oil in a wok or frying pan. Stir-fry the pork mixture for 3 minutes and then remove from pan. Wipe off the surface of the pan with paper towels.

Add remaining oil to the wok and allow to heat until slightly smoking. Pour in half the beaten eggs. Spoon ½ the pork mixture into the center of the eggs. Fold over the already firm edges to cover. Turn the omelet once until cooked through and lightly browned. Remove to a heated platter. Proceed the same way with remaining eggs and filling. Arrange on the heated platter and garnish with coriander. Slice to serve.

Stuffed Savory Pancakes

INDONESIA   Yield: 6 to 8 servings

These delicacies are eaten as snacks at Indonesian open-air market stalls. If you don't want to make your own dough, substitute wonton skins from your Oriental grocery store.

Dough

2½ cups all-purpose flour
1 teaspoon salt
2 eggs
Water to mix

Filling

1 tablespoon olive oil
2 large onions, peeled and finely sliced
2 cloves garlic, peeled and crushed
1 teaspoon coriander powder
½ teaspoon cumin powder
½ teaspoon ginger powder
½ teaspoon chili powder
½ teaspoon turmeric powder
1 teaspoon sereh (lemon grass) powder
Salt to taste
1 pound cooked lamb or beef, ground

To complete the pancake

2 to 3 eggs
5 medium scallions, chopped
¾ cup coriander leaves, chopped
Vegetable oil for shallow frying

To make the dough, place the flour, salt, and eggs in a bowl. Add enough water to make a smooth, firm dough. Sprinkle a board with cornstarch and place the ball of dough on the board. Roll out as thin as possible and cut into 3-inch squares. Refrigerate squares until you are ready to use them.

To make the filling, heat the olive oil in a deep frying pan or wok. Fry onions and garlic until soft. Add spices and salt and stir-fry for 30 seconds more. Stir-fry the meat for 1 or 2 minutes until browned. Set aside to cool for 1 hour.

To complete the pancake, break eggs into the cooled filling mixture. Add scallions and coriander and mix well.

Take 1 square of dough. On it, place 1 heaping tablespoon of filling. Top with another square and then seal all edges. Heat about 5 tablespoons oil in a frying pan, add the square, and press down flat with a spatula. Fry for just 1 minute on each side. Remove from pan and drain on paper towels. Add more oil if needed during cooking.

These may be served either hot or cold. They may also be cut into triangles.

Rice & Noodles

Apple Rice

INDONESIA   Yield: 4 to 6 servings

1 small onion, peeled and chopped
2 apples, peeled, cored, and diced
2 tablespoons oil
3 tablespoons raisins
2 tablespoons almonds, blanched and slivered
2 tablespoons fresh mushrooms, sliced
2 tablespoons black olives, halved
1 teaspoon salt
1 tablespoon sugar, or more to taste
Curry powder to taste
½ pound cooked rice

Place onions and apples in oil and cook together for 3 minutes. Add raisins, almonds, mushrooms, and olives and stir until all are tender but not overcooked. Add salt, sugar, and curry to taste. Adjust seasonings if needed.

Last, stir in cooked rice with a fork to keep it fluffy and mix gently until blended and hot. Transfer to a serving bowl and serve at once.

Chicken Rice

JAPAN   Yield: 4 servings

6 ounces chicken meat
3½ tablespoons soy sauce
2 tablespoons mirin (sweet rice wine)
4 cups chicken stock
4 cups rice

Thinly slice the chicken; marinate it for 30 minutes in a sauce made from the soy sauce and mirin. If substituting sherry for the mirin, add 1 tablespoon sugar to the sauce.

Remove the chicken; mix the sauce with the chicken stock. Use this mixture, instead of water, to boil the rice in, adding a little water if necessary to thin the mixture.

Serve the rice in 4 individual bowls, with the chicken slices on top.

Chinese Fried Rice I

CHINA   Yield: 10 to 12 servings

½ cup dried mushrooms, sliced
¼ cup olive oil
¾ cup green onions, sliced
2 cups long-grain rice
4 cups chicken stock
⅛ teaspoon dry mustard
1 tablespoon soy sauce
½ cup white bean curd, cut in cubes
¼ cup safflower oil
¾ cup cooked green peas

Soak the mushrooms in cold water for 5 minutes, then drain well. Heat the olive oil in a wok or deep skillet over medium heat. Add the onions and stir-fry until the onions are limp and transparent. Add the rice and stir-fry until the rice is golden. Add 1 cup of the stock and the mustard and stir-fry for 2 to 3 minutes or until the liquid is absorbed. Add another cup of the stock and the soy sauce and stir-fry until this liquid is absorbed. Add 1 more cup of the stock and reduce the heat to low. Stir in the bean curd, and cook, stirring occasionally, until the liquid is absorbed. Add the remaining stock, safflower oil, peas, and mushrooms. Cover and cook, stirring occasionally, for about 20 minutes or until the rice is tender. Place in a serving dish and garnish with Radish Flowers (see Index).

Chinese Fried Rice II

CHINA   Yield: 6 to 8 servings

1-1½ cups rice
2 stalks celery, diced
2 onions, diced
2 tablespoons oil
1 egg
Garlic powder
Salt
MSG, optional
3 tablespoons soy sauce

Cook rice. Dice 2 stalks celery and 2 onions. Put the oil in a large frying pan. Beat egg and add to oil, cutting into strips. Add garlic powder, salt, MSG, and soy sauce. Mix well and add cooked rice, stirring until browned by the soy sauce. Add celery and onion to the rice.

Fried Rice I

THAILAND   Yield: 4 servings

4 cups cold steamed rice
3 tablespoons peanut oil
2 medium onions, peeled and finely
   chopped
1 large pork chop, diced
½ pound raw shrimp, shelled and
   deveined
1 6-ounce can crabmeat
3 eggs, beaten
Salt and pepper to taste
2 tablespoons fish sauce
1 tablespoon chili sauce, optional
2 tablespoons tomato paste
1 cup spring onions, chopped, tops
   included
3 tablespoons fresh coriander leaves,
   chopped

Spread out the cooked, steamed rice and allow it to cool. Heat oil in a wok or skillet. Using medium-low heat, fry the onions until soft and transparent. Increase heat to high. Add pork, shrimp and crab meat and fry, stirring constantly, for 3 minutes. Season eggs with salt and pepper and pour into center of pan. Stir until egg mixture begins to set. Add rice and continue to stir.

When the rice is heated, sprinkle with fish sauce; add chili sauce and tomato paste and toss well so that rice is red in color. Remove from heat. Stir in spring onions, mixing well. Place on serving platter and sprinkle coriander leaves over all. Serve at once.

Fried Rice II

CHINA   Yield: 4 servings

½ pound long-grain rice
½ pound cooked ham, cut into strips
1 6-ounce can shrimp, drained
3 tablespoons oil
2 tablespoons soy sauce
1 leek, sliced
4 eggs
Freshly ground black pepper

Cook rice according to package directions. Cut ham into strips. Drain shrimp.

Heat oil in a large skillet. Add ham and shrimp; cook until lightly browned, approximately 5 minutes. Add rice and soy sauce; cook for another 5 minutes. Add leek; cook for 5 minutes more, stirring occasionally.

Lightly beat eggs with pepper. Pour over rice; cook until eggs are set. Serve on a preheated platter.

Fried Rice III

CHINA   Yield: 4 to 6 servings

Chinese roast pork, available from Chinese food stores, is ideal for this dish.

1 cup long-grain rice
Boiling salted water
2 strips bacon, diced
½ pound cooked pork, thinly sliced
2 eggs
2 tablespoons water
½ teaspoon salt
Generous dash of pepper
6 tablespoons oil
6 shallots, finely chopped
1 teaspoon ginger, grated
½ pound shrimp
1 teaspoon soy sauce

Cook rice in boiling salted water for 12 minutes. Drain well. Spread on tray; allow to dry out overnight.

Finely dice bacon; slice pork thin. Beat eggs with water. Season with salt and pepper.

Heat 1 teaspoon oil in pan. Pour in enough egg mixture to make 1 pancake. Turn and cook other side; remove from pan. Repeat this with remaining mixture, using 1 tablespoon oil for each pancake. Roll egg pancake; slice into thin strips.

Finely chop shallots. Shell and devein shrimp. Fry bacon until crisp. Add remaining 2 tablespoons oil to pan. When oil is hot, add rice, pork, ginger, shallots, and shrimp. Add egg strips last. Stir lightly. When completely heated through, add soy sauce; mix well.

Fried Rice IV

CHINA   Yield: 4 servings

2 tablespoons oil
1 green pepper, chopped
½ cup fresh mushrooms, sliced
3 cups cooked cold rice
½ cup cooked chicken or beef (leftover)
Soy sauce to taste

Heat oil in skillet to medium-high heat. Sauté pepper and mushrooms until pepper just begins to get soft. Add rice and chicken or beef and sauté until hot, approximately 5 minutes, stirring frequently. Sprinkle with soy sauce to taste.

Fried Rice V

CHINA   Yield: 4 servings

3 tablespoons vegetable oil
1 medium onion, chopped (or scallions)
1 green pepper, thinly sliced
3-4 cups cold, cooked rice
1-2 tablespoons soy sauce
3 eggs

Heat oil in the wok. Stir-fry the onion until it is translucent. Remove it from the wok and set aside. Stir-fry the green pepper for about a minute. Return the onions to the wok. Add the rice (and the ham, shrimp, etc., if you wish). Stir-fry the mixture until the rice is golden. Make a well in the middle and add the eggs. Cook them, stirring, until they are scrambled, then mix them with the rice. Sprinkle with soy sauce.

Fried Rice VI

CHINA

This is an excellent recipe for using left-over rice. Use the amount of mushrooms and scallions suitable for whatever amount of rice you have. You may also add leftover chicken. Experiment putting in different ingredients and different amounts of ingredients until you discover how your family likes it best.

> Oil, salad or peanut
> Rice, cooked and chilled
> Mushrooms, fresh or canned
> Scallions, chopped
> Soy sauce
> Beaten egg

Heat oil in skillet. Add rice, mushrooms, drained if canned or sliced if fresh, scallions, and soy sauce. Cook over low heat about 10 to 15 minutes, stirring occasionally. Add beaten egg; cook and stir another 2 to 3 minutes. Serve with additional soy sauce.

Fried Rice (Nasi Goreng)

INDONESIA   Yield: 8 servings

Side dishes—such as spiced pickles, fried banana slices, soy sauce, relishes, and roasted peanuts—can be served in bowls on the table for each person to dip into as he prefers.

> 1 2-pound chicken from a can
> 4 cups water
> Pinch of salt
> 3 cups long-grain rice
> 6 tablespoons oil
> 4 medium onions, peeled and chopped
> 3 cloves garlic, peeled and chopped
> 1 red pepper pod, seeded and cut into strips
> 1 pound canned shrimp, drained
> ½ pound crab meat
> ½ pound cooked ham, cut into strips
> 2 tablespoons oil
> 3 eggs
> 1 teaspoon sambal ulek
> White pepper
> Curry
> Ground ginger
> Ground caraway
> Coriander
> Ground nutmeg
> Saffron
> Parsley for garnish

Remove chicken from can. Skin and loosen meat from bones. Cut into small pieces. Set aside. Place the juice and fat from the can in a big pot. Add water and salt. Bring to a boil. Place rice in boiling broth and reduce heat. Simmer for 12 minutes. Drain rice and set aside.

Heat 6 tablespoons oil in a large pot. Cook onions, garlic, and pepper pod for 5 minutes. Add the rice. Steam for 10 minutes and stir often. Mix shrimp, crab meat, ham, and chicken into rice. Stir to mix well.

Heat 2 tablespoons oil in a skillet. Whisk eggs until frothy and then scramble until firm. Mix your choice of spices with 1 tablespoon water in a cup. Add this to the rice along with the scrambled eggs. Allow to blend for 10 minutes. Then dish rice mixture on a platter. Garnish with parsley and serve with your choice of side dishes.

Fried Rice Cantonese Style

CHINA   Yield: 4 servings

2 or 3 eggs
½ teaspoon MSG, optional
½ teaspoon dry sherry
3 tablespoons cooking oil
2 tablespoons onions, minced
4 cups cold cooked rice
1 cup bean sprouts
2 teaspoons salt
1 teaspoon Chinese brown gravy syrup

Beat eggs with MSG and sherry. Pour oil in hot skillet over medium-high heat. Stir in onion, then add egg mixture. Scramble and break into small pieces until quite dry. Add rice and other ingredients. Stir constantly until well blended and thoroughly heated, about 10 minutes. One-half cup diced or shredded cooked meat or shrimp may be added to the rice if desired.

Fried Rice with Catsup

JAPAN   Yield: 3 to 4 servings

2 cups cooked leftover rice
½ tablespoon oil
Leftover meat or seafood, cut into
    small pieces
1½ tablespoons catsup (more or less,
    to taste)
2 tablespoons frozen or fresh peas

Heat rice in oil for 5 minutes, stirring occasionally. Add rest of ingredients; mix thoroughly, while heating, for another 3 minutes.

Fried Rice with Chicken and Ham

CHINA   Yield: 4 to 6 servings

3 tablespoons vegetable oil
4 ounces cooked chicken, finely
    chopped
4 ounces cooked ham, finely chopped
2 scallions, sliced
2 to 3 cups cold, boiled rice (prepared
    a day ahead and chilled)
1 tablespoon soy sauce
¼ teaspoon salt
1 to 2 eggs, beaten
2 tablespoons cooked peas
1-egg omelet, optional garnish

Heat oil in wok and stir-fry the chicken and ham 1 to 2 minutes. Add scallions and rice and continue to stir-fry until rice is hot and golden in color. Add soy sauce and salt. Make a well in the rice and pour in the beaten eggs. Stir and heat until the eggs are coagulated. Add peas and heat for 1 minute longer. Garnish with a 1-egg omelet cut into ¼-inch strips.

Fried Rice with Ham

CHINA   Yield: 4 to 6 servings

3 tablespoons vegetable oil
1 medium onion, chopped
2 stalks celery, cut into ¼-inch slices
2 cups cold, boiled rice
3 ounces cooked ham, cut into small
    strips
2 eggs, beaten with salt and pepper

Heat oil in wok and stir-fry onion and celery 3 to 4 minutes, until they are translucent. Add the rice and ham and stir-fry together 4 to 5 minutes, until rice is golden. Pour eggs into a well in the rice. Heat and stir until all the egg is coagulated. Serve at once.

Fried Rice with Mushrooms

CHINA   Yield: 10 servings

½ cup dried mushrooms, sliced
¼ cup olive oil
¼ cup green onions, sliced
2 cups long-grain rice
4 cups chicken stock
⅛ teaspoon dry mustard
1 tablespoon soy sauce
½ cup white bean curd, cut into cubes
¼ cup safflower oil
¾ cup cooked fresh green peas
Radish flowers for garnish

Soak mushrooms in cold water 5 minutes; drain well.

Heat olive oil in a wok or deep skillet over medium heat. Add onions; stir-fry until onions are limp and transparent. Add rice; stir-fry until rice is golden. Add 1 cup stock and mustard; stir-fry 2 to 3 minutes or until liquid is absorbed. Add 1 cup stock and soy sauce; stir-fry until liquid is absorbed.

Add 1 more cup of stock; reduce heat to low. Stir in bean curd; cook, stirring occasionally, until liquid is absorbed. Add remaining stock, safflower oil, peas, and mushrooms. Cover; cook, stirring occasionally, about 20 to 25 minutes or until rice is tender. Spoon into serving dish; garnish with radish flowers.

Crab and Pork Fried Rice

KOREA   Yield: 4 servings

2 tablespoons oil
1 clove garlic, peeled and grated
1 teaspoon fresh ginger, finely grated
½ cup cooked crab meat, flaked
½ cup cooked pork, chopped
4 cups hot cooked rice
½ cup spring onions, chopped
1 teaspoon salt to taste

Using a wok or heavy skillet, heat the oil. Add garlic, ginger, crab, and pork and stir-fry until hot and well mixed. Add rice and continue to stir until rice is crisp and brown. Last, put in spring onions and sprinkle with salt. Mix well and add more salt if desired. Transfer to warmed serving dish and serve at once.

Shrimp and Egg Fried Rice

CHINA   Yield: 4 to 6 servings

1 slice bacon
2 scallions, sliced
1 clove garlic, minced
3 ounces shrimp, cut into small pieces
2 cups cold, cooked rice
1 egg beaten with salt and pepper
1 to 2 tablespoons soy sauce

Fry bacon in wok until crisp. Remove and set aside. Add scallions and garlic to wok and stir-fry in the bacon fat for 1 to 2 minutes. Add shrimp and stir-fry until pink (if frozen or canned shrimp are used, add while stir-frying the rice). Add the rice and stir-fry 4 to 5 minutes, until rice is golden. Pour the beaten egg into a well in the rice. Stir and heat until all the egg is coagulated. Crumble the bacon and add to the rice with the soy sauce. Combine well.

Green Jade Fried Rice

CHINA   Yield: 4 to 6 servings as a side dish

6 tablespoons peanut or other salad oil
4 eggs, beaten
1 10-ounce box frozen chopped spin-
    ach, thawed and drained or ½ bunch
    pele, washed and chopped
2 teaspoons salt
4 cups cooked rice (1½ cups raw rice,
    cooked)
1 tablespoon soy sauce
½ cup ham, Chinese sausage, bacon,
    or spam, chopped
3 scallions, finely chopped

Heat 3 tablespoons oil in wok or skillet over high heat until very hot. Add eggs, stir-fry for ½ minute or until firm (same as scrambled eggs). Remove and finely chop.

Heat remaining 3 tablespoons oil in wok or large skillet over high heat. Add spinach or pele and stir-fry for 2-3 minutes, until spinach dries. Add salt and rice, stir-fry for 2 minutes. Add soy sauce, ham, scallions, and chopped egg. Mix well and serve hot.

To prepare ahead: Prepare the day before serving, cover, and refrigerate. When serving reheat in 350°F oven for 15-30 minutes or stir-fry until hot.

Stir-fried Rice

CHINA   Yield: 4 servings

8 tablespoons vegetable oil
2 eggs, beaten
½ cup small shrimp (cooked or fresh)
½ cup roast pork or ham, diced
2 tablespoons peas
1 tablespoon green onion, chopped
4 cups cooked rice
2 teaspoons salt

Heat 2 tablespoons oil in pan. Pour in the beaten egg and stir-fry quickly until eggs are in tiny pieces. Remove from pan.

Heat another 3 tablespoons oil. Stir-fry shrimp, pork, and peas. Fry about 1 minute and remove from pan.

Heat another 3 tablespoons oil in same frying pan; fry the onion and cooked rice. Mix well. Add salt. Reduce heat and stir until rice is thoroughly heated. Add all previously prepared ingredients. Combine well and serve.

Chinese Rice

CHINA   Yield: 4 servings

1 cup medium or long-grain rice
Cold water

Put rice in heavy pan that has a tight-fitting lid. Add cold water until it is about 1 inch above the rice. Place pan over high heat and boil, uncovered, until most of the water has been absorbed, stirring often to prevent sticking. Turn heat to lowest setting, place lid on pan, and let rice steam for approximately 20 minutes, depending upon how soft you like rice. (Do not lift the lid while rice is steaming.)

Rice Ring

CHINA   Yield: 8 to 10 servings

1 cup converted rice, cooked
3 eggs, well beaten
½ cup melted butter
½ cup green onions, diced
⅓ cup pimientos
Pinch salt
1 can bean sprouts, drained

Cook rice as directed. Sauté other ingredients in a frying pan until softened. Fold everything into rice. Put in a well-greased round ring mold. Put ring mold on a large baking or roasting pan filled with 1 inch of water. Heat in oven about 20 minutes. Unmold and serve hot.

Coconut Rice

BURMA   Yield: 4 to 6 servings

2¼ cups long-grain rice, washed and
    drained
4½ cups water
6 tablespoons thick coconut milk
1 medium onion, peeled and quartered
½ teaspoon salt
1 teaspoon vegetable oil

Place rice and water in a large saucepan. Add the rest of the ingredients in the order given. Bring this to a boil over high heat. Reduce heat, cover pan tightly, and simmer for about 20 minutes.

Remove the lid and stir lightly with a fork. Rice is finished cooking when liquid is absorbed and grains are fluffy.

Compressed Rice Cakes

MALAYSIA   Yield: 6 servings

Here is a simple Western way of preparing Malaysian rice cakes.

1 pound short- or medium-grain rice
4 cups water
Aluminum foil

Allow water and rice to come to a boil in a large saucepan. Cover the pan and reduce heat to a simmer. Cook for 35 minutes or until all the water is absorbed. Stir with a wooden spoon. Press rice into a pie plate until it is in an even layer about 1-inch high.

Cover pie plate with greased aluminum foil, which should be resting on the rice. Weight this down with a plate and press firmly. Add more weight on top of the plate and let stand at room temperature several hours. When very firm, remove weights and foil. Cut with a wet knife into 2-inch squares.

Glutinous Yellow Rice

MALAYSIA   Yield: 6 servings

1 pound glutinous rice, washed and
    drained
2 cups water
2 teaspoons salt
1 clove garlic, peeled and crushed
1 teaspoon ground turmeric
½ teaspoon ground black pepper
1 pandanus leaf
2 cups hot coconut milk
Crisp fried onion flakes for garnish

Place rice, water, salt, garlic, turmeric, pepper, and pandanus leaf in a large saucepan. Allow mixture to come to a boil; reduce heat and cover. Simmer for 10 minutes. Do not lift lid during this time.

Uncover and stir in hot coconut milk with a fork. When rice is mixed with coconut milk, cover and simmer for 10 more minutes. Transfer to a serving bowl and garnish with onion flakes.

Rice in Sugar and Vinegar

JAPAN   Yield: 2 to 4 servings

- 1¼ teaspoons salt
1¾ tablespoons sugar
1½ tablespoons mild white vinegar
½ tablespoon dry sherry
Pinch MSG, optional
1 cup Japanese or short-grain rice, washed and drained

Combine the salt, sugar, vinegar, and sherry in saucepan and bring to a boil. Stir in the MSG and cool to room temperature.

Combine the rice with 1¼ cups of cold water. Soak for ½ hour. Bring to a boil and cook for 10 minutes over moderate heat. Reduce the heat and simmer for another 5 minutes of cooking; let the rice rest off the heat for another 5 minutes. This process steams the rice rather than boils it. Do not remove the cover until finished. Place the hot rice in a glass or ceramic bowl and pour on the vinegar dressing; mix thoroughly. The rice is ready when cooled to room temperature.

In Japan, this is eaten as a snack or a lunch, and garnished with many different things, including raw fish, caviar, seaweed, omelet strips, and sliced vegetables.

Long Rice with Chicken and Bamboo Shoots

INDOCHINA   Yield: 6 servings

1 pound chicken pieces
1 clove garlic, peeled and crushed
8 ounces cellophane noodles, soaked in hot water 15 minutes
1 tablespoon peanut oil

1 medium onion, peeled and cut into wedges
2 cans bamboo shoots, cut into strips
1 tablespoon fish sauce
¼ teaspoon black pepper
½ cup chicken stock

Cut chicken meat from bones and use bones to make stock. Meat should be prepared in bite-size pieces, as should the skin. Mix with crushed garlic.

Place presoaked noodles in lightly salted boiling water and cook for 5 minutes. Drain and cut into 2-inch lengths.

Use a wok or skillet to heat the peanut oil. Stir-fry chicken in the oil until meat is white. Push cooked chicken to side of pan. Add onion and bamboo shoots and fry for 1 minute, then mix with chicken. Add fish sauce, pepper, and stock and cook for 2 more minutes. Last, add the well-drained noodles and stir until very hot. Serve from heated platter.

Molded Rice

INDOCHINA   Yield: 4 servings

½ cup pork fat, chopped
½ cup lean pork, chopped
½ cup chicken meat, chopped
3 cloves garlic, peeled and finely chopped
3 spring onions, finely sliced
4 cups hot cooked rice
Fish sauce to taste
Hearty dash of freshly ground black pepper

Heat a wok or large skillet and cook pork fat until it is crisp and fat melted. Add pork, chicken, garlic, and onions and stir-fry until everything is well cooked. Add cooked rice and season with fish sauce and pepper. Toss with a large fork to mix well.

Press rice mixture into a greased mold. Cover with foil and keep warm until ready to serve. Turn out onto a platter and serve with extra fish sauce if desired.

Oil Rice

BURMA   Yield: 4 to 6 servings

    2 cups glutinous rice, washed, drained,
        and allowed to dry
    3 large onions, peeled and thinly sliced
    1½ teaspoons turmeric
    6 tablespoons oil
    4 cups hot water
    2 teaspoons salt
    4 tablespoons toasted sesame seeds
        mixed with a little salt

Prepare rice and onions as directed. Sprinkle onions with turmeric, mixing lightly. Heat oil in saucepan and brown the onions. Remove two-thirds of the onions and set them aside for garnish.

Add rice to the pan and mix well with the remaining onions and oil. Add water and salt and stir well. Bring to a boil; lower heat and simmer, covered tightly, for about 20 minutes. Water will be absorbed. If you prefer slightly crusty rice, leave on simmer for about 5 minutes more. Garnish the cooked rice with onion and sprinkle with lightly salted sesame seeds. Serve at once.

Oriental Rice I

CHINA   Yield: 6 servings

    3 tablespoons butter or margarine
    Dash cloves

¼ teaspoon cinnamon
¼ teaspoon cardamom
⅛ teaspoon allspice
⅛ teaspoon saffron
⅛ teaspoon black pepper
2 teaspoons garlic salt
2 tablespoons instant minced onion
1 cup long-grain rice
3 cups boiling water
½ cup raisins
½ cup toasted, slivered almonds

Melt butter or margarine in large saucepan. Add cloves, cinnamon, cardamom, allspice, saffron, pepper, garlic salt, onion, and rice; mix well. Stir in boiling water; cover and simmer 25 minutes.

Add raisins and let stand, covered, 5 minutes. Sprinkle the almonds over the top before serving.

Oriental Rice II

CHINA   Yield: 4 to 6 servings

    1 tablespoon butter or margarine
    1 cup white rice
    ½ cup white wine
    1½ cups chicken broth
    ½ teaspoon salt
    ¼ teaspoon pepper
    1 cup mushrooms, sliced
    1 tablespoon parsley, chopped

Place all ingredients in a pressure cooker in the order given. Cover the cooker and put pressure control in place. When pressure is reached, remove cooker from heat and allow pressure to drop of its own accord.

Stir the hot rice gently with a fork to fluff it. Serve at once.

Pot Roasted Rice

INDOCHINA   Yield: 4 to 6 servings

    2 cups medium-grain rice
    2 tablespoons peanut oil
    1¾ cups hot water

Wash rice well and drain thoroughly until quite dry. Heat oil in a heavy saucepan. Put in rice and stir with a metal spoon until rice is golden, about 10 or more minutes. Add hot water and bring to a boil. Place a tight-fitting lid on the pot; reduce heat and simmer for 20 minutes. This basic recipe goes with many of the main dishes from Indochina.

Rajahmundry Rice

INDIA   Yield: 4 servings

    4 cups hot cooked rice
    1 teaspoon curry powder
    ½ cup cooked celery, finely chopped
    ½ cup toasted slivered almonds

Combine the rice, curry powder, and celery in the top of a double boiler. Place over boiling water and heat through. Place in serving dish and sprinkle with almonds. Serve with pork, chicken, or seafood.

Rice and Bean Sprouts

KOREA   Yield: 4 to 6 servings

    1 cup canned bean sprouts, drained
    1 clove garlic, peeled and minced
    2 green onions, chopped
    2 teaspoons sesame seeds
    1 teaspoon sesame oil

    2 cups rice
    3 tablespoons soy sauce
    3 cups cold water

Mix bean sprouts, garlic, onions, sesame seeds, and oil together in a large saucepan. Stir constantly over medium heat for 5 minutes. Add rice, soy sauce, and water. Cover the saucepan tightly and bring to a boil. Reduce heat to a simmer and allow to steam for 30 minutes. Do not remove lid or stir rice during this cooking period.

Remove from heat, stir with a fork, and put in a serving dish; serve at once and very hot.

Rice and Dates

KOREA   Yield: 4 to 6 servings

The addition of dates to the rice makes this a delightful taste contrast to other Korean foods. The sweetness of the rice will complement other more spicy dishes.

    ½ cup dates, pitted
    2 cups rice, washed and drained well
    3 cups water

Cut dates into small pieces. Place in a large saucepan with the rice and water. Bring to a quick boil. Then cover the pan with a tight-fitting lid and reduce heat to a simmer. Allow to steam for 35 minutes. Do not lift lid or stir rice until 35 minutes are up.

Rice and Lentils

INDIA   Yield: 4 to 6 servings

    1 cup long-grain rice
    1 cup red lentils
    2½ tablespoons ghee

2 medium onions, peeled and finely
sliced
5 cups hot water
2½ teaspoons salt
1½ teaspoons garam masala

Wash rice and drain well. Wash lentils
and drain well also. Heat ghee in a large
saucepan and fry the onions until they are
golden brown. Remove half the onions and
set aside for garnish.

Put rice and lentils in pan with the remaining onions, stirring well to mix. Stir for
about 3 minutes. Add hot water, salt, and
garam masala. Bring this to a boil and cover
the pan tightly. Reduce heat and simmer for
25 minutes. Do not lift the lid until cooking
time is over. Rice and lentils will be the
consistency of porridge. Garnish with reserved onions and serve hot.

Rice Balls

JAPAN   Yield: 4 large rice balls

2 cups hot cooked rice
Goma sio (black sesame seeds and salt)
Raw or smoked fish, optional, cut into
thin strips

Cook rice and allow it to become cool
enough to handle. Wet your hands and form
a ball with ½ cup of the rice. When firm
and about 3 inches in diameter, insert 1 strip
of fish into the center of the rice ball,
molding the rice around it. Roll the finished
rice ball in goma sio. In Japan, rice balls frequently take the place of bread and are a
good picnic item.

Rice in Coconut Milk

INDONESIA   Yield: 6 servings

1 pound long-grain rice, washed and
drained
4½ cups coconut milk
2½ teaspoons salt
1 onion, peeled and finely chopped
2 cloves garlic, peeled and chopped
1 teaspoon ground turmeric
1 teaspoon ground cumin
2 teaspoons ground coriander
½ teaspoon dried shrimp paste (trasi)
1 teaspoon lemon rind, finely
chopped, or 1 stem of lemon grass

Place all ingredients except rice in a
saucepan with a tight-fitting lid. Uncovered,
bring the mixture slowly to a boil, stirring at
intervals.

Add rice; stir and bring back to a boil.
Cover the pan tightly, reduce heat to its
lowest possible point, and steam for 20
minutes. Uncover. Use a fork to stir rice
from sides of the pan, mixing in any liquid
not yet absorbed. Replace lid and steam for 5
minutes more.

Rice Indienne

INDIA   Yield: 4 to 6 servings

1 cup raw rice
2 cups bouillon
2 tablespoons butter or margarine
½ cup white raisins
½ teaspoon salt
¼ cup toasted almonds, slivered

Combine rice, bouillon, butter, raisins,
and salt in saucepan. Bring to a boil and stir.
Cover, simmer 15 minutes. Add almonds
and mix lightly.

Rice Banquet

INDONESIA   Yield: 10 servings

A typical Indonesian rice banquet consists of 9 or 10 dishes attractively set up on the table. Each guest assembles the food he wants on this own plate.

Roast grated coconut

½ cup grated coconut
4 tablespoons shelled raw peanuts
1 teaspoon sugar
1 teaspoon salt

Mix ingredients together in the order given. Brown in a hot dry frypan for 5 minutes, stirring constantly. Divide into small dishes.

Roast peanuts

1 cup shelled raw peanuts
1 tablespoon oil
Salt to taste

Heat oil and fry peanuts for 10 minutes on moderate flame. Salt while cooking. When nuts are a golden brown, remove from heat and divide into serving bowls.

Shrimp bread

Oil for deep fat frying
1 package shrimp bread

Shrimp bread, made from shrimp and tapioca meal, can be bought at an Oriental grocery store. The thin pieces become double in size when cooked. So prepare just a few at a time.

Heat oil in deep-fat fryer. Cook shrimp bread one or two pieces at a time until the pieces swell. Do not let them brown. Dish up on a platter and set aside.

2 or 3 kinds of sambal

2 dishes small pickled cucumbers
2 dishes marinated beets
2 dishes pearl onions
2 dishes sweet-and sour ginger
Hard-boiled eggs, cut into halves, 1 per person
2 dishes boiled, diced chicken

These may be made in your own home or purchased ready-made at your Oriental store.

Curry soup

3 red and 3 green pepper pods, seeded and finely chopped
3 tablespoons oil
5 shallots, chopped
½ teaspoon ground coriander
1 teaspoon caraway seeds
Salt to taste
1 clove garlic, peeled and chopped
1 teaspoon ground ginger
1 teaspoon laos powder
1 2- to -3-pound chicken, boned and diced
4 tablespoons butter
3 pieces bleached celery (canned), finely chopped
1 bay leaf
6 cups hot water
Juice of 1 lemon

Heat oil in soup pot. Steam pepper pods, shallots, coriander, caraway seeds, salt, and garlic, stirring constantly. Add ginger and laos and brown for 15 minutes, stirring occasionally. Add celery.

Place chicken and celery in soup pot and add bay leaf and seasoning mixture. Put in hot water and cook for 30 minutes. Add lemon juice and adjust salt if needed. Remove bay leaf and keep warm.

Meat dumplings

1 pound ground beef
1 teaspoon ginger powder
2 tablespoons bread crumbs
5 tablespoons cold water
1 teaspoon crushed coriander
1 teaspoon caraway seeds
Pinch of dried mint
1 onion, peeled and chopped
2 teaspoons salt
1 clove garlic, peeled and chopped
4 tablespoons oil
1 cup hot beef broth
1 teaspoon curry powder
2 teaspoons cornstarch
¼ cup cold water

In a pot, mix ground beef, ginger, bread crumbs, and cold water into a thick mass. Place on medium heat and cook, stirring constantly, for 5 minutes. Remove from heat. Add coriander, caraway, mint, onion, salt, and garlic. Knead this mixture to mix well. Add extra salt if needed.

Rinse your hands under cold water and roll meat into small dumplings. Heat fat in a skillet and fry dumplings for 10 minutes until brown. Remove from pan and keep warm.

Make a gravy by adding hot broth to skillet. Add curry powder. Mix cornstarch with ¼ cup cold water and add. Bring this to a boil and, when slightly thickened, pour over the meat dumplings.

Baked shrimp

1 pound frozen shrimp
2 egg yolks
4 tablespoons bread crumbs
5 tablespoons oil

Flatten the thawed shrimp with spatula. Dip in beaten egg yolks, then roll in bread crumbs. Heat oil in skillet and fry shrimp for 10 minutes until brown in color. Set aside and keep warm.

In addition to the dishes above, serve 1 large bowl of grainy cooked rice. Another nice accompaniment would be bananas fried in butter.

White Rice in Coconut Milk

MALAYSIA   Yield: 4 to 6 servings

1½ cups long-grain rice, washed and drained
2½ cups coconut milk
½ teaspoon salt

Place rice and coconut milk in a heavy saucepan. Add salt and bring to a boil. Then lower heat and simmer uncovered until liquid has been absorbed. Stir once or twice to prevent rice from sticking to bottom of pan. Cover saucepan with tight-fitting lid and reduce heat to simmer. Cook for 10 minutes more. Serve at once.

Rice with Potatoes

KOREA   Yield: 4 to 6 servings

1 cup potatoes, peeled and cubed
2 cups rice, washed well and drained
1 teaspoon salt
3 cups cold water

Place all ingredients in a large saucepan in the order given. Cover the pan with a tight-fitting lid and allow to come to a boil. Then reduce heat to a simmer and cook for 30 minutes. Do not lift lid or stir rice until steaming time is complete.

Rice Platter

INDIA   Yield: 8 servings

2 cups long-grain rice
2 teaspoons salt
2 quarts water
4 tablespoons butter or margarine
½ cup sultana raisins

Curry sauce

6 tablespoons butter or margarine
½ cup flour
2 cups hot beef broth
Salt and white pepper to taste
2 heaping tablespoons curry
Pinch of sugar
½ cup white wine
2 tablespoons cream

For the entrées

1 pound pork fillets
Salt and pepper to taste
4 tablespoons oil
½ pound fillet of sole
Juice of 1 lemon
½ pound shrimp, canned or frozen
6 tablespoons butter
1 small can pineapple slices, cut into
   bite-size pieces
1 small jar red marinated paprika pods
½ cup black olives, seeded and sliced
½ pound fresh mushrooms, washed
   and quartered
2 teaspoons lemon juice
6 bananas, halved lengthwise and
   sliced
½ cup sliced almonds, toasted in 2
   tablespoons butter

Place rice in boiling salted water and allow to boil for 10 minutes. Drain and rinse with cold water. Drain again. Use half the butter to grease baking dish and spread rice out evenly. Dot with remaining butter and bake at 350°F for 15 minutes.

Meanwhile, soak raisins in water and prepare curry sauce.

Heat butter or margarine in saucepan. Stir in the flour and hot beef broth until very smooth. Season lightly with salt and pepper. Add curry, sugar, and wine. Bring to a boil and remove from heat. Stir in the cream. Keep sauce warm.

Cut pork fillets into even strips. Season with salt and pepper. Heat 2 tablespoons oil in a frying pan. Add pork and stir constantly for 5 minutes. When meat is browned all over, set aside and keep warm.

Wash and dry the fish with paper towels. Sprinkle with lemon juice. In a different skillet, heat 2 tablespoons oil. Fry the fish for 5 minutes on each side. Add the shrimp and cook until it is hot through.

Heat 3 tablespoons of butter in a saucepan. Add raisins, pineapple, paprika pods, and olives. Stir until all are hot. Set aside and keep warm.

Heat remaining 3 tablespoons butter and fry mushrooms for 10 minutes. Season with lemon juice. Keep warm.

Finally, heat remaining 2 tablespoons butter in a skillet and fry the bananas to a golden brown, about 10 minutes. Keep turning bananas as they cook.

To serve, spread rice on a large platter. Alternately add meat, sole-shrimp mixture, raisins, pineapple, paprika and olives, mushrooms and bananas. Garnish with almonds. Offer the curry sauce separately.

Rice Mixed with Fingers

BURMA   Yield: 6 servings

  1 cup long-grain rice, cooked dry and
    fluffy
  2 fresh red chilies or 1 teaspoon chili
    powder
  2 tablespoons oil
  2 tablespoons water
  4 ounces rice vermicelli
  2 ounces cellophane noodles
  4 ounces fine egg noodles
  3 large potatoes
  8 ounces bean sprouts

Accompaniments

  3 eggs
  10 medium onions, peeled
  20 cloves garlic, peeled
  1 cup oil
  1 cup powdered dried shrimp
  1 cup roasted chick-pea powder
  2 tablespoons chili powder
  ½ cup fish sauce
  ½ cup dried tamarind pulp

Make a paste of the chilies and cook with oil and water over low heat until it smells cooked. Mix with the cooked rice and set aside.

Boil rice vermicelli for 2 minutes or until tender. Drain and set aside. Boil cellophane noodles; drain and set aside. Boil egg noodles until tender; drain and rinse with cold water. Boil potatoes, then peel and slice. Pour boiling water over bean sprouts and let stand for 10 minutes. Drain. Since all of these are served cold, arrange them on a platter in separate mounds. The accompaniments will be served in separate bowls.

To prepare the accompaniments, first fry the eggs as for an omelet. When firm and cooked, cut into shreds and set aside. Thinly slice half of the onions and put them into an individual bowl. Slice the remaining onions and half of the garlic. Fry them in oil until both are light brown. Put in a serving bowl, oil included. Peel remaining garlic and put the raw garlic into a small bowl. Place shrimp, chick-pea powder, and chili powder in individual bowls. Make tamarind liquid by soaking pulp in 1½ cups hot water. When cool, squeeze to dissolve the pulp and strain, keeping the water and discarding seeds and fibers.

Rice with Fresh Green Peas

INDIA   Yield: 4 to 6 servings

  1 tablespoon ghee or oil
  4 whole cloves
  1 small cinnamon stick
  2 cardamom pods
  1 teaspoon cumin seeds
  ½ teaspoon ground turmeric, optional
  1¼ cups long-grain rice, washed and
    drained
  1¼ cups shelled green peas
  2 teaspoons salt
  2½ cups hot water

Using a heavy saucepan, heat the ghee. Fry cloves, cinnamon, cardamom, and cumin on medium heat for 1 minute, stirring well. Add turmeric and rice and stir-fry for 2 more minutes. Put in peas, salt, and water and bring to a boil. Reduce heat to a simmer, cover the pan, and cook for 25 minutes. Do not lift the lid or stir during cooking time. Remove spices and use a fork to fluff the rice with the peas. Serve at once.

Rice Vermicelli with Sauce

THAILAND   Yield: 4 servings

Vegetable oil for deep frying
6 ounces rice noodles, broken into
   pieces

Sauce

1 tablespoon vegetable oil
1 onion, peeled and finely chopped
2 cloves garlic, peeled and finely
   chopped
½ pound shrimp, shelled and deveined
½ cup crab meat
2 teaspoons brown sugar
2 teaspoons tamarind water
1 teaspoon salt
1 tablespoon soy sauce
2 teaspoons orange rind, grated, for
   garnish
2 red chilies, shredded, for garnish
2 cups fresh bean sprouts

Use a deep-fat fryer or wok to fry rice noodles, a few at a time, for about 30 seconds per batch. The noodles will swell and float. When done, remove from fat, drain on paper towels, and set aside.

Heat 1 tablespoon oil in a wok or deep skillet; add onion and garlic and stir until lightly brown. Then add shrimp and crab and cook until they turn pink. Stir in remaining ingredients except for garnishes. Add noodles and mix well. Adjust seasonings if needed. When heated through, place on a serving dish. Surround vermicelli with bean sprouts and sprinkle all with orange rind and chilies.

Rice with Mushrooms

KOREA   Yield: 6 servings

½ pound fresh mushrooms, washed
   and sliced
1 tablespoon vegetable oil
1 tablespoon sesame oil
2 medium onions, peeled and finely
   sliced
½ cup lean steak, finely shredded
1 pound short-grain rice
3 cups hot water
1 teaspoon salt
¼ teaspoon ground black pepper
2 tablespoons toasted, ground sesame
   seeds

Prepare mushrooms and dry on paper towels. Heat both oils in a large saucepan. Fry onions, steak, and mushrooms for 2 minutes, stirring constantly. Add rice and stir-fry for another minute. Put in remaining ingredients and bring to a boil.

Cover the saucepan and reduce heat to a simmer. Allow to steam for 20 minutes. Do not lift lid or stir during this time. Fluff with a fork when cooking time is over and transfer to a serving dish.

Rice with Vegetables

INDIA   Yield: 4 to 6 servings

2 tablespoons ghee
2 tablespoons oil
2 medium onions, peeled and finely
   sliced
1 clove garlic, peeled and finely
   chopped
2 cups long-grain rice
4 cups hot water
2 teaspoons salt
1 teaspoon garam masala

2 carrots, cut into matchstick pieces
12 green beans, thinly sliced
½ cup diced red or green chili
1 small potato, peeled and cubed
½ cup fresh or frozen peas
1 teaspoon salt

Heat ghee and oil in a heavy saucepan with a tight-fitting lid. Cook onions slowly for about 10 minutes. Add garlic and cook for 2 minutes more. Add rice and increase heat to medium. Stir-fry for 2 minutes. Add hot water, salt, and garam masala. Bring to a boil and then reduce heat to lowest possible simmer. Cover and cook for 10 minutes.

Place vegetables on top of rice; do not stir. Sprinkle with a teaspoon of salt. Replace lid and cook for 12 minutes more. Uncover pan and allow steam to escape. Then use a folk to fluff up the rice and stir vegetables through. Transfer to a serving platter, using a slotted spoon to dish the rice.

Saffron Rice

INDIA   Yield: 4 servings

¾ cup ghee
2 large onions, peeled and sliced
1½ cups rice, washed thoroughly and
    drained
1 teaspoon whole cloves
4 whole cardamoms
1 teaspoon salt
1 teaspoon freshly ground black pepper
½ teaspoon saffron threads, soaked in
    1 tablespoon boiling water for 30
    minutes
3 cups water
Varak to garnish

Melt ghee in a large saucepan. Fry onions gently until soft. Add drained rice to the pan

with spices and seasonings and stir-fry for 3 minutes.

Add saffron and the liquid it has soaked in, and mix well. Put in water and allow to come to a boil. Reduce and simmer for 15 to 20 minutes. Drain rice well. Transfer to a serving bowl and garnish with varak. Serve very hot.

Savory Yellow Rice

INDONESIA   Yield: 4 to 6 servings

1½ cups long-grain rice
2 tablespoons vegetable oil
1 teaspoon turmeric powder
2½ cups chicken stock
1 teaspoon coriander powder
½ teaspoon cumin powder
1 cinnamon stick
1 whole clove
1 salam leaf or 2 bay leaves

Soak the rice for 1 hour in cold water. Then wash it under cold running water and drain thoroughly.

Heat oil in a saucepan and fry the rice for 2 minutes, stirring constantly. Add turmeric and stir for 2 minutes more. Add remaining ingredients in the order given and bring mixture to a boil. Allow to boil gently until the rice has absorbed the liquid. Stir the rice and reduce heat. Cover pan tightly and cook for 10 minutes more. Serve at once.

"Sizzling" Rice

CHINA   Yield: 5 to 6 servings

To get the "sizzling" effect, food, rice, and container must be hot.

  1 cup long-grain rice
  4 cups water
  2 teaspoons salt
  Oil for deep frying

At least a day in advance, combine rice, water, and salt in a 2-quart saucepan. Let stand 30 minutes. Bring to boil; cover. Simmer 30 minutes; drain. Spread evenly on heavily greased cookie sheet. Bake in 250°F oven 8 hours, turning occasionally with spatula. Break crusty rice into bite-size pieces. Can be stored in airtight containers in refrigerator several weeks.

Just before serving time, heat oven to 250°F; warm serving platter. Pour oil about 2 inches deep in a 6-quart saucepan (or deep-fryer). Heat to 425°F. Fry rice, stirring with slotted spoon, until golden brown, approximately 5 minutes. Drain quickly; place in warmed serving platter.

Spiced Rice

INDIA   Yield: 4 to 6 servings

  2½ cups long-grain rice, washed, and
     drained dry
  ½ teaspoon saffron strands, soaked in
     2 tablespoons boiling water for 10
     minutes
  2 tablespoons ghee
  4 cardamom pods, bruised
  1 small cinnamon stick
  4 whole cloves
  10 black peppercorns

  4 cups hot water
  2½ teaspoons salt
  Rind of 1 orange, finely grated
  2 tablespoons raisins
  2 tablespoons sliced almonds
  2 tablespoons pistachios, halved

After rice and saffron are prepared, heat oil in a heavy saucepan. Gently stir-fry cardamom, cinnamon, cloves, and peppercorns for 2 minutes. Add the rice and continue to stir for 3 minutes more. Put in hot water, salt, saffron and the liquid it has been soaking in, and orange rind. Bring quickly to a boil; then reduce heat, cover, and cook for 20 minutes. Lift lid long enough to scatter raisins on top of rice. Replace lid and simmer for 5 minutes more. Then garnish with almonds and pistachios and serve at once.

Sweet Rice with Black Beans

THAILAND   Yield: 4 servings

  1¼ cups thick coconut milk
  1¾ cups water
  ½ cup dried black beans, soaked in
     cold water for 12 hours
  ¼ cup glutinous rice
  2 tablespoons coconut sugar or brown
     sugar

Place coconut milk and water in a saucepan on low heat. Stir frequently.

Put drained beans, rice, sugar, and coconut milk in a bowl and mix well. Pour into a baking dish and cover. Bake at 250°F for about 3 hours. Stir after 2 hours. Serve hot.

Steamed Rice

THAILAND   Yield: 6 to 8 servings

1 pound long-grain rice
3 cups water

Wash rice thoroughly and allow to drain. Then put it in a large saucepan with the water. Bring water to a boil and lower heat. Cook uncovered. When water is absorbed and holes appear on the surface of the rice, the texture is right.

Remove from heat and place in a steamer. Steam over water, which is at a rolling boil, for 25 minutes or until the grains are firm and separate. Serve at once or use in any recipe that calls for steamed rice.

Rice and Noodles Cantonese

CHINA   Yield: 2 to 4 servings

1 stick butter
1 cup raw rice
1 package thin, fine noodles
1 can beef consommé
1 can water

Brown rice in ½ stick butter in heavy pot. Brown noodles in remaining ½ stick butter in another heavy pot. Combine and add consommé and water. Cover and simmer until done.

Cellophane Noodles

BURMA   Yield: 6 to 8 servings

Since cellophane noodles are fairly bland in taste, they are usually served with a spicy accompaniment, which can be anything from roasted chick peas to soup or curry.

12 ounces cellophane noodles
Boiling salted water

Cut noodles into short lengths, 1 to 2 inches long. Bring salted water to boil in a large saucepan. Put in noodles and cook for 20 minutes, uncovered. Drain and serve in a large bowl. Allow diners to dish separate bowls of the noodles topped with the accompaniment of their choice.

Soft-fried Noodles with Mushrooms

China   Yield: 8 servings

1 5-ounce package fine egg noodles
2 tablespoons safflower oil
1 cup bamboo shoots
1 cup fresh mushrooms, sliced
1 cup sliced almonds
½ cup chicken broth
3 tablespoons soy sauce
Salt to taste

Cook noodles in a large pot in boiling, lightly salted water for 8 minutes; drain well.

Heat oil in a wok or skillet over low heat. Add noodles; stir-fry 4 minutes. Stir in bamboo shoots, mushrooms, and almonds; mix thoroughly. Stir in broth, soy sauce, and salt. Reduce heat to low; simmer, covered, 20 minutes or until liquid is almost absorbed.

Chilled Noodles

JAPAN   Yield: 4 servings

This unusual way of serving noodles is particularly good during the hot summer months, served with bowls of your favorite sauce as a dip.

  1 pound wheat vermicelli
  6 or more cups boiling water

Sauce

  2 cups chicken broth
  ½ cup light soy sauce
  ¼ cup sake
  1 tablespoon sugar

Garnish

  A few ice cubes
  Cherry tomatoes, quartered
  Scallions, finely shredded

Cook wheat vermicelli in boiling water for 5 minutes until just tender. Drain and rinse under cold running water. Drain again. Then place in a large shallow serving dish, preferably glass, and chill in the refrigerator for at least 1 hour.

Put all sauce ingredients in a pan and bring to a boil, stirring constantly. Reduce heat and simmer for 2 minutes; allow to cool. Divide into individual bowls and chill in the refrigerator for at least 1 hour.

When ready to serve, garnish vermicelli with ice cubes, tomatoes, and scallions. Serve bowls of sauce separately.

Deep-fried Crispy Noodles

CHINA   Yield: 4 to 5 cups

  1 5-ounce package fine egg noodles
  Vegetable oil

Place noodles in a large saucepan in enough water to cover; bring to boil. Cook, stirring occasionally, 5 minutes; drain well.

Fill deep-fat fryer half full with oil; heat to 350°F. Return noodles to fryer; cook until golden brown and crisp. Drain well on paper toweling; separate noodles if necessary.

Fried Noodles

Indonesia   Yield: 4 servings

  8 ounces fine egg noodles
  1 large pork chop, diced
  8 ounces shrimp, raw or cooked,
      shelled and deveined
  4 tablespoons peanut oil
  1 onion, peeled and finely chopped
  3 cloves garlic, peeled and finely
      chopped
  1 fresh red chili, seeded and sliced
  ½ teaspoon dried shrimp paste
  2 stalks celery, finely sliced
  Small wedge of cabbage, finely
      shredded
  1 teaspoon salt
  ½ teaspoon pepper
  1 to 2 tablespoons light soy sauce
  4 spring onions for garnish, chopped
      greens and all
  Thinly sliced cucumber for garnish

Put a large saucepan of water on the heat to boil. While water is coming to a boil, soak the noodles in hot water. Drain and drop into the boiling water. Cook for 1 to 3 minutes, testing so that noodles do not overcook. They should be tender but firm. Drain and run cold water over them until they are cool. Set aside. Prepare pork and shrimp and set aside.

Heat oil in a wok or large skillet. Fry onion, garlic, and chili until onion is soft and golden. Add shrimp paste, pork, and shrimp and stir-fry until all are cooked through. Add celery, cabbage, salt, and pepper and stir-fry for 1 minute more. Put in the noodles and stir until noodles are hot. Season with soy sauce.

Put in a serving dish. Garnish with spring onions on top and arrange cucumber slices around the edges.

Fried Noodles with Mixed Meats

PHILIPPINES   Yield: 6 to 8 servings

    1 pound raw shrimp
    1½ cups lightly salted water
    1 pound thin egg noodles
    3 to 4 tablespoons lard or oil
    5 cloves garlic, peeled and crushed
    2 onions, peeled and finely sliced
    1 cup cooked chicken, diced
    1 cup cooked pork, cut in thin strips
    ½ cup ham, cut in thin strips
    1 cup cabbage, shredded
    3 tablespoons light soy sauce
    Salt and pepper to taste
    Lemon wedges for garnish

Cook shrimp in water until it just turns pink. Allow to cool; then shell, devein, and cut into pieces. Reserve 1 cup of stock.

Soak noodles in warm water. While they are soaking, bring a large pan of water to a boil. Drain noodles and put in boiling water. Cook for 2 minutes only. Drain and spread on a large pan lined with paper towels. Sprinkle with oil and allow to dry for at least 30 minutes.

Put 1 tablespoon lard into a large wok or skillet. Fry the noodles, a few at a time, until golden on both sides. Add more lard if needed and continue until all noodles are fried. Set aside.

Add more lard or oil to the pan. Separately, fry garlic, onion, shrimp, chicken, pork, and ham. Use ¼ of each of these for garnish. Return remainder to pan along with cabbage, soy sauce, shrimp stock, salt, and pepper. Cook uncovered until most of the juices have disappeared. Return the noodles to pan and mix well. When good and hot, arrange on a serving platter surrounded with reserved ingredients and wedges of lemon.

Egg Noodles with Mushrooms

CHINA   Yield: About 8 servings

    8 ounces fine egg noodles
    2 tablespoons oil
    1 cup bamboo shoots
    1 cup sliced almonds
    1 cup fresh mushrooms, sliced
    ½ cup chicken broth
    3 tablespoons soy sauce
    Salt to taste

Cook noodles according to package directions for 8 minutes. Drain. Heat oil in a wok. Stir-fry noodles for 3 minutes. Stir in the bamboo shoots, almonds, and mushrooms, and mix thoroughly. Stir in the broth, soy sauce, and salt. Simmer, covered, until the liquid is almost gone.

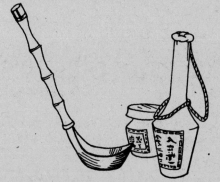

Fried Rice Noodles

MALAYSIA   Yield: 6 to 8 servings

2 pounds fresh rice noodles
¼ pound barbecued pork
½ pound small raw shrimp
2 Chinese sausages
1 cup fresh bean sprouts
4 tablespoons lard or oil
4 small onions, peeled and sliced
2 cloves garlic, peeled and finely
   chopped
4 fresh red chilies, seeded and chopped
2 tablespoons dark soy sauce
2 tablespoons light soy sauce
1 tablespoon oyster sauce
Pepper and salt to taste
3 eggs, beaten
4 spring onions, chopped

Cut rice noodles into ¼- to ½-inch widths. Thinly slice the pork. Shell and devein shrimp. Steam the sausages and cut into thin, diagonal slices. Pinch tails off bean sprouts.

Using a wok or skillet, heat half of the oil; fry onions, garlic, and chilies over medium heat until they are soft. Add pork, shrimp, and sausage and stir-fry until seafood is cooked, just a few minutes. Add bean sprouts and mix well. Remove from wok.

Put in remaining oil. When very hot, stir-fry the rice noodles until they are heated through. Add seasonings and mix well. Pour in beaten egg, stirring constantly until egg is set and firm. Return the fried mixture to the wok and toss well until it is hot. Garnish with spring onions and serve at once.

Noodles with Meat and Vegetables

PHILIPPINES   Yield: 4 to 6 servings

½ pound wide egg noodles
¼ cup vegetable oil
1 clove garlic, peeled and ground
1 cup lean pork, thinly sliced
1 cup chicken breast meat, thinly
   sliced
1 cup fresh shrimp, shelled, deveined,
   and diced
1 medium onion, peeled and thinly
   sliced
1 cup cabbage, shredded
2 tablespoons fish sauce
¾ cup chicken stock
Pinch of paprika pepper
½ teaspoon salt
Freshly ground black pepper, to taste

Garnish

2 hard-cooked eggs, shelled and
   quartered
2 scallions, chopped
Lemon wedges, optional

Boil noodles for just 2 minutes. Drain; rinse with cold water and drain again. Put noodles in a bowl with 1 tablespoon oil and mix well. Set aside.

Using moderate heat, place 1 tablespoon oil in a wok or heavy skillet. Add noodles, stirring to brown on all sides. Set aside and wipe pan clean with paper towels.

Fry garlic in 1 tablespoon oil until brown. Add pork and fry for 5 minutes. Add chicken and shrimp and stir-fry on high heat for 2 minutes. Remove from pan and set aside.

Wipe pan clean again with paper towels. Return pan to heat for 1 minute. Put in remaining oil, onion, and cabbage. Stir-fry for 4 minutes. Onion should be transparent and cabbage crunchy.

Add the remaining ingredients and the cooked meat and fish mixture to the pan. Stir constantly for 2 minutes. The juices will evaporate while you stir. Return noodles to pan, stirring and tossing gently until all is hot. Transfer to serving dish and garnish with eggs, spring onions, and lemon wedges. Serve at once.

Doughs

Baked Leavened Bread

INDIA   Yield: 6 to 8

2 cups flour
½ teaspoon baking powder
1 teaspoon salt
1 teaspoon sugar
1 teaspoon active dry yeast (1 package)
⅔ cup milk
⅔ cup unflavored yogurt
1 egg, beaten
2 teaspoons poppy seeds

In a large bowl, sift flour, baking powder, salt, and sugar. Take 2 tablespoons of milk and mix them with the yeast to make a smooth paste. Use a whisk to beat yogurt into the remaining milk and heat until luke-warm. Stir in the yeast paste. Gradually, add the liquid to the dry ingredients and mix to a dough. Knead well and then add the egg. Knead again, cover with a damp cloth, and allow to rise until doubled in size, at least 2 hours.

Divide dough into 8 pieces, rolling each piece into a small ball. Flatten each ball with your hand and press poppy seeds into top. Bake at 450°F for 12 minutes; bread will be puffed and blistered. Serve hot.

Deep-fried Whole Wheat Bread

INDIA   Yield: 8 to 10

1½ cups whole wheat flour
½ teaspoon salt

¾ cup water
⅓ cup melted ghee or butter
Vegetable oil for deep frying

Sift flour and salt together and gradually add water. Blend well into a firm dough. Add the ghee and knead well. Allow dough to rest for 20 minutes.

Divide dough into 8 or 10 pieces and shape into 1-inch balls. On lightly floured surface, roll into rounds about ⅛-inch thick.

Heat oil and deep-fry the rolled-out balls, one at a time. Cooking time is about 1½ minutes or until bread puffs up and floats on surface. Remove and drain on paper towels. Transfer to a warmed platter and keep hot in oven until ready to serve. Serve hot with your favorite chutney.

Stuffed Puri

INDIA   Yield: About 10

Mix dough as for deep-fried whole wheat bread (puri; see preceding recipe), rolling it into smaller balls. You may want to double the recipe to make more stuffed puri.

Cauliflower filling

2 cups cauliflower, finely chopped
2 teaspoons salt
¼ teaspoon ground cloves
¼ teaspoon ground cinnamon
¼ teaspoon ground cardamom
¼ teaspoon pepper
½ teaspoon ground cumin
¼ ounce grated ginger, dried or fresh

Mix finely chopped cauliflower with spices in a bowl. Take 1 rolled-out ball and put stuffing in center. Cover with a second rolled-out ball and seal edges tightly. Deep-fry until bread puffs up and floats on surface. Remove and drain on paper towels. Keep hot in oven until ready to serve.

Doughs

Fried Besan Bread

INDIA   Yield: 4 to 6

Besan is chick-pea flour and must be kneaded well to form the smooth dough for this bread.

  2 cups besan
  1 teaspoon salt
  1 cup water
  ½ cup ghee
  ¾ cup melted butter

Sift flour into a bowl, straining out lumps with a spoon pressing through sieve. Add salt. Gradually add water. The mixture will be stiff. Use hands to knead in the ghee and work until dough is very smooth. Divide the dough into 4 to 6 pieces and shape into 3-inch balls. Roll on a lightly floured surface to ¼ inch thickness.

Heat melted butter in a skillet. Cook each rolled ball separately for 3 minutes on each side, using a low heat. Keep finished balls warm in oven while you continue to cook. Brush all with melted butter on top when ready to serve.

Unleavened Bread

INDIA   Yield: 20 to 24

Known as chapati in India, this bread is made with ata or whole-wheat flour.

  3 cups fine whole wheat flour
  1½ teaspoons salt
  1 tablespoon ghee or oil
  1 cup lukewarm water

Set aside ½ cup flour. Place remainder in mixing bowl with salt. Then rub in ghee with your fingers. Add the water and mix to a firm dough. Knead for at least 10 minutes, the longer, the better. Form the dough into a ball; cover and let stand for at least 1 hour. (If possible, do this much the night before, so that chapati will be as light and tender as possible.)

Shape the dough into balls about the size of a walnut. Sprinkle reserved flour on a board and thinly roll out each ball into a circle. When all balls are rolled, heat a griddle or heavy frying pan. Place each chapati on the griddle for 1 minute. Turn and cook the other side, pressing down edges to form air bubbles and make the chapati light. Keep warm until all the chapati are finished cooking. Serve with butter.

Sweet Bread Rolls

PHILIPPINES   Yield: 18 rolls

  1 ounce compressed yeast
  ¼ cup lukewarm water
  3 teaspoons sugar
  4 cups flour
  1½ sticks (6 ounces) butter or
    margarine
  ½ cup powdered sugar
  6 egg yolks
  ½ cup milk
  1 extra stick (4 ounces) butter, melted
  4 ounces cheese (Dutch Edam
    preferred), finely grated
  2 to 3 tablespoons extra powdered
    sugar

Dissolve yeast in warm water. Stir in sugar until dissolved. Sprinkle 1 spoonful flour on top and set aside in a warm place.

Cream butter and powdered sugar until light. Add egg yolks, singly, beating well each time. Alternate flour and milk with yeast mixture and beat until smooth. The dough should be soft but not sticky. Form

320

into a ball and let stand on floured board for about 10 minutes. Wash a bowl in hot water, dry it, and grease it lightly. Place dough in bowl, cover, and let rise until doubled in size, about 1 hour.

Divide dough in half and roll into 2 rectangles, 18 × 15 inches. Brush with melted butter and sprinkle with half of the cheese. Cut each rectangle into 3 strips and roll from the long end. Cut each roll into 3 pieces. When both rectangles are rolled and cut, you will have 18 pieces.

Roll each piece on floured board until the width of a pencil. Twist well. Place on greased baking sheet, allowing space for them to rise; cover with a dry cloth and put in a warm place for 40 minutes.

Bake in a preheated 350°F oven for 10 minutes or until golden brown. Remove from oven; brush with melted butter and sprinkle with powdered sugar. Serve warm or at room temperature.

Wonton Rolls

CHINA   Yield: 16 rolls

⅓ cup orange marmalade
1 tablespoon lemon juice
2 tablespoons soy sauce
2 tablespoons margarine
½ cup cornflake crumbs
2 tubes crescent rolls

Combine all ingredients except the rolls. Open the rolls and separate them into triangles. Spoon some of the marmalade mixture into the center of each triangle. Stretch and fold the points up around the filling, shaping the roll into a pocket. Place on greased cookie sheets and bake at 400°F for 10 minutes. Serve warm.

Shrimp Crisps

INDONESIA   Yield: As many as you fry

Krupuk or shrimp crackers are pink and measure about 4 inches in length. They are obtainable in Oriental stores.

Shrimp crackers
1¼ cups vegetable oil

Heat oil in a wok or deep frying pan. Separate crackers and drop one at a time into the hot oil. They will swell up several times their original size. Flatten immediately with a spatula. Fry each cracker for a few seconds only and remove from the pan. Drain on paper towels. Allow to cool before serving.

Fried Dumplings

VIETNAM   Yield: About 48 dumplings

12 dried Chinese mushrooms, optional
2 eggs, slightly beaten
1 tablespoon vegetable oil
1 tablespoon fish sauce or soy sauce
1 tablespoon lemon juice, strained
½ teaspoon salt
⅛ teaspoon black pepper
Pinch of chili powder (or 1 teaspoon red pepper flakes if you like hot foods)
1 small onion, minced
1 cup ground, lean pork
1 cup cooked vermicelli, minced, or cooked rice
1 clove garlic, peeled, minced
2 cups raw shrimp, shelled, deveined, minced
1 cup bean sprouts, rinsed
3 cups oil (for deep-fat frying)
Shredded lettuce
Sweet-and-sour sauce

Doughs

Soak the mushrooms in warm water for 20 minutes, drain, and mince. Place in a medium bowl and mix with ½ the egg, 1 tablespoon oil, fish (or soy) sauce, lemon juice, salt, pepper, chili powder (or red pepper), onion, pork, vermicelli (or rice), garlic, shrimp, and bean sprouts. Place a spoonful of this mixture into the center of a dough circle and fold into a dumpling suitable for frying. Seal with the rest of the beaten egg and set on oiled waxed paper until ready to cook. Add the 3 cups of oil to the wok and heat to 350°F. Deep-fry the dumplings for 2 or 3 minutes, until golden brown; drain and serve hot with shredded lettuce and sweet-and-sour sauce.

Fried Cakes

KOREA   Yield: 4 to 6 servings

1 cup flour
1 teaspoon baking powder
½ teaspoon salt
3 tablespoons sugar
Water
6 dates, shredded
Small amount of oil for frying

Put the dry ingredients in a bowl. Add only enough water to make a firm dough. When the dough is firm, roll it out on a floured board to ⅛-inch thick. Cut into 2-inch circles.

Press bits of the dates into the circles of dough. Heat oil in a skillet and brown the cakes on each side. These delicacies are best served hot, so keep the cooked ones warm until all are fried.

Golden Bean Cakes

THAILAND   Yield: Varies

8 ounces mung beans
1 cup white sugar
½ cup water
Confectioners' sugar

Sugar syrup

⅓ cup sugar
1 tablespoon water

Soak beans for 24 hours in cold water. Wash the soaked beans several times until all the green skins float away. Put them into a saucepan with water and cook until soft. Drain and mash cooked beans into a smooth paste.

Heat white sugar and water over medium heat until sugar is dissolved. Add bean paste. Stir occasionally in the beginning; when the paste begins to thicken, you must stir constantly. When the mixture pulls away from the side of the pan, it is ready. Allow it to cool. When cool, roll the mixture into small balls. Make a syrup of the sugar and water. Dip cooled balls in sugar syrup and roll in confectioners' sugar. Allow them to dry fully before putting them in small paper cases or a cookie tin.

The amount this recipe makes depends on the size of the balls.

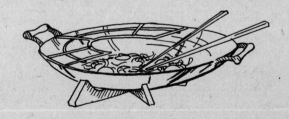

Desserts

Orange Shaped Cakes

INDOCHINA   Yield: 12 cakes

Filling

¾ cup yellow mung beans
¾ cup water
½ cup sugar

Wrapping

2 cups glutinous rice flour
1 teaspoon baking powder
½ teaspoon salt
½ cup sugar
2 medium potatoes, boiled, peeled,
   and mashed
½ cup boiling water

½ cup toasted sesame seeds
2 cups oil for deep frying

Use cold running water to rinse mung beans thoroughly. Place beans and ¾ cup water in a small saucepan and bring to a boil. Cover the pan, reduce heat, and simmer for about 30 minutes. When the beans are tender and dry, and the water cooked away, remove from heat. Mash well; add sugar and mix well. Set aside.

Mix well the dry ingredients for the wrapping, including the mashed potatoes. Gradually add the boiling water. Then knead well until dough forms a smooth ball.

Form a small ball from about 2 tablespoons of the dough. Flatten this into a 3-inch circle. Place a teaspoon of the filling mixture into the center and cover this as you reshape the dough into a sealed ball. Repeat this wrapping procedure until all balls are made.

Toast sesame seeds in a dry skillet by stir-frying until they are well browned and not oily at all. Roll prepared balls into the seeds until well coated.

Heat oil in a small skillet; cook only a few balls at a time. Drop the balls into the oil and flatten slightly with a circular motion of a spoon or spatula. Cook for about 10 minutes until golden brown. Remove from the pan and drain on paper towels. Keep warm until all the balls are fried and serve at once.

Almond Torte

CHINA   Yield: 6 servings

2 eggs
1½ cups sugar
¼ cup sifted flour
2½ teaspoons baking powder
¼ teaspoon salt
2 teaspoons almond extract
½ cup almonds, slivered
1 medium apple, finely chopped

Preheat oven to 350°F.

Beat eggs until light. Gradually add sugar; beat until thick and lemon-colored.

Sift flour, baking powder, and salt together. Fold into egg mixture. Add almond extract, nuts, and apple; fold in gently. Pour into 8-inch-square greased baking pan. Bake 25 minutes.

Teething Cake

BURMA   Yield: About 6 servings

This cake is so named because it is served to celebrate when a baby gets his first tooth.

1 cup flour
1 cup rice flour
Pinch salt
½ teaspoon baking soda
1 tablespoon light sesame oil or corn oil
Scant ⅔ cup water
1 cup fresh coconut, grated
½ cup palm sugar, grated
4 cups coconut milk
1 tablespoon or more sugar

Mix flours, salt, and baking soda. With your hands, rub the oil. Add just enough water to make a paste and then knead well to form a smooth dough. Mix the grated coconut and palm sugar together. Pull off pieces of the dough and flatten to a circle. Dot the center with a little of the coconut and palm mixture and roll up to make a ball.

Bring the coconut milk and sugar to a boil in a large saucepan. Drop in the balls. They will sink to the bottom but, as they cook, will slowly rise to the top. Stir gently in case some of the balls stick to the bottom of the pan. Allow to simmer for 10 minutes after the balls float. Serve hot or cold with a little of the liquid in which the balls were cooked.

Peanut Brittle

INDONESIA   Yield: About 50 pieces

These unusual snacks are made with very fine rice powder. They will keep in an airtight container for two weeks.

2 kemiri, chopped
1 clove garlic, peeled and chopped
2 teaspoons coriander powder
1 teaspoon salt
1 cup rice powder
1 cup water
1 cup whole, shelled peanuts, halved if large
1¼ cups vegetable oil

Pound the kemiri and garlic to a very smooth paste. Add coriander and salt and stir well to mix. Add rice powder and water and stir until batter is smooth and liquid. Last, add the peanuts.

Heat 5 tablespoons of oil in a heavy skillet. Drop batter by spoonfuls into the oil. Fry for 1 minute. Remove from pan with a slotted spoon and drain on paper towels. Continue in this way, adding oil as needed, until all the batter is used. Stir batter from time to time, adding a little water if it gets too thick.

Pour remaining oil into the skillet for deep frying. Fry the peanut brittle again for 1 minute until golden brown, turning during the frying time. Drain again on paper towels and allow to completely cool before storing.

Banana Cake with Cashews

INDONESIA   Yield: 8 or more servings

3 eggs
1 cup sugar
¾ cup cream
1½ cups flour
4 pounds of ripe bananas
1 cup fresh cashews, coarsely chopped
1 cup fresh coconut, grated

Use an electric mixer on low to beat eggs and sugar together. When thick and pale, add cream and mix for 1 minute more. Add sifted flour to the bowl and blend in with a wooden spoon. Peel and very coarsely mash bananas and add them and the nuts and coconut to the batter. Do not overstir. Mix only until all the ingredients are combined.

Grease two 8-inch pans and dust lightly with flour. Pour mixture into pans and bake in a preheated oven at 350°F for 1 hour. When cake is done, it will be golden brown and springy on top. Serve warm or cold.

Oriental Nut Torte

CHINA   Yield: 1 8-inch cake

    4 eggs, separated
    1 cup sugar
    ½ teaspoon almond extract
    1 cup matzo meal
    ¼ teaspoon salt
    1 teaspoon baking powder
    ¾ cup walnuts, coarsely chopped
    ¼ cup sesame seeds

Beat egg whites until stiff but not dry. Beat egg yolks with almond extract and sugar until thick. Mix matzo meal with salt and baking powder. Fold egg yolk mixture, matzo meal mixture, nuts, and sesame seeds into egg whites.

Pour into ungreased 9-inch round or 8-inch square pan which has been lined on the bottom. Bake in a slow oven (325°F) about 1 hour. Cool in pan. Cut into portions and serve with ice cream or pareve sherbet.

Sponge Cake

JAPAN   Yield: 1 9-inch cake

    5 eggs, beaten
    ⅔ cup sugar
    ¼ cup honey
    ¾ cup flour
    ¾ teaspoon baking powder
    2 tablespoons confectioners' sugar

Beat eggs, sugar, and honey together for about 10 minutes until thick and pale. The electric beater helps here. Sift flour and baking powder and fold into the egg mixture.

Pour this into a greased and floured 9-inch square pan. Bake at 350°F for 30 minutes. Allow the cake to cool in the pan for 10 minutes. Then remove from pan and place on a wire rack. Cool completely. When ready to serve, dust with confectioners' sugar and cut into squares.

Date Candy

KOREA   Yield: 6 to 8 servings

    1 cup pitted dates
    3 tablespoons honey
    ½ teaspoon cinnamon
    Pine nuts, whole
    ½ cup pine nuts, chopped

Chop the dates in a bowl until they are very sticky. Add the honey and cinnamon and stir until well mixed. Use a teaspoon to take out portions of this mixture. The shapes will be somewhat rounded. Put 1 pine nut into the center of the date mixture. Then roll it in the chopped pine nuts and put on a serving dish. Continue in this way until all the candies are made.

Desserts

Christmas Candies

CHINA   Yield: 1 dozen candies

½ can Chinese noodles
½ can salted peanuts
1 bag chocolate chips
½ bag maple or butterscotch chips

Melt chocolate and butterscotch chips together. Mix noodles and peanuts with melted chips. Drop onto a cookie sheet or tin foil and refrigerate.

Crispy Orange Cookies

CHINA   Yield: About 36

1¼ cups flour
¼ cup rice flour
½ cup butter or margarine
⅜ cup white sugar
Grated rind of 1 large orange
1 egg, separated
½ cup brown sugar

Preheat oven to 350°F.
Sift flour and rice flour into bowl. Rub in the butter until the mixture resembles fine bread crumbs. Add sugar, orange rind, and egg yolk; mix well. Knead until smooth; wrap in foil. Refrigerate ½ hour.
Roll dough to about 12 inches square. Brush with lightly beaten egg white; sprinkle with brown sugar. Fold corners to center. Form into ball; knead lightly. Cut in half; shape each half into roll about 9 inches long. Cut rolls into slices about ½ inch thick; place on greased baking sheets. Bake about 20 minutes; remove to cooling trays. Store when quite cold.

Almond Cookies

CHINA   Yield: About 4 dozen

1 cup shortening
1 cup sugar
1 egg, beaten
3 cups sifted flour
1½ teaspoons baking soda
3 tablespoons almond extract
4 tablespoons honey or corn syrup
1 cup blanched almonds

Cream the shortening and sugar together. Add the egg. Slowly add flour, baking soda, almond extract, and honey and blend until smooth. Take a small piece of dough and roll it into a ball. Repeat until all the dough is used. Flatten each ball to about ½ inch thickness. Place an almond in the center of each. Bake on greased cookie sheet in a preheated 375°F oven for about 15 to 20 minutes.
In China, lard is the usual ingredient in Almond Cookies, but you may substitute margarine.

Indian Nut Heaps

INDIA   Yield: About 60 cookies

2 tablespoons flour
2 tablespoons sugar
Pinch of salt
2 egg yolks
6 tablespoons butter or margarine
4 ounces candied ginger, finely diced
4 ounces grated cashew nuts
Pinch of ground cardamom

Put flour in a bowl. Make a hollow in center. Place sugar, salt, and egg yolks into the hollow and mix well. Cut butter into this mixture. Knead into a smooth dough on

326

a floured board. Mix ginger, cashew nuts, and cardamom into the dough. Cover and refrigerate for 30 minutes.

Grease a cookie sheet. Shape the dough into small balls about 1 inch in diameter. Place on cookie sheet. Bake at 350°F for about 10 minutes. Let cookies cool on a rack after baking.

Sesame Cookies

CHINA　　　Yield: About 3 dozen cookies

　1 cup sifted cake flour
　½ stick butter
　½ cup sugar
　¼ teaspoon salt
　1 egg
　1 egg yolk mixed with 1 tablespoon
　　water
　Sesame seeds

Combine flour, butter, sugar, salt, and egg in bowl and knead well until it forms a soft dough. Place on well-floured board and form into a long roll about 1½ inches in diameter. Cut into approximately 36 pieces and flatten each with bottom of a glass dipped in flour.

Brush one side of cookie with egg-yolk and water mixture. Sprinkle sesame seeds on brushed side and press sesame seeds into cookie. Place on greased cookie sheet and bake at 350°F for 10 to 12 minutes.

Chinese Chews

CHINA　　　Yield: About 48 chews

　1 cup sugar
　¾ cup sifted all-purpose flour
　1 teaspoon baking powder
　¼ teaspoon salt

　2 eggs, beaten
　1 cup dates, chopped
　1 cup walnuts, chopped
　1 teaspoon vanilla
　½ cup powdered sugar

Sift together sugar, flour, baking powder, and salt. Combine eggs, dates, nuts, and vanilla. Combine the two mixtures; mix well. Place mixture in a greased baking pan 8 × 8 × 2 inches and bake in a 350°F oven for 40 minutes. While hot cut in small squares and roll each in powdered sugar.

Tay Doy (Chinese Doughnuts)

CHINA　　　Yield: About 3 dozen

　1¼ cups brown sugar
　1½ cups water
　3¾ cups (1 pound) no mei fun, mochi
　　flour
　½ cup sesame seeds
　Oil for deep frying
　Filling
　½ cup coconut, grated
　½ cup roasted peanuts, crushed
　3 teaspoons sugar

Dissolve brown sugar in hot water. Cool. Stir enough water into flour to make a stiff dough. Do not knead. Shape into a roll 1½ inches in diameter. Cut in ½-inch pieces. Flatten. Work dough, shaping it into a hollow ball. Place small amount of filling in hollow ball. Slowly close opening by pinching edges together. Dip lightly in sesame seeds.

When all the dough has been formed into filled balls, deep-fry in hot oil, stirring until the balls (which expand gradually into round balls) are golden brown. Remove from deep-fry pan and place in receptacle lined with paper napkins to absorb excess oil.

Banana Fritters

INDONESIA   Yield: 4 to 6 servings

This can be served as an accompaniment to a meal, but it is a delicious dessert as well.

    4 ripe bananas, mashed
    ¾ cup flour
    ½ teaspoon salt
    3 tablespoons sugar
    Oil for deep frying
    Cinnamon sugar (1 teaspoon cinnamon
        to ⅓ cup sugar)

Make a batter of the mashed bananas, flour, salt, and sugar, Mix well until the batter is fairly smooth. Heat oil in a deep frying pan. Drop 1 tablespoon of the batter into the fat for each fritter. Cook a few at a time, being sure not to crowd the frying pan, until golden brown on both sides. Drain on paper towels. Sprinkle with cinnamon sugar and serve at once.

Indian Fritters

INDIA   Yield: 5 to 6 servings

    ¾ cup flour
    Pinch of salt
    Boiling water
    2 eggs
    2 egg yolks
    Frying fat
    Jam or jelly

Sift the flour into a bowl with a pinch of salt. Stir in a good ¼ cup of boiling water and beat to form a very stiff, smooth paste. Let cool slightly. Beat in the eggs and egg yolks gradually and thoroughly.

Have ready a deep-fat fryer, heated to 375°F. Half-fill a tablespoon with the mix-

ture and put a teaspoon of jam or jelly in the center; cover with more of the batter mixture; drop this into the hot fat. Cook until golden brown, about 3 minutes. Drain well. Dredge with sugar or serve with a sauce made from the same jam or jelly as the filling.

Rice Fritters

PHILIPPINES   Yield: About 20

These fritters can be served as a dessert or as a between-meal snack.

    1 cup cooked medium-grain rice
    2 eggs, beaten
    3 tablespoons sugar
    ½ teaspoon vanilla extract
    ½ cup flour
    1 tablespoon baking powder
    Pinch of salt
    ¼ cup sweetened coconut, shredded
    Vegetable oil for deep frying
    Confectioners' sugar for sprinkling
        on top

Mix rice, eggs, sugar, and vanilla in a large bowl. Gradually stir in the flour, baking soda, and salt. Last, add the coconut.

Heat oil in a deep-fat fryer. Drop the rice mixture by tablespoons into the heated oil. Fry until golden brown on both sides. Drain on paper towels. Place cooked fritters on a heated platter until all are done. Sprinkle with confectioners' sugar and serve at once.

Banana Chips

PHILIPPINES   Yield: 6 or more servings

   1 cup sugar
   ⅓ teaspoon salt
   20 unripe bananas, peeled and sliced
   Fat for deep-frying

   Mix sugar and salt together. In another bowl, place 3 cups of the sliced bananas. Add 3 tablespoons of the sugar-salt mixture. Repeat until bananas are used up.

   Heat fat in a deep-fryer. Drop a few banana slices in the hot fat and cook until golden brown. Remove and separate if the pieces are stuck together. Allow to cool before serving.

Bananas Cooked in Coconut Milk

INDOCHINA   Yield: 6 servings

   6 to 8 large, ripe bananas
   2 cups thick coconut milk
   2 tablespoons sugar

   Peel the bananas and cut into 2-inch pieces, about 3 or 4 pieces per banana. Put coconut milk and sugar in a saucepan and simmer until thick and creamy. Add bananas and cook on low heat until bananas are soft but not mushy. Transfer to individual serving dishes and serve warm.

Banana Dessert I

BURMA   Yield: 6 servings

   2 tablespoons water
   1 cup sugar
   6 large firm bananas
   Pinch of salt
   1⅓ cups coconut cream

   Make a syrup of the water and sugar by cooking them over low heat, stirring. Peel the bananas and place in the bottom of a deep saucepan. Pour the syrup over the bananas. Bring this to a boil. Add the pinch of salt and coconut cream and simmer gently until the liquid is absorbed. Turn the bananas while they cook. Serve at once.

Banana Dessert II

INDIA   Yield: 4 to 6 servings

   8 bananas, peeled and sliced
   6 tablespoons butter
   2 cups water
   ½ cup sugar
   3 tablespoons rose water
   1 heaping teaspoon cardamom
   Pinch of saffron
   3 tablespoons chopped almonds

   With a fork, mash banana slices in a bowl. Heat butter in saucepan. Stir bananas into butter and cook for 5 minutes. Add 5 tablespoons water and boil lightly for 3 minutes, using medium heat.

   In another saucepan, melt sugar in remaining water. Stir this into the bananas and simmer for 10 minutes, stirring occasionally. Add the rose water. When mixed and hot, place in a preheated serving dish. Mix cardamom, saffron, and almonds in a bowl and sprinkle this over the top. Serve at once, hot.

   This dessert can be made ahead of time, stored in the freezer, and thawed when ready to serve. Slightly frozen, it has a very delicate taste.

Banana Dessert III

INDIA   Yield: 4 servings

    4 large bananas
    3 tablespoons butter or margarine
    Juice of 1 lemon
    3 tablespoons grated coconut
    4 tablespoons raspberry preserves

Peel and slice the bananas and place in a pudding dish that has been well greased. Dot with butter. Sprinkle with lemon juice and cover with grated coconut.

Bake at 350°F for 10 minutes. Remove from oven and divide dessert into individual serving dishes. Top each portion with 1 tablespoon preserves and serve warm.

Caramel Bananas

KOREA   Yield: 4 servings

    4 bananas, peeled and cut into
        1-inch rounds
    2 tablespoons flour
    2 egg whites, beaten with a fork
    2 tablespoons cornstarch
    Oil for deep-frying

Caramel sauce

    ½ cup sugar
    2 tablespoons butter
    2 tablespoons water
    2 tablespoons sesame seeds

After preparing bananas, place flour on a plate. Combine beaten egg whites with cornstarch. Roll bananas first in flour and then in egg-white mixture. Heat oil in skillet. Fry bananas for 3 minutes to a golden brown color. Remove and drain on paper towels.

In a pan, allow sugar and 1 tablespoon butter to become golden brown. Stir in water and sesame seeds. Gently place bananas in this and turn to cover with the sauce. Use remaining butter to grease serving dish. Place bananas on greased serving dish and serve at once.

Carrot Dessert

INDIA   Yield: 4 to 6 servings

    1½ pounds carrots, grated or finely
        mashed
    2½ cups milk
    Pinch of saffron
    6 tablespoons butter
    1 teaspoon cardamom
    3 tablespoons sugar (or to taste)
    2 tablespoons raisins
    2 tablespoons honey
    1 cinnamon stick
    2 tablespoons chopped almonds

Put grated carrots in a bowl; add just enough milk to cover them and soak for 30 minutes. Heat remaining milk in a saucepan and add carrots. Allow to come to a boil and cook for 90 minutes, stirring occasionally. Add saffron, 3 tablespoons butter, cardamom, sugar, raisins, honey, and cinnamon stick. Cook on medium heat for 15 minutes more. Add remaining butter and cook for 15 more minutes. The dish is done when it is a nice orange color. Remove cinnamon stick and put carrot dessert into large bowl for serving. This tastes good hot or cold and, once made, can be reheated.

Pickled Crab Apples

CHINA   Yield: About 5 pints

    4 pounds ripe crab apples
    4½ cups sugar
    2½ cups vinegar
    2 cups water
    1 teaspoon salt
    ½ tablespoon whole cloves
    ½ tablespoon allspice
    1 1½-inch piece fresh gingerroot
    2 sticks cinnamon
    Red food coloring, optional

Wash and rinse apples; drain. Remove stem end; prick apples with a large needle. Place sugar, vinegar, water, and salt in a saucepan.

Tie spices in a muslin bag; drop into pan. Cook, stirring constantly, until sugar dissolves. Add one layer of apples; boil gently 7 minutes. Remove from pan; place in a large bowl. Repeat until all crab apples are cooked; add a few drops of color to the syrup. Pour syrup over crab apples; add spice bag. Cover; let stand in cool place 48 hours. Pack crab apples to within ½ inch of top of hot sterilized fruit jars.

Heat syrup to boiling; pour over crab apples. Place lids on jars; screw bands tight. Process pints and quarts 20 minutes in boiling water.

Deep-fried Date Buns

CHINA   Yield: About 48 buns

    1 pound pitted dates
    1 cup shelled walnuts
    4 tablespoons frozen orange juice
        concentrate
    4 tablespoons grated orange rind
    2 to 3 cups oil for frying
    Confectioner's sugar

Cut dates into chunks about 1-inch square. Place in blender ¼ at a time, with ¼ of the walnuts. At high speed, blend into finest particles. Turn into a large bowl, add orange juice and rind, and knead into a large ball. Place a spoonful into the center of a dough circle and twist into bun form. Roll in the hands until smooth.

Heat oil in the wok to 375°F. Fry the buns 6 to 8 at a time until just golden brown. Drain well, cool, and sprinkle lightly with confectioner's sugar before serving.

Steamed Date Buns

CHINA   Yield: About 48 buns

    ½ cup lard or hydrogenated shortening
    2 cups canned red-bean paste
    1 pound pitted dates, finely chopped
    Red food coloring, optional

Melt the lard in the wok at moderate heat, add the canned bean paste and chopped dates, and cook, stirring constantly, for 8 to 10 minutes. Transfer the contents of the wok pan to a bowl and cool thoroughly.

Place a spoonful of the mixture into the center of a dough circle and twist into a bun form. Roll in the hands until a smooth ball is formed. Steam the smooth buns in bamboo steamer trays above boiling water in the base of the wok for 10 minutes. Serve hot directly in the steamer tray placed on a pan.

Pickled Figs

CHINA   Yield: About 6 pints

5 quarts firm ripe figs
1 cup soda
4 to 5 cups sugar
2½ cups vinegar
1 teaspoon salt
¼ teaspoon ground nutmeg
2 teaspoons whole cloves
2 teaspoons whole allspice
1 medium piece fresh gingerroot
3 sticks cinnamon
Green food coloring, optional

Place figs in a large bowl; sprinkle with soda. Add 6 quarts boiling water; let stand 5 minutes. Rinse figs thoroughly in cool water; drain.

Combine 2½ cups sugar and 2 quarts water in a kettle; bring to a boil. Add figs; cook 30 minutes or until tender. Add remaining sugar, vinegar, salt, and nutmeg.

Tie whole spices in a bag; drop into the syrup. Cook until figs are clear. Let stand in a cool place overnight. Add coloring if desired. Pack figs to within ½ inch of top of pint jars.

Bring syrup to a boil; pour over figs. Place lids on jars; screw bands tight. Process 15 minutes in boiling water.

Spiced Kumquats

CHINA   Yield: About 3 pints

1 quart kumquats
3 cups sugar
1 cup vinegar
1 stick cinnamon
1 tablespoon whole cloves
1 tablespoon whole allspice

Wash and slit kumquats; place in a pot. Cover with water; bring to a boil. Cook 10 minutes; drain. Combine sugar, vinegar, and 3 cups of water in a large saucepan; bring to a boil.

Tie spices in a small piece of muslin; drop into syrup. Cook 5 minutes. Add kumquats; cook 10 minutes. Discard spice bag. Let kumquats stand overnight. Bring to a boil; cook until syrup is thick. Pack kumquats into hot sterilized jars; cover with syrup. Place lids on jars; screw bands tight. Process jars 10 minutes in boiling water.

Lichees

CHINA   Yield: About 4 servings

1 can lichees

For a totally unique and delightful taste treat, try a dessert of lichees. This is a canned fruit in syrup, usually imported from Hong Kong. They can sometimes be purchased in your local supermarket, for sure at a Chinese food store. Try lichees mixed with other fruits: experiment with different combinations.

Spiced Mandarin Oranges

CHINA   Yield: About 4 servings

1 small tangerine (an orange may be substituted)
2 11-ounce cans mandarin oranges
¼ cup water
⅓ cup firmly packed brown sugar
1 2-inch piece of stick cinnamon

Cut the peel from the tangerine in paper-thin strips. Squeeze the juice and strain. In medium-size saucepan, combine the peel and juice with the rest of the ingredients. Simmer for 15 minutes. Remove from heat and remove the peel and cinnamon. Chill for several hours. Serve in small dessert dishes.

Peach Coupe with Cherries Jubilee

CHINA   Yield: About 6 servings

1 can (1 pound 14 ounces) pitted black Bing cherries
1 tablespoon sugar
1 tablespoon cornstarch
1 cup cherry juice
1 3-inch piece lemon peel
2 tablespoons cherry liqueur
6 canned cling peach halves
1 pint vanilla ice cream
⅓ cup warmed brandy

Drain cherries and reserve juice. Mix sugar with cornstarch and add 1 cup cherry juice a little at a time. Add the lemon peel and cook gently, until clear and thickened, about 5 minutes. Remove from heat. Take out the lemon peel and stir in the cherry liqueur and the cherries. This may be prepared ahead.

To serve: Have the dessert dishes ready on a tray at the table. Place a peach half and some ice cream in each. Transfer the sauce to an electric wok and heat gently. Pour the warm brandy over the hot sauce, without stirring. Set ablaze and spoon over the peaches and ice cream.

Fried Pineapple

INDONESIA   Yield: 4 servings

2 tablespoons flour
1 egg
Dash of salt

6 to 8 slices of pineapple, ½ inch thick, drained
Oil for deep frying
Cinnamon sugar (1 teaspoon cinnamon to ⅓ cup sugar)

Use a whisk to mix the flour, egg, and salt in a bowl. Dip each pineapple slice in this mixture. Heat oil in a heavy skillet or deep-fryer and fry the pineapple until golden brown. Drain on paper towels. Sprinkle with cinnamon sugar and serve.

Pickled Pineapple

JAPAN   Yield: About 3 to 4 pints

2 pineapples, peeled and sliced in 1-inch rings
2 tablespoons cloves
2 cups water
4 cups sugar
2½ cups white vinegar
2 sticks cinnamon

Peel and slice pineapple, then core and cut into 1-inch pieces. Tie cloves in small piece of cheesecloth. In large saucepan, combine water, sugar, vinegar, cinnamon, and cloves. Bring to a boil and cook over low heat 20 minutes. Add the pineapple, cover, and cook over low heat 15 to 20 minutes, or until pineapple is tender and clear. Pack in sterile jars.

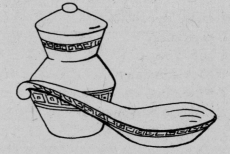

333

Dessert Yams

CHINA   Yield: 3 to 4 servings

    1½ pounds yams
    Oil
    4 tablespoons water
    4 tablespoons soy sauce
    ½ cup sugar
    4 tablespoons sesame seeds

Peel yams; cut them into bite-size pieces (irregular shapes). Fry yams in oil until just tender. Remove from oil.

In a saucepan, combine water, soy sauce, and sugar; simmer together. Put yams into this mixture for about 2 minutes; gently mix. Remove yams to lightly oiled serving platter. Sprinkle with sesame seeds that have been lightly toasted.

Dessert Tempura

JAPAN   Yield: 4 servings

This is a fun dessert to do at the table in a fondue pot or wok.

    Fruit for 4 (apples, bananas, pears)
    Tempura batter
    Powdered sugar

Peel the fruit; cut it into chunks. Dip it into tempura batter; fry it in oil. Drain on paper towels. Sprinkle with powdered sugar. Delicious with hot tea.

Pickled Watermelon Rind

CHINA   Yield: 4 quarts

    5 pounds watermelon rind
    1 tablespoon salt
    8 teaspoons alum

    9 cups sugar
    1 quart cider vinegar
    2 lemons, thinly sliced
    4 2-inch pieces cinnamon stick
    2 teaspoons whole allspice
    2 teaspoons whole cloves

Cut off and discard green and red portions from watermelon rind; leave only white inner rind. Cut into 1-inch pieces, about 4 quarts. Place rind in a large stainless-steel or enamel pot. Add water to cover. Stir in salt; bring to a boil. Reduce heat; simmer 20 minutes or until the rind can be easily pierced with a fork. Remove from heat. Stir in alum; cool. Cover; let stand 24 hours. Pour off water. Rinse; drain well. Add sugar, vinegar, lemon, and cinnamon sticks.

Tie allspice and cloves in a cheesecloth bag. Add to rind mixture; mix well. Bring just to boil, stirring constantly. Remove from heat; cool, uncovered. Cover; let stand 24 hours.

Drain off syrup into a large pan; bring just to boil. Pour over rind; cool. Cover; let stand 24 hours. Heat rind in syrup, but do not boil. Remove and discard spice bag. Pack rind and cinnamon in hot sterilized jars. Heat syrup to boiling; fill jars with boiling syrup. Seal immediately. Store 4 weeks or longer before serving.

Fruit Bowl

JAPAN   Yield: 2 servings

    1 can mandarin oranges, drained
    1 apple, peeled and sliced
    1 banana, sliced and sprinkled with lime
      or lemon juice
    6 dates, cut in half
    ⅛ cup walnut chips

Place drained mandarin oranges in glass bowl. Combine with apple, banana, and dates. Sprinkle with walnut chips.

Fruit Dessert

JAPAN   Yield: Varies

This is an ideal dessert to enjoy after a Japanese meal. Use the amount of fruit needed for the number of guests you are serving. Approximate a generous amount per person, for instance 10 to 12 pieces.

> Watermelon
> Cantaloupe
> Bananas
> Lime or lemon juice
> Grapes
> Strawberries
> Pineapple

Cut slices of watermelon and cantaloupe into chunks. Slice bananas into 4 pieces each; sprinkle with lime or lemon juice to prevent darkening. Wash grapes; leave in small bunches. Wash and hull strawberries; leave whole. If using fresh pineapple, cut into bite-size pieces. If canned pineapple is used, you may purchase tidbits, chunks, or slices cut into quarters.

Arrange all fruit attractively on serving platter; serve with a small bowl or pitcher of Fruit Dressing (see next recipe), to be poured over the fruit.

Fruit Dressing

JAPAN   Yield: About 1 pint

This is delicious poured over any kind of fruit.

> 1 cup sugar
> 1 egg, well beaten
> Juice and grated rind of 1 orange,
>   1 lime, and 1 lemon

Combine all ingredients in saucepan and blend well. Cook over medium heat, stirring constantly, until mixture comes to a boil. Boil 1 minute. Remove from heat, cool, and store in refrigerator in covered jar. Serve as an accompaniment to a dessert of fresh fruit.

Malayan Compote

MALAYSIA   Yield: 6 servings

> 3 green tipped bananas
> 1 No. 2½ can peach halves
> 1 No. 2½ can pear halves
> ½ cup maraschino cherries
> ½ cup brown sugar
> ½ teaspoon curry powder
> 3 tablespoons lemon juice
> 2 tablespoons butter

Peel bananas; cut in half lengthwise, then again crosswise. Arrange bananas and drained peach and pear halves on bottom of well-greased shallow baking dish. Sprinkle with drained cherries. Spread brown sugar mixture over fruit. Dot with butter. Cover; bake at 350°F for 15 minutes.

Combine curry powder, lemon juice, and butter and use to baste the fruit mixture once. Bake another 15 minutes. Serve hot with meat. Use orange or lime slices on top for extra flavor.

Desserts

Fruit Kabobs

JAPAN   Yield: Varies

This is a nice dessert for guests to make themselves.

Pineapple chunks, canned or fresh
Bananas, cut into large pieces
Mandarin oranges
Brandied peaches, cut into halves,
    or large pieces
Spiced crab apples, left whole

Skewer fruits; cook on a hibachi. There is an endless list of fruits suitable for this. Use the fruits that appeal to you and that are available to you. Make approximately 6 to 8 pieces of fruit per serving.

Mandarin Fruit

CHINA   Yield: 4 to 6 servings

2 11-ounce cans mandarin oranges
1 1-pound 4-ounce can lychees
    (available in Oriental-food stores)
1 tablespoon lemon juice
2 slices gingerroot

Combine oranges and lychees with the syrup from both. Add lemon juice and the slices of ginger. Chill for a few hours before serving and remove slices of gingerroot.

Orange-Cup Dessert

JAPAN   Yield: Varies

This is a very pretty and refreshing dessert.

Oranges with unblemished skin,
    as many as are needed, 1 per person

Fruit such as:
    Pineapple
    Orange sections
    Grapefruit sections
    Bananas
    Maraschino cherries
    Walnuts

Cut slice from top of orange so that the insides may be scooped out.

Combine any of the above fruits, or others of your choice, and spoon into the orange shells; refrigerate until serving time. The same thing may be done with grapefruit or bananas. If desired, a small amount of your favorite liqueur may be added to the fruit.

Pickled Fruits

JAPAN

½ pound canned pineapple slices
½ pound canned apricots
½ pound canned figs
½ pound canned peaches
1¼ teaspoons allspice
1 clove (whole)
2 pieces stick cinnamon, about
    4 inches long
4 tablespoons sugar
½ cup vinegar
Pinch of salt
1 small jar maraschino cherries (4 to
    5 ounces)
2 jiggers brandy

Drain fruits thoroughly, reserving juices. Place spices in a cheesecloth, tie securely, and place in saucepan together with reserved fruit juices. Add sugar, vinegar, and salt; boil for 10 minutes. Add fruits and maraschino cherries; simmer over very low heat for 1 hour.

Remove cheesecloth with spices. Pour in brandy. Cover saucepan, remove from heat, and let cool. When cooled, place in refrigerator for at least 24 hours before serving. Will keep for 3 weeks when refrigerated.

Spun-Sugar Fruit Dessert

CHINA   Yield: 4 servings

Apples, peeled, cored, and cut
  into wedges
Fresh whole strawberries
Fresh pineapple, cubed
Small clusters of seedless grapes
Cantaloupe balls
Watermelon balls

Glaze

1 cup sugar
1 slice of gingerroot to flavor the glaze
¼ cup water

Prepare and attractively arrange the fruit on a lightly oiled serving dish. Bring the sugar, ginger, and water to a boil over high heat. Stir just until the sugar dissolves. Continue to boil the syrup until it reaches 300°F as determined by a candy thermometer. This is the hard-crack stage, when a small amount of syrup dropped into cold water immediately forms a hard, brittle thread. At once dribble the syrup over the arranged fruit to coat each piece as much as possible. The syrup quickly hardens to a crunchy, clear, sparkling glaze on the fruit. This is a delicious contrast to the soft fruit beneath.

Rice Dessert

CHINA   Yield: About 4 servings

1 cup leftover rice
1 cup drained fruit (canned or frozen,
  thawed, may be used) such as
  pineapple, peaches, oranges, berries,
  mixed fruit, etc.
2 cups whipped cream
Nuts for garnish, optional

Mix rice with drained fruit (cut up if necessary); fold in whipped cream. Serve in dessert dishes. Garnish with fruit and/or nuts, if desired.

Sweet Coconut Rice

THAILAND   Yield: 6 to 8 servings

1 pound glutinous rice
Water
2½ cups coconut milk
⅔ cup sugar

Soak rice overnight in enough water to more than cover it. When ready to begin cooking, drain and steam the rice for 45 minutes until very tender. Place rice in a saucepan. Add coconut milk and sugar and simmer until all liquid is absorbed.

Turn the rice mixture out onto a plate and press down with the back of a spoon or a spatula. Allow to cool. Cut into squares or diamond shapes. Serve as a dessert or as an accompaniment to fruit.

Sweet Rice and Custard

THAILAND   Yield: 4 servings

Custard

  2 tablespoons rose water
  2 tablespoons brown sugar
  1¾ cups thick coconut milk
  4 eggs, beaten

Sweet Rice

  1 cup glutinous rice
  1¾ cups coconut milk
  1 teaspoon salt
  1 tablespoon sugar
  Lime slices to garnish

Mix rose water and brown sugar with the thick coconut milk. Stir in eggs and beat well. Put in an ovenproof bowl. Place bowl in a baking dish of water and bake at 275°F for about 1½ hours or until custard has set.

Use a bowl on top of a steamer or a double boiler to make the sweet rice. Mix coconut milk with salt and sugar and pour over the rice. Steam for 30 minutes or until rice is cooked.

To serve, put cooked custard on top of the rice and garnish with lime slices. This dish can be served either hot or cold.

Vermicelli and Nut Dessert

INDIA   Yield: 4 servings

  ½ pound vermicelli
  Water to cover
  ⅓ cup ghee
  1 tablespoon seedless white raisins
  1 tablespoon almonds, slivered
  1 tablespoon pistachios
  1 tablespoon rose water
  2½ cups heavy cream

  2 tablespoons coconut, shredded
  Sugar for sprinkling

Cover the vermicelli with water in a large saucepan. Bring to a boil, then lower heat to simmer and cook for 10 minutes. Drain off just enough water to leave the vermicelli covered but not drowning.

Add ghee and return mixture to boil. Reduce heat and cover the pan. Allow to simmer for 10 minutes. Do not stir this, as you might break the vermicelli. Gently fold in raisins and nuts. Add the rose water and transfer to a serving dish. Pour the heavy cream over the mixture. Sprinkle with coconut and sugar and serve either hot or cold.

Ice Cream

INDIA   Yield: 4 servings

  3¾ cups milk
  ½ cup rice flour
  1¼ cups light cream or evaporated
    milk
  ½ cup sugar
  1 tablespoon pistachios, chopped
  1 tablespoon almonds, chopped and
    blanched
  Green food coloring, optional
  Pistachio nuts and varak to garnish,
    optional

Allow the milk to come to a boil. Reduce heat and simmer until it is reduced to ⅔ original volume. Gradually stir in rice flour followed by the cream. Return this to a boil. Then reduce heat and simmer for 15 minutes. Add sugar, stirring until it is well dissolved. Set aside to cool.

When mixture has cooled, stir in nuts and food coloring if desired. Transfer to freezer containers and freeze until partially frozen. At this point, beat ice cream vigorously, then return to freezer until firm. Serve garnished with nuts and varak.

Mango Ice Cream

PHILIPPINES   Yield: 6 servings

- 2 cups milk
- 2 eggs, separated
- ½ cup confectioners' sugar
- 1 teaspoon unflavored gelatin
- 1½ to 2 cups mango pulp, fresh or canned
- 2 tablespoons water
- 1 cup cream

Bring milk slowly to a boil in a saucepan. In a bowl, beat the egg yolks and half of the sugar. Stirring constantly, add a little of the hot milk to the yolks. Put yoke mixture in saucepan with the rest of the milk and cook over hot water on a very low heat. Stir constantly to prevent the custard from curdling. When mixture lightly coats the back of your spoon, remove from heat but continue to stir until it cools slightly. Pour into a freezer tray and freeze until mixture is mushy.

Put 2 tablespoons cold water in a cup and sprinkle gelatin on top. Place cup in a saucepan of water and bring water to a boil. When gelatin is dissolved, stir this into the mango pulp. Whip the cream until it holds soft peaks. Beat the egg whites until they hold in soft peaks as well. Add the remaining sugar to the egg whites and beat until well blended.

Remove half frozen custard from freezer tray into a bowl. Beat with a rotary beater until smooth but not melted. Fold in mango

pulp, egg whites, and whipped cream and return to freezer. Freeze until firm.

Tempura Ice Cream Balls

JAPAN   Yield: 4 servings

- Oil for frying
- 4 ice-cream balls frozen very, very hard (vanilla, or another flavor of your choice)
- Tempura batter
- Sugar and cinnamon or powdered sugar

Heat oil to medium high. Remove balls from freezer; immediately dip them into tempura batter, and fry until golden brown.

Serve immediately, sprinkled with cinnamon and sugar or powdered sugar.

Steamed Banana Pudding

INDONESIA   Yield: 4 servings

- 3 eggs, well beaten
- 1 cup sugar
- 1 cup coconut milk
- 1 teaspoon vanilla
- 3 bananas, sliced

Add sugar, coconut milk, and vanilla to beaten eggs and mix well. Stir in the bananas. Put this mixture in a heavy saucepan with a lid. Steam on low heat for about 30 minutes or until the sauce has thickened. Dish into individual serving bowls and serve hot.

Carrot Pudding

INDIA   Yield: 4 servings

This pudding, known as kheer in India, is a very rich dessert, but very delicious and easy to make.

1 pound carrots, peeled and grated
1 cup sugar
6¼ cups milk
2 whole cardamoms
1 tablespoon seedless white raisins
1 tablespoon slivered almonds

Sprinkle grated carrots with sugar and set aside. Place milk and cardamoms in a saucepan and bring to a boil. Allow to boil for about 45 minutes or until the milk is reduced by half. Add the carrots and reduce heat to a simmer. When the mixture has thickened, remove from the heat. Allow to cool slightly. Stir in the raisins and almonds. This pudding may be served either hot or cold.

Baked Coconut Pudding

INDIA   Yield: 4 servings

2 whole coconuts
2 cups boiling water
1 cup sugar
1½ cups rice flour
2 eggs, beaten
½ cup slivered almonds

Break the coconuts in half, reserving the thin liquid inside. Grate the coconut meat into a large bowl and cover with boiling water. Allow to steep for 15 minutes. Then strain the liquid to get the thick coconut milk. Mix this with the liquid from the coconut and beat in the remaining ingredients in the order given.

Pour this into a saucepan and bring it to a boil. Stir constantly. Lower the heat and simmer until it thickens. Then pour into a well-greased, 8-inch, round baking tin. Bake at 350°F for about 30 minutes, until the top is lightly browned. Serve at once.

Indian Pudding

INDIA   Yield: 4 servings

¼ cup cornmeal
1 cup water
1 teaspoon salt
3 cups milk
1 egg, beaten
¼ cup sugar
½ cup molasses
1 tablespoon fat (margarine or butter)
1 teaspoon cinnamon
½ teaspoon ginger

Mix cornmeal, water, salt, and 2 cups milk in a saucepan. Bring to boiling, while stirring. Boil gently for 10 minutes. Mix egg, sugar, molasses, fat, and spices. Stir into cornmeal mixture. Pour in a greased baking pan.

Bake at 325°F (slow oven) for 30 minutes. Stir in the remaining 1 cup milk. Bake 1½ hours longer.

Rice Pudding I

INDIA   Yield: 4 servings

If you can't buy rice flour, make your own. Grind rice with a mortar and pestle or in your electric blender or food processor.

2½ cups milk
½ cup sugar
½ cup rice flour

2 teaspoons pistachios, chopped
2 teaspoons almonds, blanched and
slivered
½ teaspoon rose water

Bring the milk to a boil in a heavy saucepan. Stir in the sugar and then gradually add the rice flour. You cannot leave the stove while this pudding is cooking, because you must stir continuously. Add the nuts and allow mixture to thicken. Remove from the heat and stir in the rose water. Turn out mixture into a serving bowl and allow to cool. This pudding should be served cold.

Rice Pudding II

JAPAN   Yield: About 6 servings

1 cup converted or long-grain rice
1 teaspoon (or less) salt
4 cups milk
3 tablespoons butter
4 tablespoons sugar
½ teaspoon vanilla
½ cup raisins, optional

Wash and drain rice. In top of double boiler combine rice with salt and milk; cook for 1 hour. Add butter, sugar, vanilla, and raisins; mix.
Serve hot or cold. Good with sweet cream or whipped cream.

Sesame Semolina Pudding

BURMA   Yield: 6 to 8 servings

1⅓ cups semolina
1 cup dark brown sugar, firmly packed
½ teaspoon salt
¾ cup thick coconut milk
5 cups boiling water

¼ cup butter or margarine
2 teaspoons vegetable oil
2 medium eggs, beaten
½ cup seedless raisins
4 tablespoons sesame seeds

Use a heavy pan to cook semolina over low heat for 10 minutes, stirring from time to time. Do not let the semolina burn, but it should be toasted.
Remove from the heat and stir in brown sugar, salt, coconut milk, and water. Allow this to stand for about 30 minutes. Then return to heat and allow to simmer for 15 minutes until quite thick. Remove from heat.
Stir in butter or margarine until melted. Add oil and allow to cool for a few minutes. Stir in the beaten eggs. Return to heat and simmer for 5 minutes, stirring constantly. Add raisins and continue to cook for 5 minutes more or until the mixture is thick but not solid. Pour this into a greased, ovenproof, square dish. Sprinkle with sesame seeds.
Bake at 400°F for about 1½ hours. When the pudding shrinks away from the side of the dish, it is ready. Remove from oven and allow to cool. When completely cold, cut into squares and serve.

Tapioca Pudding

BURMA   Yield: 6 to 8 servings

    1⅓ cups tapioca
    1 cup dark brown sugar, firmly packed
    ½ teaspoon salt
    3¾ cups water
    1⅓ cups coconut, freshly grated
    2 teaspoons confectioners' sugar

Bring the tapioca, brown sugar, salt, and water to a boil. Reduce heat and simmer for about 10 minutes. Stir constantly. The mixture will be thick and the tapioca soft and transparent.

Remove from heat and pour into a greased shallow dish. Allow to cool completely.

Using a tablespoon, scoop out the mixture and roll it in coconut and then in confectioners' sugar.

Baked Custard

CHINA   Yield: 4 to 5 servings

    2 cups milk
    ¼ cup honey (or ¼ cup sugar)
    4 egg yolks (or 2 whole eggs)
    ⅛ teaspoon salt
    1 teaspoon almond extract (or vanilla)

Blend together the milk, honey, salt, and egg yolks. (If yolks are used, the custard will be creamier in texture than if whole eggs are used.) Beat well. Add the almond extract and pour into custard cups. Place the custard cups in a baking pan with an inch of hot, not boiling, water. Bake at 350°F for 30 to 40 minutes, until firm or a knife inserted near the edge comes out clean. Do not over-bake or the custard will separate and become watery and porous.

Coconut Custard I

MALAYSIA   Yield: 4 to 6 servings

    6 eggs
    ¼ teaspoon salt
    2 cups sugar
    2 cups coconut cream
    ½ cup fresh coconut, grated

Mix eggs, salt, and sugar together in a bowl until light. Add coconut cream and mix well. Last, stir in the coconut.

Pour this mixture into buttered custard cups or a buttered casserole. Place in a shallow dish filled with cold water. Bake at 350°F for 25 minutes or until a knife comes out of the custard clean. Allow to cool or chill before serving.

Coconut Custard II

PHILIPPINES   Yield: 6 to 8 servings

    1 cup brown sugar
    ¼ cup water
    2 cups coconut cream
    6 egg yolks
    4 egg whites, slightly beaten
    1 cup sugar
    1 teaspoon lemon rind, grated

Put brown sugar and water in a saucepan on moderate heat. When the sugar browns or caramelizes, pour ¾ of the sugar into a large mold. Rotate the mold so that its base and sides are coated.

Dissolve the remaining sugar with coconut cream over low heat, stirring constantly. Combine egg yolks and whites in a bowl and beat until mixed. Add sugar and lemon rind. Last, add the saucepan of coconut cream. Strain this mixture and pour it into the prepared mold.

Place the mold in a baking tin with hot water coming halfway up the mold. Bake at 300°F for 45 minutes to 1 hour, or until a knife comes out clean. When custard is done, allow it to cool, then refrigerate it for several hours. Unmold onto a serving plate and serve cold.

Steamed Custard in Pumpkin Shell

THAILAND   Yield: 4 to 6 servings

To enrich this dish, use milk instead of water when making the coconut milk.

¾ cup thick coconut milk
½ cup palm sugar or substitute
3 eggs
Few drops rose water
1 medium-size pumpkin

Beat eggs slightly; mix them with the sugar and coconut milk. Stir until sugar is completely dissolved; then add rose water.

Cut a hole in the top of the pumpkin. Remove seeds and pulpy tissue, leaving the shell about 1 inch in thickness.

Pour custard almost to the top of the pumpkin. Place pumpkin in a dish that fits into a steamer. Steam the custard for 1 hour or until a knife inserted in the center comes out clean. Cool and chill. Slice into individual portions and remove the pumpkin skin from each piece. Serve chilled.

Almond Balls in Syrup

INDIA   Yield: 20 to 25 balls

2 cups all-purpose flour
2 cups ground almonds
½ cup butter
1 teaspoon baking powder

⅔ cup unflavored yogurt
Vegetable oil for deep frying

Syrup

3¾ cups water
4 cups sugar
Pinch of cream of tartar
5 whole cloves
5 whole cardamoms
½ teaspoon rose water

Mix flour and almonds in a bowl and rub in the butter with your hands. Stir in baking powder and gradually add the yogurt until mixture becomes a firm dough. Cover and let stand for at least 2 hours.

While the dough is standing, make the syrup. Place all ingredients in a saucepan except the rose water. Do not boil. Heat gently until all sugar is dissolved. Remove from heat and stir in the rose water.

When ready to cook, divide the dough into 25 pieces and roll into 1-inch balls. use a deep-fat fryer and heat the oil. Deep-fry the balls until they are golden brown. Remove from the pan and drain on paper towels. Drop the balls into syrup while still warm. Serve either hot or cold.

Almond Delight

CHINAZ   Yield: 4 servings

    1 envelope unflavored gelatin
    3 tablespoons warm water
    1 small can evaporated milk
    1¼ cups cold water
    6 tablespoons sugar
    1 tablespoon almond extract
    1 small can mandarin oranges (drain; reserve juice)

Orange syrup

    ¼ cup sugar
    2 cups warm water
    1 teaspoon almond extract
    Juice from mandarin oranges

Dissolve gelatin in warm water. Heat milk with cold water and sugar to just below boiling. Add gelatin mixture; cool. Add almond extract. Pour into square or rectangular glass dish; refrigerate to set. Cut into squares; float in syrup with mandarin oranges.

To make the syrup dissolve sugar in water. Add almond extract and juice. Chill before serving.

Small Brandied Cakes

PHILIPPINES   Yield: 12 cakes

Syrup

    ½ cup sugar
    ½ cup water
    1 tablespoon brandy

Cakes

    ¼ cup melted butter, allowed to cool
    ½ cup flour
    ½ teaspoon baking powder
    Pinch of salt
    2 large eggs
    ½ cup sugar
    1 tablespoon brandy

Make syrup first by dissolving sugar in water in a small saucepan over low heat. Allow to boil for 2 minutes, then cool. Last, stir in brandy. Set aside.

Mix dry ingredients together in a large bowl. Beat eggs until frothy, gradually adding sugar. Add butter and brandy and fold in the dry ingredients. Use a spatula or wooden spoon for the folding process.

Drop by spoonfuls into greased muffin tins, filling them halfway. Bake at 400°F for 10 minutes or until cakes are golden brown. Remove from muffin tins and dip into syrup for just a few seconds. Allow to cool on a cake rack.

Chestnut Balls

KOREA   Yield: 4 to 6 servings

    5 cups chestnuts in the shell
    Water
    ¼ cup sugar
    4 tablespoons honey
    2 teaspoons cinnamon
    4 tablespoons pine nuts, chopped

Place chestnuts in a saucepan and cover with water. Bring to a boil and cook until the nuts are tender. As soon as you can handle the nuts, remove shells and skins. Mash the nuts into a fine paste.

Mix sugar, honey, and cinnamon with the chestnuts. When flavors are all blended, roll into small balls, about 1 inch in diameter. Roll each ball in the chopped pine nuts and serve when desired.

Ginger Mix

BURMA   Yield: 4 to 6 servings

This can be offered as a sweet snack or a dessert. In Burma, they eat it with the fingers.

4 ounces very tender fresh ginger
4 to 6 tablespoons lemon juice
2 tablespoons peanut oil
1 tablespoon sesame-seed oil
12 cloves garlic, peeled and sliced
2 to 3 tablespoons sesame seeds
Salt to taste

Scrape the skin off the ginger and slice with a very sharp knife. The younger the ginger, the better the snack will be. Cut the slices even finer into slivers. Soak in lemon juice for 1 hour.

Heat both oils in a small skillet and fry garlic until it is golden. Remove from skillet with slotted spoon and drain on paper towels. Using a clean, dry skillet, fry the sesame seeds until golden brown, stirring constantly. Turn out to a plate to cool.

When ready for dessert, drain ginger and put it in a bowl. Add salt to taste and sprinkle garlic and sesame seeds over all. Toss to mix and serve.

Indian Dessert

INDIA   Yield: 4 servings

½ cup margarine
1 cup uncooked farina or cream of wheat
1 cup brown sugar, packed
5 cups water
½ cup raisins

½ cup chopped nuts or wheat germ, if you like
½ teaspoon vanilla, if you like

Melt margarine in a large pan. Add farina or cream of wheat and cook over low heat until lightly browned. Bring sugar and water to boiling. Add raisins. Add to farina slowly while stirring. Add nuts or wheat germ (if used). Cover and boil gently about 5 minutes until done. Add vanilla (if used).

Pour into large baking pan or dish. Cool and cut into squares.

Seaweed Jelly I

BURMA   Yield: 6 to 8 servings

1 ounce dried agar-agar
½ cup thick coconut milk
1 cup granulated sugar
5 cups water

Place the agar-agar in enough water to cover and soak it for 3 hours. Strain and discard the water. Then measure the agar-agar. Set aside ¼ of the thick coconut milk.

Put the remaining coconut milk in a pan. Add the agar-agar and sugar. In another pan, bring water to a boil. You'll need 5 cups of water for every 2 cups of agar-agar. Add the water to the first pan and simmer gently for about 10 minutes. When the mixture is smooth, it is ready. Transfer to a shallow square dish and allow to cool slightly. Pour over the reserved coconut milk. Leave in a cool place for at least 1 hour until jelly is set. Cut into diamond shapes and arrange on a serving dish.

Seaweed Jelly II

BURMA   Yield: About 18 pieces

This very firm jelly can be picked up with the fingers — it's a popular accompaniment in Burma.

¼ ounce agar-agar strands
4 cups coconut milk
½ cup sugar
Few drops rose flavoring

In cold water, soak the strands of agar-agar at least 1 hour, preferably overnight. Drain and measure. You should have about 1½ cups. Place this with coconut milk in a saucepan and stir constantly as the mixture comes to a boil. Add sugar and continue to stir.

Reduce the heat to a simmer for 20 minutes or until all the agar-agar is dissolved. Last, add the rose flavoring. Take a square, 8-inch, ovenproof dish and rinse it with cold water. Then pour the mixture into the chilled dish and allow it to set. Cut it into squares and serve.

Spiced Semolina Dessert (Halwa)

INDIA   Yield: 4 servings

1⅓ cups semolina flour
¼ cup coconut, shredded
2 cups sugar
1 tablespoon poppy seeds
Seeds of 6 cardamoms
2½ cups water
½ cup melted ghee

In a heavy pan, mix the semolina, coconut, sugar, poppy seeds, and cardamom. After this is well mixed, stir in the water. Bring to a boil, still stirring. Lower the heat and allow to simmer for 1 hour until the mixture is consistently soft. Stir frequently during the cooking process. Last, add the ghee and mix well.

Transfer the mixture to a shallow pan, spreading it out evenly. Allow to cool. Then cut into triangles. The halwa should be about ¼ inch thick. It may be stored in an airtight container.

Accompaniments

Chinese Nuts

CHINA

3 tablespoons butter or margarine
4 teaspoons soy sauce
¼ teaspoon onion salt
⅛ teaspoon white pepper
¼ cup slivered almonds, toasted
Cabbage, broccoli, asparagus, or green
    beans, cooked and drained

Melt butter or margarine. Stir in soy sauce, onion salt, and white pepper. Heat. Add slivered almonds. Mix with cabbage, broccoli, asparagus, or green beans.

Glazed Chestnuts

CHINA   Yield: About 24

2 cups chestnuts
¾ cup honey
2 cups sugar

Place chestnuts in a bowl with water to cover. Soak overnight; drain. Remove shells, dry on paper toweling.

Combine honey and sugar in a saucepan. Cook over low heat for 1 hour, stirring often. Add chestnuts; cook 2 hours, stirring often. Separate chestnuts on cookie sheets; cool.

Coconut Milk

Yield: 1⅔ cups thick coconut milk

Since so many countries in the Orient include coconut milk in their recipes, this particular recipe cannot be attributed to any one country. Some Oriental stores carry canned coconut milk. This is not the fluid that comes out of the coconut when the husk is broken. Coconut milk is made directly from the flesh of fresh coconuts. In the absence of fresh coconut meat, dried coconut or desiccated coconut may be used.

2 cups coconut meat, grated
2½ cups hot water

In a large bowl, pour water over the coconut. Set aside until it cools to lukewarm. Knead the mixture firmly with your hands for a few minutes. Strain through a fine strainer or fine cheesecloth, being sure to squeeze out as much liquid as possible.

Use the same coconut to make thin coconut milk by adding 2½ cups hot water to the same flesh of the coconut. Repeat the process above and the yield will be about 2 cups thin coconut milk.

Coconut milk should not be stored for more than 24 hours.

Toasted Coconut

ORIENTAL   Yield: ½ cup

½ cup coconut, grated
1 tablespoon butter
2 tablespoons confectioners' sugar

Mix the coconut with butter and sugar; spread on baking sheet. Bake in preheated 350°F oven 8 to 10 minutes, until browned.

Accompaniments

Coconut Relish

MALAYSIA   Yield: 4 servings

    1 slice dried shrimp paste, fried or
        broiled
    2 cloves garlic, peeled and chopped
    3 to 5 lombok rawit (hot chilies),
        chopped
    1 small piece brown palm sugar
    1 tablespoon tamarind water
    7 tablespoons white coconut flesh,
        freshly grated
    Salt to taste

Make a very smooth paste of the dried
shrimp paste, garlic, chilies, and sugar. Use a
mortar and pestle, electric blender, or food
processor to make the paste. Stir in the remaining ingredients except for the salt.
When well mixed, add salt to taste. Chill
and serve on the same day made.

Hot Relish

INDONESIA   Yield: 4 servings

    20 red chilies, seeded and chopped
    10 shallots, peeled and chopped
    2 cloves garlic, peeled and chopped
    5 kemiri, chopped
    1 slice trasi
    2 tablespoons vegetable oil
    1 teaspoon ginger powder
    1 teaspoon brown sugar
    3 tablespoons tamarind water
    Salt to taste
    ⅔ cup thick coconut milk

Use a mortar and pestle to pound chilies,
shallots, garlic, kemiri, and trasi to a fine
paste.

Heat oil in a skillet and fry this smooth
paste for 2 minutes, stirring constantly. Add

all the remaining ingredients except the coconut milk and simmer for 15 minutes. Stir
occasionally. When the relish is thick and
oily, increase the heat and stir-fry for 3
minutes. Serve hot or cold.

Indian Relish

INDIA   Yield: 3 to 3⅔ pints

    2 quarts green tomatoes, peeled,
        chopped
    ½ cup salt
    3 cups cabbage, finely chopped
    3 cups vinegar
    ½ cup onion, finely chopped
    ½ cup green pepper, chopped
    ¼ cup pimiento, diced
    1½ cups sugar
    1½ teaspoons celery seed
    1½ teaspoons mustard seed
    1 teaspoon whole cloves
    Small piece (¼ inch) cinnamon stick

Sprinkle tomatoes with salt; leave overnight. Strain off liquid. Put tomatoes into a
kettle. Add cabbage and vinegar; boil gently
25 to 30 minutes.

Add onion, pepper, pimiento, sugar, celery seed, and mustard seed. Add cloves and
cinnamon tied loosely together in piece of
cheesecloth. Mix well; cook over gentle heat
until the onion is tender and the relish a
good consistency. Pack in hot sterilized jars;
seal at once.

Cucumber Pickle

Burma   Yield: 6 servings

    2 large, green cucumbers, peeled
    ½ cup malt vinegar
    2 cups water

348

1 teaspoon salt
¼ cup peanut oil
2 tablespoons sesame oil
8 cloves garlic, peeled and sliced
1 medium onion, peeled and finely
   sliced
2 tablespoons sesame seeds

Cut peeled cucumbers in half the long way. Scoop out the seeds and cut the cucumbers into strips about ½ inch thick. Then cut the strips into 2-inch pieces.

Put vinegar, water, and salt in a saucepan and bring to a boil. Add cucumber pieces and allow to boil until just transparent. Drain and allow to cool.

Heat the oils in a skillet and fry the garlic until golden. Drain and set aside. Fry the onion until golden and drain. Allow oil to cool. Toast sesame seeds in a dry skillet, stirring constantly until they are golden brown. Turn out on a plate to cool.

When the oil is completely cool, pour 3 tablespoons of it over the cucumbers. Mix gently with your fingers. Put in a small serving dish with the onion, garlic, and sesame seeds. Toss lightly. Chill if desired.

Cumin and Tamarind Water

INDIA   Yield: 4 to 8 servings

This is frequently served at the start of a meal, much the same way as tomato juice is served here.

½ cup dried tamarind pulp
2 cups hot water
3 teaspoons fresh ginger, finely grated
2 teaspoons ground cumin
Pinch of chili powder, optional
½ teaspoon garam masala

3 teaspoons sugar, or to taste
Salt to taste
Ice water and crushed ice for serving
Mint sprigs for garnish
Lemon slices for garnish

Cover the dried tamarind pulp with 2 cups hot water and allow to stand overnight. Squeeze to dissolve the pulp. Strain through a sieve, discarding the pulp and seeds. Add the ginger, cumin, chili, garam masala, sugar, and salt to the tamarind water, stirring well to be sure all flavors are blended. Strain again through a fine sieve or muslin. Refrigerate until ready to use. Dilute this with desired amount of ice water and pour over crushed ice. Garnish with mint and lemon.

Guava Paste

PHILIPPINES

To make guava paste, you must reserve the pulp of the fruit used to make jelly. This is a tasty sweetmeat.

Guava pulp
Sugar
Juice of 1 lemon

Strain the pulp through a nylon sieve, discarding seeds and skins. Weigh the pulp and add ¾ of its weight in sugar. Heat pulp and sugar with the juice of 1 lemon and allow to thicken, stirring constantly. Use a long-handled spoon and cook over low heat, as this spatters while cooking.

When the mixture is stiff and pulls away from the sides of the pan, turn it out onto a well-greased dish. Flatten it with a buttered spoon and allow it to cool and become firm. Using a sharp knife, cut into thin slices and serve.

Accompaniments

Guava Jelly

PHILIPPINES   Yield: Several jars of jelly

4 pounds slightly underripe guavas
4 green cooking apples
Sugar (¾ cup to each cup of juice)
Lemon juice

Wash guavas and cut into quarters. Core and quarter apples. Place in a large saucepan with enough cold water to cover. Allow to cook uncovered for at least 1 hour or until fruit is soft and colorless. Wet 3 layers of muslin and wring it out. Then strain the cooked liquid through the muslin. Measure how much liquid there is and discard the fruit or use it to make guava paste. (See previous recipe.)

For each cup of juice, allow ¾ cup sugar. Put no more than 5 cups liquid in a saucepan and bring to a boil. Add sugar and 2 tablespoons lemon juice and stir until all sugar is dissolved. Allow the jelly to cook without stirring, but skin off any froth that rises to the top. When the liquid thickens on the side of a spoon, it is ready. Pour into sterile jars and seal with paraffin.

Garam Masala

INDIA

Garam masala is a combination of spices and is not usually found in a food store. Variations from individual cooks range from the sweet to the hot. The recipe included here can be adjusted to your personal taste.

4 tablespoons coriander seeds
2 tablespoons cumin seeds
1 tablespoon whole black peppercorns
2 teaspoons cardamom seeds (measure after removing pods)

3-inch cinnamon stick
1 teaspoon whole cloves
1 whole nutmeg

Roast each of the spices above, except the nutmeg, separately. To roast, place the spices on a small pan in a moderate oven and let them roast until you begin to smell a delicate fragrance. Turn out on a plate to cool. Remove the pods from the cardamom and discard, keeping only the seeds.

When the roasting process is over, blend the spices into a fine powder with a mortar and pestle or an electric blender or food processor. Last, finely grate the nutmeg and mix in. Place the spice mixture, well mixed, in an airtight jar and store until needed.

Indian Salad Dressing

INDIA   Yield: 1 jar

Yolks 2 hard-cooked eggs
¾ teaspoon salt
½ powdered sugar
¼ teaspoon paprika
Few grains cayenne
Few grains white pepper
1 tablespoon lemon juice
2 tablespoons vinegar
½ cup olive oil
1 tablespoon red pepper, finely chopped
1 tablespoon green pepper, finely chopped
1 tablespoon pickled beets, cut in small cubes
1 teaspoon parsley, finely chopped

Force egg yolks through a strainer and add salt, sugar, paprika, cayenne, white pepper, lemon juice, vinegar, and olive oil. Shake thoroughly and add remaining ingredients.

Mint Chutney

INDIA   Yield: 4 servings

This refreshing chutney goes well with most dishes—and it is easy to put together.

⅔ cup unflavored yogurt
3 cups mint, chopped
2 green chilies, finely chopped
Juice of 1 lemon
½ teaspoon salt
Pinch of chili powder for garnish

Mix all of the ingredients in the order given except for the garnish. Stir well to blend the flavors. Chill well in the refrigerator. When ready to serve, garnish with chili powder.

Peach Chutney

INDIA   Yield: 2 or 3 jars

2 pounds thoroughly ripe peaches
½ cup seedless raisins
3 onions, peeled and finely chopped
1 cup dark brown sugar
½ teaspoon saffron
1 cup wine vinegar
1 teaspoon ginger
1 teaspoon chili powder

Peel peaches and cut into thin slices. Cut slices in half again. Pour hot water over raisins in a sieve and drain.

Place peaches together with raisins, onions, sugar, and saffron in a pot. Stir and bring to a boil. Allow to boil for 10 minutes. Add wine vinegar and ginger. Cover and reduce heat to simmer. Simmer for 30 minutes. Last, season with chili powder. Fill jars that have been rinsed with hot water. Seal with paraffin and allow to cool completely. Store in a cool place for up to 3 months.

Tomato Chutney

INDIA   Yield: 2 half-pints

1 tablespoon salad oil
1 whole red chili pepper, crumbled
½ teaspoon cumin seed
¼ teaspoon nutmeg
¼ teaspoon mustard seed
4 tomatoes, peeled, sliced ⅛ inch thick
½ lemon, quartered
⅓ cup raisins
½ cup sugar

Heat oil; add chili pepper. Add cumin, nutmeg, and mustard seed. When seeds start to jump, add tomatoes and lemon. Simmer 15 minutes; stir frequently. Stir in raisins and sugar. Simmer, stirring frequently until thickened, about 30 minutes; chill. Pack in sterilized jars; seal.

Note: This chutney is from Bengal. It is sweeter and milder than most. If made ahead of time and refrigerated, allow it to warm to room temperature before serving.

Teriyaki Marinade

Japan   Yield: About 1 cup

¾ cup pineapple juice
2 tablespoons soy sauce
2 tablespoons lemon juice
2 cloves garlic, finely chopped
1 small bay leaf
⅛ teaspoon ground cloves

Combine pineapple juice and remaining ingredients in a pint-sized jar. Cover jar tightly and shake well. Use immediately or store in the refrigerator until ready to use.

Accompaniments

Oily Balachaung

BURMA   Yield: 1 jar

Once made, this will keep for weeks.

    20 cloves garlic, peeled and thinly
      sliced
    4 medium onions, peeled and finely
      sliced
    2 cups peanut oil
    1 8-ounce packet of shrimp powder
    2 teaspoons chili powder, optional
    2 teaspoons salt
    1 teaspoon dried shrimp paste
    ½ cup vinegar

After garlic and onions are prepared, heat oil in a skillet. Fry garlic separately until it is golden. Lift out with slotted spoon and set aside. Repeat this procedure for the onions, setting them aside as well. When cool, onions and garlic will be crisp and dark.

Fry the shrimp powder in the same oil for 5 minutes. Mix remaining ingredients together and add to shrimp powder. Stir well and fry until crisp.

Add the onion and garlic and stir well to mix. When cool, store in an airtight container.

Roasted Salt and Pepper

CHINA   Yield: About 8 servings

    5 tablespoons salt
    1 tablespoon whole Szechuan
      peppercorns
    ½ teaspoon whole black peppercorns

Pour the salt and peppercorns into a hot wok. Turn the heat down to moderate and cook, stirring constantly, for 5 minutes or until the mixture browns lightly. Don't burn

it! Crush the browned mixture to a fine powder. Strain it through a sieve and serve as a dip with Szechuan Duck.

Shrimp Paste Sambal

THAILAND   Yield: About 8 servings

    3 tablespoons dried shrimp paste
    2 tablespoons onions, finely chopped
    1 tablespoon garlic, finely chopped
    2 tablespoons dried shrimp powder
    ¼ cup lime or lemon juice
    1 tablespoon palm sugar or substitute
    Fish sauce to taste
    1 teaspoon lime or lemon rind, finely
      shredded
    Fresh red chilies, chopped for garnish

Make a flat cake of the shrimp paste and wrap it in foil. Roast under a hot grill for 5 minutes per side. Allow to cool completely.

Using mortar and pestle, make a paste of the onions, garlic, dried shrimp paste, shrimp powder, and lime juice. When the paste is smooth, add the sugar and fish sauce. Place on a serving plate in a large, rounded mound. Garnish with citrus rind and chilies.

Batters

Tempura Cornstarch Batter

JAPAN   Yield: About 2 servings

The kinds of food suitable for dipping in tempura batter and frying crisply can range from small pieces of seafood to vegetables to ice cream. This recipe and the ones to follow show a number of ways to make tempura batters and sauces, and give a number of suggestions for tempura ingredients.

  1½ cups cornstarch
  ¾ teaspoon salt
  ¾ cup cold water
  1 egg
  Peanut or vegetable oil for frying

Blend ingredients together, but do not overmix. Dip fresh vegetables or seafood into the batter, then fry in hot peanut or vegetable oil. The foods you are frying should be cut into bite-size pieces. You may use a frying pan or a wok.

Beer Tempura Batter

JAPAN   Yield: Approximately 2 cups

  2 eggs
  1⅓ cups sifted all-purpose flour
  1 teaspoon salt
  1 cup flat beer

Place the eggs, flour, and salt in a bowl and mix well. Gradually stir in the beer. Beat just until smooth. Let stand 1 hour or refrigerate overnight.

Tempura Flour Batter

JAPAN   Yield: About 2 servings

  2 eggs, beaten
  1 cup cold water
  ¾ cup flour
  Pinch of salt

Beat the eggs with cold water until frothy. Blend in flour. Add salt. Blend well. Keep batter cool while using it by setting it in a bowl of ice.

Use a variety of vegetables, or seafood, cut into bite-size pieces. Dip into batter and fry in hot peanut or vegetable oil in wok or frying pan.

Extra-Light Tempura Batter

JAPAN   Yield: About 2 servings

  1 egg, separated
  ½ cup sifted flour
  2 tablespoons cornstarch
  ¼ teaspoon salt
  ½ teaspoon pepper
  ½ cup cold water

In a small bowl, beat the egg white until stiff peaks form. In another bowl, sift the flour, cornstarch, salt, and pepper together.

In a separate bowl, beat the egg yolk and water until frothy. Gradually add the flour mixture to the egg yolk and water, mixing constantly. Blend until smooth. Fold egg white into yolk mixture. Blend thoroughly.

Batters

Light, Fluffy Tempura Batter

JAPAN   Yield: Approximately 2 cups

1 cup sifted all-purpose flour
½ teaspoon baking powder
¼ teaspoon salt
1 tablespoon oil
2 eggs, separated
⅔ cup milk

Combine flour, baking powder, salt, oil, egg yolks, and milk in a bowl. Beat until smooth. Let rest 1 hour. Whip egg whites and fold them into the batter just before use.

Golden Tempura Batter

JAPAN   Yield: Approximately 2 cups

1 large egg
1 cup water
1¼ cups sifted all-purpose flour

Beat the egg and water together. Add the flour all at once and beat just until smooth. Let stand 1 hour or refrigerate overnight.

Thin and Crunchy Tempura Batter

JAPAN   Yield: About 2 cups

1½ cups cornstarch
¾ teaspoon salt
¾ cup cold water
1 large egg

Combine all ingredients in a small bowl and beat until smooth. This one is thin and crackly.

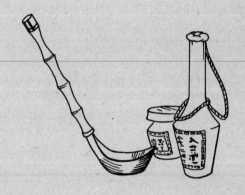

Beverages

Green Tea

JAPAN   Yield: 4 cups

    Green tea
    Boiling water

Place a good-size pinch of tea into a tea-pot. You may have to experiment with the amount that is palatable for you. Add enough boiling water for 4 cups; let steep for a few minutes. Have another pot of just-boiled water on the table, so that when you pour the tea your guests may add more water, if necessary.

Indian Fruit Punch

INDIA   Yield: 6 servings

    1 cup sugar
    1 pint water
    1 small can pineapple
    1 small bottle maraschino cherries
    3 oranges, cut into pieces
    2 cups grape carbonated beverage
    2 cups lime carbonated beverage
    1 cup strawberry carbonated beverage

Make a syrup of the sugar and water, boiling for five minutes. Cool. Add the fruits. Thoroughly chill. When ready to serve, add the carbonated beverages thoroughly chilled; ice cubes may be made of lemon carbonated beverage or fruit juices.

Sweet Fruit Drink

KOREA   Yield: 4 to 6 servings

Although this is called a drink, it is usually served in individual bowls with a spoon.

    1 grapefruit
    1 cup sugar
    5 cups water
    ¼ cup whole pine nuts
    Fresh or maraschino cherries

Peel the grapefruit; remove the pulp and put it in a bowl. Add ¼ cup sugar and set aside for a half hour.

Bring the remaining sugar and water to a boil in a saucepan until all the sugar is dissolved. Allow to cool. Place 1 tablespoon of grapefruit pulp in a glass bowl, making a portion for all those at the table. Add about 1 cup of sugar-water mixture to each bowl. Top with pine nuts and some cherries.

Strawberry Drink

KOREA   Yield: 4 to 6 servings

    2 cups strawberries, washed, stemmed, and sliced
    1½ cups sugar
    1 quart water
    3 tablespoons whole pine nuts

Sprinkle the prepared strawberries with 1 cup of sugar and set aside. Make a syrup of the water and remaining sugar by bringing them to a boil until the sugar is fully dissolved. Divide the berries into dessert bowls and add sugar syrup to each bowl. Top with pine nuts and serve with a spoon.

Glossary

A

Aburage. A Japanese fried bean curd, which comes in thin sheets, square or rectangular. This is usually sold frozen and can be stored in the freezer for several months.

Agar-Agar. A type of seaweed widely used in Asia. Available in strands or in powdered form. It is used in small quantities, as a little makes a lot of liquid. It can be found in Oriental stores and in health food shops.

Ajowan. Used in Indian cooking, particularly in lentil dishes. The seeds resemble parsley but give the flavor of thyme.

Akamiso. Japanese soy-bean paste, which is reddish in color. See Miso.

Anise pepper (Chinese pepper or Szechwan pepper). This is used in Five Spice Powder and comes from dried berries. Roasted over heat in a dry skillet, pounded and mixed with salt, anise pepper makes a good seasoning by itself.

Annatto seeds. Small red seeds used in the Philippines for color as well as for flavor. Paprika and turmeric serve as good substitutes.

Asafetida. Endowed with the medicinal property of preventing flatulence, this is used in minute quantities in Indian cooking. In addition, it adds a special flavor of its own.

Ata. A fine whole-wheat flour used in making Indian unleavened breads. Can be purchased at stores specializing in Oriental foods.

Azuki. Beans that vary in color from dark red to cream. Available in cans. As a substitute, use red kidney beans.

B

Bamboo shoots, dried. No substitute for fresh or canned bamboo shoots, dried bamboo shoots have their own special flavor. Available in cans at your Oriental store; can be stored for 2 weeks in a bowl in refrigerator if water is changed daily.

Basil. Herb sometimes called Sweet Basil and used primarily in Indonesian cooking.

Bean curd. A soft white, cheese-like cake made of pressed soy beans, which will keep refrigerated for several days if stored in water. Sometimes sold in instant powdered form in Oriental stores.

Yellow bean curd, also fresh, with slightly different flavor, will also keep refrigerated.

Dried bean curd is available in flat sheets and must be soaked before using.

Beans, salted. Black soy beans that have been processed and preserved in salt. Available in cans and packets. Can be stored in the refrigerator in airtight container for up to 1 year.

Bean sauce. Made from yellow soy beans, which have been crushed and mixed to a paste with flour, vinegar, spices, and salt. Comes in jars and cans. Sometimes called yellow bean sauce or black or brown bean sauce.

Bean threads. See Mung bean threads.

Beni-Shoga. Pickled ginger, usually red and used as a garnish or for additional flavor.

Besan. Made from ground chick-peas, this fine flour tends to become lumpy and must be passed through a sieve before using. Because of its unusual flavor, ordinary wheat flour cannot be substituted.

Black beans, salted. These heavily salted soy beans are sold in cans and jars. Rinse before using to avoid over- seasoning your recipes. Will keep in the refrigerator in a covered jar for 6 months or longer.

Bombay duck. This salted and dried fish, sold in packets in Oriental stores, should be served in small 1-inch pieces. When deep-fried or grilled, it can be served with a meal of rice and curry. The diner should nibble very small pieces at a time.

Boo. A long white radish with very mild flavor but do not substitute Western radishes for boo. If unable to find in your Oriental store, white turnips will serve as a substitute.

C

Candlenut. Pale yellow nuts used in Indonesian and Malaysian curries, about the size of a chestnut. Since they are imported shelled and broken, when a recipe calls for 2 whole nuts, you will need to know the original size of the candlenut to approximate amount required.

Cardamom. A spice grown mainly in India and Ceylon and a member of the ginger family. Although they are expensive, both cardamom pods and ground cardamom are generally available. A little goes a long way in most recipes and adds a very special flavor.

Cashew nuts. This refers to raw cashews rather than roasted or salted ones. The nuts are usually available raw where Oriental ingredients are sold.

Cellophane noodles (also known as Bean thread vermicelli). Fine dried noodles made from mung bean flour, sold in packets. Must be soaked in hot water before using. Sometimes called transparent noodles.

Chili powder. Made from ground chilies and much hotter than the Mexican-syle chili powder.

Chili sauce. Available in either the Chinese style or Malaysian. Both have a hot flavor and both are readily found at your Oriental store.

Chilies, bird's eye or bird peppers. Usually used for pickling but occasionally included where a very hot flavor is desired. Use with care.

Chilies, capsicum or peppers. A milder variety with a large enough pod to be used in stuffed meat or fish recipes.

Chilies, green. Used ground in sambals or sauces. Many times, the hot seeds are removed and not used. They can also be substituted or used with red chilies.

Chilies, red. Used for flavoring throughout the Orient. They may be served whole, finely chopped, or sliced for garnish.

Chinese bean sauce. Made of ground soybeans in a thick paste, about the consistency of ketchup. Available in bottles or cans.

Chinese parsley. See Coriander.

Chinese sausages. Dried and filled with spiced lean and fat pork. To cook, allow to steam for about 15 minutes when the fat is translucent. Serve by themselves, cut in thin slices, or include in recipe as indicated.

Chinese-style fish cakes. Available and ready to use at Oriental stores. Heat through and serve as is.

Chenna dal. See Dal.

Chrysanthemum choy. Edible chrysanthemum leaves available at Oriental stores. Use only the tender top leaves, before the plant has bloomed.

Cinnamon. A spice native to the Orient and best used in stick form rather than in ground form. The ground spice may lose its flavor if kept too long.

Cloves. A spice that has been used for more than 2,000 years. It not only flavors food but helps to preserve it as well.

Coconut cream. To make, use 2 cups of grated coconut. Pour over 1 cup of boiling water. Allow to stand for 30 minutes. Squeeze the flesh of the coconut and then strain before using. Use within 24 hours.

Coconut milk. To 1 cup grated coconut meat, add 2 cups of boiling water. Allow to stand for 30 minutes. Squeeze the flesh of the coconut and then strain before using. Use, like the coconut cream, within 24 hours. Sometimes available in cans.

Coconut sugar. See Palm sugar.

Coriander. Sometimes called Chinese parsley or Cilantro, all parts of the coriander plant are used including leaves, roots, stems, seeds, and powder. While parsley is sometimes substituted for fresh coriander, it does not give the same flavor. Easily grown in a garden or a window box in a sunny location.

Creamed coconut. Sold in packets, tubs, slabs, and cakes, this is more concentrated than coconut milk. To use, cut up, heat with water and stir until melted. Then use as needed in recipe.

Cumin. An essential ingredient for curry powder and available in seed or ground form. Used throughout the Orient.

Curry leaves. Although used fresh in Asia, they are sold dried here and can be found where Oriental supplies are purchased.

D

Daikon. Large white radish used both raw and cooked in Japan.

Dal. The Indian name for a variety of pulses or edible seeds, which form the staple diet along with rice. Although there are several different varieties, the lentil is the most familiar.

Dashi. An essential for Japanese cooking, where it is used as a clear soup or as stock. Made from dried bonita flakes and seaweed and available in Oriental stores.

Daun pandan. Turmeric leaf.

Dried mushrooms. See Mushrooms, dried.

Dried shrimp paste. Although it has a different name in the countries of the East where it is used, it is always a pungent paste made from shrimp. It keeps indefinitely without refrigeration and is know as "blachan" commercially.

F

Fish paste. Made from fermented fish or shrimp and salt. Used frequently as a relish in the Philippines and Indochina.

Glossary

Fish sauce. A thin, salty, brown liquid used to bring out the flavor of food in much the way salt is used in the West. Available in Oriental stores.

Five spice powder. Essential in Chinese and some Malaysian cooking. A reddish brown powder that includes anise, fennel, cloves, cinnamon, and Szechuan pepper. For best results, the powder should be ground from the ready-mixed whole spices sold in Oriental stores when ready to use.

Fried bean curd. See Aburage.

G

Garam masala. A mixture of ground spices necessary for Indian cooking. See index for recipe.

Garlic. Used throughout Asia for its flavor and health-giving properties. Many different varieties create flavors from strong to very mild.

Ghee. Clarified butter or pure butter fat with all milk solids removed. To make your own ghee, heat unsalted, sweet butter in a heavy pan. Skim off any floating impurities and maintain heat for 1 hour. Strain through several layers of cheesecloth and store in a cool place. Ghee will keep for several months. Also available in Oriental stores.

Ginger. A pungent-flavored root, which is used all over the Orient. When fresh ginger is called for, it should be used. The root can be kept by scraping the skin from the outside, dividing into sections and packing in a glass jar with lid. Pour dry sherry to cover the ginger, seal the jar and refrigerate.

Glutinous (sweet) rice. This short-grain rice becomes very sticky when cooked and is used in stuffings, cakes, and puddings. Sometimes known as "sticky" rice, it is available at Oriental stores.

Glutinous (sweet) rice flour. Made from ground glutinous sweet rice; has no real substitute. Can be purchased where Oriental foods are found.

H K

Hoisin sauce. Also known as barbecue sauce, it is made from soy beans, flour, sugar, spices, and red food coloring. Available in jars or cans at Oriental stores and keeps indefinitely in a closed container.

Kemiri nuts. See Candlenut.

L

Laos powder. Made from the root of a plant resembling ginger.

Lemon grass. The bulb-like base of the plant is used when chopped or sliced lemon grass is required. Dried lemon grass can be purchased at Oriental stores. Twelve strips dried are equal to 1 fresh stem. A good available substitute is 2 strips of thin lemon rind.

Lentil flour. When needed, this can be made from ground or pounded lentils. An electric blender works well but if you do not have one, use mortar and pestle.

M

Mint. A refreshing flavor for many curries and sambals. Although there are several varieties, spearmint is usually preferred.

Miso. Japanese name for soy-bean paste. See Soy-bean paste.

Moong dal. See Dal.

Mung beans. Small, green in color with green husks. When husks are removed, beans are yellow. Dried split peas may be used as a substitute but mung beans are usually available at health food stores.

Mung bean flour. Used basically in the making of sweets, this fine smooth flour is made from mung beans.

Mung bean threads. See Cellophane noodles.

Mushrooms, dried. Used in both Chinese and Japanese cooking as well as in the cuisine of other Oriental countries. They must be soaked in warm water for 30 minutes before using and there is no substitute for them. Available where Oriental foods are sold.

N O

Nam pla. The Thai name for fish sauce. See Fish sauce.

Noodles, Japanese. Several different varieties of noodles are used ranging from very fine, made from bean starch, to thick wheat-flour noodles.

Oyster sauce. Made from oysters and soy sauce and used to add delicate flavor to all kinds of dishes. Keeps indefinitely.

P

Palm sugar. A strong-flavored dark sugar from the sap of coconut palms and Palmyrah palms. Usually sold in round, flat cakes or in a ball shape. Substitute dark brown sugar if unavailable.

Peppers, red and green. Known as a capsicums, sweet or bell peppers, they are used in many vegetable and salad dishes.

Plum sauce. Used primarily as a dip in China, this sauce keeps indefinitely in a covered jar.

Prawn powder. Finely shredded dried prawns or shrimp. Available in packets at specialty food stores.

Puri. Deep-fried whole wheat bread native to India.

R

Rice flour. Comes from ground rice and can be made at home with an electric blender or using a mortar and pestle.

Rice, ground. More granular than rice flour, this adds texture when used in batters. Available in many grocery stores and Oriental food stores.

Rice papers, dried. A thin pancake used as a wrapper for a variety of foods. Must be moistened with water to make them flexible and easy to use. Available at Oriental stores.

Rice powder. Finer than rice flour and when required in a recipe, there is no substitute.

Rice vermicelli. Known as rice sticks or rice noodles and come in a variety of sizes. Can be soaked in hot water for 10 minutes for most uses. Deep-fried, they can be used without soaking.

Rose water. Can be obtained commercially or made at home by floating rose petals in water overnight. Remove rose petals from liquid and use as directed in recipe.

S

Sake. Rice wine used primarily in Japan and Korea. Dry sherry can be substituted.

Salam. Native to Malaysia, these leaves are frequently used in Malaysian recipes. As a substitute, use bay leaves.

Sambal bajak. An accompaniment to rice and curry dishes made of chilies and spices. Commercially made sambal can be purchased where Oriental foods are sold.

Sambal ulek. Used widely in Indonesia as an accompaniment to main dishes and in cooking. Like Sambal bajak, this can be purchased at Oriental stores.

Santen. See Coconut milk.

Sereh powder. See Lemon grass.

Sesame seed. Easily available in most supermarkets, these seeds are used in sweet dishes in the Orient. To toast, dry fry in a skillet with no fat, shaking the pan until the seeds "jump."

Shrimp paste or shrimp sauce. Thick and gray in color, this is an essential flavor for Oriental foods. Anchovies mixed with vinegar may be subsituted, but it's best to buy the real thing in jars from an Oriental store.

Shrimp paste, dried. See Dried shrimp paste.

Snow peas. Small flat pods, bright green in color and cooked for 1 or 2 minutes. Eaten whole. Available in supermarkets as well as Oriental stores.

Soy-bean paste. Called Miso in Japan. This is a basic seasoning used in China, Japan, and Korea. Made from cooked soy beans, malt and salt. Sold in plastic packs at Oriental stores.

Soy sauce. A basic ingredient in Asian cooking, which comes in several different forms. Light soy, dark soy, and sweetened soy are all available and keep well without need of refrigeration.

Szechuan vegetable. Preserved in salt and chili, this can be used as a relish or included in cooking for flavor. Available in cans.

T

Tamarind. An acid-tasting fruit, which is dried and sold in packets. To use, soak a small piece, size of a walnut, in ½ cup of hot water for 10 minutes. Squeeze until the tamarind mixes with the water, then strain out seeds and fibers. What remains is the tamarind liquid called for in so many recipes.

Tauco. See Beans, salted.

Terasi, trasi, or trassi. All names for dried shrimp paste. See Dried shrimp paste.

Transparent noodles. See Cellophane noodles.

Tree ears. Delicate, black mushrooms that are dried and sold in plastic bags. Will keep indefinitely without refrigeration.

Glossary

V W

Vindaloo. A blend of spices similar to curry powder. Available at specialty food stores.

Wasabi. A strong, green horseradish used in Japan. Available in powdered form and can be reconstituted with cold water. If unable to obtain, substitute dry mustard mixed to a paste with water.

Water chestnuts. Can sometimes be purchased fresh but generally available canned at supermarkets and Oriental stores.

Wonton wrappers. Known sometimes as wonton skins, they come in paper-thin squares or circles of dough. Although they can be made at home, they are available in Oriental stores.

Wun sen. A transparent vermicelli made from mung beans.

Index

Index

Index

Index

Index

Index

Index

Index

Index